The Daring Muse

No weak, no common Wing shall bear
My rising Body thro' the Air;
    Now chang'd I upward go.   Horace, *Odes* II. xx

THE DARING MUSE

AUGUSTAN POETRY RECONSIDERED

MARGARET ANNE DOODY

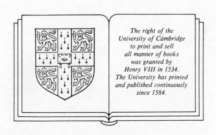

The right of the
University of Cambridge
to print and sell
all manner of books
was granted by
Henry VIII in 1534.
The University has printed
and published continuously
since 1584.

CAMBRIDGE UNIVERSITY PRESS

CAMBRIDGE

LONDON   NEW YORK   NEW ROCHELLE
MELBOURNE   SYDNEY

Published by the Press Syndicate of the University of Cambridge
The Pitt Building, Trumpington Street, Cambridge CB2 IRP
32 East 57th Street, New York, NY 10022, USA
10 Stamford Road, Oakleigh, Melbourne 3166, Australia

First published 1985

Printed in Great Britain at
the University Press, Cambridge

Library of Congress catalogue card number: 84–17061

British Library cataloguing in publication data
Doody, Margaret
The daring muse.
1. English poetry – Early modern, 1500–1700
– History and criticism 2. English
poetry – 18th century – History and criticism
I. Title
821'.009   PR561
ISBN 0 521 25825 1 hard covers
ISBN 0 521 27723 X paperback

This book is dedicated
to
my sister
Freda

Frontispice.   Lud. Du Guernier inv. et Sculp.

Ye sacred Nine! that all my Soul possess,
Whose Raptures fire me, and whose Visions bless
(Pope, *Windsor Forest*)

Beat not the dirty paths where vulgar feet have trod,
  But give the vigorous fancy room
(Swift, "To Mr. Congreve")

Contents

Illustrations

Figures 1 to 10, 19, 20 and 25 are from works in the Rare Books
    collection of the Green Library, Stanford University, and
    were photographed by the Green Library photographic ser-
    vice.

Figures 11, 12, 13, 16, 17, 18, 21, 23 and 24 are from works in the
    collection of the Bancroft Library, University of California at
    Berkeley, and were photographed by the Doe Library photo-
    graphic service.

The frontispiece, the illustration on p. vi and figures 14, 15, 22, 26
    and 27 are from works in the Rare Books collection of the
    Firestone Library, Princeton University, and were photo-
    graphed by the Firestone Library photographic service.

Figure 28 is from a work in the collection of Robert Taylor,
    photographed by the Firestone Library photographic service.

A note on editions

The following works by these authors (frequently cited in this book) are quoted throughout as they appear in the modern editions given here. A note will be supplied only when the text referred to differs from that on this list.

Marvell *The Poems and Letters of Andrew Marvell*, H. M. Margoliouth, ed., 2 vols. (Oxford: Clarendon Press, 1927).

Butler *Hudibras*, John Wilders, ed. (Oxford: Clarendon Press, 1967).

Rochester *The Complete Poems of John Wilmot, Earl of Rochester*, David M. Vieth, ed. (London and New Haven, Conn.: Yale University Press, 1968).

Dryden *The Works of John Dryden*, H. T. Swedenberg, General Editor, with numerous other editors, 19 vols. (Berkeley, Los Angeles and London: University of California Press, 1958–).

Swift *Swift, Poetical Works*, Herbert Davis, ed. (London: Oxford University Press, 1967).

Philips, John *The Poems of John Philips*, M. G. Lloyd Thomas, ed. (Oxford: B. Blackwell, 1927).

Gay *John Gay Poetry and Prose*, Vinton A. Dearing and Charles E. Beckwith, eds., 2 vols. (Oxford: Clarendon Press, 1974).

Pope *The Poems of Alexander Pope*. A one-volume edition of the Twickenham text, John Butt, ed. (New Haven, Conn.: Yale University Press, 1963).

Thomson *The Seasons*, James Sambrook, ed. (Oxford: Clarendon Press, 1981).

Gray *Thomas Gray and William Collins, Poetical Works*, Roger Lonsdale, ed. (Oxford University Press, 1977).
Collins

Johnson *The Lives of the Poets*, George Birbeck Hill, ed., 3 vols. (Oxford: Clarendon Press, 1905).

Cowper *The Poetical Works of William Cowper*, H. S. Milford, ed. (London: Oxford University Press, 1950).

Chatterton *The Complete Works of Thomas Chatterton*. A bicentenary edition, Donald S. Taylor, in association with Benjamin B. Hoover, eds., 2 vols. (Oxford: Clarendon Press, 1971).

Preface

In this work I have endeavoured to describe and account for the peculiar complexity and strange richness of the poetry of one important period of England's literary history. The "period" is in this work generously defined. There is another kind of profit in cutting the age into segments, but on this occasion I wish to pursue resemblances and connections, to see what can be said to unite Butler and Gray, what threads connect Rochester with Crabbe.

The book is as richly illustrated as I dared to hope; I am indeed grateful to the Cambridge University Press for allowing me to include the illustrations. Augustan poetry is highly (if often oddly) visual. Illustrators during the period interpreted the poems and their images for their contemporaries, and can help us to see what is there. I hope that looking at my book can give the modern reader some idea of what looking at eighteenth-century books of poetry can be like – an experience far removed from the sensation of grey unbroken columns which some anthologies have inflicted as the essential effect of Augustan poetry.

I wish here to express my sense of indebtedness to a number of people. First, I wish to acknowledge the inspiration offered by Rachel Trickett, since I trace the true origin of this book to a seminar she gave in Oxford to graduate students in eighteenth-century studies. I have always admired *The Honest Muse*, and I am sure the Principal of St. Hugh's will be entertained at seeing I have in my title forsaken honesty for daring.

Like all who teach, I am indebted to my students, and in particular to the graduate students who attended seminars on Augustan poetry in Berkeley and Princeton. To the students in the class held at Princeton in the spring of 1982 I am especially grateful.

I am also very much obliged to many librarians, including those in the Bodleian Library, Oxford; the Rare Books section of the Green Library, Stanford; the Bancroft Library, Berkeley; the New York Public Library; the Firestone Library, Princeton. I owe my thanks also to Robert Taylor who is always so generous in allowing use of the Taylor Collection, and to Nancy Coffin, his librarian. I would like to express very warm thanks to the Librarians of the Firestone Library Rare Books department, who hunted up works with zeal and held books on "my" trolley for a time generously made boundless to an almost Augustan extent. I wish to mention in particular Charles Greene, Jean Preston and Ann Van Arsdale. I am of course especially obliged to those libraries which allowed photographs to be taken of illustrative material, and to the various photographic departments which took the pictures.

I should not wish this book to see the light without inscribing in it the names of those who have so kindly helped me by reading part or all of it in sundry phases. In particular I wish to express my gratitude to the following: Zelda Boyd, Carol Christ, Deborah Laycock, Thomas P. Roche Jr., Steven Shankman, Steven Volentir. Claudia Johnson read the whole manuscript in first draft as each chapter appeared and supplied detailed comments and encouragement at an early stage; I have very much appreciated her continued interest in the project. Florian Stuber has been an acute and supportive reader of the work throughout its progress, offering informed comment on eighteenth-century matters and capably pointing out possible solutions to stylistic problems. I value his contribution as a reader, and hope the final version pleases him. My colleagues and friends have enlightened me as to errors or omissions; any mistakes that remain are my own responsibility.

In conclusion, I would like to express my appreciation to my editor, Andrew Brown, for his tact, cheerfulness and encouragement. And I am most grateful to him for putting into my head the notion of writing my projected book on Augustan poetry not in some hazy future but (in true Augustan fashion) in the immediate hazardous present.

Margaret Anne Doody
Princeton, N.J.
March 1984

Introduction

English poetry of the late seventeenth century and the eighteenth century has attracted many faithful readers and a number of good critics, but it still seems, among college students and the public at large, to be at a disadvantage, to labour under a certain unpopularity. It may be that Matthew Arnold's condescending damnation, "Dryden and Pope are not classics of our poetry, they are classics of our prose,"[1] has done its work so well as to leave lingering effects a century later. General notions of the period have not helped. "The Age of Reason" is a phrase that arouses dislike, perhaps because the hearer conceives him or herself to be less devoted to reason, or less capable of using it, than those who would seem to flourish it about. Attempts have been made to substitute other descriptions of the period, e.g. "The Age of Exuberance," "The Age of Passion," but the older term has stuck.[2] And we have not time to explain quite what our writers meant by "Reason" before a large part of our potential audience wanders away. The term "Augustan" puts off students and other readers, as it seems to refer to something high and arcane, something so Roman and classical as to remain ever obscure to a modern mind.

The novelists of the eighteenth century have by now been largely rescued from the opprobrium in which the whole period once seemed sunk. Novelists write about characters, about adventures and money and sex; they are entertaining, and not really "Augustan." Besides, the novel as a genre was not classical, not a regulated or traditional form; writers could invent and experiment as they went along. But was not poetry in the period subject to set ideas of correctness, enslaved to rules, and directed not (like the novel) to the mass of readers but to well-read gentlemen? How then could such poetry appeal to us?

Something like this reasoning (crudely put here) would seem to have inhibited the study and, more important, the general enjoyment of poetry of the period between the flourishing of the Metaphysicals and the rise of the Romantics. Our modern poets, too, have in general not been notably eager to talk about their relation to Augustan poets, even if real relationships may be seen to exist. T. S. Eliot experimented with couplets somewhat in Pope's manner in the original version of *The Waste Land*, but Ezra Pound told him to take them out, remarking "Pope has done this so well that you cannot do it better."[3] With direct imitation suppressed, the influence of Pope (and of others of the period just before and just after Pope) on Eliot remained obscured. Eliot is better known as the champion of the Metaphysicals, whom he helped to raise into new favour; despite his essay on Dryden,[4] he did not do much for the reputation of the Augustans. Indeed, they remain the poor fragmented victims of "dissociation of sensibility."

No cure is here offered for this state of affairs. But it seems right that those of us who do like "Augustan" poetry should speak out. The time would seem to be right for offering new reasons for liking the poems. Too much talk about "decorum" and "correctness" can only depress the uninitiated, and even among the initiated some of us may feel there are matters of more importance to be discussed first. The time seems propitious. There have been many excellent new studies of poets of the period, some of them indicating a more lively and stirring view of our Augustans. To single out new works would be invidious, but I would like to pay a special tribute to Donald Davie's discussion of Watts and Wesley.[5] The placement of hymns within the canon of eighteenth-century literature is welcome and long overdue; the new interest may indicate a welcome amplification of the canon in general. There are a number of indicators that the period (or rather, our view of what constituted the literary work of the period) is getting bigger, is broadening so as to include more of what was written – by Dissenters, for instance, or by women. Studies of Restoration and eighteenth-century literature are at present in a more restless and mobile state than formerly. Now would seem to be the time to persuade not only college students but also general readers to take another look at the poetry. It also seems possible now to hazard some speculations, to take up some positions even at the risk of being wrong – to become, in short, controversial about Augustan poetry, a topic that has seldom been truly controversial because the poems have been too seldom read, or read widely.

What I propose is not a complete discussion of Augustan poetry (that would be impossible) but a discussion of some major points of interest. I do not deal with only one poet, nor do I take up a group of writers hitherto little regarded (female poets, hymn writers) though these may figure in my discussion. It is my major purpose to restore the sense of excitement that can come from a reading of Augustan poetry.

It is true that "Augustan" is not a really satisfactory term for the poetry I am describing. It is both too specific and too vague. It meant various things to contemporaries; in 1709 Anne Finch, Countess of Winchilsea, thought the *"Augustean Days"* in England had gone with the age of Charles II.[6] Some modern critics have tried to do without the word. Donald Greene treats "Augustan" and "Augustanism"[7] (a "maddeningly opaque term") to a memorable rejection. Yet, if it is not a satisfactory term, it is the term we have, the one we have used for years, the one that inspires recognition. It is partly my object to change slightly what "Augustan" means, so that certain forms of poetic excitement become associated with the term. It is not a novelty to point out that there is a resemblance and a relationship between the works of very diverse poets from Butler and Dryden to Cowper and Crabbe, and that poets from 1660 to the end of the following century (or even slightly beyond that) come into the same story. The relationship between a poet like Dryden (or

Thomson or Pope) and a Romantic poet like Wordsworth (or Coleridge or Keats) also exists, but that is another story; it is, however, true that English literature can in one light be seen as a continuum and that all breaks of "periods" and so forth are somewhat artificial. The "Augustans" were what the Romantics knew.

I wish, however, to stress qualities that I think are peculiar to or characteristic of this poetry which is often too little regarded. My emphasis will be on the excitement of the works, and on their strangeness. That is not because strangeness is all that could be found in the poetry, but because precisely these qualities have received least attention, and are least associated with the poetic work of the age. Even "irony" or "wit" (topics which have been much talked about in this connection) could, at least momentarily, become clearer or more engaging if seen in stimulating association with other matters. I take the liberty of ranging in time and in hierarchies. That is, the discussion is not primarily chronological, and "minor" or almost unknown works will be quoted as well as the works of the established poets.

After first discussing in general some of the most salient characteristics of the adventurous Augustan poetry, I shall turn in the second chapter briefly to the past, the past of the Civil War, to examine the origins of the new poetry which, as the following chapter observes, was marked by stylistic versatility, generic self-consciousness and distrust of set forms. The fourth chapter deals with what the English Augustans found useful or congenial in the great Roman poets, particularly in those who were markedly versatile in use of styles and experimental in genre. The fifth chapter, "Charivari and metamorphosis," discusses the Augustan poem in the light of its energies of transformation. The sixth chapter traces out connections between the English eighteenth-century novel and the poetry of the age in terms of similarities in modes of proceeding, in transformations and in formal distrusts. The eighteenth-century English novel has long been felt by students to be more accessible than the poetry; I wish to show how closely related they are and to point out that understanding the one assists comprehension of the other. The last chapters deal with more purely "poetic" topics, ultimately bringing the entire previous discussion to bear on a detailed examination of the use and significance of that great poetic achievement, the Augustan couplet.

I do not believe that my discussion will provide a final statement on Augustan poetry. I could not even hope for that – should not, as Augustan poetry is greater than any (or all) of its critics. ("Critic" is a portentous word in the period, and the Augustans gave us much good advice about "*Pride, the never-failing Vice of Fools*.") I do hope, however, that some new suggestions will be found stimulating, will arouse some argument and response, and, in so doing, will help push Augustan poetry to the forefront of the consciousness of those who like English poetry. Some of my suggestions may seem peculiar, others rash, but literary rashness, as the Augustans themselves were fond of pointing out, is not always a fault if it serves some worthy end.

I

Appetite, imperialism and the fair variety of things

Pope had likewise genius; a mind active, ambitious, and adventurous, always investigating, always aspiring; in its widest searches still longing to go forward, in its highest flights still wishing to be higher; always imagining something greater than it knows, always endeavouring more than it can do.   (Johnson, *Life of Pope*)

Johnson's statement about Pope which here serves as epigraph can be taken as a description of the eighteenth-century idea of poetic genius. In a sentence whose structure echoes the sense (the clauses still longing to go forward) Johnson defines the poetic mind, and poetry itself: it investigates, aspires, goes wide and high, always tries to surpass the point where it is. Without this adventurous excitement there is no great poetry. In defending Pope against detractors (like Joseph Warton), Johnson is appealing to standards recognized throughout the age from Dryden to Crabbe. Poetry is active, experimental (endeavouring more than it can do) and vitally energetic. At the end of the previous century Swift (or his Apollo) makes a similar statement in his exhortation to Congreve; the "vigorous fancy" has to have room to move about in, and must not be forced into depressing conformity, or yield in subjection to academic or other regulation:

> *Beat not the dirty paths where vulgar feet have trod,*
>   *But give the vigorous fancy room.*
> For when like stupid alchymists you try
>   To fix this nimble god,
>   This volatile mercury,
> The subtil spirit all flies up in fume;
>   Nor shall the bubbl'd virtuoso find
> More than a fade insipid mixture left behind.
>
> ("To Mr. Congreve," 1693)

Swift's own verse here exhibits the daring he is urging upon the dramatist. The verse form has altered for this prophetic or oracular stanza into an imitation "Pindaric" mode (the rest of the "Ode" is "Horatian"). The image alters suddenly, so we move from footpaths to alchemy; the alchemical imagery in a profusion of technical terms is played with in the metaphysical manner. There seems to be, as well, a slight comic allusion to Volpone's mountebank speech describing unsuccessful competitors (*Volpone* II. i), and to various parts of *The*

5

Alchemist (e.g. II. i; IV. iii). Such transplanted reference, put to new and original use, is far from being mere imitation or conformity, as Swift shows.

The whole of Swift's "To Mr. Congreve" exhibits the force of "vigorous fancy." In it, the poet, speaking with confidence though with assumed bashfulness (at times) to another writer (a contemporary), ranges through the world for metaphors, employs a number of styles and devices; he includes fables, and short narratives, and social vignettes after the manner of Rochester; his Muse among critics is like a "bright country virgin" caught up in a knot of rallying town beaux who offend her – much as the Yahoos are later to disgust Gulliver:

> *But with the odious smell and sight annoy'd*
> *In haste she does th'offensive herd avoid.*

Swift is nothing if not sensuous and particular, even in (or especially in) the sensuousness of satiric aversion. But such distasteful if fascinating images of disgust as "th'offensive herd," or "beds of dung," or worms which grow into city butterflies ("other kind of things / Than those with backs of silk and golden wings") are mingled in the poem with images of poetic beauty:

> Here by a mountain's side, a reverend cave
> Gives murmuring passage to a lasting wave;
> 'Tis the world's wat'ry hour-glass streaming fast,
> Time is no more when th'utmost drop is past;
> Here, on a better day, some druid dwelt,
> And the young Muse's early favour felt;
> Druid, a name she does with pride repeat,
> Confessing Albion once her darling seat.

The first two lines of this passage foreshadow Thomson. The second two lines compose a complete metaphysical image: a waterfall audaciously compared to an hour-glass. The last four lines here quoted also foreshadow Thomson's fondness for "druids" as representing the original vitality of English poetry. Swift's early poem can, as we look at it, become, like many "Augustan" poems when closely looked at, an archetype of the work of the whole period from the Metaphysicals to Crabbe. It surprises us with its range, its variety and its ability to mix likes with unlikes. Swift was not alone in finding the world *miscible* – or at least the poetic, the literary world.

The last verse-paragraph of "To Mr. Congreve" is a statement in four lines containing at once a riddle, an exhortation and a Biblical prophecy.

> In this descending sheet you'll haply find
> Some short refreshment for your weary mind,
> Nought it contains is common or unclean,
> And once drawn up, is ne'er let down again.   (lines 231–4)

Swift tells Congreve, then, that the sheet (of verses) produced by his Muse may offer his fellow-writer refreshment, something to feed on, presumably not only because of the encouragement and advice it contains but also because of the poetic entertainment it offers. It is, as Swift has said all along, a production for once and once only, as the poet rarely has such fire, and could write only under the inspiration of Congreve's own muse, borrowed (or prostituted) for the occasion. Yet Swift's conclusion is far from humble, certainly. The most outrageous thing about this poem is its ending. Swift's poem is compared, not to an offering, but to a vision supplied by God. The whole of these four lines is a sustained allusion to the apostle Peter's vision before he went to Cornelius the centurion, as recorded in Acts 10: 9–16. Peter fell into a trance

11   And saw heaven opened, and a certain vessel descending unto him, as it had been a great sheet knit at the four corners, and let down to the earth:
12   Wherein were all manner of four-footed beasts of the earth, and wild beasts, and creeping things, and fowls of the air.

A voice told Peter "Rise, Peter; kill, and eat" but the apostle was unwilling, "for I have never eaten any thing that is common or unclean." To this objection (a reference of course to the Jewish dietary laws) the voice from heaven replied "What God hath cleansed, *that* call not thou common." We are told "This was done thrice" (not just once) and then "the vessel" (or sheet) was "received up again into heaven."

Swift in his poem is making an impudent allusion to Holy Writ – impudent and serious. Though we are often told that the "Augustans" disliked puns, and certainly they were often willing to censure puns or "quibbles," Swift is not alone among Augustan writers in employing them; here the whole is a conceit, depending on the outrageous pun on "sheet" (of paper) and the "sheet" in Peter's vision. Swift says that his own work, like the sheet in Peter's vision, contains nothing that should be called "common or unclean." The poem ends by announcing a freedom from law and restriction (with Scriptural backing). The ending is a defence both jocular and spirited of that mixed quality (mixed in style, images, topics) of Swift's works. The traditional interpretation of Acts 10 (an interpretation supplied in the New Testament) is that Peter's vision told him that Jewish Christians must not despise the Gentiles, that the old rules against a Jew keeping company with people of another nation were no longer applicable, and that Jewish dietary laws need not obtain for Gentile converts to Christianity. Nothing is prohibited, nothing is to be shunned; everything can be taken in superabundance – mixed superabundance – and consumed. In Swift's poem, the implication is that all is open to the poet, all can be taken; no mixture of styles, no images of sources "clean" or "unclean" can be disdained. The poet under the New Law is not prohibited from the use of anything; all, including creeping things, can go into the poetry that fills his sheet. What God, or the Muse, hath cleansed, that call not thou common.

Swift's "To Mr. Congreve" could be called a late manifesto of Restoration poetics. Written thirty-three years after the Restoration, it gives voice to governing principles already recognizable and indeed set forth elsewhere by

Restoration poets. I have dwelt upon it because it gives such a succinct account of some major principles of daring, and because its final conceit clearly sets out one of the central characteristics of poetry we have come to call "Augustan." Liberty and audacity, adventure and experiment are central principles of our major poets of the period. Above all, they value the restless reaching of poetic desire. Poetry, or a poem, must be allowed to consume whatever in the cosmos it finds refreshing or appropriate at the moment.

The poetry of the Restoration and of the period which followed is strongly *appetitive*. If we miss this quality in Augustan poetry, we risk misunderstanding statements about decorum, propriety and so on, for the notion of limitation is introduced only on the understanding that the appetite is there, almost ungovernably strong, and is in itself a good, though it may require occasional restraint. The urge of Restoration poets in particular is very visibly to reach out and grab the world – and any reference to anything like rules is only a reminder that the grasping, the taking, the deglutition must be done effectively. Decorum is occasional; appetite, permanent. Lack of daring, the timidity that refuses to "*Snatch* a *Grace* beyond the Reach of Art" is the crowning poetic sin. Failure to reach, to go forward, to endeavour to have and be more is lamentable. Johnson praises Pope precisely for exemplifying the opposite of such feebleness, such timid respect for limits. Pope's genius always wanted to take in more than it already had. It did not produce what Swift called "fade insipid mixture," the product of the cautious vulgar (poets and critics) who try to fix fancy's mercury.

Appetite and expansive movement come naturally to the mind of the writers of this period whenever they are talking of poetry or of poetic genius. Dryden's famous simile describing poetic wit has often been discussed, and perhaps sometimes wrongly discussed as presenting a dull and mechanistic notion of the poetic mind (in contrast to the notions of the Romantics):

wit in the Poet, or wit writing ... is no other than the faculty of imagination in the writer, which, like a nimble Spaniel, beats over and ranges through the field of Memory, till it springs the Quarry it hunted after ...

("An Account of the Ensuing Poem [i.e. *Annus Mirabilis*] in a Letter to the Honourable Sir Robert Howard," 1667)

It is worth pointing out that the "Account" of *Annus Mirabilis*, written twenty-six years before Swift's "Ode to Congreve," expresses the same idea; the poetic imagination is nimble, ranging and appetitive. The connection of the spaniel to appetite (and to human appetite) may be half-forgotten by those of us who do not engage in field sports, but Dryden, a country man originally, knew these field sports well, and his spaniel springing its quarry is naturally connected with the idea of killing and eating. Imagination searches quickly, disdaining bounds; it ranges over large spatial territory until it finds what can be snatched and consumed. The imagination is a hungry hunter. In an earlier preface, Dryden had said that "Imagination in a Poet is a faculty so Wild and Lawless that, like an High-ranging Spaniel it must have Cloggs tied to it, least it out-run the Judgment" ("To the Right Honourable Roger, Earl of Orrery," Preface to *The Rival Ladies*, 1664). By the "Cloggs" Dryden here means the practice of rhyme, which disciplines poetry; blank verse is too luxurious, leading to prolixity and looseness. But the imagination, the high-ranging spaniel, is approved of; imagination ought to be, centrally, "Wild and Lawless" or it isn't imagination at all. In the *Annus Mirabilis* preface, Dryden uses the spaniel image again, to concentrate on the splendour of the free-ranging poetic appetite.

The idea of appetite comes naturally to Dryden when discussing poetry. We find the idea – and the word itself – strikingly and slightly differently applied later in a preface of 1693. We may take it that Dryden's tribute to Dorset, however undeserved a piece of flattery in relation to its particular object, expresses what Dryden thinks are the most delightful and admirable qualities of poetry:

'tis Your Lordships particular Talent to lay your Thoughts so close together, that were they closer, they wou'd be crouded, and even a due connexion wou'd be wanting. We are not kept in expectation of two good lines, which are to come after a long Parenthesis of twenty bad; which is the *April* Poetry of other Writers, a mixture of Rain and Sun-shine by fits: You are always bright, even almost to a fault, by reason of the excess. There is continual abundance, a Magazine of Thought, and yet a perpetual Variety of Entertainment; which creates such an Appetite in your Reader, that he is not cloy'd with any thing, but satisfy'd with all. 'Tis that which the *Romans* call *Coena dubia*; where there is such plenty, yet withall so much Diversity ...

> ("Discourse concerning the Original and Progress of Satire," dedication of
> translation of Juvenal, "To the Right Honourable Charles, Earl of *Dorset* and
> *Middlesex*," 1693)

Good poetry should be close-crowded with good things, bright even to a fault, offering "perpetual Variety," surprising by a fine excess – and good poetry creates "such an Appetite in your Reader," creates the appetite by which it is to be enjoyed. Good poetry, appetite-provoking, is produced by the appetitive imagination which it then stimulates in others. Hunger provides a major Augustan metaphor for artistic creation and for the psychological workings of imagination. Over sixty years later, Samuel Johnson spoke of "that hunger of imagination which preys incessantly upon life" (*Rasselas* [1759], ch. 21). This is not, for Johnson, a personal defect or virtue of the individual mind, just a fact; without being hungry, imagination is not imagination.

"Rise, kill, and eat" might be taken as the motto of English poets of the Restoration, from Butler on, and, to only a slightly lesser extent, of all the succeeding poets to the end of the eighteenth century. Nothing is so common, so bizarre, so "unclean" – or so grand – that it can't be apprehended and consumed by the poetic process. Everything that has being, physical or mental, is available to the poet. Our tendency, inculcated in schools (when Augustan poetry is talked of at all), to think of the poets of the time as "neo-classical" and hence bound by a notion of some abstract classic dignity can lead to serious misreading. The poets were not in love with some marble-cool, remote and stiff dignity, some bare white essence of unassailable grandeur. "Neo-classicism" has its place, as a new movement, emanating from France and promising philosophic and aesthetic possibilities of considerable interest – rather like structuralism or semiotics in our own time. Strange things happen, however, to Continental theories when they are taken up in English-speaking lands. We will misunderstand the neo-classical enthusiasm (to use that typical figure of the Augustans, an oxymoron) if we do not see first the appetitiveness and excitement that underlay all interest in new literary movements, techniques, or forms of criticism.

The poets who were young in the late years of the Interregnum or the early years of the Restoration did not think of themselves as old classical poets, or as musty classics of English literature, or as correct and stiff "Augustans." They (and the generations who came after them) thought of themselves (rightly) as new poets, and as part of a new movement in English poetry. The idea of a "movement" is of course a modern one, coming from the late nineteenth century. At least, the phrase is modern, but the sense is visibly there in the late seventeenth century, a sense sharpened by a new and heightened feeling of the importance of time, a new idea of historical period. Earl Miner has pointed out that in Dryden's *Essay of Dramatic Poesy* "the concept of historical periods of literature emerges ... for the first time in English criticism, along with a sense of historical movement or development – and of a period of literature as something related to the other events of the time."[1] Men now spoke of "the age"; they could see difference between historical periods, even the relatively minute periods of generations, or decades. The experience of the Civil War had given Englishmen a sharpened and modern sense of the historically possible, of change in history, and had led to a sense of the characteristic qualities of a period. "The new" has a new indicative and prophetic meaning. Changes of fashions, the possibilities of degeneration, had been noted, often gloomily, since classical times (*O tempora! o mores!*) and the Renaissance furnished a heightened sense of the possibility of what we call progress, as well as (heavily stressed) processes of deterioration. But our whole way of thinking about time (which includes our habit of trying to explain social and other change historically, and our endeavours to predict the future on the basis of assumptions about inevitable change) can be seen as a direct inheritance from the latter part of the seventeenth century.

One by-product of this way of thinking about time, of considering the new, is an urgent sense of possibility and adventure in undertaking novel literary forms and techniques, in writing new poetry. Like Wyatt and Surrey (and the other contributors to *Tottel's Miscellany*), like Philip Sidney writing *Astrophel and Stella* or the *Arcadia*, like Donne producing Songs and Sonnets, the writers of the Restoration were conscious of bringing something new and adventurous to English literature. Indeed, it is less of an anachronism to speak of a "movement" when referring to Butler, or Dryden, or Rochester, or (to move up in time) to Swift and Pope than when referring to Wyatt or Sidney or Donne, since novelty, and the sense of some kind of forward movement through history, were notions now central to consciousness. The feeling that one is contributing something to one's own "age," both reflecting that age and being reflected in it, is visible throughout the period, and is part of that Augustan self-consciousness which I shall deal with later.

The new poets thought of themselves as new poets of new movements always do – as dashing and experimental. They would, to say the least, have been disappointed to hear that we think of them as less colourful or less adventurous than the Elizabethans and Jacobeans – however great their respect for their predecessors. They would have been deeply chagrined had they known that their works were considered by anybody, even by schoolchildren, as charac-terized by dull correctness. And once one gets to know those works, such a view cannot hold. Certainly, these poets, both those of the Restoration and those of the later generations who succeeded them, thought they had opened up the field of poetry. In their eyes, the great Elizabethans, and the so-called (by us) "Jacobeans" and "Metaphysicals," had produced wonderful poetry but their works were much too limited in scope to be satisfactory contemporary models. The new poets felt the exaltation which all poets in new movements always feel, of breaking through old limits, doing away with old rules, tossing antique blueprints out of the window. They were excited by the idea of doing more than their great forebears. Poetry had a licence to range, to grab, to take, to consume more of the world than the elder poets had allowed themselves. Until recently, so many of us have been brought up on Wordsworth's Preface to *Lyrical Ballads*, the manifesto of another new movement, that we have tended to take Wordsworth's opinions of Augustan poetry too much as truth. Or at least we did so when we were in school, and found the indoctrination hard to outgrow, because Wordsworth got his word in first. We then missed the comedy of seeing the parallel between Wordsworth's eager assumption that he and some of his contemporaries could write in the *real* language of men and the early Augustans' own ardent protests that that was exactly what *they* were doing, in contradistinction to an older poetry that had got timid and crouched within the palings of its own set limits.

Dryden in his "Account" of *Annus Mirabilis* gives us one of the early (1667) manifestos of the new poetry, in drawing attention to his expanded use of language.

In general I will onely say, I have never yet seen the description of any Naval Fight in the proper terms which are us'd at Sea; and if there be any such in another Language, as that of *Lucan* in the third of his *Pharsalia*, yet I could not prevail my self of it in the *English*; the terms of Arts in every Tongue bearing more of the Idiom of it than any other words. We hear, indeed, among our Poets, of the thundring of Guns, the smoke, the disorder, and the slaughter; but all these are common notions. And certainly as those who, in a Logical dispute, keep in general terms, would hide a fallacy, so those who do it in any Poetical description would vail their ignorance ... For my own part, if I had little knowledge of the Sea, yet I have thought it no shame to learn ...

Dryden is proud of having included the real language of the navy and ships, the "Idiom" of the terms of art. He has got rid of the old language, the mere "general terms." He is writing in the real language of men. The passages to which he refers include verses like this:

> Some the gall'd ropes with dawby Marling bind,
> Or sear-cloth Masts with strong Tarpawling coats:
> To try new shrouds one mounts into the wind,
> And one, below, their ease or stifness notes.   (stanza 148)

A reader might complain that some of these words were not known to him; Dryden would retort that the full expanse of English must be at the poet's disposal, and that only "the proper terms which are us'd at Sea" can convey to us the real experience of Englishmen involved in a naval war. What may seem at first more strange, Dryden does not shrink from incorporating such terms of the practical arts into a poem which also contains such stanzas as the sixteenth, which, as Jean Hagstrum has noted,[2] works in the terms of Baroque painting:

> To see this Fleet upon the Ocean move
> Angels drew wide the Curtains of the skies:
> And Heav'n, as if there wanted Lights above,
> For Tapers made two glareing Comets rise.

Dryden makes his poem draw upon all possible and imaginable levels of reality and ways of seeing. The heavenly host watching the outcome of a human sea-battle like spectators at a solemn cosmic theatre are no less and no more real than the "strong Tarpawling." What is almost more fascinating about stanza 16 is the way that it is picked up in the ensuing stanza, which entertains scientific speculation about the exact nature of comets:

> Whether they unctuous Exhalations are,
>   Fir'd by the Sun, or seeming so alone,
> Or each some more remote and slippery Star,
>   Which looses footing when to Mortals shown.

That third line is one of the most beautiful Dryden ever wrote, but its effect depends on its context. In these two stanzas we can see that the new mixture includes some old elements. The effect of the last part of stanza 16 is dependent partly on a metaphysical conceit, with an elaborated homeliness in "as if there wanted Lights above" (heaven in a domestic need for candlelight) that reminds us of Shakespeare and of Donne. The scientific speculation of the first two lines of stanza 17 belongs to the age of Dryden (which is also the age of Milton's *Paradise Lost*, a poem embodying similar scientific queries).[3] But the combination of the serene grandeur with economy, of nicety of touch with sumptuous fullness of effect (as in the alliteration), the mixture of the splendid with the delicately homely ("slippery"; "looses footing") can certainly remind us of Spenser. All the resources of English poetry are being brought together with new elements to make something new. Each stanza in *Annus Mirabilis* is a complete movement in itself, a factor which slows down the action – probably the reason why Dryden never again used this verse form (derived from Davenant's experimental unfinished epic, *Gondibert*, 1651). But each stanza also expands as it moves into the next one; meanings change and develop, and the whole creates a "true" history – which we must admit is propagandistic history – of a series of actions. The actions are not lost in the mist of the past but are known to poet and reader alike as recent developments, the current events of the last two years. The poem covers two great sea-battles against the Dutch, and then the Great Fire of London – disparate elements which Dryden manages to make into a unity, a unity based on the principles of historicity and of expansiveness.

Dryden's poem has several immediate practical and political purposes: it expresses nationalism against the Dutch, royalism against Puritan political views. The poet was vitally concerned with developing an optimistic interpretation of history and making hopeful prophecy to counter the sternly negative interpretations and prophecies of Puritan astrologers who saw in the comets emblems of horrific disaster connected with the ominous year 1666, associated with 666, the number of the Beast in Revelation 13.[4] *Annus Mirabilis* expresses the hope for England's imperial peace, and is one of the clearest Restoration utterances of the imperial theme. The poet prophesies that London will rise cleansed and beautified from its ashes, and will, like England herself, become famous and rich through wealth derived from her sea-trading.

> Now, like a Maiden Queen, she will behold,
>   From her high Turrets, hourly Sutors come:
> The East with Incense, and the West with Gold,
>   Will stand like Suppliants, to receive her doom.   (stanza 297)

Fairy-tales, the story of the Three Wise Men, and the idea of Queen Elizabeth (here transferred to London) combine here in a picture of beauty, wealth and power united in a sort of innocence – for Dryden wants us to think that the new power of England will be founded on the arts of peace. English ships will sail round the world, and the world's fleets will sail here. The last image combines the completion of the poem itself with the completion of England's recent and present trials, and the completion of a sea-journey on the spice route:

> Thus to the Eastern wealth through storms we go;
>   But now, the Cape once doubled, fear no more:
> A constant Trade-wind will securely blow,
>   And gently lay us on the Spicy shore.   (stanza 304)

Dryden has predecessors and successors in this vision of England's accession of pleasure and power through trade. Denham in *Cooper's Hill* (first published 1642) had seen the promise offered by the Thames (personified), who

Visits the World, and in his flying towers
Brings home to us, and makes both Indies ours;
Finds wealth where 'tis, bestows it where it wants,
Cities in deserts, woods in Cities plants.
So that to us no thing, no place is strange,
While his fayre bosome is the worlds exchange.[5]

The imperial – or rather, imperial-commercial – theme is picked up effectively by Pope in *Windsor Forest*, in which the god of the Thames speaks, prophetically like the poet of *Annus Mirabilis*, of the good time to come, when Britain shall be free of war, and will rule the earth by trade. Pope emphasizes a belief that prosperous commerce will put an end to divisions between peoples of East and West, of new worlds and old, and will end barbarism, cruelty, slavery and conquest, giving each nation its own glory:

Thy Trees, fair *Windsor*! now shall leave their Woods,
And half thy Forests rush into my Floods,
Bear *Britain*'s Thunder, and her Cross display,
To the bright Regions of the rising Day;
Tempt Icy Seas, where scarce the Waters roll,
Where clearer Flames glow round the frozen Pole;
Or under Southern Skies exalt their Sails,
Led by new Stars, and born by spicy Gales!
For me the Balm shall bleed, and Amber flow,
The Coral redden, and the Ruby glow,
The Pearly Shell its lucid Globe infold,
And *Phoebus* warm the ripening Ore to Gold.
The Time shall come, when free as Seas or Wind
Unbounded *Thames* shall flow for all Mankind,
Whole Nations enter with each swelling Tyde,
And Seas but join the Regions they divide;
Earth's distant Ends our Glory shall behold,
And the new World launch forth to seek the Old.
Then Ships of uncouth Form shall stem the Tyde,
And Feather'd People crowd my wealthy Side,
And naked Youths and painted Chiefs admire
Our Speech, our Colour, and our strange Attire!
Oh stretch thy Reign, fair *Peace*! from Shore to Shore,
Till Conquest cease, and Slav'ry be no more:
Till the freed *Indians* in their native Groves
Reap their own Fruits, and woo their Sable Loves,
Peru once more a Race of Kings behold,
And other *Mexico's* be roof'd with Gold.   (lines 385–412)

The world displayed by Pope here is one of great richness, energy and activity. Everything is active, even the foreign products: Balm bleeds, Amber flows, Coral and Ruby redden and glow of their own accord – in lines which seem to borrow their pearl-and-golden sheen from the late Elizabethans. Things sparkle or shimmer (the aurora borealis round "the frozen Pole") or gush in an irresistible natural impulse round the world and into Britain ("Whole Nations enter with each swelling Tyde"). The impulse which stirs the world negates divisions and mixes the ingredients of the world so that war, hostility, conquest – anything that insists on the old conventions, hierarchies and placements – seem antique.

It must be admitted that Pope's vision appears naive, politically. The poet avoids exploiting the coercive connection between Britain's cannons (her "Thunder") and her Cross. And Pope here seems unwilling to recognize what is now so plain to us, that the desire for world trade is one of the central causes of war and conquest, not a preventive. Pope himself lost faith in this idea, and was to become one of the sharpest critics of the new capitalism. *Windsor Forest* is an early poem, written while a Stuart still reigned; under the Hanoverians, and particularly after the advent of Walpole, Pope took a much more critical and angry look at Whig beliefs and at the politics of mercantilism.[6] James Thomson, in *The Seasons* (written in the 1730s), is still able to be complacent about England's financial and commercial progress in a way that Pope is not. Nevertheless, Pope did not forsake the humanistic vision that is, for us, the best idea in the passage quoted above. He desired, as we do in our day, a world united, with its peoples capable of communicating with each other, and all nations equally valid, respected and self-governing. His imagined future world is one which has not forsaken differences but acknowledged them without letting them be obstacles. Even the elements which are still, to our ears, unfortunately patronizing, in the references to "Feather'd People," "naked Youths and painted Chiefs," are almost redeemed by the cultural relativism imposed in the reversal: these visitors, coming of their own free will for peaceful purposes, will have their own comments to make on our strange language, racial colouring and dress. This vision of the great world brought together not only pleases Pope – it thrills him.

What Pope shows is a world of activity, of sumptuousness ("Balm," "Amber," "Coral," "Ruby," "Pearly Shell"), of opposites united ("clearer Flames glow round the frozen Pole") and space conquered through expansive movement and reaction. By a paradoxical new geometry, as new as the "new Stars" Englishmen will see in Southern skies, what divides will also join. Nothing is to be cut off, left separate and isolated, from East to West, from Pole to Pole. Nothing is left to itself in all this hurly-burly of glory – and so we may say of *Annus Mirabilis*. The appetite for wealth and glory is an appetite for the great globe itself, for space and all the products of earth and sea – an appetite which Pope assumes will be happily shared by Peruvians, Mexicans, American Indians and others, who will all, like us, rush forth to consume space.

It is a fact, however disagreeable or embarrassing it may be both to people of other nations and to the British now when we are at the end of Britain's imperial history, that the poetry of the "Augustan Age" is the poetry that arose during England's first great age of imperialism. Before the end of the eighteenth century Britain (and perhaps we should more truthfully say

England) had lost one set of colonies in North America, but had also, after steady efforts, gained large control over India, as well as the West Indies and various other parts of the world. The poetry of the period under discussion, from the Restoration (or just before it) to the end of the eighteenth century, reflects that large historical truth. Dryden's prophecy in *Annus Mirabilis*, Pope's in *Windsor Forest*, and a number of explicit lines in Thomson's *The Seasons* are full statements about the new commercial and territorial enterprise and hopes. It should also be held in mind that Britain's drive toward empire during this period has not too much to do with the "British Empire" as that puzzling entity came to be known in the imperial heyday of the nineteenth century, when it was managed by large centralized governmental organizations producing earnest District Officers and involving much regulation. The "empire" of the earlier period was an unofficial one, and except for North American settlements had little to do with colonies, but much to do with trade.

The search for wealth in the rise of the new capitalism stimulated the enterprise of empire, which can be seen as just another aspect of emerging capitalism itself – old capitalism with all its stout flaws and bustling qualities. The 1690s saw the establishment of the Bank of England, and the country under William III became accustomed, if never quite resigned, to a National Debt. The system of credit, risk, insurance, paper money and all the other things we associate with capitalistic activity had their flowering in England at this time – and we were soon to learn about boom-and-bust stock markets and other entertainments offered by the developing financial system. The imperial drive, financed by private brokers in London but supported by Government in the supply of troops and navies for a number of trade wars, was a drive for wealth, even glamorous wealth. The figure of a "nabob," returned from India or the West Indies with a jaundiced complexion, a bad liver and bags of gold, is a stock figure in plays and novels from the early eighteenth century to the Regency. Empire made its way in an expansiveness which was also a kind of cruising, as individuals, supported by communal approval, made their way to foreign coasts, "Spicy shores" (there is a touch of the erotic in that phrase), looking for what they might pick up. Some of the toughest criticism of this whole process comes from the writers, very much including the poets. But that does not mean that the writers were not in any way affected, both for ill and for good, by the mentality and mood that produced this rather swashbuckling and impressive (if in some respects morally dubious) England – or Britain.

The idea of "empire" figures importantly in many minor works of the Restoration and the eighteenth century; the English empire and other empires were examined, and drawn upon for metaphor, imagery, allegory. Dryden's *The Indian Emperor* is about empire – and about the Western conquest of Mexico; his *Aureng-Zebe* is about the Mogul empire of India. But *MacFlecknoe* is about empire, too, as Marvell's earlier *Fleckno* is not, and its successor, Pope's *Dunciad*, is about empire, the anti-Virgilian anti-Augustan Empire of Dulness. The prevalence of empire as a powerful idea is, however, less important in itself than the unconscious presence in poetry (and poetics) of the same qualities or mental dispositions that made, in the practical or historical sphere, for England's expansion and domination of trade. The defects and – more strikingly – the qualities of Augustan poetry can more clearly be seen if we are willing, at least for one reading, to relate what is going on in that poetry to one of the principal historic facts about the period. We have spoken much in the past about the Peace of the Augustans, noticing, as we ought, the memory in Englishmen of the time of the Civil War and their acute anxiety at the symptoms of anything like it happening again. Previous critics have written, and have written well, about the Augustans' "rage for order," their concern to make a balanced and controlled society, accommodating differences in order to prevent any breaking-out of the divisive forces, so very visible in the events of the early and mid seventeenth century. We have been taught that men and women of the Restoration and eighteenth century feared and despised "enthusiasm" (meaning religious "enthusiasm"), and have sometimes mistakenly been led to believe that they thus despised enthusiasm (in the modern sense) about anything at all. I believe that we should notice, along with the compromise, the scepticism, the humanism, another impulse, or set of impulses – perhaps not so unrelated to these other things as we might at first think.

That impulse is the impulse of expansion. Expansiveness is a fact of this literature, both in form and style. The expansiveness is related to the desire to mix things, to exclude nothing, to combine what was hitherto separate: "And seas but join the Regions they divide." The idea of importing and exporting (which visibly excites Dryden and Pope so much in the passages quoted) as a poetically, i.e. imaginatively, attractive idea depends on a notion of the attractiveness of mixing things, of bringing things not native to the soil together and sending our own people, ourselves, out to unknown climes to fetch them, while receiving persons from unknown climes in our native harbour. Unknown and disparate wealth is sought and gathered, fastidiously but greedily, and brought home for use, adding essential colour and flavour to life, and also making possible new activities. Pope doesn't use "Tea" in his catalogue of exotic nouns; "Balm," "Ruby," "Coral" carry the sensuous appeal – but in the poem of the previous year (amplified in 1714), *The Rape of the Lock*, "Tea," "Coffee" and "Chocolate" are vividly celebrated, and the reference to the teacup as "*China*'s earth" is more than an elegant variation; it is a reminder of imports and trade. Indeed, as Louis Landa has shown us, much of the poem alludes to trade and economic theory: "Belinda as a consumer, the embodiment of luxury ... was ... recognizably the final point in a vast nexus of enterprises, a vast commercial expansion which stirred the imagination of Englishmen."[7] Belinda and her set wear imported silks and Arabian perfumes; they take tea and coffee from oriental cups. That the English became accustomed to tea- and coffee-drinking in the later seventeenth century may not be a major historical fact, but it is not a little fact. The importation of tea-leaves and coffee beans had, and was to have (and still has), important effects on the world's economy. One of the effects was the rise of England's china manufacture in the eighteenth century. It seems one of history's ironies that the Wedgwoods, respectable kings of china manufacture, should have become leading propagandists against slavery, when the product which led to the demand for their own successful product was the result of vigorous commercial imperialism, and when the other import, used to sweeten the tea or coffee the Wedgwood cups were made to contain, depended very directly for its cultivation on the use of slave-labour. Our elegancies and our rage for dominion – our greed – seem intertwined.

This reference to the tea-trade is used only as a short parable to illustrate the pervasiveness of appetitive activities during the period under discussion. It is not my purpose here to enter into the now familiar censure of the English past, or even to lament human wickedness overmuch. It is useful here to impress these things on our memories in order to look at the literature with fresh eyes. For the stylistic qualities of "Augustan" poetry are metaphorically and more than metaphorically related to the qualities and activities of that energetic and greedy time, and the qualities of appetite and expansiveness can be seen in the poetry of the period, along with the desire to mix, to import, to remake and remodel. The vices and virtues of Augustan poetry are the vices and virtues of buccaneering millionaires, intelligent, ingenious and insatiable. At least, such a view makes a refreshing change from the view of the Augustans as tame and pedantic. If we look at them suspiciously, it should be for other reasons.

It is hardly necessary to add that I do not mean that the poets were morally piratical, or that their views are commercial or imperialistic, or that they wrote about trade and empire all the time. I am speaking of the style and language of their poetry, a poetry which seeks expansively for new language, invents new forms, adds new colouring.

The poets could, when they wished, back up some of their claims with justifying references to the antique critic known as "Longinus." But the popularity of this author of a treatise on the sublime (*Peri Hypsous*) after the late seventeenth century is presumably best explained by his noticeable congeniality to the age. Longinus was fundamentally suited to their enterprise (whether they were or were not trying at a particular moment for a "sublime" effect); Longinus disdains safety and admires daring faults:

I readily allow, that Writers of a lofty and tow'ring Genius are by no means pure and correct, since whatever is neat and accurate throughout must be exceedingly liable to Flatness. In the Sublime, as in great Affluence of Fortune, some minuter Articles will unavoidably escape Observation. But it is almost impossible for a low and grov'ling Genius to be guilty of Error, since he never endangers himself by soaring on high, or aiming at Eminence, but still goes on in the same uniform secure Track, whilst its very Height and Grandeur exposes the Sublime to sudden Falls.
. . .
Is the Poet *Eratosthenes*, whose *Erigone* is . . . not chargeable with one Fault, to be

esteem'd a superior Poet to *Archilochus*, who flies off into many and brave Irregularities; a godlike Spirit bearing him forwards in the noblest Career, such Spirit as will not bend to Rule, or easily brook Controul?

(*On the Sublime*, Section xxxiii, trans. William Smith)[8]

The obvious answer to that last question is "certainly not." Or, as Swift put it, *"Beat not the dirty paths where vulgar feet have trod."* Longinus could be called upon, when wanted, to support adventure and experiment, the daring that risks imperfection. He gave to poets and critics a language to express much of what the poetry of the age most desired to achieve: "fire," intensity, expansiveness,

Fig. 1

freedom from unwanted "Controul." The poets were determined not to be content poetically with a small lot. This is the period in which we began to talk about "Genius."

The sense of confidence, the desire for expansiveness, for moving away from some "secure Track" can be found in the poet's references to the role of the poet. The authority and the ambition are caught in the visual icons used to illustrate the poet's role in the period, such as portrait frontispieces to collected works (all those portraits surrounded by Fame, Muses, angels) or in particular illustrations such as those to Pope's poems in Warburton's great edition of the *Works* (1751); see Figs. 1, 2 and 3. In the illustration to the *Essay on Criticism*, lines 189–96 (Fig. 1), we see the bardic Pope being inspired by the *"Bards triumphant"* who have apparently made a point of coming to visit him. The humility of the reference to "the meanest of your Sons" is counteracted in the verse by the poetry itself, and, in the picture, by the contrast between the standing group, who seem agitated, and the seated Pope, who regards them attentively but serenely while he writes. Pope is inspired, but certainly not overcome. The poet is seated in a grotto, like the womb of a mind, but his grotto is open to the sky, to the regions of history, art and life (the tree and the temple) beyond.

In the illustrations to the second "Epilogue to the Satires" (one for lines 210–11; the next for lines 212–15), the first shows the poet seated and writing in a classical building like a great theatre – again in a circular structure open to the sky, to an infinity beyond. Before the poet divine messengers display Donne and Horace, and offer the inspiration of wit and music, the caduceus and the lyre. Pope, pensive, with the strange mongrel dog (Satire) at his feet, exhibits a lively interest combined with a calm which reflects his undoubted authority; this poet, poised over his writings, has a right to be classed with Donne and Horace. In the illustration to the next lines, the Muse of Satire, unmasking, gives Pope the sacred weapon, the pen, which is at the same moment touched by the spear of the goddess leaning from her cloud. Behind him, as in need of his defence, stands Truth (or perhaps Justice) blindfolded, while Pope kneels at the altar and receives what the verses say are needed, the gift of the weapon and the direction of heaven. There is a good deal that could be said about this serious and playful picture, regarding, for instance, the use of faces and parts of faces, and most notably the odd use of sexual gender and of objects. Suffice it to note that despite the prayerful humility of posture, Pope kneeling at the altar has his eyes wide open and appears to be in command of these transactions, which seem to be no more than his due. Above the poet is the great expanse of limitless sky, and the zig-zag movement indicated by the composition of figures and objects indicates movement into space, expansion, the going up and forward into the limitless.

It is true that Hayman's and Grignion's pictures were drawn for the posthumous edition of Pope, celebrating a poet who had now entered that eternal literary world where he joins Donne and Horace. But we are rather

Fig. 2

reminded of the Pope who is speaking to us from the present of his verse, and the pictures certainly manifest the idea of the poet as his age saw him. Roving to the interior of the world, to past ages, to the heavens, dealing with the strange and with the eternal, the poet lives an expansive and symbolically rich life, trafficking with all manner of inspiring powers and forms. We remember that to Johnson these pictures would have been familiar long before he wrote Pope's *Life*. In the pictures, as in the poems themselves, the poet, or his genius, is indeed presented as "active, ambitious, and adventurous, always investigating, always aspiring; in ... highest flights still wishing to be higher."

Fig. 3

The poetry of the Augustan Age is ambitious and adventurous. It has confidence in its own authority. It imports new languages and remodels old ones. Refusing to be flawless in mere limitation, the poetry is both fastidious and gluttonous; some profit can be made of almost everything, nothing is too common or unclean for use, nothing too exotic or wonderful for apprehension.

In their interest in discovering (not to say forcefully grabbing) and containing new images and ideas, the Augustans owed a great debt to the Metaphysicals. Although they never quite acknowledged this fully, we have helped to acknowledge it on their behalf. Ian Jack has usefully pointed out that much of

Samuel Butler's effect depends on the use of "the Metaphysical idiom."[9] A couplet such as

> And like a *Lobster* boyl'd, the *Morn*
> From *black* to *red* began to turn

is "metaphysical" in its unexpected, and even strained, but at the same time appropriate, use of an image. Indeed it was probably inspired by John Cleveland's "The Mixt Assembly" (1647), a satire on the reforming synod of churchmen and laity set up by the largely Presbyterian parliament of 1643. In that poem Cleveland makes play with the coloration of this mixture, the black coats of the clergy and the ceremonial red gowns worn by aldermen:

> Strange Scarlet Doctors these, they'l passe in Story
> For sinners half refin'd in Purgatory;
> Or parboyl'd Lobsters, where there joyntly rules
> The fading Sables and the coming Gules.

Indeed, if we want to know what "metaphysical" poetry meant to the Augustans, we ought to look closely at Cleveland, who was closer to the Restoration poets (and thus to their successors) than was Donne, closer in time, and in political interest and passion. Cleveland (whose works were republished in 1668) also exhibits, much more than Donne, an interest in packing in all possible images, everything that might be said about a matter and everything that might be done with an image, and in this he is congenial to his successors, many of whom were political as well as poetic successors.

Marvell is of course our big example of the metaphysical poet *par excellence* who turned into an "Augustan" in writing his satiric poetry after the Restoration. Later, I wish to deal more extensively with what happened to metaphysical poetry under the stress of the Civil War and the Interregnum. But we ought here to note Marvell's qualities as a metaphysical Augustan. In "Last Instructions to a Painter" he includes couplets playing with one image, like Cleveland or like his earlier poetic self:

> Draw next a Pair of Tables op'ning, then
> The *House of Commons* clatt'ring like the Men.
> Describe the *Court* and *Country*, both set right,
> On opposite points, the black against the white.
> Those having lost the Nation at *Trick track*,
> These now advent'ring how to win it back.   (lines 105–10)

In the same poem he can produce a couplet composed of a quiet colloquial sentence, casual and clear, yet depending on the various metaphorical (and slangy) connotations of two utterly common words:

> Thick was the Morning, and the *House* was thin,
> The *Speaker* early, when they all fell in.   (lines 235–6)

Even more strange, in the very same poem he can include the moving, highly strained and baroque description of the dying Archibald Douglas who stayed with his burning ship, the *Royal Oak*, and died amid the flames:

> His shape exact, which the bright flames infold,
> Like the Sun's Statue stands of burnish'd Gold.
> Round the transparent Fire about him glows,
> As the clear Amber on the Bee does close:
> And, as on Angels Heads their Glories shine,
> His burning Locks adorn his Face Divine.   (lines 679–84)

Despite Marvell's own religious sympathies, he is unafraid of the high style, even the Continental high style; the description of Douglas is like the description not only of Catholic saints, but of saints in art; it seems related to the ornament of Roman Catholic churches, and the whole hyperbolical pyramid of tropes reminds us of Crashaw. We can take that, I think, though our own sensibilities may shrink at such a method of describing a human being dying in a fire. But the grand passage in which this occurs is preceded by a rough and disparaging (but effective) joke in the contemptuous reference to the officers who escaped from the burning ships:

> *Captain*, *Lieutenant*, *Ensign*, all make haste,
> E're in the Firy Furnace they be cast.
> Three Children tall, unsing'd, away they row,
> Like *Shadrack*, *Mesheck*, and *Abednego*.   (lines 645–8)

The Biblical story and reference are put to unexpected use, and the comicality of the rhyme in its context would do credit to Butler.

In "Last Instructions" Marvell exploits an enormous number of styles and devices, eliciting, in rapid succession or simultaneously, a variety of impressions while covering a large historical subject. The poem keeps expanding to include new topics or subordinate subjects, some of which we could not possibly have anticipated from the work's beginning. It traffics happily and richly in images, registers, tones and effects, joining in new combinations what was held asunder. Marvell is taking advantage – of his new position and freedom as an Augustan poet. Johnson criticizes the Metaphysicals for making "far-fetched" comparisons and yoking unequals violently together. When the Augustans want less violence in an effect they supply an easier transition to conduct the reader through the comparison, but they can still be violent and often wish to be surprising; they too still delight in *discordia concors*. They glory in the various relations of likes and unlikes. It is in fact the Augustans who amplify the spaces poetry could cover so that nothing has to be excluded. They literally fetch things (language, images) from afar, ranging from Peru to the slums. Theirs is a free-trading and ambitious literature.

Johnson, like other Augustan writers, knew the Metaphysicals; he certainly knew the later ones such as Cleveland better than we tend to do. What bothered Johnson most about the Metaphysicals was what seemed to him an absence of both sensuousness and passion, and a lack of range. In his view "they wrote rather as beholders than partakers of human nature . . . impassive and at leisure . . . without interest and without emotion" (*Life of Cowley*). "In forming descriptions they looked out not for images, but for conceits." What we think of as the Metaphysicals' images, Johnson sees as illustrative reference ("nature and art are ransacked for illustrations, comparisons, and allusions"). He misses the fullness of an object or scene brought for the reader to enjoy and existing in itself, poetically, in its own right and not as a metaphor or simile for something else. Some deep sources of entire pleasure are missing, which is why "the imagination is not always gratified." Metaphysical poetry is too tight, too narrowly held within the boundaries of the wits. It lacks the explosive and expansive effect:

they never attempted that *comprehension* and *expanse* of thought which at once *fills* the whole mind, and of which the first effect is *sudden astonishment*, and the second rational admiration . . . Their attempts were always analytick; they broke every image into fragments; and could no more represent by their *slender* conceits and *laboured* particularities the prospects of nature, or the scenes of life, than he who dissects a sun-beam with a prism can exhibit the *wide effulgence* of a summer noon.

(*Life of Cowley*; italics mine)

Johnson's whole paragraph here is implicitly a comparison of an old kind of poetry with the modern. In that last sentence, Johnson plays with his similes, making the first (for the inferior style) a fidgety metaphysical image and then rushing into the second, the simile for superiority, a simile very much in the style – indeed almost an echo – of Thomson. Johnson's own play of wit here shows that he understands and can handle both Cowley's and Thomson's style of imagery, but that the modern manner, which comprehends the other but is not bound by it, is greatly preferable. It is also altogether bigger, more – not less – surprising. Metaphysical poetry is "analytick," "slender," "laboured." Good poetry, i.e. modern Augustan poetry, is full, large and pleasurable. It offers "expanse," it "fills the mind." And it is modern Augustan poetry that supplies the electrifying jolt: "sudden astonishment." Disdaining boundaries and the timidity of the study, Augustan poetry (such as Thomson's at its best) bursts upon us with "wide effulgence" and the hot richness of "a summer noon."

Johnson is here giving voice to the (often implicit) poetic theories of other Augustan poets, as well as imitating in his prose sentences the range of their imagery and the force of their ideas. The Augustan poets retained the yoking of unequals, the surprise effects, even increasing the resources of astonishment because their poetics encouraged both the inclusion of a number of sources of language, including popular language (colloquialism, slang), and the exploration and exploitation of an increased number of sources of imagery. The poets and theorists insisted, however, on the presence of emotion, of passion (it may often be political passion), and they were never willing to forsake sensuousness for the rather dry effect they found in much of the Metaphysicals' poetry. If an

Augustan poet refers to rich things – Ruby or Gold – he wants to make you feel them, as the Elizabethans wish to make you do. If an Augustan poet refers to commonplace or ugly things, he wants you to sense those clearly also:

> Or hast thou mark't how antique Masters limn
> The Aly roof, with snuff of Candle dimm,
> Sketching in shady smoke prodigious tools,
> 'Twill serve this race of Drunkards, Pimps, and Fools.
>
> (Marvell, "Last Instructions," lines 9–12)

Graffiti are not only alluded to, but to be described so fully as to be seen. It is a mark of Augustan poetry that the reader is required to contemplate with his senses, to take in direct sense impressions. Eric Rothstein in his recent excellent book on Augustan poetry argues that "eighteenth-century readers had especially acute sensory reactions to poetic images when the idiom of the verse invited them to do so," and talks of the eighteenth century's attempt to create in reading a Kamesean "ideal presence." Rothstein holds that eighteenth-century readers read very differently from ourselves, in their endeavour to make everything on the page come alive to their eyes and senses, and the poets' techniques, in particular the cultivation of synecdoche, were cultivated "to make the reader see the context for details and visualize personifications."[10] It may be true that "no modern critic could write as Kames did" but that does not mean what Kames was referring to does not exist now; I would be much more cautious than Rothstein in attributing to "our forebears in the eighteenth century" an entirely different mode of reading from our own. Still, it is true that eighteenth-century poets desired a special vividness of effect, which their readers appreciated. It was the poet's task to bring all the universe before your eyes, or thought. The evocation of sense impressions was important. More remarkably, perhaps, the sense impressions evoked are often complex, finely roused by mixing the ugly and the beautiful, or the expected and the unexpected:

> Here, *Mummies* lay most reverendly stale,
> And there, the *Tortois* hung her Coat o' Mail;
> . . .
> Aloft in Rows large Poppy Heads were strung,
> And near, a scaly Alligator hung.
> In this place, Drugs in musty Heaps decay'd,
> In that, dri'd Bladders, and drawn Teeth were laid.
>
> (Garth, *The Dispensary*, Canto II)[11]

> Sweepings from Butchers' Stalls, Dung, Guts, and Blood,
> Drown'd Puppies, stinking Sprats, all drench'd in Mud,
> Dead Cats and Turnip-Tops come tumbling down the Flood.
>
> (Swift, "A Description of a City Shower," 1710)

> And Polyanthus of unnumber'd Dyes;
> The yellow Wall-Flower, stain'd with iron Brown,
> And lavish Stock, that scents the Garden round.
>
> (Thomson, *The Seasons*, "Spring," lines 532–4)

It is customary for Augustan poets to appeal to a number of different senses in quick succession or even combination.

But the chief mark of Augustan poetry, a symptom found unmistakably in "Last Instructions," is the desire to call upon different styles and to treat different topics in the same work. Various styles, tones, topics are mingled in one large space-exploring and spacious statement which takes in experience at a variety of levels or in a variety of moods. In "Metaphysical" poetry generally, we find in each poem a single topic, treated with concentration; the topic is unremittingly pursued, even harped on, played with and finished. In "Augustan" poetry the topic chosen is customarily a large one, capable of almost infinite extension to include all sorts of other topics, and an expanding number of styles or tones. An Augustan poem characteristically bears the interposition of lyric beauty, satiric description, pathos, parody and high late baroque emotiveness. Presumably contemporary readers felt cheated if their poet did not offer variety and expansion.

Each Augustan poem is thus entitled to be called "experimental," just as we say approvingly of individual metaphysical poems that they are experimental. But the experiment had different interests. In each poem the poet found new combinations of topics, tones, styles and emotions, never thus put together before. Each important poem announced itself as presenting an entirely new mixture, a peculiar variety, in an *expansive* and unrestricted treatment of large and ever-ramifying subjects. We might remind ourselves of some favourite if unobtrusive tropes of Augustan poets. One of their favourite ideas is that of the mixture or blend (rather like the tea-merchant, again). Thomson speaks of light's "mingling Ray" ("Autumn," line 695); the lights of the aurora borealis "mix and thwart, extinguish, and renew, / All Ether coursing in a Maze of Light" ("Autumn," lines 1113–14). Pope speaks of the view from Windsor as a mixture:

> Here Hills and Vales, the Woodland and the Plain,
> Here Earth and Water seem to strive again,
> Not *Chaos*-like together crush'd and bruis'd,
> But as the World, harmoniously confus'd.
>
> (*Windsor Forest*, lines 11–14)

Another favourite idea is freedom, the removal or transcendence of limits. "Unbounded" is a typically Augustan word, and we find it in the passage by Pope on trade quoted earlier; throughout that passage Pope rings the changes on the word "free." "Free" is one of Thomson's favourite words; we might expect that in a poet who wrote a five-part poem called *Liberty*, but the word is all over *The Seasons*, as are the words "all," "vast" and "unbounded." God is "boundless Spirit all / And unremitting Energy" ("Spring," lines 853–4) and one suspects that the attributes of the Deity who created the joys of Spring's "unbounded Beauty" are coveted and imitated by the author of unbounded "Spring." Mark Akenside in *The Pleasures of Imagination* (1744) makes the connection more explicit. The mind of God is the source of all that the imagination knows, and the mind of man is created to behold and recreate it, with "resistless ardour, to imbrace / Majestic forms" (Book I, lines 170–1). The human mind, like the imagination (and Akenside's own imagination, as he shows us), is "impatient to be free" and "Proud to be daring" (Book I, lines 171, 174).

Yet a third constant is the idea of *variety* – and the word. Nature offers "Order in Variety," but the idea of order is actually secondary, for without "variety" the concept of order would have no meaning. Akenside's Deity Platonically contemplates "the uncreated images of things" and then smiles them into being:

> Hence the breath
> Of life informing each organic frame,
> Hence the green earth, and wild resounding waves;
> Hence light and shade alternate, warmth and cold;
> And clear autumnal skies and vernal showers,
> And all the fair variety of things.
>
> (*Pleasures of Imagination*, Book I, lines 73–8)[12]

The "fair variety of things" pleased Augustan poets, perhaps a little too much. I cannot now remember who first said that Thomson's list of spring flowers ("Spring," lines 529–55) sounds like a seedsman's catalogue, but there is a touch of truth in that remark. And that sense of beauty combined with homely particularity, that mixture of memory and hope, and that delight in what seems to be an almost inexhaustible source of treasure which are the pleasures of reading a seedsman's catalogue are not, as the Augustans certainly felt, inappropriate to poetry. There is of course in Thomson's *Seasons* the danger of the reader's feeling overstuffed and exhausted, but that is a danger lurking in, for instance, Pope's *Dunciad* also: think of the fertile list of scatological games in Book II, or the apparently endless train of dunces (a variety indeed) in Book IV.

It is one of the potential defects of Augustan poetry that the poet may offer us too much, that the poem goes beyond the bounds of what the reader wants. Readers' appetites have, however, to be educated. We may suspect at times that the poet lingers too lovingly on catalogues of things in nature or of the mind, pushing at us a surplus of varieties of topic, style or tone. We may also find we can grow accustomed to and then enjoy this quality. There is, it must be admitted, a tendency at times for Augustan poets to seem like millionaires totting up their (nearly inexhaustible) assets aloud. But after all, these are assets that they offer us for sharing. They offer "continual abundance" from a sublime "great Affluence." It seems to me that it is this quality, rather than the famous love of order and desire of clarity, that has put real readers off the Augustan poets, though the objection has rarely been voiced, and has no precedent in most available modern academic criticism of the period. We have to get into the mood to enjoy such amplitude and affluence. We have to get used to the imperious and imperial command over all that is in earth and sky and sea, and over multifarious poetic effects and ideas. Like St. Peter, we have to become converted into a willingness to eat at the unusual, mixed and various banquet, a willingness which involves the removal of inhibitions, a delight in the novel and boundless. Our appetites have, in short, to match the poetic appetites of the poets and their appreciative original readers. Once we educate ourselves into this frame of mind (rather like going off a diet) we can proceed. It is harder for us, who have been bred in the sparer tradition of modern lyric poetry, to regain such a mood, to take the gargantuan courses of poetry. But once we realize that it is our appetite that is being commanded first, and not our fasting, that richness instead of austere control is the order of the day, then the extraordinary nature of what we are offered can make its appeal. Or, to change to the other metaphor, we realize that we are not asked to share in the kingship of some small "Province in Acrostick Land," but to participate in aspiring empire, the empire that Fleckno and MacFlecknoe missed, and Dryden (and Pope, Thomson, Cowper and others) found.

II

Some origins of Augustan practice: Civil War verse and its implications

In order to understand Augustan poetry and how it works, we should enquire, if only briefly, why it is what it is. We ought to look at the origins of Augustan poetry and Augustan poetic manners. Some of the antecedents of Augustan poetry are "low" rather than "high." We cannot explain the complexities of Augustan poetic work by alluding only to Milton and Virgil: some roots lie tangled deeper in the ground. The mixture of styles to which I have alluded as a feature of Augustan poetry can be seen as largely the result of what happened to English poetry just before, during and just after the Civil War of the 1640s. I ought to say, rather, what happened to *some* English poetry, but the "some" includes much of importance. The poets, like other Englishmen, were engaged in the internecine conflict, and many of them put their talent to work in writing poetic propaganda. Milton, the great Puritan apologist, did his major propaganda work in prose rather than poetry, but a number of his contemporaries wrote partisan poetry that was meant to circulate. Poets deliberately set out to be catchy; a lot of their works were intended to be singable. What might have been court poetry, or metaphysical lyric, or polished well-cadenced verse in the manner of Jonson turned into street-ballad, or ale-house or army-camp entertainment. Even those writers who did not participate in this popular movement, this reversion to a kind of "folk-poetry," could not remain unaffected by such a noticeable alteration in manner, subject and approach.

The best discussion of the Civil War partisan verse is still C. V. Wedgwood's *Poetry and Politics in the Age of the Stuarts* (1960), which first informed many undergraduates and general readers of the existence and significance of a body of work that should certainly be examined. The modern reader will not, however, readily obtain more than a limited number of the Civil War and Interregnum pieces.[1] Undoubtedly a number perished in the few ephemeral sheets in which they appeared, and a number of those that survive must lie unpublished in collections – or in attics. There is, however, a sufficient amount of Civil War verse available to the general reader to tell us a good deal. A major collection is found in *Rump: Or an Exact Collection of the Choycest Poems and Songs relating to the Late Times* By the most Eminent Wits, from *Anno* 1639 to *Anno* 1661, and on this I have drawn for many of my quotations. Like the bulk of surviving Civil War propaganda verse, which survived because it was published after the Restoration, *Rump Songs* is Cavalier in sympathies, even violently partisan. The one-sidedness of the surviving material is a pity, but

matters less in a literary context because the more immediate successors of the
Cavalier balladeers were for the most part Royalist or Tories, and the literary
influence is traceable in a more or less direct alignment with political sympathies.

Not all of the surviving Civil War verse is Cavalier, however. John Lookes's
ballad celebrating the execution of Strafford (1641) takes a jovial and sinister
pleasure in the event. The verse form is a well-wrought example of a short-line
stanza; with an irregular number of lines (seven in verse and four in the
refrain) and some unrhymed lines it seems free in form, though it is actually
strict. The fifth and sixth lines of this first stanza can, even today, cause a
shudder:

> Though Wentworths beheaded,
> Should any Repyne,
> Thers others may come
> To the Blocke beside he:
> Keepe thy head on thy Shoulders
> I will keep mine;
> For what is all this to thee or to mee?
> *Then merrily and cherrily*
> *Lets drink off our Beere,*
> *Let who as will run for it*
> *Wee will stay heere.*

The verse conjures up a strange vision of men in a pub, perhaps in town,
perhaps in the country, roaring out "Keepe thy Head on thy Shoulders" and
keeping time with their beer-mugs. Strange indeed, but not too strange to be
true, especially in areas where it would be safe to sing such an anti-Court
ballad. The concessions made, or apparently made, to censorship are only
intensifications of the general effect. The next object of Parliament's wrath was
to be Archbishop Laud, referred to in mock-guarded manner in the fifth
stanza:

> A man to doe evill
> And have too much Grace,
> Me thinks its a wonder
> Most strange for to see,
> So little in person,
> Yet great by his place:
> But what is all this to thee or to me,
> *Then merrily and cherrily*
> *Lets drinke off our wine*
> *Keepe thy head on thy shoulders,*
> *I will keepe mine.*

The code is easy to decipher, and the energy involved in decoding the reference
to (and description of) Laud is an aspect of the general aggressive energy
summoned up in the reader – or hearer or singer – by the ballad. The whole of
"Keepe thy Head on thy Shoulders" describes political events and amplifies a

mood; in its own way it is discursive, as it runs through topics of interest, enumerating the high-placed courtiers who have run away to escape Parliament's wrath ("many hath catched / The Running Disease"), prophesying the expulsion of all priests, Jesuits and "false Traytors" and looking forward to better times. Almost all such Civil War verse has a prophetic element.

What is really odd about "Keepe thy Head on thy Shoulders" is the peculiar combination of such a grim tone and such charged matter with such a form. The ballad is a drinking-song, thus belonging to a well-established genre with classical Greek forebears in the "high" style and light-hearted popular lyrics in the "low." Encouragement to drink is usually expressed in praise of wine or of John Barleycorn, or combined with praise of love and sex (romantic or bawdy). There are well-established topics and tones, and this ballad avoids almost all of them while still maintaining its identity as a drinking-song. The form seems to be invited to do something foreign to its nature. Yet the effect doesn't seem primarily disjunctive, though it is certainly striking. The camaraderie and all-togetherness summoned up by drinking-songs which belong in the friendly fug of the ale-house are here identified with political camaraderie cemented by a common hatred and contempt. Patterns of drinking-song style are sustained, but the style is turned to a new use.

This ballad succinctly illustrates a fact which all Civil War writers and readers had in some way to recognize. There is no style or form which will not be capable of being used by the enemy. No style or form is so simple and so pure as to resist the infection of the adversaries' thoughts and feelings. If we think that drinking-songs belong to Cavaliers, anti-Puritans and good fellows, we must think again. All styles and all forms are capable of betrayal.

Civil War verse questioned the genres which had been worked out from the time of the Tudors to that of the Metaphysicals and the tribe of Ben. Genres lose their safety and perfection; that a form or style is suited to only one set of uses becomes questionable. This has far-reaching implications for Restoration poetry and poetics. The question of genres has to be worked out again, and all style is recognized as concealing lurking dangers.

One way of getting around the problem newly posed by the new treachery of styles and forms is to withhold endorsement of the style one writes in by choosing a language and manner different from what one would choose to express one's own beliefs. Civil War poetry sees a surge of poems and verses rendered as if in the enemy's voice. The form of the ballad and its styles are thus acknowledged as already polluted, taken over by the repulsive Other, and a style cannot be considered responsible for keeping its innocence or its cool. Usually the ridicule of the view expressed is made clear from the outset, but the ridicule may be saved up for some telling point after the verse has proceeded for a while. It is clear at the beginning of "The Humble Petition of the House of Commons" that the speakers are ludicrous, that their assumed modesty

and rags of remaining formal politeness hardly bother to conceal the preposterous greed of their demands:

> If *Charles* thou wilt but be so kind
> To give us leave to take our mind,
> Of all thy store.
> When we thy Loyal Subjects, find
> Th'ast nothing left to give behind,
> Wee'l ask no more.

The verse creates an outrageous flat blandness, an impudence that has forgotten that it is impudence. In later stanzas the most outrageous demands or
commands are expressed casually, almost breezily, in perfect colloquial tones,
like throw-away lines on stage:

> Next, for the State, we think it fit
> That Mr. *Pym* should govern it,
> He's very poor.

But in other satiric poems of the time the beginning establishes the "serious"
language and thoughts of the supposed speakers, and the revelation of their
ugliness or absurdity is postponed for a space. One "Song" begins

> Know this my Brethren Heaven is clear,
> And all the clowds are gone,
> The righteous men shall flourish now
> Good dayes are comming on;
> Come then my Brethren and be glad,
> And eke rejoyce with me,
> Lawn sleeves and Rochets shall go down,
> *And hey then up go we.*

The first six lines of this first verse seem to contain nothing that could not be
said by a genuine Puritan; indeed a genuine Puritan might have looked at the
"Song" with some interest for those first few lines, unless he was struck by the
words at the head of the ballad: "To the Tune of *Cuckolds all a-row*." The saucy
vulgarity of the refrain, in its delineation of stupidly vaulting ambition, gives
the game away completely, though still not stepping out of the voice of the
imagined enemy speaker(s) or singer(s). The refrain makes its final point at
the very end of the ballad, "Except the *Gallows* claim his due, / *And hey then up go
we.*" The real writer of these verses, and the persons who would really speak or
sing them, take a vicious delight in imagining the execution of the supposed
speakers; the ballad which begins so easily is actually lethal, and the baleful,
jaunty inner humour depends partly on imagining the bad persons, the enemy,
still celebrating their own destruction to the very end. It is one of the ironies of
this ballad that whoever sings it has to impersonate the identity of a Puritan,
even to the point of celebrating the hanging of the supposed speaker whose
identity is temporarily fused with that of the reciter. Singing the ballad is not
only highly aggressive, but also oddly suicidal.

A number of Cavalier poems depend on this effect, the speaker damning himself and the celebratory verse form working against its own apparent grain. The style that might be used quite seriously and genuinely by the enemy is perverted, twisted out of common meaning by the context. "Collonel *Vennes* Encouragement to his Souldiers" by Alexander Brome begins heroically, with a trope familiar to us from genuinely ancient ballads like "Johnnie Armstrong." Again, it is only the end of the verse that reveals the true meaning of the whole, and thus reinterprets the beginning:

> Fight on brave Souldiers for the Cause,
>   Fear not the Cavaliers,
> Their threatnings are, as senceless as
>   Our jealousies and fears,
> 'Tis you must perfect this great Work
>   And all Malignants slay,
> You must bring back the King again
>   The clean contrary way.

The last line tells us that the supposed speaker, the Parliamentary Colonel Venn, works by mad reversal, and that the whole poem is to be read "the clean contrary way." Again we have the lethal game at the end, the speaker imagining his and his party's own damnation:

> But when our Faith and Workes fall down,
>   And all our Hopes decay,
> Our Acts will bear us up to Heaven
>   The clean contrary way.

It is of course absurd to suppose that the enemy would so damn himself; the art of such lethal satire in disguise as imitation folk-poetry is to make such self-accusation in some way credible, by excluding the tone, manner, style, beliefs and feelings of the antagonistic speaker or speakers. Genuine speakers for the real side (e.g. here the Puritan Party) should not be able to reject everything as entirely unrealistic or unrepresentative. The art is partly an art of mimicry.

The art of mimicry is pushed to a new boundary in Thomas Jordan's "The Rebellion" which jeers at the threatening democracy by employing the voices of (supposed) common and illiterate people:

> Come Clowns, and come Boys, come Hoberdehoys,
>   Come Females of each degree,
> Stretch out your Throats, bring in your Votes,
>   And make good the Anarchy;
> Then thus it shall be, sayes *Alse*,
>   Nay, thus it shall be, sayes *Amie*,
> Nay, thus it shall go, sayes *Taffie*, I trow,
>   Nay, thus it shall go, sayes *Jemmy*.

The voices are full of unashamed excitement and confusion:

> Speak *Abraham*, speak *Hester*,
> Speak *Judith*, speak *Kester*,
> Speak tag and rag, short coat and long:
> Truth is the spell that made us rebell,
> And murder and plunder ding dong;
> Sure I have the truth, sayes *Numphs*,
> Nay, I have the truth, sayes *Clem*,
> Nay, I have the truth, sayes reverend *Ruth*,
> Nay, I have the truth, sayes *Nem*.

The true speaker can be heard behind the mad Puritan democrat; with some subtlety, and intermittently, the illusion of the other voice is broken. The Other, the enemy thus mimicked, would not speak of his cohorts as "tag and rag" nor identify what appealed to them as "murder and plunder." The busy jollity of the whole carries us over such points; they make their impact, but we don't linger over them. The poem exhibits some kind of action in progress; the group decides not to fall out among themselves over religious differences, and agrees that religion is of secondary or even trifling importance compared to the main object, which is disposing of the Crown. The first of these points is got over in the second verse:

> Well, let the truth be whose it will
> There is something else in ours,
> Yet this devotion in our Religions
> May chance to abate our Powers:
> Then let's agree on some new way,
> It skills not much how true,
> Take P— and his club, or *Smec* and his tub
> Or any Sect, old or new;
> The Devil is in the pack, if choyce you can lack,
> We are fourscore Religions strong,
> Then take your choice, the Major voice
> Shall carry't right or wrong;
> Then let's have King *Charles*, sayes *George*,
> Nay, we'll have his Son, sayes *Hugh*;
> Nay, then let's have none, sayes gabbering *Jone*,
> Nay, wee'l be all Kings, sayes *Prue*.

The doggerel manner of the irregular lines adds to the effect of jabbering and illiterate confusion. So well did Jordan carry out his mimicry that he thought it advisable to pull back. The last verse is in another voice, drawing the moral ("Thus from the Rout who can expect / Ought but confusion . . .?") and firmly encouraging his own side: "Come Royalists, then, do you play the men, / And Cavaliers give the word." This exhortation could come only at the end of something else; if left to stand alone, it would itself be susceptible of parody, ambiguous, like the beginning of "Collonel *Vennes* Encouragement."

The only safe way, indeed, of expressing one's own opinions seems to have become the method of mixing them with mimicry of the other side's beliefs and

manner. Marchamont Nedham, who has some claim to be called England's
first journalist, could be taken as the first strong and widely read exponent of
what were to be the important new literary techniques. Nedham (for whom the
inevitable adjective is "versatile") was an expert in all current beliefs and
manners; he first wrote the journal *Mercurius Britanicus* against the King and in
favour of the Parliamentary army, then turned to writing *Mercurius Pragmaticus*
in favour of the King and against Cromwell and at last became editor and
writer of *Mercurius Politicus* in support of Cromwell. In his journalistic work
Nedham early discovered the uses of mimicry and the effectiveness of ridicule
through a *persona*. When, for instance, his Royalist opponent, the writer of the
King's official journal *Mercurius Aulicus*, published a letter supposedly from the
wife of a soldier in the Parliamentary army, lamenting the war, Nedham of the
Britanicus responded with a comic and profane equivalent as from the wife of a
Cavalier.²

The journalism of the time was strongly related to the ballad, and shared its
interests – even its writers. When Nedham was editor of the Royalist *Pragmaticus* (during the confused period from the defeat of the King to his execution) one of his assistants was the poet John Cleveland. Nedham himself then
regularly turned his talents to verse as well as prose. Each number of *Mercurius
Pragmaticus* opened with four four-line stanzas, neat and memorable satiric
utterances – Nedham's poem of the week, as it were. Nedham became, if only
for a while, one of the best or at least most effective popular poets on the
Cavalier side. In an effort to win favour after the Restoration, Nedham
published these sixty-four editorial poems as one long poem, *A Short History
of the English Rebellion* (1661; reprinted 1680). His verse would certain have
been known to Butler and the other Restoration writers, if they didn't recall
seeing the verses in *Pragmaticus*. The conceits and even the rhymes of Nedham's
verse³ invective can remind us of the work of better poets who followed, of
Butler, e.g.

> When ev'ry *Priest* becomes a *Pope*,
>   Then *Tinkers* and *Sow-gelders*
> Nay, if they can but 'scape the *Rope*,
>   Be Princes and *Lay-Elders*

or of Dryden as in

> Our States men (though no Lunaticks,
>   No *Wizards*, nor *Buffo[o]ns*)
> Have shewn a hundred Changeling Tricks,
>   In less than three New Moons.

(Compare the description of Zimri.)

Nedham's best verse exhibits a sneering irony, imitating the opposition's
slogans, voice, views, while suggesting succinctly the context that makes these
slogans, those views, so repulsive and even terrifying:

> These both agreed to have *no King*;
> The *Scotchman* he cries further,
> *No Bishop:* 'tis a godly thing
> States to reform by Murther.

Nedham was happiest in his role as a Cavalier street-poet when he could attack the Scots and the Presbyterians, and the "Puritan" attitudes he could not approve (Nedham was always a better Commonwealthsman than Puritan). His capacity for mimicry stands him in good stead in this example, for instance, where he mocks the Puritan prohibition of Christmas:

> All *Plums* the *Prophets Sons* defie
> And *Spice-broths* are too hot;
> Treason's in a *December-Pye*
> And *Death* within the *Pot*.
>
> *Christmas*, farewel; thy day (I fear)
> And merry-days are done:
> So they may keep *Feasts* all the year,
> Our *Saviour* shall have none.

Slang, mimicry, comic exaggeration, the yoking of the great with the little – all these combine oddly but effectively with elegiac feeling. The elegiac sense is found in a simpler, more old-fashioned ballad on the same topic, "The World is Turned Upside Down," which appeared in 1646, over a year before Nedham's verses were printed in *Pragmaticus*. "The World is Turned Upside Down" laments the loss of the festival, "Old Christmas is kickt out of Town," and decides that "Christmas was kil'd at *Nasbie* fight: / Charity was slain at that same time." The fifth verse of "The World is Turned Upside Down" is a delightfully descriptive account of an old hall or manor-house suffering under monotonous and hungry deprivation:

> The serving men doe sit and whine,
> And thinke it long ere dinner time:
> The Butler's still out of the way,
> Or else my Lady keeps the key,
> The poor old cook,
> In the larder doth look,
> Where is no goodnesse to be found,
> *Yet let's be content, and the times lament,*
> *You see the world turn'd upside down.*

The description provides a social vignette, like pared-down Jonson, though the striking thing here is that the poem is made up of absences; the emphasis is on something missing, and the verse moves from anticlimax to anticlimax. Nedham's verses are full of particulars (*"Plums"* and *"Spice-broths"*) and comic diminishing hyperbole, depending on an absurd imagined action (*"Prophets Sons"* defying *"Plums"*). The anonymous ballad is milder, moving on a level without employing the projected voice of the enemy. The description seems to

be made by an observer, rueful and even lamenting, who yet maintains a kind
of resigned serenity. It is indicated on the broadsheet that the ballad is to be
sung to the tune of Martin Parker's ballad, "When the King Enjoys His Own
Again."[4] That most popular and long-lived of propaganda songs (it was to
become an anthem of the Jacobites) has its own elegiac sense, a lament for the
past, the sense of empty and cold rooms. But it also mocks Roundhead
astrologers, prophesies change, and aggressively imagines the downfall and
death of enemies:

> Though for a time we see White-hall
> With cobweb-hangings on the wall,
> Instead of gold and silver brave,
> Which, formerly, 'twas wont to have,
> > With rich perfume
> > In every room,
> Delightful to that princely train;
> > Which again shall be,
> > When the time you see
> That the king enjoys his own again.

> Did Walker no predictions lack,
> In Hammonds bloody almanack?
> Foretelling things that would ensue,
> . . .
> > And also, foreknow
> > To th'gallows he must go,
> When the king enjoys his own again.

The aggressiveness of the position ultimately behind "The World is Turned
Upside Down" is largely expressed through the quotation of the other title and
the employment of the tune with all its associations. The elegiac meaning is
"turned upside down" by the appeal to Cavalier confidence conveyed in the
melody.

The Civil War ballads supply many of the common topics and even images
to be found in poetry of the Restoration, and later. Samuel Butler in *Hudibras* is
an immediate successor to the Cavalier balladeers. We find him picking up
and amplifying the point made by Nedham's poem. Butler's Puritans

> Quarrel with *minc'd Pies*, and disparage
> Their best and dearest friend, *Plum-porredge*;
> Fat *Pig* and *Goose* itself oppose,
> And blaspheme *Custard* through the *nose*.
>
> (*Hudibras*, Book I, Canto I, lines 225–8)

The association of Puritans with the death of Christmas and thus with the
death of charity, hospitality and housekeeping persists long after the Civil
War. Puritans, and what were seen as their later avatars, the early Whigs, were
associated with domestic coldness in place of an old manorial warmth. Dryden's Shimei (Slingsby Bethel, Whig Sheriff of London), noted for "Zeal to

God, and Hatred to his King," provides a portrait largely composed in terms familiar from Civil War propaganda; he wisely refrains from "Expensive Sins" like merrymaking and hospitality:

> His Cooks, with long disuse, their Trade forgot;
> Cool was his Kitchen, tho his Brains were hot.
>
> (*Absalom and Achitophel*, lines 620–1)

At a long remove, but still recognizable as springing, if indirectly, from the same ultimate source is the portrait of Pope's miser, Cotta (based on Sir John Cutler, a wealthy London merchant):

> What tho' (the use of barb'rous spits forgot)
> His Kitchen vy'd in coolness with his grot?
>
> (*Epistle to Bathurst*, lines 181–2)

What was once "the good old Hall" stands silent, and inert, barren of all festivity in a monotonous imprisonment of dull frugality,

> Silence without, and Fasts within the wall;
> No rafter'd roofs with dance and tabor sound,
> No noontide-bell invites the country round;
> ...
> Benighted wanderers, the forest o'er,
> Curse the sav'd candle, and unop'ning door.   (lines 190–6)

The "good old Hall" has lost its real identity in losing its function. Pope is here very close to the spirit and at times even the manner of "The World is Turned Upside Down"; the passage moves through negatives, absences, with an elegiac sense of deprivation and desolation tempered by anger at this obtrusiveness of denial.

Some of the Civil War ballads and poems ought to be included in any anthology which professes to introduce the reader to Restoration and eighteenth-century poetry, and any "course" given to students on this subject should probably include some references to and some reading of such verse. Readers could then trace the progress and meaning of certain important *topoi*, such as the hospitality theme just discussed, and could then also recognize that certain vigorous satiric treatments of images have predecessors. Dryden's *The Medall* (1682), for instance, contemplates the medal struck by Whigs to celebrate and commemorate Shaftesbury's acquittal:

> So like the Man; so golden to the sight,
> So base within, so counterfeit and light.
> One side is fill'd with Title and with Face;
> And, lest the King shou'd want a regal Place,
> On the reverse, a Tow'r the Town surveys;
> O'er which our mounting Sun his beams displays.
>
> (*The Medall, A Satyre Against Sedition*, lines 8–13)

Dryden, examining this detested medal, venomously and wittily rings the changes upon all possible derogatory meanings of its symbols and of itself as symbol. In doing this, he is following the example of the author of the Interregnum ballad, "The States New Coyne," which examines the significance of the new coin issued under Cromwell:

> Saw you the States mony new come from the Mint?
> Some People do say it is wonderous fine;
> And that you may read a great mystery in't,
> Of mighty King *Nol*, the Lord of the Coyn.
>
> They have quite omitted his Politick head,
> His worshipfull Face, and his excellent Nose;
> But the better to tempt the sisters to bed,
> They have fixed upon it the print of his Hose.
>
> For, if they had set up his Picture there,
> They needs must ha' crown'd him in *Charles* his stead;
> But 'twas cunningly done, that they did forbear,
> And rather set up his Ar— than his head.
>
> . . .
>
> On this side they have circumscrib'd *God with us*,
> And in this stamp and Coyn they confide;
> *Common-wealth* on the other, by which we may guess
> That *God* and the *States* were not both of a side.

Dryden's poem is much wittier, and more venomous and less vulgar than the ballad, but yet it seems to remember its predecessor; contemporary readers of *The Medall* might recall it too, since the collection of *Rump Songs* had such wide circulation after their first printing. The ballad depends on readers trained in Elizabethan and Jacobean methods of reading symbols and applying meaning to images. It also has the metaphysical characteristic of using images with strained or unexpected meaning and effect.

One of the major literary events of the seventeenth century was the conversion of metaphysical devices and manner to popular and public use. Metaphysical poetry could no longer stay in the closet, to be read with private appreciation by the chosen few; if the poet wanted to write about what was going on, he had to be able to speak to the many. Private events and feelings no longer made sufficient subject matter for the use of poetic skill – at least they did not if the poets, like their fellow-countrymen, were drawn into the conflict. Ballad writing would seem to be more congenial to members of the graceful and ostensibly plainer and clearer writers of the "tribe of Ben," but a number of metaphysical poets, including Cleveland, devoted a large body of their work to public affairs, and wrote poems actively intended to influence the outcome of history. (Some of Cleveland's works are included in *Rump Songs*.) The metaphysical moments in the propaganda poetry, even that which is obviously intended as street-poetry, are often surprisingly effective:

When Temples lye like batter'd Quarrs,
Rich in their ruin'd Sepulchers,
When Saints forsake their painted Glasse
To meet their worship as they passe,
When Altars grow luxurious with the dye
    Of humane bloud,
    Is this the floud
    Of Christianity?

When Kings are cup-boarded like cheese,
Sights to be seen for pence a piece,
When Dyadems, like Brokers tire,
Are custom'd reliques set to hire,
When Sovraignty & Scepters loose their names,
    Stream'd into words,
    Carv'd out by swords
    Are these refining flames?
                ("A Hue and Cry after the Reformation")

The quick play of images illustrates the destruction of all that is right, beautiful and spiritually powerful; churches have become battered quarries, Kings are shut up (i.e. imprisoned) as if of no more importance than cheese in a cup-board. The new power is everywhere taking over in its work of iconoclasm, reversal and destruction. Even names change. "Sovraignty" and "Scepters" have no meaning, and are altered into the language of the sword. Beauty is presented only to be transformed into destruction. The saints in the old stained glass are broken and tossed out in favour of the new Puritan "Saints" (self-styled) who greet each other with pious unction and terms of undeserved honour. Much meaning is packed into this series of transformations in a poem in which the elegiac sorrow struggles with surprise, and surprise with indignation.

The idea emphasized at the end of both stanzas quoted above is (like Nedham's "'tis a godly thing / States to reform by Murther") recognizably the same as that in Butler's lines on the Presbyterian true-blue errant saints:

Such as do build their Faith upon
The holy Text of *Pike* and *Gun*;
Decide all Controversies by
Infallible *Artillery*;
And prove their Doctrine Orthodox
By Apostolick *Blows* and *Knocks*.
            (*Hudibras*, Book I, Canto I, lines 193–8)

C. V. Wedgwood has noted

Hudibras was the final product of Civil War satire, the strong-water ultimately distilled from the plentiful coarse, angry, comic, impulsive, ingenious, quick-off-the-mark rhymes that the Cavalier wits had written against their opponents as the conflict proceeded.

Repeatedly Butler took up, sharpened and perfected ideas and themes which had been roughly sketched out before.[5]

This is very right, except that *Hudibras* is not the *final* product. of Civil War verse. A number of other poems are, if not as directly as *Hudibras*, products of the poetry of the Civil War. There are abundant instances of passages which re-work themes and devices familiar to Civil War verse. More important than individual *topoi* or devices is the lasting effect on the next hundred years of English poetry. Civil War verse and its interests, poetic as well as political, had a part in shaping what we know as Augustan poetry.

What happened in the Civil War was that poetry, or much of it, Jonsonian and metaphysical, went out into the streets. When metaphysical poetry moved from the closet to the pavement, it changed its habits, and its manner of living. One of the most important results of metaphysical poetry's hitting the street was John Dryden's poetry in the new generation, a poetry that is often both metaphysical and public. The survival of the metaphysical style was to a certain extent assured if it proved it could alter when it had to. Poetry had to prove its ability to deal not with 'real experience' (when had the metaphysical poets claimed to do otherwise?) but with experience as we know it in political and communal activity. Streets, markets, battlefields could no longer be used as sources of images for developing some more private topic – they became central subjects. Civil War poetry gave evidence of metaphysical poetry's willingness to change. But it could not go out into the world in this manner without losing its purity. In some sense, it ceased to be itself. Poets had to be willing to explain their images, at least to a certain extent, to suit them to a public ear; elaborate intricate verse form was too difficult to catch in the hearing to be suited to public verse, sung or read. Metaphysical poetry died – but rather, we should say it was transformed, and went on to a new existence, once the metaphysical mode was willing to act as a co-partner, co-operating with other modes and devices, subordinating itself to other fashions of poetic speech and to moods foreign to the old customs of meta-physical expression.

Metaphysical poetry survives in Augustan poetry in parts and in moments, always indicating its willingness to be transcended by other moments and to be governed by statements which could not be satisfactorily expressed by recourse to the metaphysical style. It is present, the metaphysical poetic manner, in the works of Augustan poets, even of those who are so outstand-ingly of their period as often to be cited as representative. Metaphysical devices can be found not only in Dryden (where the case is obvious) but also in Pope, and even in Thomson and Cowper. We find metaphysical conceits in Thomson's great work of the late 1720s and 1730s, *The Seasons*, as in this description of ice which "gathers round the pointed Stone, / A crystal Pave-ment, by the Breath of Heaven / Cemented firm" ("Winter," lines 728–30). Plant-conception is carried on by "the Father Dust" ("Spring," line 541);

vegetation under the ground is "a twining Mass of Tubes" (*ibid.*, line 566). There is an even greater abundance of metaphysical devices in Cowper, who shows in *The Task* (1785) that he can be both succinct and striking: e.g. "And spreads the honey of his deep research" (IV, line 112). "Variety's the very spice of life" (II, line 606). When a reverie is broken, interruption comes "snapping short/ The glassy threads, with which the fancy weaves/ Her brittle toils" (IV, lines 305–7). Cowper's deployment of such conceits identifies his inheritance from the Metaphysicals. That quiet legacy was still yielding interest in 1785. But it was only a part of the richness of English poetic tradition which the Augustans were eager to use in their own way.

It is not my purpose to stress the survival of metaphysical poetic practice, as if a contemplation of the fact could somehow rescue Augustans from being Augustans. They didn't want to sound like Donne or Vaughan. In the work of poets like Cleveland and the later Marvell, poetry had leaped into the public arena, acquired new combative devices and rejected or modified old techniques. Metaphysical turns of poetic wit had proved that they could, when modified, accommodate the language of public passion and the rhythms of the streets – as in "When Temples lye like batter'd Quarrs, / Rich in their ruin'd Sepulchers." Poets such as the satiric Marvell or Samuel Butler could adapt the devices to suit their purposes, creating a new style of poetry which in its full bloom was to seem to a true Augustan critic like Johnson fuller and more flexible and infinitely less limited than the old metaphysical style had been (see chapter I, above). The metaphysical strain is a traceable element among the many which went into the new poetry. Augustan poetry is made of our variousness. A mixture of styles and manners exists in it; the job of a true Augustan poet is to get these styles to co-operate. The effect may, however, partly depend on styles and manners being required to co-operate visibly against their usual inclinations, e.g.:

> *Synods* are mystical *Bear-gardens*,
> Where *Elders, Deputies, Church-wardens*,
> And other Members of the Court,
> Manage the *Babylonish* sport.
> . . .
> Both are but sev'ral Synagogues
> Of *carnal Men*, and *Bears* and *Dogs*:
> . . .
> The Question then, to state it first,
> Is which is *better*, or which *worst*,
> *Synods* or *Bears*.
>
> (*Hudibras*, Book I, Canto III, lines 1095–267)

The new Augustan modes necessitated a great self-consciousness about habits of language, about style – a consciousness educated by the combats and debates of the mid-century. Writers during and after the Civil War, especially the poets, were endowed with or haunted by a persistent sense of the parodic.

Parody had become their most acute and flexible device for registering and expressing irony.

The combative ballads of the Civil War introduced emphatic irony, or rather did not so much introduce as lodge in English poetry of the next phase a particular and aggressive use of irony. Irony has always existed in our literature, but the poets of the Civil War took something previously occasional and intermittent, one manner of irony, and brought it to the fore in a continuous parodic use of the enemy's voice. We have seen before in poetry the use of the antagonist's or butt's voice and thoughts, in Chaucer's rendition of the Monk in the Prologue to the *Canterbury Tales*, for instance ("upon a book in cloystre alwey to poure"), but the Civil War ballads introduced an uncommon and really novel concentration of such mimicry. A poem like "Collonel *Vennes* Encouragement" is apparently entirely given over to the speaker of the opposing side. As we have seen, "Hey Then Up Go We" establishes the "serious" or seemingly serious language and thoughts of the assumed speaker ("Come then my Brethren and be glad, / And eke rejoyce with me"). The technique is something between *style indirect libre* (first noted in France in the seventeenth-century works of La Fontaine, but not supposed to arrive in England until Jane Austen's era) and the dramatic monologue. I suggest calling this technique "ventriloquism"; the voice of the "real" speaker (speaking for the poet, and his audience) is momentarily cast into the personification of the Opposite or Other; a dummy or puppet-speaker is given a strange voice. When the poet wishes, the whole piece can be carried on as a kind of dialogue between a ventriloquist's dummy and the ventriloquist as personal speaker.

A great deal of what we recognize as Augustan irony is based on such ventriloquism. Swift is famous for his exploitation of this technique in his prose works, notably in *A Tale of a Tub* but also in shorter essays such as his reply to Collins or *An Argument to Prove that the Abolishing of Christianity in England May . . . be Attended with Some Inconveniences* (1708). *Gulliver's Travels* is an amplification and refinement of this technique. His poems exhibit a fair amount of ventriloquism, as in, for example, "The Speech":

> The Duke shew'd me all his fine House; and the Duchess
> From her Closet brought out a full Purse in her Clutches
> . . .
> But, some will cry, *Turn-Coat*, and rip up old Stories,
> How I always pretended to be for the *Tories*:
> I answer; the Tories were in my good Graces,
> Till all my *Relations* were put into *Places*.
> But still I'm in Principle ever the same,
> And will quit my best Friends, while I'm *Not in game*.
> ("An Excellent New Song, being the Intended Speech
> of a famous Orator against Peace," lines 15–26)

It is interesting that this poem, a satire against Nottingham published in a broadside half-sheet in 1711, is called "An Excellent New Song"; it not only pays homage to its literary ancestry in street poetry, but is itself a sophisticated street-poem. Swift was always interested in mimicry, even on non-political occasions and in non-satiric verse. Verses like "Mrs. Frances Harris's Petition" exhibit his fascination with the use of a garrulous, unpoetical voice, inadequate but assured.

No one would deny that Swift is a mimic, a ventriloquist. But it is worth considering how many important poems of the period, particularly but not only in the Restoration, depend on the self-exposition by the absurd enemy of his absurd point of view. An example is Ralpho's and Hudibras's argument about the relative iniquity of "*Synods* or *Bears*," quoted above, but the whole of *Hudibras* depends on this device. The pseudo-speaker, the dummy, damns himself and his style simultaneously, as from his own mouth. Dryden controls his dummies, but at the same time gives them a lot of room in which to speak, and in a leisurely fashion, in favour of themselves and their notions of things. Flecknoe speaks (five times) praising himself and Shadwell. Achitophel makes speeches at the centre of *Absalom and Achitophel*. The Panther carries on at length in *The Hind and the Panther*, being allowed to tell her own fable to illustrate her views (as she thinks – really to damn herself more thoroughly). Cibber speaks in the *Dunciad*, the Goddess of Nonsense speaks, and in the late Book IV a whole train of dunces put in their self-approving words, each in his or her own manner. The enemy's self-praise is mimicked everywhere, and the enemy's style.

Self-praise or self-exposition can be rendered by characters or voices that are not simply to be recognized as the enemy. Some of the "dummies" may be sympathetic, or partly sympathetic. Rochester's Artemisia is certainly not an enemy, nor is her friend, the gossiping fine lady. Pope's Belinda is not an inimical force to be rejected. Almost all Crabbe's characters are sympathetic to some extent. Yet with all of these we are, I think, made conscious that they are being mimicked, their personal views and manner and style parodied, that they are, in short, in some measure being "sent up" – as is not true of, for instance, Browning's Fra Lippo Lippi or Andrea del Sarto, whatever the visible defects of the characters or the degree of comedy extracted from their limitations or plight. In Augustan poetry, even mixed characters who are not enemies are treated rather as if they were, and we know that it is part of our job as readers (as with "Hey Then Up Go We," though in a much more subtle and refined manner) to catch the style out, to shoot the folly as it flies and recognize the source of the ventriloquy – even when we're not quite sure where exactly the ventriloquist would stand if he became personal speaker.

The Civil War was a war of *styles* – so much so that in the popular mind style in its more superficial sense has largely taken the place of historical ideas, and the Cavaliers are associated with long locks, lace and licentiousness, and the Puritans with short hair, dark clothes, hypocritical sermons and a kill-joy attitude to almost everything. This caricature would grieve Jeremy Taylor and John Milton, but the terms of the caricature were set at the time. Both sides –

one should really say "all sides" – were extremely conscious of the characteristic styles of the enemy in sermons, oratory, poetry and general expression as well as in mode of living. Marchamont Nedham helped to set the clichés about the Cavaliers even while drawing upon them as he parodied Cavalier language and mocked their style of living in his pamphlet *News from Brussels*. In a Letter From A Neer Attendant on His Majesties Person (1660). This mock-letter, pretending to come from Charles II's court, was intended to make England turn back at the eleventh hour from contemplating a Restoration. The letter makes us feel that it is embarrassingly and unguardedly accurate:

O *Jesu, Jack*! I want an iron hoop to keep my sides from splitting, to see my poor Prince bite's lips for halfe an hour long, while that *Dulmano* begs a blessing (as he calls it) as our Mech-beggers [*sic*] do their Bacon at the Farmers doors: *G*. got behinde him yesterday and made mouths which the Puppy by an unhappy turn of his head perceived; but His Majesty seeing all, prudently anticipated his complaint, and with a Royal gravity, not onely rebuked *G*. but immediately dismist him his service.

We all made application to the Parson to mediate to our Master for *G*. his restoration ... *M. H.* and *J.* were in the presence at night, but I thought we should have split our spleenes a laughing ... *H.* bid me hand his service to thee, he swears he hath horn'd 15 Cuckolds within this 14 dayes.[6]

The evocation of frivolous, silly and idle young men creates a sense of outrage when the reader realizes that these are the people who want to come back and take revenge on all the "Traitors." "Hug them you cannot Hang, at least until you can ..." Cavalier style betrays lack of any cause beyond self-interest.

The Cavaliers were not the only object of Nedham's mockery, even in his Cromwellian days. After June 1650 the former Cavalier propagandist and poet of *Mercurius Pragmaticus* was engaged in editing and writing the Cromwellian newspaper, *Mercurius Politicus*. When we remember that Nedham had practically a monopoly of the journalistic press for a decade (Cromwell not approving of opposition papers) there is reason to consider him if not the best the most influential of English writers in mid-century. In his work mimicry is thoroughly developed, and he makes his readers aware of what he is doing. He overtly describes and defends his journalistic mimicry of the Presbyterian clergy:

Nor have I introduced any expressions of a *sacred Character*, in a jocular way, with intent to profane them ... but rather to shew how they are profaned by those *weekly Praters*, to guild their *Hypocriticall Orations*, and promote a *Faction*. It was their *Part* which I *Acted*, not my own, and therefore it could not be amiss to borrow a little of their own language, to represent them in the same Apparel that they use in those *Parochiall Trage-Comedies*, which they Act every *Sabbath*, to amaze the People.

(*Mercurius Politicus*, No. 3, 20–27 June 1650)[7]

The now disgruntled Presbyterians were seen as Royalists opposed to Cromwell, and Nedham, never favourable to Presbyterians, turns upon them with a range of stylistic mockery. Describing the hearing of the case of a Presbyterian minister (here called Rabbi Jenkins) who had refused to observe the fast-day proclaimed by Parliament, Nedham bursts not only into invective but into jocular ventriloquism, culminating in a ballad, turned off as if *extempore*:

Here the *Priest* . . . began to preach by way of Peroration, with a use of *Information* . . . and of *Reprehension* to *Politicus*, that merciless *Pamphleter*: which being pulled out of his Pocket, he cryed out, *Persecution. For here*, Gentlemen, *I desire you to take notice, how I have been abused by that wicked* Politicus, *who saith, I confessed that I preached and I prated, and I prated and I preached.* Gentlemen, *I beseech you*, Gentlemen, *did I say so? And do you not perceive how he speaks against the yong [sic] man of* Scotland? *And tells how he must be purged upon the Stool of Repentance*; and thus he proceeded, with his Scotch Bagpipe, to the tune of Tom. Triplet, *I defie thee, with heigh and with heigh*; which I had best turn into a *Catch*, for the use of the proud *Presbyters* in every Parish.

> *Politicus, we hate thee with heigh, and with heigh;*
> Politicus, *we hate thee with ho.*
> *Thou call'st us prating Rabbies,*
> *And mak'st poor* Charls *a Babie*;
> *Sing, heigh-tara noni-noni-no.*
> (*Mercurius Politicus*, No. 5, 4–11 July 1650)[8]

When Jenkins objects to what the newspaper has said he said – i.e. how it has ventriloquized him – the gratified Nedham sees the chance to undertake more ventriloquism and to carry it further. He can also enjoy in his official role as *Politicus* the pleasure of being hated for his power by an enemy whom he can render ever more impotent and absurd. The poor speaker, the "Rabbi," the "Priest," becomes a singer, and then the new catch is offered, as if Jenkins had sung it. In an unusually cruel and effective piece of ventriloquism, the now-fictionalized Jenkins is an ineffectual balladeer; his ballad, in attempting to ventriloquize the enemy, fails and topples over altogether into *Politicus'* own camp – the enemy has no language left. Such a "taking off," such displacements and plays of style, render the opponent helpless, and his true style, that which for him expresses theological, historical and psychological truth, is profaned and injured. A style can not only be rendered less effectual in the public forum through such ridicule; it can also be made less acceptable, less comfortable even to a mind which wants to think in that style, or in terms of the beliefs and attitudes that style customarily conveys. There comes to be no easy way of thinking, no mode of discourse, or of self-presentation, in private or public speech that won't cause a twitch in the mind. The English had twenty years of stylistic attack and counter-attack. Writers had learned in a very practical school the meaning of parody and of ventriloquism.

One of the results of the Civil War was that English literature of the Restoration is marked by an extremely active sensitivity to style and its implications or possibilities. Constant inspection of styles, and play with them, had made styles – all sorts – of deep interest. Most poets could say, with Nedham, "it could not be amiss to borrow a little of their own language" as they tried to act in words the part of others: "it was their *Part* which I *Acted*, not my own." Poets could not resist trying out the different voices and different styles for enemy dummy, or representative dummy (a fool or knave but sympathetically resembling the rest of us) or even for friendly dummy (like Dryden's David/Charles in *Absalom and Achitophel*, or his James I I/farmer in *The Hind and the Panther*). The job of a poet was to find answerable style for a character, his terms, point of view, manner of life – or, conversely, to find a character for whom a mimicked style would be appropriate. The point did not need always to be political, especially later in the period.

A notable example of a virtuoso use of answerable style in creating a representative sympathetic dummy is John Philips's *The Splendid Shilling* (first published 1701, authorized publication 1705). In this poem the speaker is a poverty-stricken poet, mournfully singing the joys of the man who retains "A Splendid Shilling," joys from which he is debarred. Its epigraph is "Sing, Heavenly Muse, / Things unattempted yet in Prose or Rhime, / A Shilling, Breeches, and Chimera's Dire." The dummy who is the pseudo-actor of this poem renders his lament on his own condition, and a description of his days and ways (as we might say, his "life-style") entirely in Miltonic verse. *The Splendid Shilling* is the first extensive successful example of mock-Miltonics:

> But when Nocturnal Shades
> This World invelop, and th'inclement Air
> Persuades Men to repel benumming Frosts,
> With pleasant Wines, and crackling blaze of Wood;
> Me Lonely sitting, nor the glimmering Light
> Of Make-weight Candle, nor the joyous Talk
> Of loving Friend delights; distress'd, forlorn,
> Amidst the horrors of the tedious Night,
> Darkling I sigh, and feed with dismal Thoughts
> My anxious Mind; or sometimes mournful Verse
> Indite, and sing of Groves and Myrtle Shades,
> Or desperate Lady near a purling Stream,
> Or Lover pendent on a Willow-Tree:
> Mean while I Labour with eternal Drought,
> And restless Wish, and Rave; my parched Throat
> Finds no Relief, nor heavy Eyes Repose:
> But if a Slumber haply does Invade
> My weary Limbs, my Fancy's still awake,
> Thoughtful of Drink, and Eager in a Dream,
> Tipples Imaginary Pots of Ale;
> In Vain; awake, I find the settled Thirst
> Still gnawing, and the pleasant Phantom curse.
>   (*The Splendid Shilling. An Imitation of Milton*, lines 93–114)[9]

Of course the comedy of this style rests on the fact that on the obvious level it isn't answerable at all. The tone, the grand blank verse, the solemn inversions of Milton's *Paradise Lost* were never invented to serve such common purposes. But then – we know the speaker is a "dummy" because he doesn't question or notice the tension between subject matter and style; evidently for the ventriloquized puppet-character the grand style feels right for his egotism. We feel sure that there is a "real" poet, a ventriloquist, casting his voice over into the pretended speaker, and we have this certainty because we can imagine that the poet who can carry on the Miltonic lines so well must understand their original use, and also because we presume that the "real" poet would have more sense and discretion than to speak of his pastoral poems in such a flippant manner ("Or Lover pendent [*sic*] on a Willow-Tree"). We should be embarrassed if a real "I" were to speak solemnly and almost obsessively of his dreams of "Pots of Ale." At the same time, of course, there is an obverse side to this effect. The picture created is vivid, the speaker sympathetic, and we can see that the puppet-character is a joke-self, perhaps of the "real" poet who could find relief from his own situation in laughing at it. The situation might, for an individual truly involved in it, seem serious enough from his point of view almost to merit Miltonic grand treatment. We are also reminded of the homelier moments in Milton's own poem, like the description of Eve's housekeeping. The style here is the central subject; we are entertained at seeing what can be done with it. But the style loses its original purpose and implication when it is used like this; we may even wonder if Milton will seem quite the same after. Both ventriloquist and dummy seem gaily prodigal of stylistic resources.

It is no accident that the age of ideological and stylistic mimicry of the Civil War journals, broadsides and street-ballads preceded what is noticeably the great age of parody, or perhaps more properly the beginning of parody as we most commonly think of it today. Parody is an element constantly present in literature, and in poetry, especially in comic poetry; it is known to antiquity, which invented the mock-heroic. There are numerous touches of parody in Horace, references to the *Odyssey*, for instance, or mimicry of grand poems praising Augustus which Horace evidently considers fustian. Chaucer's "Rime of Sir Thopas" is parodic. In general, however, before the Restoration parody in English literature consisted most largely in the parody of a genre, rather than of the work and style of an individual poet. Touches referring to an individual poet are slight and brief when they do occur, which is rarely, and they are customarily subsumed into the larger parody of a generally well-known kind of literature. After the Restoration, parody becomes dominant, and whole works can be based on it. It also becomes much more individually referential. Buckingham, Butler and the others in writing *The Rehearsall* are not just getting at the heroic play as a genre; they are parodying the work of John Dryden, as is vividly apparent in Dryden's own appearance as Bayes in the play. Later, Fielding's *Shamela* parodies Richardson specifically and unremittingly. Johnson mimicking Warton, Jane Austen's sketches on Mrs. Radcliffe — these are parodies of particular writers, as well as the literary kind they represent. *The Splendid Shilling* is not just a parody of the grand style, but a parody of Milton, very specifically. It is now a point to be noted, even suspiciously noted, about individual writers — that they do have *style*.

The new interest in parody supplemented, rather than cancelled out, a previous interest in burlesque. Literary burlesque seems a seventeenth-century preoccupation both on the Continent and in England. Essentially, burlesque consists in rendering a subject that is grand or romantic or pathetic in terms in such violent contrast to that subject that the grand or pathetic effects are totally destroyed. A subject or theme shows that it cannot sustain itself when deprived of appropriate style.

A desire to burlesque even great works of literature may have been in the seventeenth century an impulse to escape the Renaissance; burlesque (the word itself is seventeenth-century) may have been a method of signifying farewell to that earlier and very powerful cultural phase. Burlesque and, later, parody in both France and England seem related also to the experience of civil war. The most striking example of seventeenth-century literary burlesque is Paul Scarron's *Le Virgile Travesti* (1648–62), the most effective and lasting of a number of burlesques which took France by storm for about twenty years. A nineteenth-century editor of Scarron connects the popularity of burlesque poetry with the French civil war, the Fronde: "The reign of the burlesque is, as has been said, in our literary history what the Fronde is in our political history, that is to say a revolt against a tyrannical yoke, a basically legitimate protest, if often ridiculous in form, against an excessive authority."[10] *Le Virgile Travesti* is a sharp if playful revolt against a poet often thought the world's greatest and a poem of enormous importance to the Renaissance sensibility. Scarron's poem is a rendition of the *Aeneid* (or extensive parts of it) in flippant and tripping short rhyming verses, with insistent reminders of the commonplace. Aeneas is reduced to a lachrymose fool, and Dido to a lascivious wench – of course the tears and sensuality are present in Virgil, but they certainly come out differently here. This pious Aeneas is a comic dolt:

> Alors, Æneas le pieux,
> Regardant tristement les cieux,
> Lâcha ces pieuses paroles:
> «Je serai donc mangé des soles!
> Cria-t-il, pleurant comme un veau,
> Et je finirai dedans l'eau!»

(Then the pious Aeneas, sadly regarding the skies, let fall these pious words: "I shall be eaten by the soles!" he cried, weeping like a calf, "and I will finish up in the water!"; Book 1)

The burlesque keeps close to its original in its movement from topic to topic, even maintaining – and exaggerating – some of Virgil's images (as in the description of the work being done on Carthage) but topics and images are maintained only in order to reduce the matter to jolly banality at each point. In England, Charles Cotton produced a translation-imitation of Scarron's work in his *Scarronides, or, Virgile Travestie* of 1664. It is shorter than Scarron's, dealing only with the first and fourth books of the *Aeneid*, and Cotton's work is ruder or more violent. In Cotton's work for instance, as not in Scarron, Aeolus at Juno's request looses the winds ("a sedibus imis" as the note reminds us the original has it) from his guts, by farting:

Æol, who all the while stood gapping,
At her fine Peacocks gawdy-trapping,
Seeing her mount *Olympus* Stair-case,
Began t'untruss to ease his Carcase.
...
    Have you not seen below the Sphear,
A mortal Drink call'd Bottle-Beer,
How by the Tapster when the Stopple
Is ravished from the teeming Bottle,
It Bounces, Foams, and Froths, and Flitters,
As if 'twere troubled with the Squitters?
Even so, when *Æol* pluckt the Plugg,
...
    Æneas, and his wand'ring Mates,
Were, at that time, Angling for *Sprats*:
Thinking no harm no more than we do,
(For all was fine and fare to see to)
When all o' th' sudden; oh who would think it,
...
It grew so dark, that wanting Light
They could not see the Fishes bite;
And strait e'er one could say, what's this?
The Winds began to howl and hiss.   (*Scarronides*, Book I)[11]

The edition of 1715, "Illustrated with many curious Cutts, all new design'd, and engraved by the best Artists," offers an illustration of that passage as one of the "curious Cutts" (Fig. 4). Goupy and Van der Gucht display Aeolus and attendant spirits or cupidons all letting off farts; Juno observes from above, in the heavens with her peacocks, while below on the seas Aeneas' ship receives the force of the blast. The lines of the picture itself are pleasing (one can observe a Hogarthian curve of beauty) but the subject is startling, in every way a surprise. The picture mocks serious illustrations of classical subjects in the Renaissance style, just as the poem mocks the seriousness with which such subjects had been taken. We should observe the poem (and the picture) before applying any of the usual clichés about "a neo-classical age." Scarron's and Cotton's works signify a revolt against the classical. And nothing keeps a poet like Cotton (a good and elegant poet too) from profaning a master, turning a classic into a kind of street-ballad. It strikes us forcibly that no subject is safe. The powers of style seem also to have been freshly discovered in releasing such aggressive style, a comic style of destruction.

Cotton's *Virgile Travestie* can be set beside Butler's *Hudibras*, a contemporary and in some ways similar work. *Hudibras* is partly a burlesque; the motifs of chivalric romance epic are rendered in aggressive colloquial slangily rhyming tetrameters. But *Hudibras* mingles burlesque with parody, and with political ventriloquism (the views of the Presbyterian knight and the Independent Ralpho). Most writers after the Restoration prefer parody to sheer burlesque; though they mingle burlesque with their parody, almost always, they prefer

Fig. 4

not to rely only on burlesque for satiric or comic purposes. Burlesque produces a style which opposes its subject. The stylistic range allowed in burlesque is limited, for it usually means a certain low manner which sets its own bounds. Parody is much closer to its subject. In fact, parody has to get under the skin of the writer it mimics, or adopt the voice whose views are presented. Pure parody in the modern manner (one writer aggressively and carefully imitating one other writer for comic purpose) does strictly what ventriloquism does loosely and more freely – it moves into the dummy's voice and makes that voice dissolve its own views by expressing them. The stylistic range open to parody, as to literary ventriloquism, is almost boundless – the parodist-ventriloquist can employ as many voices or styles as he chooses to imitate. But the presence of burlesque hovers behind most effective parody and ventriloquism; somewhere behind the perverse self-exposition there are clues that alert us to a ghostly voice behind the dummy, saying "Nonsense, nonsense," and rendering the effect banal. The Civil War poems had shown how effective the mingling of parodic ventriloquism and parodic burlesque could be:

> Next, for the State, we think it fit
> That Mr. *Pym* should govern it,
> He's very poor.

This poem, "The Humble Petition," perpetually turns parodic ventriloquism into parodic burlesque, the burlesque effect coming most often in the short lines, as here, where the preposterous pseudo-reason for Pym's right to govern the state is given as his need for the money the job would bring, indicated in the flat colloquial line (in a reasonable tone, too) "He's very poor"; Pym (who to the real poet's mind is a greedy anarch) is mockingly excused in this burlesque of him as a job-candidate in exigent circumstances.

English poets of the Restoration and later were fascinated by the possibilities of combining parody and burlesque, and combining them in ventriloquism which could permit a wide range of effects even when only one character is composed and presented. We can have parody-ventriloquism and burlesque-ventriloquism operating in the same character (e.g. Artemisia's gossiping visitor in Rochester's poem). Parody-ventriloquism, or imitation of what this kind of character actually would say, is mixed with burlesque-ventriloquism, thoughts and attitudes appropriate to the character presented in exaggeratedly low expression or otherwise unsuitable style – as in the fine lady's exclamations as she kisses the monkey. Parody and burlesque may co-operate within a sympathetic ventriloquism, as in the creation of Artemisia herself, the author of her letter. (We are also here invited to admire Rochester's virtuosity in creating a female speaker as the "I" of the poem.) We can have an alien but sympathetic character produced by ventriloquism, with the character's set of beliefs, general views and style of living imitated and indicated by the use of direct parody or mimicry of the sort of things that character would think of or would say. Such a characterization can be combined with the burlesque – with the introduction of a parodied style which would be alien to the "dummy," the ventriloquized person, considered on one realistic level. This is the case with Pope's Belinda. Belinda is realistically described, and appropriately ventriloquized. Yet she is also made to speak in parody-burlesque of Virgil's Dido:

> Happy! ah ten times happy, had I been,
> If *Hampton-Court* these Eyes had never seen!
> (*The Rape of the Lock*, Canto iv, lines 149–50)

Belinda, the girl who wears the diamond cross and flirts and plays cards, would not have heard of or identified herself with Dido – she would certainly never have quoted her. Nor would Dido have identified herself with Belinda. A style which is poetically appropriate for Virgil's character is not only parodied but transformed; it has to do another kind of job when it is turned to work on Belinda's lock and Hampton Court. The burlesque here doesn't drop the grand Virgilian style too far into vulgarity or triviality. The danger of burlesque is that once the vulgar subject takes over, all styles but one disappear. Scarron's and Cotton's travesties become monotonous if one reads them through, though individual lines and passages seem very funny. For Augustan writers the trick is to keep style going, even while burlesque is in operation. Stylistic vivacity and variety and appeal must be maintained. Sometimes in Augustan mimicry style is kept going almost free of subject matter altogether. Rather than relying on the perpetual burlesque effect of denuding subject matter and tone of all ornamental play and graces of style, Augustan writers may prefer to go in the other direction, keeping style up, spinning along, crazily, almost free of the gravitational pull of content – at least of overt content. Belinda's long speech at the end of Canto iv is not, strictly speaking, necessary to the poem's narrative or its moral. It is a stylistic *tour de force*, a conceit of ventriloquism – and it finds its subject again in the memorable verbal conceit at the end:

> Oh hadst thou, Cruel! been content to seize
> Hairs less in sight, or any Hairs but these!   (iv, lines 175–6)

The pun not only brings us back to the sexual content and subject matter of the poem, but reminds us that everything that preceded it has been a play on style and words out of place. Belinda's Dido-esque speech has betrayed her in the end to what has anachronistically been called her Freudian slip. She reminds us at the end that what has been concealed through her actions and her speech-aria may be of more concern than the language in which she has apparently been saying something, or trying to say something. That is, Belinda's style, not only her Dido-style but her personal style here and throughout the poem, is an artifice, a betrayal of self which leads her in the end after so much strain to betray herself. This is not, whatever moralists have said, a pointer to the "moral" of Pope's poem (that we should eschew cosmetics and elegance and "be ourselves" – what a tawdry banal vision that would be!) but an element in the pleasures the poem offers. The poem explores and exploits style and styles. There isn't any "right" style to tell Belinda's story in, except exactly the "false" playful parodic styles, the mixture the poet is using.

Discussion of parody and irony in the work of Augustan poets usually revolves around one single topic: satire. The effects of the Civil War on poetry might seem to provide only a means once again to go over the same old ground about satire. Was it not the propagandists' object to satirize their enemies? It is no wonder that satire has been seen as so significant in the period. A significant amount of major work, both poetry and prose, of the Augustan Age is satiric. I do not, however, intend to deal with satire as a main subject, nor as a single and separable topic. There is, after all, so much able work on satire I need hardly attempt it, but I have other fish to fry. Satire, though important, is not the whole of Augustan literature, nor is its story the whole story. The Civil War satiric ballads have larger implications than for satire alone; they made an impact on the poetic practice of an age. The interest in parody and burlesque, an interest in England strongly related to political developments in the mid seventeenth century (and later), had effects on all literature – on all poetry, not just some poetry.

The flowering of ballad literature and popular poetry, poetry cast for the street and the ale-house, meant an upheaval of form and style. The ballads and songs exhibited a militant use of forms and styles; idioms turned away from their original meaning or customary purpose. To put it shortly, the Civil War poetry, ventriloqual and parodic (or burlesque), meant that poetically nothing was safe any more. There was no form so stable that it could not be turned to inimical or at least strange purposes. There was no voice that could not be mimicked. No style was sacrosanct, no subject off-limits to abusive treatment. A drinking-song could turn into a Puritan curse, an apparently pious hymn into a bawdy announcement dramatizing vulgar ambition. All styles could be used for hostile, or at least quite alien, purposes. The major Royalist work right after the Restoration itself burlesques traditional themes and idioms of Spenserian romance, turning knight-errantry into nonsense, while at the same time ventriloquizing quite other voices, picking up the styles, catchwords, idiom, terms, languages of the enemy Puritans and giving them at large and at length.

The major literary implication of Civil War verse is that styles are not trustworthy. It is a theme of Civil War poetry, as of Augustan poetry in general, that words are inadequate and slippery, that great words "loose their names / Stream'd into words / Carv'd out by swords." Words won't stay put – what is a sacred word to one's own group or party can be turned into a derisive catchword used in mockery by the other side, or by some other writer. Styles won't stay put. And genres won't stay put either; they can't be trusted to define the work and keep it safe from defiling usage or mocking interpretation.

Augustan poetry is marked by an acute, almost embarrassed, consciousness of style and language. No poet can trust any one style to do its work without some interference. For one thing, the reader's mind may itself provide interference in the form of spontaneous parodic response – a possibility the poet cannot but anticipate. If the grand style can be used to take in the wash, if the greatest epic of the sophisticated West can be reduced to the story of a tearful lout comically tripping (and tripping up) around the Mediterranean – then what is left? The answer is that nothing is left, and everything. No kind of style need be thrown away; such wastefulness wouldn't render life – the life of poetry – any better insured. At the same time, no style alone can be trusted to do its own work through the force of association because the associations have got crossed and mingled; associations, profaned or subject to profanation, are always questionable. The early years of the Restoration saw the completion of the work the Civil War and Commonwealth period had begun, in destroying the holiness or purity of style and genre.

The poets who wrote during the sixties or seventies threw everything into question, and illustrated at the same time the most sensitive reaction to the possibilities of styles and genres by refusing to proceed without a multitude of experiments with styles and genres. The work of the early Restoration is (to borrow a now popular critical word) deconstructive at the practical working level of poetry-making. The poets dismantle genres, and dissect all poetic effects. At the same time, the work of the early Restoration is constructive in suggesting the new enterprise of creation through ventriloquial multiplicity, through multiplicity of styles and the recreation of the concept of genre. The Augustan poets who followed continued that enterprise and built their own poetry up from that shattered and remodelled foundation. The whole period exhibits extreme generic self-consciousness, and a constant search for new and mixed genres, as well as an extreme stylistic self-consciousness born out of seeing the possibilities of parody, burlesque or alienation in every poetic idiom or voice.

III
Generic self-consciousness: from closed to open forms

One of the difficulties Augustan poetry poses for the modern reader is a generic unfamiliarity. Augustan poets don't write the kind of poetry we are most used to. Most mid-twentieth-century readers are trained first and trained best in reading short poems, modern or metaphysical. Augustan poetry seems at first so much the less accessible partly because there is such a lack – at times, it seems, an absence – of lyric verse. After the age of Dryden this lack becomes especially noticeable, and most of Dryden's own best lyric verse is found in the big "Pindaric" Ode. True, all our major poets wrote a few short poems. But these are not many, nor, on the whole with a few notable exceptions (such as some of the hymns), are they very good. They seldom if ever represent the best work of even a minor poet. Augustan poets on the whole threw out the short versatile lyric forms that had served Jonson, Donne and Herbert – and even some of the Civil War balladeers. Their generic inventiveness did not mean the kind of generic inventiveness that caused Donne or Herbert or Marvell to create for almost every poem a new and complete short verse form.

What are the reasons for this eclipse of the lyric? The best answer, if there is one, would seem to be found in an examination of the poems of John Wilmot, Earl of Rochester; he was the genius among the "Mob of Gentlemen who wrote with Ease,"[1] and he produced a number of memorable lyrics in the early years of the Restoration. His work on the lyric was part of the process of dismantling, of de- and re-creation, that is the most striking poetic activity of the Restoration period.

Rochester takes as his model the love-lyric as it had been developed from the Elizabethan period to the beginning of the reign of Charles II, from the elegant solidity of Jonson to the famous ease of Suckling or the refined simplicity of Lovelace. He thus defines a basic kind of lyric and makes lyric seem a distinct kind of poem. Lyric poetry is to be simple, passionate, graceful, emotive. It is written as a short series of singable four-line (or six- or eight-line) stanzas, with unobtrusive rhymes and gracefully pleasing modulations of sound and image. In thus fixing our attention constantly on one type of lyric and making it stand for all, Rochester by a kind of sleight of poetry convinces us that his lyrics provide a test case for all lyrics. After all, almost any one among the mob of gentlemen, and some among the mob of ladies, could turn out an elegant and graceful love-lyric, a simple, satisfying and predictable statement of love, or of love-complaint. Rochester implies that if this kind of lyric, composed of such

57

simple and regular elements as to seem nearly indestructible, could stand out against pressure and pollution, then there might be hope for lyric verse altogether. But if this kind cannot, for all its naive and blooming advantages, escape seduction, then no lyric verse is capable through the soundness of its form of retaining purity and clear meaning. I may seem to exaggerate or even to import the significance of Rochester's implied debate, but the fact that he wrote such a number of closely similar and perverse love-lyrics would seem to indicate that he himself felt a special meaning in his activity. There is a debate going on which he feels confident of winning, even if at moments, like the rake in his progress, he may regret the universal lack of formal innocence his victory implies. Sexual imagery comes naturally when speaking of Rochester, who himself could hardly speak without it. His triumph over love in his love-lyrics has more than a little tinge of *machismo*. Yet in a sense he always plays fair, seducing the form rather than raping it. He is faithful to the musical flow and rhythm of his verse, to the stanza form, and to the traditional curve of argument – but here, as in a sort of sexual Jabberwocky, the lines come out quite differently, and the argument curves in quite a different direction from that traditionally expected by and through the operation of the form.

There are a number of illustrative choices among Rochester's poems (and among these a number of versions, published and unpublished, some more, some less, obscene).[2] To deal with just one example of his fallen lyric, take "To a Lady in a Letter" (first published 1676) which begins

> Such perfect bliss, fair *Chloris*, we
> In our enjoyments prove,
> 'Tis pity restless jealousy
> Should mingle with our love.

A governing word in line 1 is "bliss," the central word in line 4 is "love," and the stanza seems to move appropriately from "bliss" enjoyed together through "jealousy" back to "love," as if anticipating the union of the lovers which ought to be worked out by the end of the lyric. The argument seems to be already apparent – a lover pleads with his lady not to be jealous of him; traditionally, his plea should involve the assurance of his fidelity amplified in the course of the poem – or at least, the assurance that the rival loves mean nothing. The lovers are already really united, their love is "perfect bliss"; surely nothing can alter that. As all readers of Rochester know, the poem doesn't proceed in the conventional vein, or even the several conventional veins. The second stanza is a shock:

> Let us, since wit has taught us how,
> Raise pleasure to the top:
> You rival bottle must allow,
> I'll suffer rival fop.

The rival to the lady, to the female partner in the pair who enjoyed "perfect bliss," is not (here) other ladies, but the bottle. Cause for jealousy would seem to exist on the man's side, as he has to endure "rival fop" – and although the noun is in the singular, the metonymic use of "bottle" (for a number of bottles) implies an equal plurality of fops. A bargain of mutual tolerance is here suggested, cutting short any expectation of assurance of fidelity, or promises of amendment. Guilt, if any, would seem to belong to the lady but the lover makes no accusations or demands. This second stanza follows the rhythm pattern of the first (iambic tetrameter followed by iambic trimeter) but the hard crisp sounds stress the vulgarity of the two nouns in the last two lines, and contradict the effects of harmony, grace and sentiment suggested by sounds and language of the first stanza. Yet the tone and language of traditional love verse are not rejected; they reappear in stanza 3:

> Think not in this that I design
> A treason 'gainst love's charms,
> When, following the god of wine,
> I leave my *Chloris'* arms.

This stanza has the first suggestion of the parody of Lovelace's "To Lucasta, going to the Warres," which appears fully in stanza 7.[3] The language of love and love-lyric is used for a declaration that the lover intends to leave his mistress's arms for his own pleasure, and that pleasure drink, at any time. And the lady has compensation – she too drinks – but at the nether end of her body:

> Since you have that, for all your haste
> (At which I'll ne'er repine),
> Will take its liquor off as fast
> As I can take off mine.

Stanzas 5 and 6 might seem to accuse the lady of tasteless promiscuity – but it is accusation with a shrug, if accusation at all, and the emphasis is on the tastelessness, not the promiscuity. She constantly marks for her own any "brisk insipid spark," as the most inane admirer will fulfil her purpose:

> Nor do you think it worth your care
> How empty and how dull
> The heads of your admirers are,
> So that their cods be full.

The poem refrains, entirely and ostentatiously, from railing, lamentation, or love-agony. The lady's activities are approved and endorsed by the lover who traditionally ought to feel jealous, forsaken and angry. The last two stanzas pick up the tone of love-eulogy, and love's idealism:

> All this you freely may confess,
> Yet we ne'er disagree,
> For did you love your pleasure less,
> You were no match for me.

Whilst I, my pleasure to pursue,
Whole nights am taking in
The juice of lusty grapes, take you
The juice of lusty men.

The governing word has turned out to be the "pleasure" of stanza 2, not the "love" or even "bliss" of stanza 1. Yet the promises of stanza 1 have been fulfilled, and what was prophesied has come to pass. The lovers, once separated by jealousy, are now (through argument) again united in serenity and harmony, reconciled through the enjoyment once again of equal "bliss" – though the sharing of bliss, here defined as the taking in of juice, is pursued separately. The conceit which equalizes their joys (and thus restores the grace of love-harmony) is also a conceit which separates and disunites. The couple are at the end promised independence of each other, though without an end to their love – there is no ending to this pair of lovers' story. Nothing has changed, and what conventionally should be a reaffirmation of love turns out to be a negotiated settlement of individual appetites. The verses see nothing wrong with this but advance through disharmony to mock-harmony as easily as if everything were as it should be in a true love-lyric whose reconciling functions and statements of passion are so well known.

Rochester's "To a Lady in a Letter" is a burlesque; divine and human characters and actions have changed, as is the case with Cotton's Aeneas, or his farting Aeolus. But love poetry and the styles of love poetry are here delicately burlesqued; traditional or conventional love-poetry language has not been thrown out – rather, something has been added. Styles now mingle: "love's charms"; "brisk insipid spark." Parody refers us back to the love-lyric as seriously employed by a master; Lovelace's apology "I could not love thee (Deare) so much / Lov'd I not Honour more" is twisted several times here. First it is applied to the *woman*, who is here the person who ought to love an abstract good (in this case pleasure, not honour) more than any single individual. It is then extended to the love of pleasure which is the measure of both parties' fitness for each other. The lovers' power of loving each other is connected with their capacity for loving something else more. That capacity is found here in both partners – an implicit comment on the sexual inequality inherent in Lovelace's high-sounding statement; at the same time the poem is a comment on, and question about, high Cavalier values subject – so terribly easily subject – to casual debasement. But the rhythm, cadences and line length are in keeping with rhythm, cadences and line lengths in Lovelace's poem.

Lovelace's own lyric is questioned and twisted out of shape by this casual-seeming parody.[4] Moreover, Rochester's whole poem, like so many of his lyrics, proves that a conventional form cannot resist re-stating itself, parodying and overthrowing itself. A genre like the love-lyric formally conceived cannot escape calumny and self-betrayal. The generic designs and expectations prove powerless to ensure one type or set of meanings. Genre, so to speak, is worthless; it cannot stand on its own feet.

Rochester's lyric (like a number of his other lyrics) is a triumphant piece of early Augustan art by a poet who was one of the first and most intelligent successors of the writers of the Civil War and Interregnum. "To a Lady in a Letter" moves from style to style, employs poetic and colloquial mimicry, burlesque and parody, in the creation of an impure and novel mixture which dissolves even while it exploits the charms of form. This lyric explodes the conventions of genre. After such work had been done on the lyric in its most simple and unified manifestation, no writer – and no reader – could be confident that genre had saving power, that genre was going to maintain stability so that meaning could be carried by it. Lyric itself becomes suspect, once you find out that simple lyric, instead of being right where you want it, is over in the corner doing something you'd never have imagined or expected. Lyric, simply considered, is in effect shot up, wasted, not just because someone is able to write parody lyric (which is also a true and effective lyric) but because the new use or abuse illustrates the instability and impurity of such generic forms. Lyrics depend on being able to make an impact at once – but that impact can evidently be muffled, or diverted. It is too unsettling to read a lyric wondering if you're meant to take the effects seriously or whether the next lines won't explode them, and lyric forms don't allow room for the poet to comment on or guard against that possibility. Lyrics, serious ones, must become so heavily armoured that quick motion would be impossible; the charm of reading or writing new ones is lost.

Rochester's generic self-consciousness, inherited from the immediate past generation of verse-writers, contributed to the self-consciousness about genre which affects all Augustan writers. In their self-consciousness, Augustan writers turn away from the serious short lyric as from a lost cause; short poems become satiric or parodic (like Carey on Ambrose Philips, or Johnson on Warton). And in forsaking the lyric which in its various modes had served the seventeenth century so well, Augustan poets were also forsaking the idea of the conventional formal genre as a model, and, progressively, the idea of the poem as closed formal unit. It is obvious, for example, that the sonnet, loved by Elizabethans and Jacobeans (and later picked up again by Romantics and Victorians) is almost wholly unused by the Augustans. Closed forms are highly *formal* forms, depending greatly on generic trust being kept, and on trust in genre. Generic trust had been lost. The Augustans had to work at creating new kinds of poetry that would not depend for support on formal expectations and restrictions.

There are, presumably, other reasons for the Augustans turning from the short poem to the long, reasons distinct if not disconnected from the distrust of lyric forms and kinds fostered by knowledge of their instability. For one thing, the Augustans seem to have wished, in reaction to the restrictions of seventeenth-century verse, to flow out and expand, to press against and go beyond barriers, in defiance of the enclosure of their grandfathers' poetry. Perhaps poetry seemed not best served by the frustration found in limited short forms – at least, not once the frustration was felt. Certainly we notice in tropes, metaphors and narrative in Augustan poetry from the very early Restoration a fascination with space, and with the idea of space. Moving through space and through changing locations in space is important in Milton's *Paradise Lost* and Cowley's *Davideis*, and in poems that aren't epic at all, such as the "Ode on Mrs. Anne Killigrew," or Pope's *Epistles* to Bathurst and Burlington, or Akenside's *Pleasures of Imagination*. Augustan poetry frets against boundaries. Rochester's "To a Lady in a Letter" oddly illustrates that, the poem fretting against both the boundaries of love-lyric as lyric form and the boundaries of the love affair, conventionally conceived. Rochester proposes a paradox, that a lovable lady ought to have a boundless appetite for pleasure. He strikes the true notes of Augustanism in his insistence on appetite and in empire, both of which disregard bounds and limits. The love of the boundless, the unlimited, which we notice in Augustan poetry can be traced back to the Restoration. The adjectives "irreverent" and "obscene" are traditionally applied to Restoration literature (and Rochester's poems). This was a literature whose style was often deliberately shocking, setting limits at defiance, and mocking order. It knocked over fences, and left the Augustans free to wander or "roam" (a favourite word) through the limitless. The sense of the boundless in these early Augustans would seem to arise from the feeling that boundaries and settled ways had betrayed them, both in history and in poetry.

Restoration writers, living in a world patched together from pieces of old régimes, knew too that there was more than one side to any cause, or any story. Stories are seldom pure and rarely simple. Stories require, as Rochester's lyric does, argument, opinions, mixed styles. When Restoration poetry is not defying or parodying lyric, it tends (like Charles II's conversation[5]) to become narrative, and the narrative tends towards elaboration and ventriloqual complexity. Post-Civil War poets have an urgent desire to tell a whole story, to discourse at length about the whole course of political and moral conflict. This retrospective urge can be seen as early as Davenant's unfinished experiment in epic, *Gondibert* (1651). Hobbes praised *Gondibert* highly because the author does not employ the magic and wonders of Renaissance epic, but even in his imaginary world sticks to a story of political and historical forces in opposition to each other; modern poets should recreate a whole political story.[6] It is an irony that *Gondibert* (now almost unreadable, save to specialists) remained unfinished. So did Cowley's more poetically successful political epic, *Davideis, A Sacred Poem of the Troubles of David* (1656). Cowley's epic was an attempt to tell the whole story of King David's rise to power – a political-theological-historical subject of sufficient magnitude. It should be emphasized that Cowley's *Davideis* was read from the Restoration to the Age of Anne; it was reprinted regularly with Cowley's *Works*, of which the eleventh edition appeared in 1710. The David story was symbolically a Royalist story, though Cowley never lets any ideas, including the ideas of monarchical absolutism or divine right, slide by without question. He seems to consider it part of his poetic task to create spokesmen for various points of view, and a number of political opinions are presented, even comically presented, as still in formation, or inadequate. The Moabite king, for instance, the monarch who befriends David, unconsciously indicates the weakness of certain defences of monarchy in his complacent and contemptuous objection to Samuel's opinion of kings (based on 1 Samuel: 8). He interrupts David's own narrative to express his opinion:

> Methinks (thus *Moab* interrupts him here)
> The good old *Seer* 'gainst *Kings* was too severe.
> 'Tis *Jest* to tell a *People* that they're *Free*,
> *Who*, or *how many* shall their *Masters* be,
> Is the sole doubt; *Laws guide*, but cannot *reign*;
> And though they *bind* not Kings, yet they *restrain*.
> I dare affirm (so much I trust their *Love*)
> That no one *Moabite* would his Speech approve.
> But, pray go on.   (*Davideis*, Book IV)[7]

Moab's self-love is evident and his theories seem unexamined; his untested life (he is not one of the chosen people) has not seen what politics or Civil War can do. Cowley ventriloquizes, in a manner almost worthy of Marchamont Nedham, creating a satiric or at least partly comic characterization of a man with inadequate political views (even if he is in some sense on the right side). Cowley ornaments every corner of his narrative, and fills all the interstices of the Biblical story with yet more debate, yet another review of tensions and beliefs. The project ramifies so much under the poet's treatment that it is little wonder he never completed his great work. It is also little wonder that the poem with its intellectual manner appealed to Dryden who drew upon it and who could count on many readers being sufficiently familiar with Cowley's poem to recognize allusions to and plays upon passages from it.[8] For Cowley's large poem of serious intent itself invited burlesque and parody; variations of its lines turn up in *MacFlecknoe*.

The *Davideis* remains an unfinished epic work, or even an epic barely begun; Sprat praises it as "a better ... Beginning of a Divine Poem, than I ever yet saw," and indeed it is just a beginning.[9] At the end of its extant four books David's career has hardly started, though the reader has had much to do, particularly in pondering the voluminous notes Cowley appended to each book. The job of writing such gigantic whole stories, such lengthy retrospective accounts of major conflicts, obviously daunted most poets in the end. Aside from Milton, who hit on exactly the right subject matter, no poet of the post-Civil War period was able to produce a finished and effective epic. The epic itself, as a genre, was open to question. Milton in his own epic by a superb – and characteristically Restoration – feat of wit manages to question and parody all devices of former epics, both of the antique classical model and of the more modern Renaissance romance type. Not only is *Paradise Lost* a "self-consuming artifact" (to use Stanley Fish's phrase); it also consumes epic styles, devices and narrative formulae, to the point where these become unusable in any other poem. We are meant to discard them, and with them all epics save this one alone. Even while he uses epic allusions and devices, Milton reminds us that such stories and such devices are only "feign'd," poor shady ineffectual ornament or weak fables substituted for the grand reality which only he can convey and which can only be told once for all. After that, the epic had better shut up shop and keep quiet. Milton deconstructed the epic as thoroughly as Rochester did the love-lyric. Again, a genre *qua* genre was shown up as absurd and impossible. The only way to use it after this is in burlesque and parody, in mock-heroics and satire.

The Milton of *Paradise Lost* can quite seriously be taken as one of the first Augustan poets of the Restoration period. He participates in the Restoration-Augustan task of exploding genres. At the same time, he exhibits the typical Augustan desire for complexity and inclusiveness. All sides, all sorts of voices, should be heard. The representation of all voices, including, ventriloqually, that of the Opposition, is extremely noticeable in *Paradise Lost*, particularly in some of Satan's sarcastic sneers and lethal puns, which oddly resemble the voices of the Civil War ballads, too. Some readers have thought that Milton gave the Devil more than his due, but that is the sort of danger constantly courted by Augustan poets, who preferred that risk to the risk of limitation and exclusiveness.

It is noticeable that *debate* figures very largely in Augustan works in general, and most certainly in the poetry. Opposing sides are all given a voice. In Restoration drama, and particularly the "heroic play," debate is a staple ingredient. In Dryden's *Aureng-Zebe* (1676), for instance, we go through a number of debates, one character against one other character: the Emperor and the Empress; the Emperor and Morat; the Emperor and Indamora; Aureng-Zebe and Indamora; Indamora and Morat – to cite only some of the permutations. Most of Dryden's major poems work through the narration of debate. Sometimes his debater is arguing with an unheard but not unfelt antagonist off the scene, as it were (the same could also be said of Rochester's speaker in most of the poems, a speaker who seems to be involved in some at least implicit debate). On one occasion, in *MacFlecknoe*, and only that once, Dryden uses the brilliant device of the ventriloquized histrionic debater bombinating in a vacuum. That poem is organized around the sequence of Flecknoe's speeches, unanswered (save by the final gesture of his impatient son); the effect is that of a peculiar one-hand-clapping comedy. But *Absalom and Achitophel* and *The Hind and the Panther* exemplify extensive and multiplex (and crafty) debate – as does *Paradise Regained*. And *Absalom and Achitophel* and *The Hind and the Panther* (and *Paradise Regained*) all give us a whole history combined with prophecy of the future in a unique form crafted for the occasion and permitting a number of styles and manners, as well as of jangling voices.

The mind of the poet – of every Augustan poet – turned to long poems that could get everything in. Poets of the Interregnum and early Restoration turned hopefully to the epic, and then turned away again, after having found that it would not do. The poets needed to invent forms of narrative that were not epic; they had to contrive something suited to their particular purposes. New epic was just not possible. Milton, the one successful modern epic poet, had at the same time done the genre in – even for his own future purpose. Whatever *Paradise Regained*, that peculiar debate-narrative, may be, it is not an epic – at least if that word is to make any sense at all. In some respects *Paradise Regained* oddly resembles its arch-contrast, *Hudibras* – in its de-valorization of romance, its avoidance of meaningful action, its almost caddis-like accumulation of material which would seem fragmentary if the pieces were not so firmly and even jauntily cemented together. And of course in both *Hudibras* and *Paradise Regained* the central space is taken up by the two central characters' self-explication in talk; what these people all do is to converse. If *Hudibras* is an aggressive comic mock-epic, then *Paradise Regained* (published in 1671, seven years after the second part of *Hudibras* and seven years before the third and last instalment) is its counterpart, an aggressive *serious* mock-epic. Both works equally defy and abuse generic expectation, and self-consciously deny the values and significance of the epic. From 1671 on, the epic is left to the un-witty writers like Blackmore, who hadn't seen that the high epic road led straight to ridicule. Blackmore was not a fool; a stolid but high-flying late baroque poet, he just had not caught on to the intellectual style of what his contemporaries called "the age," to its self-consciousness and its distrust of genre.

By Pope's time, the imbecility of modern attempts to write epic was almost a commonplace. Pope himself contributed to the jokes about it even as he was preparing for the strenuous work of translating Homer – and in translation of the oldest epic lay his only hope of producing an acceptable serious epic. Even so, the difficulties were many, and Pope added to the difficulties of his task by his own witty insight into the treacheries of genre and manner. In 1713 he wrote an essay for the *Guardian*, "A Receit to make an *Epick* Poem." The essay's motto ("Docebo/Unde parentur opes, quid alat, formetque Poetam") puts the *Ars Poetica* to strange use and supplies a meaning Horace did not intend. Pope pretends to think that poets can be usefully instructed by flat recipes:

It is no small Pleasure to me, who am zealous in the Interests of Learning, to think I may have the Honour of leading the Town into a very new and uncommon Road of Criticism. As that kind of Literature is at present carried on, it consists only in a knowledge of Mechanick Rules, which contribute to the Structure of different sorts of Poetry, as the Receits of good Housewives do to the making Puddings of Flower, Oranges, Plumbs, or any other Ingredients. It would, methinks, make these my Instructions more easily intelligible ... if I discoursed of these Matters in the Stile in which Ladies Learned in Œconomicks dictate to their Pupils for the Improvement of the Kitchin and Larder. (*Guardian*, No. 78, 10 June 1713)[10]

This ventriloquized author of a literary cookery-book (appetite as metaphor again) then offers instructions as to steps and ingredients:

For the *Fable*.

Take out of any old Poem, History-books, Romance, or Legend . . . those Parts of Story which afford most Scope for long Descriptions: Put these Pieces together, and throw all the Adventures you fancy into one Tale. Then take a Hero, whom you may chuse for the Sound of his Name, and put him into the midst of these Adventures: There let him work, *for twelve Books; at the end of which you may take him out, ready prepared to conquer or to marry; it being necessary that the Conclusion of an Epick Poem be fortunate.*

. . .

For the Moral and Allegory. *These you may Extract out of the Fable afterwards at your Leisure; Be sure you strain them sufficiently.*

. . .

For the Machines.

Take of Deities, Male and Female, as many as you can use. Separate them into two equal parts, and keep Jupiter *in the middle. Let* Juno *put him in a Ferment, and* Venus *mollifie him. . . . If you have need of Devils, draw them out of* Milton's Paradise, *and extract your Spirits from* Tasso.

. . .

For the Descriptions.

For a Tempest, *Take* Eurus, Zephyr, Auster *and* Boreas, *and cast them together in one Verse. Add to these of Rain, Lightning, and of Thunder (the loudest you can)* quantum sufficit. *Mix your Clouds and Billows well together till they foam, and thicken your Description here and there with a Quicksand. . . .*

For a Battel. *Pick a large quantity of Images and Descriptions from* Homer's Iliads, *with a Spice or two of* Virgil, *and if there remain any Overplus, you may lay them by for a* Skirmish. *Season it well with* Similes, *and it will make an* Excellent Battel.

. . .

For the Language.

(*I mean the* Diction). *Here it will do well to be an Imitator of* Milton, *for you'll find it easier to imitate him in this than any thing else.* Hebraisms *and* Grecisms *are to be found in him, without the trouble of Learning the Languages. I knew a Painter who . . . had no* Genius, *make his Dawbings be thought* Originals *by setting them in the* Smoak: *You may in the same manner give the venerable Air of Antiquity to your Piece, by darkening it up and down with* Old English. *With this you may be easily furnished upon any Occasion, by the Dictionary commonly Printed at the end of* Chaucer.

Pope's comical recipes go far beyond an attack on inferior poets who write poor epics. The tenor of the whole makes it evident that the epic is, as a venture, passé. The author will be an imitator, not an original; he can assume specious originality only by trying to sound more ancient (i.e. out of date) than his predecessors. And as for all the properties of epic – its actions, its heroes, its gods, its scenes – we know them before they come up. Readers (and good writers) are wised-up ahead of time, and each reappearance of the elements most typical of the genre will be greeted, or even anticipated, with mockery. The whole structure, in *esse* and in its devices, is predictable and thus static, absurd; the new poem has been understood and parodied before it arrives. It is the very predictability and typicality of a genre as a genre that Pope here laughingly attacks. Generic expectations are ludicrous expectations, because (he feels) we ought not to be able to expect and predict from structure, formulae, and *topoi*. We can also see that Pope, cursed (like all Augustans) with too good a wit, is both afflicted and sustained by an extreme self-consciousness regarding all the devices of poetic art.

The *Guardian* essay and *Peri Bathous* show that the writer could anticipate the burlesque and parody of almost any subject or manner or device he might be about to use. The youthful Pope wrote four books of an epic poem, *Alcander* (later burnt);[11] some of the lines from it were jeeringly immortalized as illustrations of the Art of Sinking in Poetry. The mature Pope never quite gave up his projected epic poem, *Brutus*;[12] as late as 1743, if Spence can be believed, he still thought of doing it: "Though there is none of it writ as yet ... 'tis all exactly planned." But Pope never really began *Brutus*. Johnson comments "He laid aside his Epick Poem, perhaps without much loss to mankind." How could Pope have started his blank verse epic without imagining his lines, as soon as they were written, as candidates for the Art of Sinking? The ghost of an opposing parody, a ridiculing sprite, seems to have flitted between the pen and the page of almost all our best Augustan poets. The only way to success was to endeavour to incorporate the self-conscious wit within the work itself. And to rely on genre to do part of the work of communicating was to lean on a broken reed. Worse – it meant pretending to cut off one's self-consciousness about poetry, attempting to deny the poetic mind, and thus submitting to the smothering sleep of Dulness. The route to all traditional set genres was, like the road to the epic, visibly signed "No Entry." Modern poets would have to be able to manage on their own. If that meant doing without the familiar genial comforts of genre, it also meant poets could feel they were escaping from restrictions into liberty.

The new poet had to face the job of creating each poem as its own genre, anticipating within it the mockery or subversion of any of the styles it employed. If we wish to know how this could be done, we can again do no better than to look at the poems of Lord Rochester. His contemporaries and successors were quite justified in thinking him a genius; even those who objected to his immorality still thought so. Rochester not only led the critical attack on genre, intelligently voicing the intuitions of the post-Civil War period, but also provided models for the new kind of authorship. The creator of new self-sustaining occasional poems, he wrote what were among the first major poems of the new age. What he suggested could be done was perhaps even more important than what he actually achieved, but his achievement is by no means inconsiderable. "Tunbridge Wells" can be considered one of his typical new poems; it was written early enough to have considerable influence during the Restoration (written *circa* 1674, it circulated extensively in manuscript, though it was not published until 1697). "Tunbridge Wells" is not written for or about any particular public occasion, yet it feels occasional and immediate:

> At five this morn, when *Phoebus* raised his head
> From *Thetis'* lap, I raised myself from bed,
> And mounting steed, I trotted to the waters,
> The rendezvous of fools, buffoons, and praters,
> Cuckolds, whores, citizens, their wives and daughters. (lines 1–5)

The poet makes an occasion of his getting up to take the waters at dawn. The egotism of his asserting his own activities as a suitable beginning of a poem is amplified in mocking hyperbole (sun rising compared to himself rising) and acknowledged as absurd in the subsequent use of contrasting language ("I trotted to the waters") which emphasizes the vulgar banality of the occasion.

The scene then shifts to a parade of fools, such as often forms a *topos* of satire, but the poet here is well placed within his crowd, engaged in the same activity as they. Disgust and amusement mingle in the speaker's reaction to his accidental company. His almost motiveless erratic movement through the streets and centres of Tunbridge Wells provides the narrative thread. The poet as central character holds the poem together, and there is no reason to expect the poem to be of any given length, or to decide that the beginning necessitates any particular ending. The styles alter, burlesquing themselves as soon as they become recognizable, or even before: contrast "At five this morn" with the traditional "high" phrase, *"Phoebus* raised his head." The styles (of dress, of speech, of living) of the characters encountered are not only closely observed, but can vary in themselves, as we see in the seduction-conversation of the would-be fashionables:

> Here waiting for gallant, young damsel stood,
> Leaning on cane, and muffled up in hood.
> The would-be wit, whose business was to woo,
> With hat removed and solemn scrape of shoe
> Advanceth bowing, then genteelly shrugs,
> And ruffled foretop into order tugs,
> And thus accosts her: "Madam, methinks the weather
> Is grown much more serene since you came hither.
> You influence the heavens; but should the sun
> Withdraw himself to see his rays outdone
> By your bright eyes, they would supply the morn,
> And make a day before the day be born."
> With mouth screwed up, conceited winking eyes,
> And breasts thrust forward, "Lord, sir!" she replies.
> "It is your goodness, and not my deserts,
> Which makes you show this learning, wit, and parts."
> He, puzzled, bites his nail, both to display
> The sparkling ring, and think what next to say,
> And thus breaks forth afresh: "Madam, egad!
> Your luck at cards last night was very bad."   (lines 86–105)

This vignette is a piece of vivid mimesis. In the whole of "Tunbridge Wells" we can see the influence of Horace (*Satires* i, ix) and of Donne's account of the encounter with the gossiping courtier. But this poem is different. Horace and Donne dwell on the inconvenience caused to the poet by his being entrapped by a bore who insists on holding him in conversation. Rochester is, as it were, more disinterested. The fools are not bothering him; he pauses to observe and overhear, and the combination of mimesis with description confers on these personages, momentarily, the completeness of Jonsonian drama. This section of the poem is taken up with incorporating the bundle of styles available to the girl and the "would-be wit." We see in the gallant's first speech how debased the old Petrarchan or Elizabethan style of love-hyperbole has become; he sets it going mechanically, a borrowed style, while his self-consciousness is expressed in gesture. The conceited lass replies with a cliché, descended ultimately from the polite ripostes of court circles of an earlier age. This elegant (in his eyes) response throws the gallant out; he has to puzzle what to say next, and his next outburst of language completely betrays the smooth first speech, in its splutter of colloquial familiarity. At last he has come home to his real style. But as a seduction gambit, talk about cribbage will do as well as high-falutin' stylized reference to the sun. His conversation then becomes larded with oaths as blank counters while he waits for ideas ("God damn me, madam, I'm the son of a whore / If in my life I saw the like before!", lines 108–9). Style has been completely subverted and overthrown in this scene, as indeed it is in the pattern of the whole poem which this scene parallels in its opening reference to the sun.

There aren't any great grand effects any more, Rochester implies; there is only Tunbridge Wells, the way we live now with our debased language and styles. This is the conclusion to which the poet moves:

> Bless me! thought I, what thing is man, that thus
> In all his shapes, he is ridiculous?
> Ourselves with noise of reason we do please
> In vain: humanity's our worst disease.
> Thrice happy beasts are, who because they be
> Of reason void, are so of foppery.
> Faith, I was so ashamed that with remorse
> I used the insolence to mount my horse;
> For he, doing only things fit for his nature,
> Did seem to me by much the wiser creature.   (lines 166–75)

The speaker's feelings strongly resemble those of Gulliver at the end of *Gulliver's Travels*; Rochester's satire closes with this perhaps rather forced, though not unjustified, expression of disgust at humanity. But this moral comes casually, from the speaker's own experience; the conclusion just occurs to him as he is riding away in an ordinary commonplace manner, from a place which has worn out his patience. There can be no grand closure; the conclusion is only in the poet's mind, it is in itself occasional, perhaps only momentary, and does not have to fit tightly with all the impressions (delight, amusement) created by the experience. Nor does the tone of the opening lines prepare us, or have to prepare us, for this moral conclusion.

Each moment as well as the whole experience is occasional, and the poet, as "I," is the source of what is to be observed and felt. There is no prescription governing "Tunbridge Wells." It does not require any particular kind of ending, nor does the reader feel that in order to fulfil its nature certain topics or personages must be covered, nor that it should devote a certain space to any

particular character type or style. Neither the length of the whole nor the length
of the parts can be prescribed or even predicted. The poem does not require any
successors; unlike Juvenal's satires, for instance, it does not belong in some kind
of series, but speaks for itself only, on its own occasion.

Another poem by Rochester of about the same date and enjoying a more
widespread readership at the time (it was published in 1679) is "A Letter from
Artemisia in the Town to *Chloe* in the Country." This poem is more original in
both structure and manner than "Tunbridge Wells"; it is much harder to pin it
to any obvious predecessors. "A Letter from *Artemisia*" is a striking example of
the poem *sui generis*; we see the poet inventing his genre as he proceeds. This is
an epistle, but not an Horatian epistle. It is from a woman and about love, but
it is not an Ovidian heroic epistle either. The whole is carried on through the
voice – or the writing voice – of Artemisia; in the creation of his speaker
Rochester has brought off a piece of mimetic ventriloquism which is also
sympathetic ventriloquism. Artemisia is not a mere fool, nor does she exemplify the traits of women commonly portrayed in satire, i.e. lustfulness,
extravagance, conceit, empty-headedness. No doubt at the time readers were
the more struck, knowing Rochester's other verse and his life, by the fidelity
with which he had rendered the voice and idiom of the opposing party in the
sex war, as well as the ingenuity with which he manages in the poem what
Barbara Everett has called "his two-faced mask of man of wit and woman."[13]

Artemisia (whose name is a reference to Artemis/Diana and to the goddess's
bitter plant, wormwood) is intelligent, frustrated and puzzled. She is not a fool
as the butts of satire are fools, yet some of her discourse seems inconsistent –
but then, it is self-consciously inconsistent. She is discussing a topic which
reflects the inconstancy and irrationality of human beings. She laments that
love is "debauched by ill bred customs here" (i.e. in town), while speaking for
love:

> That cordial drop heaven in our cup has thrown
> To make the nauseous draught of life go down;
> . . .
> This only joy for which poor we were made
> Is grown, like play, to be an arrant trade.   (lines 44–51)

Her outlook is bleak; life is "nauseous" (a combination of lady's slang with
satiric disgust) and love, the one thing that makes life (or female life) endur-
able, has disappeared, to be replaced by its sour counterpart, an unemotive
promiscuity. Women, "Our silly sex," are largely responsible for this disturbing change; having seized on "a meaner liberty" they forget the primacy of
pleasure in pursuing the fashionable vice for its own sake:

> To an exact perfection they have wrought
> The action, love; the passion is forgot.   (lines 62–3)

This Artemis does not seem ignorant of either action or passion, though we do
not know the precise extent to which she has experienced either. At one level,

Artemisia is a country girl who has just discovered the wickedness of the town (like so many young ladies in Restoration comedy). But she is not an innocent and not a bumpkin; one respects her opinion. With all her wit, Artemisia seems disturbed in her feelings, and her disturbance is part of the poem. In a state of both comic and moving irritation she tries, self-consciously tries, to define what she means, and never quite hits the mark. The reader remains puzzled; the folly of fashionable behaviour is clear enough, but what exactly does Artemisia mean by "love" and "passion"? What should – or could – a woman do? The character's cogitations break off into description of the "fine lady," wife of a drunken country knight. This lady's conversation with Artemisia is then quoted at length, with some interjections by Artemisia, who tells her reader what she thought at the time about the lady and her speeches. The visiting lady is full of grimace and affectation; her style is that of a feminine rattle:

> "Dear madam, am not I
> The altered'st creature breathing? Let me die,
> I find myself ridiculously grown,
> *Embarrassée* with being out of town ..." (lines 95–8)

The style should betray her utterly – but it does not, as this lady has a number of styles at her command, some of them those of Butler or Rochester; e.g., jealous men do not guess "The perfect joy of being well-deceived." Artemisia considers her visitor "a fool of parts," with all good qualities that can distinguish a woman, "Except discretion only." The work of the poem is largely carried on through the lady's quoted discourses, which are equal in interest to Artemisia's written discourses, though the worldly lady speaks from another point of view, not regretting the loss of passion but observing the folly of both men and women. As a speaker for her sex (a position she holds in common with the letter-writer who describes her) the "fine lady" is not without a cynical power. The reader may suspect that her affectations are doubly affected, to disguise and soften the tough reality of what she sees and knows. The lady who can embrace the pet monkey, crying

> "Kiss me, thou curious miniature of man!
> How odd thou art! how pretty! how japan!" (lines 143–4)

is also an uncomplaining satirist of her world, though she makes no pretence of not belonging to it; we see some of her unillusioned contempt mingled with the feminine act she puts on. Artemisia is reduced to a secondary personage, recording this lady's speech and actions. She too is puzzled by the lady visitor, "So very wise, yet so impertinent," and repeats this judgment at the end of the lady's speeches: "some grains of sense / Still mixed with volleys of impertinence" (lines 256–7).

Artemisia can come to no conclusion about the lady; she merely concludes the letter, remembering that it has gone on for a long while: "since I cannot

choose but know / Readers must reap the dullness writers sow" (lines 259–60).
Yet at the same time she promises Chloe, her addressee, more "such stories"
(stories such as the lady told her, as well as the story of the visitor herself) by
the next post. She will send stories such

> As, joined with these, shall to a volume swell
> As true as heaven, more infamous than hell.
> But you are tired, and so am I.
>   Farewell.   (lines 262–5)

The ending here is a bathos, but that dropping-off is preceded by a kind of
reverse bathos, in the move from "the dullness writers sow" to "more infamous
than hell." How can what Artemisia recounts be dull and fatiguing and at the
same time as exciting as the phrase "infamous as hell" certainly suggests?
Artemisia feels a repulsion from her subject, and an attraction to it – it seems
necessary to compile a "volume" of the stories of the town, infamous as these
may be, and yet, like any self-conscious Restoration writer, Artemisia questions her own subject and effects, even in the act of writing.

"A Letter from *Artemisia*" is a difficult poem; it works through the interfolding of different voices and styles, and it refuses to arrive at one clear meaning
that the reader can be happy with. The amoral lady's account of the career of
the amoral Corinna (a long narrative of typical sexual fortune and misfortune)
could provide several "morals" – or none at all. Neither the fine lady's rattlings
nor Artemisia's cogitations come to conclusions, fulfil a formal idea, or satisfy
any generic expectations. The poem has only the simulacra of formal elements
in beginning, middle and end. The piece creates in the reader a sense of
tremendous movement and variety. The aspects of life brought up are not
trivial, nor are they ultimately treated in a trivial way. It does not feel at all like
a fuzzy poem. Yet there is no way of plotting it, nor of deciding in advance the
sort of meaning we ought to be driving to. It is up to the reader to pick out the
"sense" and discriminate it from the "impertinence" in both the lady's conversation and Artemisia's letter – and we may feel that there is more sense than
impertinence in both and yet find it hard to pin down.

Artemisia finishes her epistle, because she is tired – and aware of the various
(conflicting) effects it might have on her reader. But she does not finish her
subject. She cannot talk dismissively, in the way that Horace could chat in an
epistle to Maecenas, about a subject that bothers her so much. Nor does she
have something specific in the emotional line to utter in the way that a Dido
does to an Aeneas. She observes acutely, like a satiric speaker, but her feelings
obliquely bounce off what she observes. We have not met another character
like her in poetic epistles, nor is there any need for us to do so again. If
Rochester were to keep Artemisia's promise (or threat) of writing more letters
with such accounts as would fill up a volume, he would be falling into mere
tedious repetition. We are left with a very puzzling and inconclusive discussion
of an un-finishable subject, embodied in the one poetic letter in the voice of one

poetic speaker on a specific occasion. The poem defies its self-levelled charge of dullness, giving us many interesting experiences and surprising insights as it zig-zags along. Connection is supplied by the speaker, the pseudo-writer, the "I" of the poem. Artemisia's thoughts and associations of feeling and ideas give the poem its peculiar shape and individual form. Just so, it was the poet-as-speaker's thoughts, observations, associations, that gave shape to "Tunbridge Wells." It seems, incidentally, no wonder that in this English intellectual climate of the late seventeenth century, with its interest in inner individual consciousness, John Locke produced his speculations on the operation of the mind (the *Essay concerning Human Understanding* was published in 1690). One might argue that poets such as Rochester had not only preceded but even inspired Locke, or at least made his work possible. The age was already interested in processes of thinking, and Locke had a large ready-made audience, accustomed to considering observation and reflection, those two Lockean modes of knowledge.

Augustan poets rely on the "I" (most commonly the "I" of the poet) which is pushed forward and made to do a lot of work. It is mainly, or often only, the "I," a speaking self, that can hold the poem together once genre as a shaping idea or power has been undone. Rochester very commonly employs the "I," whether as poet-self or ventriloqual character (as in "A Very Heroical Epistle"). Pope, Thomson and Cowper employ the poet-self "I" extensively; the reader must feel with the poet, see things as he sees them, accept the mental connections and emotional associations that his recorded experience brings into play. It is almost a rule of necessity that a *sui generis* poem must have a well-developed "I" as a means of unifying the poem. If it does not, then the voices of other "I"s – like Hudibras and Ralpho, Absalom and Achitophel – must be extensively employed to do the job of unification, even if that job is against their rhetorical interests.

Even in a poem which is chiefly directed by an "I," another voice (or voices) may enter – like that of the visitor in "A Letter from *Artemisia*." The "I"-directed poem may well wish to include the entertainment of argument and debate; we are expected to enjoy hearing more voices than just one, catching at once musings, monologue, private utterance and outer-directed conversation. The Augustan interest in including voices and debate had on at least one occasion an unforeseen personal side-effect, if Joseph Warton is to be believed in his account of Lord Bathurst's reaction to Pope's *Epistle to Bathurst* as printed in the Warburton edition:

That very lively and amiable old nobleman, the late Lord B A T H U R S T, told me, "that he was much surprised to see what he had with repeated pleasure so often read as an *epistle* addressed to himself, in this edition converted into a *dialogue*; in which," said he, "I perceive I really make but a shabby and indifferent figure, and contribute very little to the spirit of the *dialogue*, if it *must be* a *dialogue*; and I hope I had generally more to say for myself in the many charming conversations I used to hold with P O P E and Swift, and my old poetical friends."[14]

Bathurst was understandably sensitive about his presentation as the secondary speaker; he found himself transformed into the dull interlocutor who gets the worst of the debate.

It is hard to be a ventriloquized character in somebody else's poem. Warburton may not have perfectly understood Pope's intentions, but his punctuation was a natural result of the interest in hearing debate, of the expectation that voices and dialogue would be introduced into the "I"-controlled poem. Even Cowper imagines voices from the outside world who address him and are present (like the Bathurst his Lordship found) to be argued down:

> 'Twere well, says one sage erudite, profound,
> Terribly arch'd and aquiline his nose,
> And overbuilt with most impending brows,
> 'Twere well, could you permit the world to live
> As the world pleases. What's the world to you?
>
> (*The Task*, Book III, lines 191–5)

In any "I"-originating poem other speakers, whether envisaged as literally present, like Artemisia's visitor, or as a product of the "I"'s own conjuring fancy, like Cowper's aquiline sage, are bound to suffer as Bathurst felt he did. The "I" has the controlling consciousness, and the others are included only because it pleases. Once an "I" is put on the job that "I" (however ignoble or fallacious or simply puzzled) can by its presence justify the enriching inclusion of all matter that could occur to such a character, whether in observation or reflection.

It may seem a far cry from Rochester's Artemisia to Cowper's poet-speaker in *The Task*, but they are related. Artemisia brings in and develops the matters, both material and emotional, that occur to her and seem to her important at the moment. So does Cowper's Cowper, roving from post-horn to politics, from the rural greenhouse to London's gambling dens, as his ideas and emotions take him. A small prompting, a miniature occasion (taking the waters at the Wells, writing a letter to a friend back home, growing a cucumber) can evoke a large response, and a complicated series of movements of mind. Augustan poets discovered one of the happiest modes of including the world and grabbing all it had to offer when they cast off genre in favour of the *sui generis* poem with the speaking "I" as its living centre. The unpredictable self (Poet or Other) may make an unpredictable poem, credibly and most richly. Rhetorical tidiness can be ignored in favour of the mind's flight, whether the flight be that of a sympathetic or unsympathetic speaker. Voices and thoughts can also be mixed, supplying fresh offerings of the unexpected at any turn where it suits the poet to be surprising.

The presence of an "I" is something to be developed at leisure and at length. If emotions can be taken as partly settled by the genre, emotional developments can come on very quickly in the poem (there is, we as readers believe, only a certain repertory that the speaker can and will undertake). In what might be called traditional objective genres, where narrative takes precedence over any personal reaction and the poet should keep at a distance, the definition of the poet's place in things is already pre-defined – as in the case of the epic. Homer and even Virgil tell us little in their epics of themselves – though later ages have insisted on speculating as to their biographical relation to their works. Spenser doesn't need and doesn't want to say much about himself in *The Faerie Queene*. But in Milton's *Paradise Lost*, in which the genre itself is under question and is being displaced, the poet creates himself not only as a persona but as a person; he speaks to us and to God about his blindness in a personal and very Augustan fashion. The poet insists on his own presence; he is entitled to speak out devoutly or satirically or intimately as his moods shift.

The presence of the "I" can also be felt in the one kind of lyric verse that succeeded brilliantly in the Augustan Age. Hymns keep to regular short verse form without the flights of an "Ode"; they maintain generic expectations, though these expectations often sit loosely on the actual state and statement of a hymn-poem. A hymn may set out to surprise, to give one that jolt of "astonishment" which Johnson approved in poetry, e.g.

> G o d moves in a mysterious way,
> His wonders to perform;
> He plants his footsteps in the sea,
> And rides upon the storm.[15]

English hymns offer the only full example of the success of a genre in the eighteenth century, and of more or less "closed" forms. Yet something has happened to this genre too. In the eighteenth century both Anglicans and Dissenters went in for a new kind of hymn, new at least in Britain. The new kind of hymn relies less than traditionally on celebration, symbol and triumph, and hardly at all on musical effect. They are close to the psalm form as known in psalms turned into hymns, yet they don't sound like Sternhold and Hopkins; they don't rely with strict closeness on the psalm as a predetermining genre. These hymns are very personal, often extremely so. The member of the congregation must (almost paradoxically) sing of his most intimate feelings (or the poet's most intimate feelings) in public (these hymns were written for congregations, most definitely, and not for choirs). We join together in singing in unison, each about himself, and emotively: "When *I* survey the wondrous Cross" (Watts);[16] "Other Refuge have *I* none, / Hangs *my* helpless Soul on Thee" (Wesley); "*I* hate the sins that made thee mourn / And drove thee from *my* breast" (Cowper); "Rock of Ages, cleft for *me*" (Toplady). Each hymn (at least each of the best ones, the great ones) goes through various emotional twists and turns; we are halfway between a strict genre and a personal discourse through association of thoughts and feelings. Without some generic allegiance, the hymns could not be sung at all, but the genre has been amplified and altered. When you begin one of these hymns you don't necessarily know how it is going to proceed, and sometimes you may be brought up short by a verse making you utter sentiments not originally foreseen when you began the song. The hymns are adventurous, risking the precipice of absurdity, even brushing against the still centre of true hyperbole where words fail and die. These poems deserve to be called (in the honourable sense) experimental. The poems are also for the poet as John Newton said his were, the "fruit and expression of my own experience";[17] the "I," however universalized, is kept at or near the centre, like Milton's "I" in *Paradise Lost*.

The poem that creates its own kind employs the mind of the "I" as speaking self, or presses into service the voices and personalities of other "I"s who in argument, assertion and emotion keep the poem going and give it its shape. Our great Augustans find different ways on different occasions of making a poem that is its own kind. Dryden has traditionally been seen as the greatest Augustan of the first generation, though some twentieth-century readers (including T. S. Eliot) have questioned the place he was once given. One of the reasons for the respect he was accorded, especially by poets, in the next century and later, is his inventiveness – not mere contrivance, but invention at a deep level. Dryden's major poems are all experimental, and each is a mixture of a number of elements put together in a new way. Reading a big Dryden poem is a little like reading Joyce's *Ulysses*; you recognize that this is a classic form and also that it has never been seen before, and is virtually unrepeatable. It has often been noted that Dryden's major works are occasional, brought into being by some specific (usually political) event or crisis. Dryden's response to crisis is a recreation of poetic crisis in his poem; elements are mixed up and stood on their heads, the wrong side seems at times to be winning the rhetorical battle, voices chime and conflict so that the reader has much serious work to do to straighten matters out. At the beginning of *Absalom and Achitophel* or *The Hind and the Panther* we don't know how long these works are to be, or how they are to proceed; there is no prescription or definition to assist us. In *Absalom and Achitophel* we have a number of voices, and reference to a number of voices; the poem moves from description to drama, rather as "A Letter from *Artemisia*" does, and here, as in Rochester's poem, the central actions are conversations. The centre of the poem is the Temptation Scene as Achitophel speaks to Absalom and Absalom replies. The poem ends with the great speech of David/Charles; all the major action has been a rhetoric of shifting styles, and now there is one last stylistic shift, as we finally listen to the King and take him seriously. The parodic presentation of David/Charles has moved from the great comic introductory lines through the perversions of Achitophel's view of him. The parody version is now discounted; the voice of the King, the last great "I" of the poem, can speak truthfully, undoing the other "I"s of counsellor and prince, and the egotism of their supporters, and all their styles.

Scholarship has provided us with good information about the use of Biblical prototypes in Civil War and Restoration literature.[18] But none of this undoes the unusualness of Dryden's poem. We have often referred to it as a species of "mock-epic," but it isn't a burlesque of any particular epic, nor does it include large epic *topoi*. The point is that epic action such as a battle should be avoided, and the whole poem is as much avoidance of epic as invocation of it. But this the reader cannot know when he starts out, any more than he can know that the tone of what seems like mock-praise of David/Charles' virile fertility at the beginning does not set a tone of mockery about the King which will continue throughout. We are pulled rapidly along through its changing styles. The fact that the poem seems so complete, convincing and strong is a triumph of Dryden's art, for there is no model for it.

The Hind and the Panther, written for a later crisis in the reign of James II, is an even more striking example of the poem *sui generis*. It defies classification. It tells a story – and, like *Absalom*, but more noticeably – an incomplete story, taking place in a still moment of emblematic history that seems to cover an almost endless amount of imaginative time. The Hind (the Roman Catholic Church) meets the perfidious Panther (the Anglican Church). Violence might seem threatened by the Panther's nature, but instead the two beasts, the one immaculate and the other spotted, engage in an extensive debate, casually set up by themselves and seeming to have no necessary end (as indeed the differences between the two churches do not). After extensive discussion of Church history, both fabulous creatures have recourse to fables, and it is in the two fables told by these characters in an incomplete fable that the story is ended, and within these, also, that the violence of the situation emerges. The whole poem disconcerts by its odd structure and mode of proceeding. Miner has called its method "discontinuous allegory" but the poem involves a certain amount of shock for most readers, from the seventeenth century to today, who expect allegory to be tighter and fable to be neater.[19] Johnson objected:

The scheme of the work is injudicious and incommodious; for what can be more absurd than that one beast should counsel another to rest her faith upon a pope and council?... The *Hind* at one time is afraid to drink at the common brook, because she may be worried; but walking home with the *Panther*, talks by the way of the *Nicene Fathers*, and at last declares herself to be the Catholic Church.   (*Life of Dryden*)

As Johnson knew, the objection had been made at the time by Dryden's political and religious opponents, Charles Montague and Matthew Prior, in *The Hind and the Panther Transvers'd to the Story of the Country and the City-Mouse* (1687).[20] The two young poets evidently enjoyed parodying the laureate's poem:

> A milk-white Mouse immortal and unchang'd,
> Fed on soft Cheese, and o're the Dairy rang'd;
> Without, unspotted; innocent within,
> She fear'd no danger, for she knew no Ginn.

As they explained in their Preface

there is nothing Represented here as monstrous and unnatural, which is not equally so in the Original. First as to the General Design, Is it not as easie to imagine two Mice bilking Coachmen, and supping at the Devil; as to suppose a Hind entertaining the Panther at a Hermit's Cell, discussing the greatest Mysteries of Religion, and telling you her son Rodriguez *wrote very good Spanish? . . . But this is his new way of telling a Story, and confounding the* Moral *and the* Fable *together.*

Johnson observed of Montague and Prior's attack, "in the detection and censure of the incongruity of the fiction chiefly consists the value of their performance." Their performance is one of the results of that typical Restoration urge to parody, burlesque and otherwise dismantle other works, but it does not take much *detection* to see that Dryden's fiction is incongruous. Dryden would seem to be deliberately playing with his incongruities, and in a sense it is these which render the poem difficult to parody or deconstruct beyond the simplest level. It is Dryden who points out to the reader that the structure of the poem is concerned with large stylistic variation:

The *first part*, consisting most in general Characters and Narration, I have endeavour'd to raise, and give it the Majestick Turn of Heroick Poesie. The *second*, being Matter of Dispute, and chiefly concerning Church Authority, I was oblig'd to make as plain and perspicuous as possibly I cou'd: yet not wholly neglecting the Numbers, though I had not frequent occasions for the Magnificence of Verse. The *third*, which has more of the Nature of Domestick Conversation, is, or ought to be more free and familiar than the two former.

There are in it two *Episodes*, or *Fables*, which are interwoven with the main Design; so that they are properly parts of it, though they are also distinct Stories of themselves.

("To the Reader," prefixed to *The Hind and the Panther*. A Poem in Three Parts, 1687)

Johnson argued that Dryden's stylistic intentions did not succeed. Large sections of the first part, however "spritely and keen," have "not much of heroic poesy." "The character of a Presbyterian, whose emblem is the *Wolf*, is not very heroically majestick." We need not believe, as Johnson appears to do, that Dryden gave a poor account of his own work, or was not in control of his style. It is just that the diversity of styles Dryden wishes to control makes for an odd mix. And, given Dryden's account, the whole poem would seem to be built on a kind of bathos; we are to go from "the Majestick Turn of Heroick Poesie" to "plain and perspicuous" dispute, and then to "Domestick Conversation . . . more free and familiar," including also the two interwoven fables. We go from level to level and from style to style, not resting in the assurance of one grand style – we pick up the grand style, and then leave it. Anyone advising Dryden at the time of writing would almost certainly have urged him to move from the familiar through the plain to the grand style, and to clear away his complicating fables in the beginning or middle. But as soon as we try to find fault with this discomfiting poem we find that we are really trying to simplify it. The poem incorporates many styles and genres since it wants the reader to remain sceptical about all styles and genres – for all, even narrative fables, obscure the truth, and raise questions not answerable on earth. Dryden offers the satisfactions of styles, of conceits, of genres (the debate as in the heroic play, the beast-fable) and then takes away these satisfactions, making us realize they depend on devices, human contrivances. The devices offer modes of thinking, ways of imagining reality for the moment, but they are not real, and we are not to be caught by them. Again, there is no way of prescribing how such a poem should proceed or end, because there is no such category as "such a poem" – there is only *this* poem. It is by unmaking styles and genres, and taking them up, refashioned, for this original and occasional purpose that Dryden succeeds. We are to doubt (rather as with *Paradise Lost*, too) all styles, devices, genres, modes of speaking, except that which is "immortal and unchanged" – and thus cannot be fully heard in the mortality and changefulness which the poem's own ranging illustrates. That there is no clear way of even reacting to the poem is shown at the very end of the piece. The Hind ends her "Fable of the Pigeons" – and there are only ten lines of the long poem left. The Panther just does not know how to react:

> Thus did the gentle *Hind* her fable end,
> Nor would the *Panther* blame it, nor commend;
> But, with affected Yawnings at the close,
> Seem'd to require her natural repose.
>
> (Part III, lines 1289–92)

The end of one work (the Hind's fable) is nearly congruent with the end of Dryden's work (loosely, another fable) and each is reflected in the other. The Hind's auditor doesn't know how to react to what has been said – either because the Panther has not taken in the meaning or because the meaning is too powerful (both might apply to Dryden's own auditors). That Dryden knew his poem was odd and difficult is humorously indicated in this ending. The secondary central character is sent to sleep (or pretends to be) by what she has heard. There can be no greater bathos (as Rochester and Artemisia knew) than the invocation of a large yawn at the end of a narrative and disputative poem (a point Pope picked up at the end of Books II and IV of the *Dunciad*). The Hind herself also goes to sleep:

> Ten thousand Angels on her slumbers waite
> With glorious Visions of her future state. (lines 1297–8)

The justification of the Hind is held in suspension, belonging to eternity. The real closure cannot be expressed here and now. The poem ends by pointing us elsewhere. As in *Absalom*, there is in the central (here intermittent) narrative no full satisfying action which expresses and resolves all the conflict. A clear worldly ending would evoke political disaster, religious war. The whole poem preaches peace, not war; its conflicts cannot be solved by anything in traditional epic or conventional fable. This non-epic non-fable shows us both splendour and absurdity, and dwells more on absurdity. Yes, what *could* be more absurd than that one beast should counsel another to rest her faith upon a pope and a council? The bathetic progression is also absurd, subtly affronting our sense of proportion. The poem emphasizes through its strangeness the strangeness of divisions within the Christian Church; we should stop accepting divisiveness and meanness as normal. Dryden gives us a poetically ab-normal view in his absurd unfulfilled quasi-fable which allows a suspension of disbelief and of fictional belief in a changeable narrative and perpetually altering stylistic formation. *The Hind and the Panther* may be taken as the great, the undeniable, *sui generis* poem of the Restoration era, and pondering on it may help us to understand others of that period, and of the Augustan Age in general. *The Hind and the Panther* was written once for all. It is its own kind of poem, it cannot be repeated (and no one has repeated it).

The Restoration poets' urge to collapse old genres and invent new ones, making a new genre for each poem and finding the style suitable to it, has very noticeable effects. Unique invention is characteristic of their best poetic works. Although the first impulse to parody styles and dismantle old genres diminished slightly with the passage of time (and after so much demolition work had already been done), this characteristic of the early Augustans (including the later Milton and Marvell as well as Butler, Rochester and Dryden) is also a characteristic of the later Augustans. Swift, Gay and Pope are consummate parodists, who mingle a number of styles in creating unique works while at the same time demolishing other poems, precedent genres. Augustan works often signal their stylistic self-consciousness by beginning with some prefatory matter, like Dryden's at the beginning of *The Hind and the Panther*, some address "To the Reader" that explains why the work is as it is, alluding to other possible styles or manners and repudiating these possibilities in order to explain the advantages of this particular piece and its own procedure. Prefatory material, which includes sub-titles, may often tease and puzzle us, alerting us in advance to a unique stylistic mixture, e.g. "*The Rape of the Lock*. An Heroic-Comical Poem." The habit the Augustans cultivated, of prefacing poetic works with discussions of that work, becomes an object of parody by the Augustans themselves. We have for instance "*Martinus Scriblerus his Prolegomena and Illustrations to the Dunciad*: with the Hyper Critics of Aristarchus," in which prefaces, explanations and various sorts of criticism are mocked and rejected as precedents. (Anything that looked so settled as to be a genre was asking for deconstruction.)

The repudiation of other styles, of precedent genres, is customarily found, implicitly or explicitly expressed, in a poem itself, especially the beginning of a poem. The rejection of other possibilities (while in some sense exploiting them) is very visible in mock-heroic works, where the open discussion of the piece is part of the fun. ("Slight is the Subject, but not so the Praise, / If She inspire, and He approve my Lays.") But such discussion and rejection are also to be found in works which are not mock-heroic; see, for instance, the opening of the *Essay on Man*, which picks up images and ideas from *Paradise Lost* and puts them to different use under the governance of a new and individual style which is the product of a mixture of styles:

> A mighty maze! but not without a plan;
> A Wild, where weeds and flow'rs promiscuous shoot,
> Or Garden, tempting with forbidden fruit.
> Together let us beat this ample field,
> Try what the open, what the covert yield;

The latent tracts, the giddy heights explore
Of all who blindly creep, or sightless soar;
Eye Nature's walks, shoot Folly as it flies,
And catch the Manners living as they rise;
Laugh where we must, be candid where we can;
But vindicate the ways of God to Man.

(Essay on Man, I, lines 6–16)

Milton's Paradise as "scene of Man" becomes a gentleman's estate and a rather surreal one, full of strange life which can be observed at leisure and laughed at by modern gentlemen who act as naturalists but also as sportsmen, shooting Folly as it flies by like some colourful but stupid pheasant. The tone, the idiom, the new style, have changed everything. We as readers are moved through parody to a recognition of the poem's new and unique quality; that is what the parody signals, and not in any way a triviality of subject or treatment. We now know that the poem is itself. The rite of parodic opening establishes the poem's claim to be *sui generis*.

George Crabbe, at the very end of our Augustan line, begins his first great poem, *The Village* (1783), with a generic question and with a parody which is a resounding attack on and demolition of the pastoral manner:

The village life, and every care that reigns
O'er youthful peasants and declining swains;
What labour yields, and what, that labour past,
Age, in its hour of languour, finds at last;
What forms the real picture of the poor,
Demand a song – the Muse can give no more.
. . .
    On Mincio's banks, in Caesar's bounteous reign,
If TITYRUS found the golden age again,
Must sleepy bards the flattering dream prolong,
Mechanic echo's of the Mantuan song?
From truth and nature shall we widely stray,
Where VIRGIL, not where fancy, leads the way?

    Yes, thus the Muses sing of happy swains,
Because the Muses never know their pains:
. . .
    No; cast by Fortune on a frowning coast,
Which neither groves nor happy vallies boast;
Where other cares than those the Muse relates,
And other shepherds dwell with other mates;
By such examples taught, I paint the cot,
As truth will paint it, and as bards will not:
Nor you, ye poor, of letter'd scorn complain,
To you the smoothest song is smooth in vain;
. . .
Can poets sooth you, when you pine for bread,
By winding myrtles round your ruin'd shed?

(The Village, Book I, lines 1–60)[21]

I should perhaps have said that Crabbe proves he is an Augustan by such a beginning. What marks him as an Augustan, more than his couplets, is his approach by an attack on a precedent genre, his entry into a poem by parody, and his declaration that *this* poem is going to be its own kind of work. He declares his refusal to be restrained by traditions of genre and by stylistic expectations, and the reader is incited to break through the tired precedent here exhibited to get at the reality and excitements which only this new style, this new poem, can supply. Pastoral manners and old styles of nature description are so sent up and exploded that we feel indeed we could not bear them any more by the time Crabbe has mimicked and discarded them. Perhaps the Augustan poets' greatest and most consistent work of ventriloquism was their mimicry of other poets, real or more often imagined, "sleepy bards" with "Mechanic echo's" of outworn songs – the poets that they did not wish to be.

If we are looking for a mark that distinguishes Augustan poetry from other English poetry we have probably found it in the voiced repudiation within the poem of other styles and kinds. Romantic poets are much more likely to insulate their works, especially at the outset, from any sound of debate or attack; they prefer not to criticize, and not to comment on alternative styles, being more busily involved in creating one unified style for their statement. Byron is of course the notable exception, especially in *Don Juan*, but then Byron consciously wished to be an honorary Augustan. It is appropriate that Byron and Johnson unite in admiring Crabbe. Byron thought Crabbe "Nature's sternest Painter, yet the best."[22] Johnson praised *The Village* to Sir Joshua Reynolds as "original, vigorous, and elegant."[23] It is both Johnsonian and Augustan to put "original" first, and to set elegance in third place, after vigour. The "vigorous fancy" is still roaming, and finding room – and elbowing old genres and styles out of the way.

It was the Augustan Age that discovered "originality" as a modern literary (or artistic) concept. Some may think this idea more of a curse than a blessing; like most important human notions it has at times led to follies. But it is not unimportant, not a little idea. It becomes dominant precisely at the time when poets questioned and pulled down past genres and styles, because these seemed incapable of serving, or of serving simply, any more. Almost every major poem questions within itself the nature of its art and its undertaking, as well as reaching out to apprehend the large external universe of people, things, ideas, history. Each poem makes room for differences, for various voices, various tones. The poets do not shy away from, but rather welcome, discord and dissonance. They seek out peculiar thematic and structural problems, self-invented and very consciously produced problems that cannot make for easy resolution. In their almost aggressively original enterprise the poets were certainly not without respect for the works of the past, from antiquity to the age of the Metaphysicals, and they did not disdain literary models. But the models had to be taken on the new poets' own new Augustan terms. This is most deeply true of their relation to the "old Augustans," the poets of Rome in the age of Augustus Caesar. Our Augustans would follow only where vigorous fancy as well as Virgil led the way. As we shall see, they found that Virgil and the roaming fancy could combine, but nobody advocated producing "Mechanic echo's of the Mantuan song." On the contrary, the Roman poets were most approved when they seemed most closely in sympathy with the new English enterprise.

IV

The new Augustans and the Roman poets

The "Augustan" writers are so called, and their period termed the "Augustan Age," chiefly because the poets – and it was chiefly the poets – found in certain Roman writers of the age of the Emperor Augustus some of their most congenial literary models. Poets, however, even those educated in seventeenth-century schools, are not schoolboys doing Latin exercises; they do not have a model imposed on them which they try dutifully to imitate. Rather, poets of all ages seek out certain models, and discard or largely discount others. Literary influence means *wanting* to be influenced.

One advantage of going back to antiquity is that the poet can get rid of some of the more harassing or irritating qualities of immediate predecessors. An admiration extended over a distance of sixteen hundred years is not constricting. Our English Augustans, who really knew their Latin poets, were not trying for a general and chilly Latinity, and their choice of models was highly selective. Some very fine Latin poets are almost ignored by our Augustans, either because their works dealt in uncongenial subject matter (Propertius) or exemplified the use of closed strict lyric form (Catullus). The poets who were the biggest "influences" on our English poets of the Restoration and eighteenth century are Ovid, Horace and Virgil. And in looking to aspects of these poets' works our new Augustans were likewise highly selective. Not all works by the same author interested them.

To begin with Ovid – in some respects the simplest case. The poet who interests the Augustans is not the amorous Ovid, the authority on love once so valued. It is true that Dryden translated short portions of the *Ars Amatoria* and the *Remedia Amoris*; he singles out those aspects the medieval readers looked askance at, and his translations create short worldly vignettes, much in the manner of Rochester. By the eighteenth century, one has to look hard for any signs of Ovid the artist, even the cynical artist, of love.

Ovid was still very much the poet of the *Metamorphoses*, as he had been for the Renaissance. One might think indeed that the *Metamorphoses* had been done almost to death as a source of literary allusion in that period, and our Augustans when they draw on the *Metamorphoses* are also often playing with and parodying the Renaissance use of Ovidian myth. Ovid's big work could notoriously be drawn on for pleasant elaborate ornament, asked to supply a kind of décor. The Augustans were not interested in the kind of Ovidian narrative poem the Elizabethans had developed; there is no new equivalent to

Hero and Leander or *Venus and Adonis*. There is still, however, a very strong interest in Ovidian narrative. This interest can be seen in Dryden's translations of individual stories in *Examen Poeticum* (1693) and in the *Fables* (1700), renditions that were later to affect the Keats of *Lamia*. Dryden gives us the narrative of Ovid's twelfth book, complete; that book goes through Aesacus' love of a nymph, the story of the Trojan war, the House of Fame, the fight of Achilles and Cygnus, and the battle between the Lapiths and the Centaurs. Book xii of the *Metamorphoses* provides a stunning example of the interweaving of different *topoi* and styles. It exemplifies all of Ovid's qualities, and that particularly sophisticated view of narrative, of story and style, that one associates with Ovid.

Dryden's partial translation had a number of successors. Various Augustan writers were pleased to translate some parts of books or a sequence of Ovidian tales. When in 1717 Samuel Garth produced *Ovid's Metamorphoses in Fifteen Books*, Translated by the most Eminent Hands, he found no lack of eminent hands to contribute. As well as including Dryden's long-known rendering of Book xii, Garth's book, a sort of anthology of translations, offered new work by Addison, Prior, Garth and others. It is noticeable what a good turn Ovid can do his translators; even Addison, whose poetry is marked customarily by a proud inanity, gains imagery and interest. He acquires vividness in dealing with Ovidian transformations, as in his description of Aglauros blasted by Envy and pining away:

> Consum'd like ice, that just begins to run,
> When feebly smitten by the distant Sun;
> Or like unwholesome weeds, that set on fire
> Are slowly wasted, and in smoke expire

or his description of the ship being changed by Bacchus:

> The sails are cover'd with a chearful green,
> And Berries in the fruitful canvase seen.

Translating Ovid was a challenge and an inspiration. As Addison says in his "Notes" on Ovid,

There is so great a variety in the arguments of the Metamorphoses, that he who would treat of 'em rightly, ought to be a master of all stiles, and every different way of writing. Ovid indeed shows himself most in a familiar story, where the chief grace is to be easie and natural; but wants neither strength of thought nor expression, when he endeavours after it.[1]

A rich variety is what Ovid has, outstandingly, to offer, as Samuel Garth stresses in a passage strongly exemplifying the Augustan recourse to imagery of appetite. (Indeed, I wonder if this passage was recalled by Fielding as he began *Tom Jones*.) The *Metamorphoses* is not a ceremonious dinner but a great disorderly feast at which one can drop in:

Since therefore the Readers are not solemnly invited to an Entertainment, but come accidentally; they ought to be contented with what they find: And pray what have they to complain of, but too great Variety? where, tho' some of the Dishes be not serv'd in the exactest Order, and Politeness, but hash'd up in haste; there are a great many accommodated to every particular Palate.

Ovid is copious and versatile. He has energy and creates striking effects; he can both move and amuse. Above all the Augustans admired Ovid's facility in keeping up a narrative while being ready at any moment to change gear in a rapid but smooth transition:

the Reader may take Notice ... how natural his Transitions generally are. With how much Ease does he slide into some new Circumstance, without any Violation of the Unity of the Story. The Texture is so artful, that it may be compar'd to the work of his own *Arachne*, where the Shade dyes so gradually, and the Light revives so imperceptibly, that it is hard to tell where the one ceases and the other begins.

(Garth, Preface to *Ovid's Metamorphoses*)[2]

As the English Augustans tended to rely on versatile narrative, often presenting short bursts of narrative of different kinds within one obliquely connected whole, they had reason to study Ovid's various styles, his narrative manners, and his transitions.

One of the striking things about the *Metamorphoses* is that it seems so expansive, so limitless. There is no reason for stopping; there never is a boundary quite to any story, as we almost immediately leap over to (or are entangled in) yet another story. We cannot say anything is incomplete, but there seems no stopping point. This is a technique particularly Ovid's own. Ovid made up his own genre, too, for this great work; any relation to Hesiod's *Theogony*, for instance, is extremely loose and almost entirely parodic. Ovid engages constantly in parody and in plays of wit and words (Dryden and Addison thought he sacrificed too much to the latter) without giving up his power to amaze or move. His work proceeds (like a Dryden Preface) at least ostensibly as the stream of attached or loosely connected thoughts emanating from the writer's gloriously fertile mind. There is a power of the mind let loose, an "Energy" of "Fancy", that had an appeal for the Augustans.

Yet at the same time, despite the praise, Ovid is often not treated with much respect. His stories are too well known; allusion to them would be feebly pseudo-Elizabethan if such allusion were not made knowingly parodic. Augustan poets, aware of his decorative uses in the past, often echo this kind of use, more or less mockingly. Ovidian illustration becomes transparent, rather than opaque as with the Elizabethans; we are meant to see through it. In *Windsor Forest*, for instance, Pope includes the story of Lodona, a mock-Ovidian tale, which we are meant to spot (unlike other parts of the poem more seriously meant) as smooth contrivance, a flourish of ornament taking in an Elizabethan habit by the way.

Even more frequently, Ovid is burlesqued – indeed there is a touch of the burlesque in the London story. All imitations have a touch of the burlesque about them. It has been suggested by Howard D. Weinbrot that in the late seventeenth century not only translation but "the comic burlesque of specific works also fostered the rise of the Imitation."[3] The most substantial and serious imitations of Horace and Juvenal, for instance, became possible only after Restoration impudence and freedom had made various sorts of parody thoroughly at home. The Restoration's first urge is to parody, and parody – or parody-burlesque – requires the sort of intimate knowledge, the ventriloquizing of the poet, which is needed for the Imitation proper much more than for translation alone. Both parody and Imitation (yes, even Pope's Imitations of Horace) have a kind of outrageousness and intimacy; they stick close to the skin whereas translation follows at a distance. The Augustan poets were familiar (in both senses) with their Roman predecessors and contemporaries. Swift's "Baucis and Philemon" is a burlesque parody both of Ovid's poem and Dryden's poetic translation of it. Gay in *Trivia* indulges in mock-Ovidian tales, fluently and with panache. We are given the origin of the pattens (I, lines 223–82), and the generation of the shoeblack, offspring of the goddess Cloacina's love for a mortal man, a collector of night soil (II, lines 103–68). There are a number of briefer Ovidian references, e.g. "Church-Monuments foretell the changing Air; / Then *Niobe* dissolves into a Tear, / And sweats with secret Grief" (I, lines 167–9); part of the fun is the quick and unusual association of Niobe (found in Ovid's Book VI) with Anglican church monuments damp with condensation. It is part of the fun Ovid himself offers that anything can be associated with almost anything else; he invites liberties which the Augustan poets happily took.

Gay could not, of course, have managed so happily had he not been very interested in Ovid. He contributed stories from Book IX to Garth's book, as well as the story of Arachne which he had previously published in 1712. At times Gay seems to strive to outdo Ovid's usual outdoing, extending the effects, whether hyperbolical or comic; the comic certainly seems uppermost in his version of the story of Arachne, and its end ("Her bloated Belly swells to larger size, / Which now with smallest Threads her Work supplies").

The poet of the *Metamorphoses* was, for our period even more than for the late Renaissance, the poet of the *Heroides*. The idea of the epistle was particularly congenial; the letter exhibits personal character, permits digressions, discourse and debate, teasing the reader with modulations and transitions. The poetic epistle is a major idea in poetry of our Augustan period. Ovid's heroines are reduced to letter-writing, that is, to inaction; their lovers are away, or have abandoned them altogether, and the women can do nothing but express memory and emotion. An "heroic epistle" is an expression of emotion which may or may not affect the addressee. Such an epistle is particularly suited, on the overt level of narrative, to feminine discourse, and, being female, it can thus forsake altogether the bounds of rhetorical styles or decorums, is not even required to be aware of generic distinctions. Ovid invented a literary kind capable of unslavish imitation, of expansion.

Heroic epistles already existed in English before our period, chiefly the

"Heroicall Epistles" of Michael Drayton, one of the most important Elizabethan poets for the Augustans.[4] Typically, the first major Restoration exercises in the heroic epistle include parodic heroic epistles. Rochester's "A Very Heroical Epistle in Answer to *Ephelia*" turns the genre upside down. This poetic letter, an answer to Etherege's more conventional "*Ephelia to Bajazet*," is the response by a man to a woman, fully betraying and traducing her while declaring his impudent infidelity in response to her lovelorn emotions. "Bajazet" (thought an allusion to the Earl of Mulgrave, noted for his conceit) is an impenitent egotist:

> What man or woman upon earth can say
> I ever used 'em well above a day?
> . . .
> In my dear self I center everything: (lines 1–7)

Rochester, by adding the adverb ("Very Heroical"), mocks the genre and the idea, though his mockery has serious meaning. He reminds us that Ovid's Aeneas, Theseus and company escape without having to exhibit themselves in an epistle and that, if they had written a response to their desperate mistresses, they might have cut a poor figure. The extremely masculinist view of love, a view of woman as disposable, is presented as monstrous though funny. Perhaps too Rochester felt, if only momentarily, the questionable nature of readers' enjoyment of the *Heroides*, which depends on our taking feminine passion and its failure for granted truths:

> My blazing star but visits, and away.
> As fatal, too, it shines as those i'th'skies:
> 'Tis never seen but some great lady dies.
>   The boasted favor you so precious hold
> To me's no more than changing of my gold:
> . . .
> But women, beggar-like, still haunt the door
> Where they've received a charity before.   (lines 21–31)

In some respects the cleansing of the "heroic epistle" by such scouring of mockery made possible its serious and varied use later. The tradition of the *Heroides* fed the new conventions of the love-novel; even Richardson,[5] who had no Latin (or very little), was affected indirectly by the popularity of this verse idea. The idea of the heroic epistle (it can only very loosely be called a form) was important, as such an epistle provided a means for the expression of subjective emotion. The writer (or speaker) is pure "I," and the reader focuses on the movements of consciousness, the world seen through this sensibility and in this crisis. It is a non-prescriptive kind of work, which ought never to smell of the lamp. The most famous Augustan example of the heroic epistle is Pope's *Eloisa to Abelard*; Gillian Beer has discussed the relation of this work to the *Heroides*.[6] Classical knowledge was not necessary for appreciation of the poem; *Eloisa* was enjoyed by many of the unlearned, including, if report can be believed, "all the kept Mistresses" of the town.[7] *Eloisa* was a distillation of passion. The poem seems so original that the reader does not pause to ask (as we do, for instance with *Hero and Leander*) "What was the model for this?" The *Heroides* provided unrestricting models, loose examples rather than tight forms. The poet, or even novelist, could go on at any length, and cover (or make his heroine cover) varied emotions or associations. The influence of the *Heroides* is to be found in the novel of the period, and also at moments in poems which aren't "heroical epistles," as in some of Belinda's rhetoric in *The Rape of the Lock*, or the thoughts and feelings of the women in *Epistle to a Lady*.

Ovid is above all the great poet of change and changefulness; he deals in change (metamorphosis). He shows how to fuse various elements in surprising combinations, and how to move through quick transitions. In the *Metamorphoses*, things and people change; in the *Heroides* people change and the world looks changed to the subjective eye. It was in this record of change and rapid alteration that Ovid was most useful to the Augustan poets. The topic of my next chapter is the Augustan poets' interest in change and metamorphosis, and there Ovidian influences figure very largely. Ovid was not the major classical model who appealed to the Augustans; they used him in combination with other things. They never used him unquestioningly, but Ovid's own inventiveness, as well as his own parodic sense of style and genre, made him an associate of considerable significance, if by no means the one most venerated.

Horace is a different matter altogether. A much clearer relationship is to be discerned between his work and that of our English Augustans. Horace had not been so extensively mined during the Renaissance as to require, like Ovid, double reference, both to the poet and to those who more recently used his style, manner and topics. That is, of course, true for only part of his work, the *Satires* and *Epistles*. The Horatian poems that had appealed to writers earlier in the seventeenth century, the *carmina*, became much less important than they had been. It is true that the whole of Horace's works, including the *Odes*, underwent translation into English during our period, the first and most important of these new Augustan renderings being Thomas Creech's *The Odes, Satyrs and Epistles of Horace* (1684).

It might be argued, against the view that the *Odes* receded in importance, that the frontispiece of Creech's book illustrates one of the *carmina*. It seems, however, significant that the illustrator introduces us to what might be called the Ovidian Horace. In this reference to *Odes* ii, xx, we see the poet in the process comically described by Horace, that of turning into a swan. This metamorphosis, Horace proposes, is a way of escaping death, becoming pure poet, immortal not earthbound. As the picture shows, the poet is in the act of changing, to the astonishment of the spectators. He is both man and immortal bird, but subject to comic distresses from which Keats's Nightingale, or Yeats's wild swans, are more happily free. The "biformis vates" or two-formed poet, still looking rather heavy in the lower body, sails into the air, daringly departing from the common world. In this picture, the bi-formed poet's long writhing bird's neck is a strange replacement for the missing male member, so noticeably absent between the naked feathery thighs. The attenuated neck with the small head at the end emphasizes what is comically strange (both potent and impotent) within this conceit. The image of the poet's metamorphosis suggests a comic pathos in the search for the inspired and eternal. In its concentration on poetic identity, and in its emphasis on both the absurdity and the daring that make the poet what he is, the illustration to Creech's *Horace* offers no bad emblem of the English Augustan view of the Poet.

After Creech's workmanlike if uninspired effort, there are several standard translations of Horace, and some passable if not exciting verse translations of various Odes. Yet on the whole, though the *Odes* were certainly read and known, they have little connection with our Augustan poetry; one is rarely aware of their presence. There is no English Augustan equivalent, and hardly any valid rendering, of, for instance, "Vides et alta stet nive candidum / Soracte" (i. ix) or "Persicos odi" (i. xxxviii). Samuel Johnson's verse translations turn Horace's poems into something else – something strong, mournful and defiant. The note struck in "dulce ridentem Lalagen amabo / dulce loquentem" (i. xxii) is not heard – save momentarily and mockingly in Gay's "Were I laid on *Greenland's* Coast," Air xvi of *The Beggar's Opera*. For the true Horatian feeling, the feeling of the *carmina*, we must turn to Jonson ("Still to be neat," "Drink to me only") or to Herrick. In Herrick indeed the Horace of the *Odes* is everywhere, and not in mere translation:

> So, when or you or I are made
> A fable, song or fleeting shade,
> All love, all liking, all delight
> Lies drown'd with us in endless night.
> Then, while time serves, and we are but decaying,
> Come, my *Corinna*, come, let's goe a Maying.

Significantly, Herrick was not read in the eighteenth century.[8] The Augustans do not seem to have shared the sensibility of the *Odes*, with their Epicurean insistence on the pleasures of love and on the fleetingness of those pleasures. The qualities which had appealed in the early or mid seventeenth century seemed unsympathetic (and of course also outdated) by the end of it. The Horace of the *Odes* seemed too inturned, too elegiac, and too resigned. Moreover, the *Odes* and *Epodes* are *carmina* – lyrics in tightly wrought if varying verse forms. They represent closed forms, a less than satisfactory kind of poetry to the Augustan mind, and the very fact that closed elegant lyrics had been so copiously written in the period just before the Augustan Age was reason in itself for not wishing to produce more of the same.

It is not true that we do not find any versions of or parallels to the true Horatian song – just that we don't find many, and what we do find is rarely successful. Pope in 1736 produced a version of part of the first Ode of the fourth book. It begins thus in the originals:

> Intermissa, Venus, diu
> rursus bella moves? parce precor, precor.
> non sum qualis eram bonae
> sub regno Cinarae   (iv. i, lines 1–4)

an opening Pope renders as

> Again? new Tumults in my Breast?
> Ah spare me, Venus, let me, let me rest!
> I am not now, alas! the man
> As in the gentle Reign of My Queen *Anne*.
> ("The First Ode of the Fourth Book of Horace, to Venus," lines 1–4)

We can hardly avoid feeling that Pope has coarsened the lines, and his endeavour to produce lines of varied length and metre sounds awkward. The conceit is also changed; the rule of Horace's Cinara was not an official political rule, but Pope's use of Queen Anne diminishes the importance of erotic relationship. In omitting the second of the two verbs "sum ... eram" Pope has cut out the elegiac feeling; the whole effect is jaunty in a way that Horace's is not. In his youth, Pope once produced a more successful Horatian *carmen*:

> Happy the man, whose wish and care
> A few paternal acres bound,
> Content to breathe his native air,
>   In his own ground.
> ("Ode on Solitude," lines 1–4)[9]

But this, as he proudly claimed, is a juvenile work. And no poet of the Augustan Age could make his name on what he produced in the manner of the *carmina*. Horace's other poems are a different matter. If the *carmina* were pushed into the background, the *Epistles* and *Satires* became of immense importance. The Horace that the new Augustans "discovered" was the Horace of the *sermones*.

In his *Satires* (less misleadingly called "sermones," i.e. chats, conversations) Horace often proclaims himself the founder of a new kind of poetry. Though he acknowledges his debt to Lucilius (how large that was we have no sure means of knowing) he makes it clear that he is writing a new sort of poetry, and is jokingly willing to entertain the question whether this kind of writing ("genus hoc scribendi") is or is not "poema," real poetry (*Satires* I. iv, lines 63–5). He speaks disarmingly if ironically of his pedestrian Muse ("Musaque pedestri," II. vi, line 17), of his chit-chat crawling along the ground ("sermones ... repentis per humum," *Epistles* II. i, lines 250–1). All this mock self-dispraise is combined with a vivid sense of the other poetic possibilities he is refusing to entertain, and with a keen desire to parody competing and established "poetic" styles. Trebatius the lawyer advises Horace against continuing to write – or, if he must write, let him tell the feats of Caesar, in high style. Horace says he cannot:

vires
deficiunt: neque enim quivis horrentia pilis
agmina nec fracta pereuntis cuspide Gallos
aut labentis equo describat volnera Parthi.

(*Satires* ii. i, lines 12–15)

His strength is lacking: it isn't given to everyone to describe armies bristling
with lances or falling Gauls with fractured spearheads or the wounded Parthian sliding off his horse. The tremendous war-picture is produced with the *élan*
of pure comedy, and a genre as well as a style is produced, questioned, laughed
at and thrown away.

Horace is always conscious of styles and genres, as in *Satires* i. x, where he
lists modern genres and their contemporary practitioners (including the
Eclogues of Virgil), imitating each briefly in the description. He admires
Lucilius for originality, for writing a new kind of poetry untouched by the
Greeks ("Graecis intacti carminis auctor," i. x, line 66). Yet he is often
somewhat critical of Lucilius, and emphasizes his own differences from him,
differences both literary and social. Horace was the son of a freedman, as he
goes out of his way to emphasize, and not the born member of an aristocratic
circle. He was on the losing side at Philippi and lost his (small) estate in the
civil war; "paupertas impulit audax / ut versus facerem," "audacious poverty
pushed me into writing verse" (*Epistles* ii. ii, lines 51–2). The Horace of the
sermones lives quietly on his little country place (and we hear about beans and
stew, not the rosy wreaths of the *Odes*) or in town, where he goes out alone,
shopping for greens and flour (*Satires* i. vi. lines 111–12). Such biographical
details put a distance between himself and both grand social style and grand
literary style; he surprises with what he is willing to put into poetry.

It is evident that the Horace of the *sermones* feels he is perfecting his own
genre, his own style, in defiance – and there is a good deal of defiance – of other
styles and the practice of both predecessors and contemporaries. Let turgid
Bibaculus carry on by himself, murdering Memnon and making muddy the
head of the Rhine; Horace will continue to play with works which are not for
recital in the Temple of the Muses or to be played over and over on stage:

Turgidus Alpinus iugulat dum Memnona dumque
defingit Rheni luteum caput, haec ego ludo,
quae neque in aede sonent certantia iudice Tarpa,
nec redeant iterum atque iterum spectanda theatris.

(*Satires* i. x, lines 36–9)

Horace says wryly "haec ego ludo": I play with this, this playful stuff, these
trifling pieces. He *is* playing a game of genres and styles; we don't have to
believe in his modesty. Each poem, as he really shows us, is a self-sustaining
work, wrought on its own without reliance on traditional genres or someone
else's style. Each of the *sermones* (both of the *Satires* and the *Epistles*) is generi-
cally its own, the result, the poet perpetually insists, of his incessant desire to

scribble something down. He pretends to rattle on with what comes into his mind, grave or gay, with a flexibility of mind that requires him to exclude nothing. As Philip Francis noted in the mid eighteenth century, those very qualities which make the Horace of the *sermones* so individual and enjoyable pose problems for any translator.[10] But the temptation to regulate Horace, to straighten him out in some manner, should be resisted:

The Difficulties of Horace in his Satires and Epistles arise, in general, from his Frequent Translations of Lines in Grecian Writers, and Parodies on those of his Cotemporaries [*sic*]; from his introducing new Characters on the Scene, and changing the Speakers of his Dialogues; from his not marking his Transitions from Thought to Thought, but giving them as they lay in his Mind. These unconnected Transitions are of great Life and Spirit, nor should a Translator be too coldly regular in supplying the Connexion, since it will be a tame Performance, that gives us the Sense of Horace, if it be not given in his peculiar Manner.

To supply coldly explanatory transitions is indeed to tame and betray Horace, as Francis justly saw; Horace offers us the "Life and Spirit" of a mind in action. Neither should his style be cramped; Francis complains that modern verse-translators "have only one style" and make Ovid, Virgil, Horace sound the same: "the freeborn Spirit of Poetry is confined in twenty constant Syllables, and the Sense regularly ends with every second Line." Such frigid regularity is indeed as Francis says "unclassical" as well as "unnatural" if we are to reproduce Horace. It is true that the mixture which is Horatian style suffers badly in any century when turned into the "one style" of most translators. We never know, when reading one of the *sermones*, what styles we are going to come upon: high style, serious middle tone, parody, odd quotations such as Cicero's wretched jingle or the cries of a children's game – or snatches of colloquial speech after the manner of Terence, e.g. "hora quota est?" "Thraex est Gallina Syro par?" ("What time is it?" "Is the Thracian Chicken up to Syrus?" *Satires* II. vi, line 44). Horace was seldom as outrageous as he is in the early satire (I. ii) in which the first hexameter line is made up of three mouthfilling preposterous words ("Ambubaiarum collegia, pharmacopolae") – but he did try that once. In each case the poem seems to sweep the board, collecting styles and rearranging or disarranging them as it goes. No poem seems fixed by any regulations which demand the maintenance of one particular style or tone, and the reader cannot be sure how the poem is to end, or how beginning and ending will be related, or how many various genres will be taken up and sliced and popped into the stew (*saturam*).

Horace's *sermones* represent an extreme literary self-consciousness. Did any poet before Horace ever write so much about writing itself, about styles and genres and the difficulty or ease of writing? In many of the *sermones* the making of the poem is part of the subject; we watch it being made before our eyes and admire the wit that can be so casually self-conscious (and conscious of the modes and choices of poetry) and yet at the same so triumphant over self-consciousness. Most of the *sermones* are triumphant memorials to generic instability. Structurally, they are wonders of apparently loose contrivance, interfolding style and manner with style and manner, introducing one discursive or narrative element after another.

One of the finest examples of Horace's techniques in the *sermones* is *Satires* II. vi, which has long been a favourite, particularly because of its treatment of the Aesopian fable of the Town Mouse and Country Mouse. The beginning, "Hoc erat in votis" etc. sounds rather like the tone of an Ode or Epode; we might be about to get a simple description of the pleasures of country life and the virtues of content, a topic which could be closed up satisfactorily in a few polished lines. But the intrusion of the foolish prayer which Horace says he does *not* utter (lines 8–13) cuts against too much simplicity; we are diverted by the comedy of the imagined petitioner who wishes Mercury would let him discover a buried treasure, and we can't quite dissociate ourselves (or Horace) from the foolish prayer. Enjoying his peace in the hills, Horace – after a sudden mock-heroic invocation to Janus – imagines his life at Rome in the early morning and then throughout the day. Abruptly, through the processes of the poet's mind in reverie and memory, we are with him, back in the big city, afflicted by summonses to business, jostlings in the street, crowds. There are conversations, questions, quick spurts of dialogue. The *mihi, me* of the first part is in this section swamped by the insistence of *tibi, tu, te*, emerging most impolitely on the street in "quid tibi vis, insane, et quam rem agis?" which might be very roughly translated as "what do you think you're doing, you idiot?" Horace has become the object of others' questions and exclamations, and longs again to be subject "O rus, quando *ego* te aspiciam?" (line 60). Being a subject, being an "I" and not a "you" is associated with being in the country. Horace is the great poet of pronouns, their use the more marked because an inflected language requires them so much less than an uninflected one.

The bustling Horace in town (originally imagined by the contented Horace in the country) then longs for home, remembering the beauty of his simple life and the conversations with his neighbours. And his neighbour Cervius would tell a tale like this – and so we go to the Fable which concludes the poem (lines 79–117). The Fable of the Town Mouse and Country Mouse occurs at the point where the memory of the Horace in town remembering the country is thus recalled or conjured up by a Horace now in his country home – Horace himself being, as it were, both mice. The major locale of the whole poem is the poet's memory – an outstanding example of the personality of the poet holding the whole poem together. Everything that happens is the effect of Horace's consciousness, which allows all of this to exist, conjures it into being. We move from the recalled crowded Roman streets (realistic descriptive comic narrative) to the fable of the two mice (pseudo-realistic surreal comic narrative). Unequals are yoked together, as they are too in the Fable itself with the homely vivid details, the humanizing of the "characters" (who are more polite to each other than are Horace's Romans in the scenes preceding), and the moments of mock-heroic style and parody, as in the philosophical discourse of the

Epicurean Town Mouse (who has made an error in his Epicureanism, unlike Horace). The Town Mouse unwittingly parodies the tone of the Odes: "carpe viam" he says encouragingly (line 93).

The whole poem works logically, but with its own logic. It is unpredictable. "Hoc erat in votis" would not necessarily lead to this ending. The transitions are easy but audacious, illustrating what Francis meant by "unconnected Transitions . . . of great Life and Spirit"; they depend on the movement of the poet's mind. As it proceeds, the poem uses up a number of genres, from prayer and invocation to Aesopian fable (remodelled).

The Horace of the *sermones* has the qualities which the English poets of the late seventeenth century and the eighteenth century valued. Historically, there was a sympathy between Horace and the English poets of the Restoration; Horace's life had crashed behind him after a civil war which meant the end of an era, literary and political. The literary problems he faced were similar to those of the English Augustans, and he solved them in a manner similar to that favoured by his much later counterparts. He capitalized on generic instability, created new genres, mixed styles. His works, self-conscious, varied and free, are held together by the personality of the poet, by the "I" of the poem. It was not only his poverty but Horace himself who was bold. His new writings are ambitious, despite his overtly ironic jokes about their low prosaic qualities. The qualities of what is "poetical" are brought sharply into question. The *sermones* allowed extreme richness; everything could be fitted in. It was no wonder that the new Augustan poets in England felt friendly to this Horace, or that they "discovered" him. We discover the writers who are close to our own concerns.

It should at some point be admitted that of course Juvenal was close to the concerns of many Augustans. The only reason for not giving him extensive separate attention here is that his kind of writing may be considered as belonging in Horace's province. Undoubtedly, Juvenal was by some – most important, by Dryden – considered Horace's superior. Juvenal is more appetite-provoking ("The Meat of *Horace* is more nourishing, but the Cookery of *Juvenal* more exquisite"), more "vigorous," "sometimes too luxuriant," always "on the Gallop" (Dryden, *Discourse of Satire*). Juvenal's poems were celebrated, and imitated, notably in Johnson's *London* (1738) and *The Vanity of Human Wishes* (1749). Juvenal could seem the more British of the two poets as well as the more sublime. He was praised as the superior moralist, politically independent of corrupt courts whereas Horace the flatterer of Augustus was, as Dryden put it, "often afraid of Laughing in the right place." The honest satirist must, it was thought, have something of Juvenal in his composition. Weinbrot has shown us how Pope mingled Horatian and Juvenalian manners, as "some of Horace's perceived conventions were foreign to Pope's satiric aims."[11]

Yet the qualities and modes of proceeding of Juvenal are related to those of Horace, whose successor he was. We enjoy in Juvenal the vividness of his images, the power and vivacity with which he can evoke a crowded urban life. There is in Juvenal a profound love of detail of the Horatian sort, if turned to different purposes. That love of detail went into the creation of such vivid sketches as the description of the small poet in his fire-menaced garret, surrounded by the poor treasures he is doomed to lose:

> lectus erat Codro Procula minor, urceoli sex
> ornamentum abaci nec non et parvulus infra
> cantharus et recubans sub eodem marmore Chiron.
> iamque vetus graecos servabat cista libellos
> et divina opici rodebant carmina mures.
> nil habuit Codrus, quis enim negat? et tamen illud
> perdidit infelix totum nihil.
>
> (*Satire* III, lines 203–9)

Here indeed is vivid realization of a scene. The passage is translated by Dryden with animated attention to the particulars, extending to amplification of them:

> *Codrus* had but one Bed, so short to boot,
> That his short Wife's short Legs hung dangling out:
> His Cup-board's Head, six Earthen Pitchers grac'd,
> Beneath 'em was his Trusty Tankard plac'd:
> And, to support this Noble Plate, there lay
> A bending *Chiron* cast from honest Clay:
> His few *Greek* Books a rotten Chest contain'd;
> Whose Covers much of mouldiness complain'd:
> Where Mice and Rats devour'd Poetick Bread;
> And with Heroick Verse luxuriously were fed.
> 'Tis true, poor *Codrus* nothing had to boast,
> And yet poor *Codrus* all that Nothing lost.
>
> (*Juvenal: Satyr III*, lines 332–43)

We can see in such clear homely detail elaborated a relation to Horace's descriptions, such as that of himself, pricing cabbage and flour, strolling round the deceiving Circus and going home to supper, to peas and pancakes, at a table adorned with a white stone slab holding two cups and a ladle, and a cheap bowl beside it (*Satires* I, vi, lines 112–18). If "*Juvenal* Excels in the Tragical Satyre, as *Horace* does in the Comical," then we must also admit that Juvenal often proceeds by use of "the Comical." Juvenal is to some extent Horatian. And praise distinguishing the later satirist must also concede that he had the advantage of coming after Horace, and "Building upon his Foundations" (*Discourse of Satire*).

Despite the opposition often posed between the two poets, their strains converge in the eighteenth century. We may find, as Weinbrot has shown us we do in Pope's *Imitations of Horace*, a Juvenalized Horace, but Horace is the essential figure, and his work is more pervasive. At the beginning of our period Rochester has his "Allusion to Horace" which allows him to enumerate and critically describe his poetic contemporaries. Rachel Trickett points out that

Horace can be heard in Rochester's *Timon*, and "in the conversational idiom of *Artemisia*."[12] Throughout the work of Swift there are Horatian touches, as well as direct imitations. In 1713 Swift imitated part of *Epistles* I. vii; in 1714 he wrote an imitation of part of *Satires* II. vi, the Town and Country poem, later completed by Pope who added a delightful version of the Fable of the Mice. As we have seen, it was that fable to which Montague and Prior turned when they wanted a comic fable to counter Dryden's; they pretend to try to turn *The Hind and the Panther* into "the Story of the Country and the City-Mouse." How close Horace seemed can be felt in Pope's *Epistles*, as well as in his *Imitations of Horace*. It is the Horatian character who is congenial, even when being corrected by Juvenal's – and even more by Pope's – political insight and moral integrity. We need not seek out particular imitations or paraphrases to sense the presence of Horace or his influence.[13]

The word "influence" is perhaps rather suspect. The word indicates lines of force working in one direction, and irresistibly. Literary influence is largely a matter of conscious choice; an older writer is in some way taken into partnership. Such a partnership can always alter, if not the older poet's works, at least the reading of them. Writers take other writers into this partnership of "influence" only if it suits them to do so, if they find in the other a useful and stimulating associate. That was the relation of the Augustan poets to the Horace of the *Satires* and *Epistles*. Even in Dryden, who professed a preference for Juvenal, there are elements like those of the sermonic Horace. And to most of the other Augustans, Horace seemed a friend they were proud to own.

The greatest of the Roman poets, however, as everyone agreed, is Virgil. The seventeenth century saw a number of translations of Virgil, culminating in Dryden's great translation of his works (final version, 1697). This superseded Ogilby's ambitious folio of the late 1650s; Dryden's folio even contains the same illustrations (by Francis Cleyn, Wenceslas Hollar and others) as those found in "Uncle *Ogleby*'s" earlier luxurious volume.[14] Dryden's magnificent translation brought Virgil to a number of readers unable to read the Latin; its presence assured the existence of an English–Virgilian manner that could be imitated, parodied, or alluded to, as well as helping to ensure that, in general, references to Virgil would be understood.

The greatest work of this greatest of Latin poets has been universally understood to be his epic, the *Aeneid*. This work had the least affinity to the new Augustan enterprise. As we have seen, the early Augustans undid the epic. Translations were paralleled, even rudely anticipated, by the burlesques. Dryden's version of the *Aeneid* had to compete with that other "translation," Cotton's *Virgile Travestie*, a work which has its own scholarly apparatus and points us to extensive passages of the original, reproduced in the footnotes. The strongest late seventeenth-century tribute to the *Aeneid* is Tate's and Purcell's *Dido and Aeneas* (1680). This opera treats the comedy of the love-relationship between the wandering Trojan and the Queen of Carthage, as well as the Ovidian passion of the Queen, loving and abandoned. It is the story of Dido and Aeneas, not of Aeneas and Dido; the Queen is central character, and Aeneas (a role relatively small) comes off as something of a lout. The musical effects, including the screeching witchy chorus, are varied and exciting, but hardly classical in tone. *Dido and Aeneas* is certainly not a burlesque, but it obviously arises from the period which produced the travesties. The opera is an example of de-genre-fication. The epic is twisted about to make that new and hybrid drama, an opera, and this comic-romantic opera is the hybrid of a hybrid, a mixture in the Restoration style. Like other references to epic in the period, *Dido* is an attack on the epic idea. The *Aeneid* is through the rest of our period useful to poets (and novelists) chiefly as the perfected example of an impossible genre. It exists as a backdrop, a source of parody and allusion, and a means of comment. The greatest eighteenth-century English tribute to the *Aeneid* is the *Dunciad*, that mock-epic which is, among other things, a mock-*Aeneid*. There was no point in reproducing style and effects and epic genre ("A Receit to make an *Epick* Poem"). As a source of allusion, the *Aeneid* was valuable. It crops up in various places, expected and unexpected, as in Belinda's passionate speech in *The Rape of the Lock*: "Happy! ah ten times happy, had I been" etc. (IV, lines 149ff).

Virgil's *Eclogues* supply a more interesting case of a model, and offer other literary possibilities. Dryden translates them with loving attention, often echoing effects of Virgil very finely, as when he tries to capture some of the sound-effects of *Eclogue* I:

> hinc tibi, quae semper, vicino ab limite saepes
> Hyblaeis apibus florem depasta salicti
> saepe levi somnum suadebit inire susurro;   (I, lines 53–5)

> Behold yon bord'ring Fence of Sallow Trees
> Is fraught with Flow'rs, the Flow'rs are fraught with Bees:
> The busie Bees with a soft murm'ring Strain
> Invite to gentle sleep the lab'ring Swain.   (I, lines 71–4)

Dryden enjoys the sensuous detail, and reproduces it, often strikingly, sometimes increasing comic effect by both elaboration and explication. For example,

> at mecum raucis, tua dum vestigia lustro,
> sole sub ardenti resonant arbusta cicadis   (II, lines 12–13)

becomes

> While in the scorching Sun I trace in vain
> Thy flying footsteps o'er the burning Plain.
> The creaking Locusts with my Voice conspire,
> They fry'd with Heat, and I with fierce Desire.   (II, lines 11–14)

There seems to be here some echo or memory of Marvell's Mower poems. Certainly Dryden is in no danger from pallor or restraint, and the common words "creaking" and "fry'd" add to surprise effect as well as to sensuous immediacy. Dryden often amplifies detail. In *Eclogue* II, Virgil's Corydon offers Alexis the flowers of the Nymphs:

> tibi lilia plenis
> ecce ferunt Nymphae calathis, tibi candida Nais,
> pallentis violas et summa papavera carpens,
> narcissum et florem iungit bene olentis anethi;
> tum, casia atque aliis intexens suavibus herbis,
> mollia luteola pingit vaccinia caltha. (II, lines 45–50)[15]

Dryden's Corydon offers all this, and, it seems, even more:

> White Lillies in full Canisters they bring,
> With all the Glories of the Purple Spring,
> The Daughters of the Flood have search'd the Mead
> For Violets pale, and cropt the Poppy's Head:
> The short *Narcissus* and fair Daffodil,
> Pancies to please the Sight, and Cassia sweet to smell:
> And set soft Hyacinths with Iron blue, ·
> To shade marsh Marigolds of shining Hue. (II, lines 61–8)

Dryden has dropped the fennel and inserted the very English "Daffodil"; he has added the pansies and described the hyacinths (there is no Virgilian equivalent of "Iron blue"). We have here an example of the richness which the eighteenth century loved; again we see how their feeling for sensuous image and sound relates them to the Elizabethans. In his prefatory Dedication Dryden paid tribute to Spenser, whose pastoral work he thought "not inferior" to that of Theocritus and Virgil, *"For the Shepherd's Kalendar of Spenser, is not to be match'd in any Modern Language."* In a passage like the flower passage above, we can also see a resemblance to the work of, say, Thomson in *The Seasons*. That cataloguing delight in variety, in colour and detail, is found in both. Thomson's "yellow Wall-Flower, stain'd with iron Brown" is related to Dryden's "soft Hyacinths with Iron blue."

Seen in this context, Pope's *Pastorals* (1709) look all the more curious. That work seems almost an anomaly in its period. The *Pastorals* represent Pope's only ambitious effort to write exactly in the centre of a genre – in itself, at that time, an odd thing to do. It is as if Pope were trying to turn the clock back, to reach some eternal idea of pastoral, anterior to the realities of Theocritus or Virgil. He disdains almost entirely sensuousness, particularity, variety of effect, homely language and objects – all for the sake of one pure effect, representing a static or uncontaminated state. He seems to believe he can arrive at the essence of pastoral by getting rid of most of the decoration and pleasures. In trying to repurify the genre he almost loses the poems. He concentrates on sweetness of numbers, the creation of pastoral music, at the expense of almost everything else. He pays tribute to Spenser, but all that he takes from Spenser is the idea of time as a unifying motif. It is no wonder that his *Pastorals* got Pope into a heated literary dispute,[16] nor that some contemporary readers preferred Ambrose Philips. Pope was never to do anything like that again, though the music of the *Pastorals* and various pastoral ideas are to be found scattered over his works.

John Gay is the great practitioner in the pastoral mode, and he succeeds by the Augustan process of subversion. His greatest creative subversion of the pastoral idea is of course his "Newgate Pastoral" (Swift's audacious oxymoron) *The Beggar's Opera*, but his pastoral sequence *The Shepherd's Week* (1714) is also a considerable achievement. It is the immediate offspring of a parodic impulse. Ambrose Philips's *Pastorals* (1708) were praised by a friend of Addison in a series of *Guardian* essays in 1713, while Pope's were neglected. Pope responded with the satiric *Guardian* No. 40. According to a tradition whose source is Pope, *The Shepherd's Week* was written to punish Philips for his angry reaction to Pope's essay. Certainly, Gay's "Proeme To the Courteous Reader" picks up and mocks Philips's Preface.[17] Philips had begun by saying "*It is strange to think, in an Age so addicted to the* Muses, *how* Pastoral Poetry *comes to be never so much as thought upon; considering especially, that it has always been accounted the most considerable of the smaller Poems ...*" This mild wonderment becomes huffingly translated into the astonishments of the pseudo-E.K. prose of Gay's first sentence:

> *Great Marvell hath it been, (and that not unworthily) to diverse worthy Wits, that in this our Island of* Britain ... *no Poet (though otherways of notable Cunning in Roundelays) hath hit on the right simple Eclogue ...*

The inventive energy of Gay's work, in the poems themselves and in the "Proeme," seems a response not just to the feebleness of Philips's style but also to his weak view of the very form he espouses. Ambrose Philips's theory might be called the tranquillizing or soporific theory of the pastoral: "*Pastoral gives a sweet and gentle Composure to the Mind; whereas the* Epick *and* Tragick *Poem put the Spirits in too great a Ferment ...*" Small poems which lull the mind seem scarcely worth championing. Gay's parodic mock-words are capable of working some ferment. Rather than putting the reader into a condition to sleep, they wake him up.

The "Proeme" claims that this poet is attempting "*the right simple Eclogue after the true ancient guise of* Theocritus":

> *Other Poet travailing in this plain High-way of Pastoral know I none. Yet, certes, such it behoveth a Pastoral to be, as Nature in the Country affordeth; and the Manners also meetly copied from the rustical Folk therein. In this also my Love to my native Country* Britain *much pricketh me forward, to describe aright the Manners of our own honest and laborious Plough-men, in no wise sure more unworthy a* British *Poet's imitation, than those of* Sicily *or* Arcadie; *albeit, not ignorant I am, what a Rout and Rabblement of Critical Gallimawfry hath been made of late Days by certain young Men of insipid Delicacy, concerning, I wist not what,* Golden Age, *and other outragious Conceits, to which they would confine Pastoral. Whereof, I avow, I account nought at all, knowing no Age so justly to be instiled* Golden, *as this of* our Sovereign Lady Queen ANNE.

Gay's "Proeme" parodies Philips's Preface, makes fun of Tickell's conten-
tions, and supports Pope's mocking criticisms in *Guardian* No. 40. Yet Pope
himself seems to be one of Gay's targets here, for Pope, chief upholder of the
Golden Age, is a chief perpetrator of the *"I wist not what."* He must be the
foremost *"young M[a]n of insipid Delicacy"* contributing to the *"Critical Gal-
limawfry."* It is evident that no other contemporary writer of pastorals could
consider himself kindly treated by this "Proeme" which lays everything low,
and is itself *"outragious."* It is a kind of manifesto, a declaration that the
pastoral genre (and hence serious critical introductions to new sets of pastorals, in Pope's manner) must be considered absurd. Gay's language creates a
pseudo-Elizabethan who is still desperately and anachronistically writing in
the Age of Anne. This poet is writing pseudo-Spenserian pastorals – which are
imitations of Virgil imitating Theocritus. The mock-mock-mock levels of the
"Proeme" guide us inescapably to the view that pastorals are all imitations,
and imitations of an unreality. The genre is an absurdity, and the only way to
manage it is to get out of it, to mix up its manners and question its conventions.

The description of *"our own honest and laborious Plough-men,"* for which Gay
speaks – or would if his "speaker" were not a mock-Elizabethan vainly
uttering a passé prose – is as much a mockery as anything else. Reality and
pastoral are shown to be mutually exclusive. But mutually exclusive opposites
can be combined in the game that stands a genre on its head, or turns styles
inside out. Gay mingles Theocritus, Virgil and Spenser in blithe confusion.
For names and structural arrangement, Gay's mock-author says he is indebted
to Spenser:

> For as much, as I have mentioned Maister Spencer, soothly I must acknowledge him a Bard of
> sweetest Memorial. Yet hath his Shepherds Boy at some times raised his rustick Reed to Rhimes more
> rumbling than rural ... What liketh me best are his Names, indeed right simple and meet for the
> Country, such as Lobbin, Cuddy, Hobbinol, Diggon, and others, some of which I have made
> bold to borrow. Moreover, as he called his Eclogues, the Shepherd's Calendar, and divided the
> same into the twelve Months, I have chosen ... to name mine by the Days of the Week, omitting
> Sunday or the Sabbath, Ours being supposed to be Christian Shepherds, and to be then at Church
> worship.

What we get are pseudo-Spenserian swains, with names like Lobbin Clout,
Cuddy, Marian, Bumkinet, Grubbinol, Blowzelinda. The topics of the
different eclogues are those of the Theocritan idyll as familiarized by Virgil:
the song contest, the love-plaint, the lament for a dead companion. But these
topics are oddly attached to the days of the week, and certainly diminished:
"Monday; or, The Squabble" (for the song contest); "Wednesday; or, The
Dumps" (the sad love-song of a forsaken maiden). The whole is a large,
deliberate and playful bathos. The high side of the pastoral tradition is got rid
of at a stroke; destroyed are the prophetic elements, the vision of a life in tune
with Nature at her highest, the Christian association so dear to Spenser (and to
Milton in *Lycidas*) of the shepherd. Because of the way of thinking so natural
to Gay and so fully expressed by him here, later generations have found

the pastoral an odd and incredible mode. And those later generations include Samuel Johnson (a child when Gay's *Shepherd's Week* first appeared), to whom pastoral poetry (as in *Lycidas*) seemed "disgusting."[18]

Yet *The Shepherd's Week*, for all its destructive capacities, is an appealing as

Fig. 5

well as a striking work. It is – in its original edition – in the most literal sense a
beautiful book. The type is handsome, the margins wide, and the whole is
illuminated by numerous and striking illustrations. The care with which the
book is got up should prevent us from the outset from treating it too lightly; it

Fig. 6

announces itself as an important work, presented with care. Compared with it, Philips's *Pastorals* dwindle into a mere pamphlet.

The illustrations by Du Guernier (see Figs. 5, 6 and 7) capture the spirit very well. The pictures are somewhat in the Flemish style, but the English nymphs and swains are not merely boors. Comic they may be, but they are not too

Fig. 7

clumsy, and not bad-looking. They are certainly energetic, whether dancing around a maypole (as in the frontispiece to the work) or crowding to attend Blowzelinda's funeral ("Friday; or, The Dirge"); the same English parish church is recognizable in both pictures. The artist has, in the frontispiece, drawn himself in the scene, drawing the dancers, as if he is attracted to them, one of them in spite of himself. In almost every one of his pictures Du Guernier has included his favourite romantic tree (a rather Rubensesque tree) such as shades the churchyard, or shelters the pensive Marian (in "Tuesday; or, The Ditty") as she ignores the spilled milk, and the gesticulating Janus-like "Goody *Dobbins*" who brings her "Cow to Bull." The world of *The Shepherd's Week* has its own beauty, as the pictures serve to emphasize. The pictures reflect Gay's development of inspiration through burlesque.

Gay's pastoral poems in *The Shepherd's Week* are real poems, with real pastoral strengths, though these are used to unmake the convention itself. Gay's poems do possess beauty. They do (even, it would appear, against their will) give us a picture of the country, and the sensuous appeal of its simple pleasures, as in forsaken Marian's memory of happier days:

> In misling Days when I my Thresher heard,
> With nappy Beer I to the Barn repair'd;
> Lost in the Musick of the whirling Flail,
> To gaze on thee I left the smoking Pail;
> In Harvest when the Sun was mounted high,
> My Leathern Bottle did thy Drought supply;
> When-e'er you mow'd I follow'd with the Rake,
> And have full oft been Sun-burnt for thy Sake;
> ...
> And when at Eve returning with thy Carr,
> Awaiting heard the gingling Bells from far;
> Strait on the Fire the sooty Pot I plac't,
> To warm thy Broth I burnt my Hands for Haste.
> When hungry thou stood'st *staring, like an Oaf*,
> I slic'd the Luncheon from the Barly Loaf,
> With crumbled Bread I thicken'd well thy Mess.
> Ah, love me more, or love thy Pottage less!
>
> ("Tuesday; or, The Ditty," lines 55–72)

It might be fashionable nowadays to say that Gay (whose poet refuses to deal like Spenser with *"Churchly Matter"*) is an un- or anti-Christian writer, in thus opposing the Christian pastoral tradition represented by Spenser and Milton. But that would not necessarily be true. Gay breaks down a traditional elegant expression of symbolic belief in order to present something just as important for Christians – for those like Samuel Johnson, for instance. Gay includes the work of the countryside, the everyday unromantic work, as well as the play and pleasures. Comically but truthfully he reminds us (as Pope and Philips do not) that there are real people in those fields, barns and church-yards. The language insistently reminds us of a contemporary real world, not a Golden Age life but a life with certain attractions as well as stubborn facts:

"misling days," "nappy Beer," "sooty Pot," "Barly Loaf." Virgilian
shepherds, being Italian, don't have to endure "misling rain," and though
they may eat and drink, they do not take "Luncheon" nor does their cook burn
her hands.

It was, I think, only a period which had produced something like Gay's
pastorals that would take kindly to the work of Stephen Duck, the real thresher
poet, who gives us the unglamorous, fatiguing and even heartbreaking aspects
of true rural labour. Duck writes, for instance, of the real exhaustion attendant
on mowing:

> With Heat and Labour tir'd, our Scythes we quit,
> Search out a shady Tree and down we sit:
> From Scrip and Bottle hope new Strength to gain;
> But Scrip and Bottle too are try'd in vain.
> Down our parch'd Throats we scarce the Bread can get;
> And, quite o'erspent with Toil, but faintly eat,
> Nor can the Bottle only answer all;
> The Bottle and the Beer are both too small.
> Time flows: Again we rise from off the Grass;
> Again each Mower takes his proper Place;
> . . .
> We often whet, and often view the Sun;
> As often wish, his tedious Race was run.
> At length he veils his purple Face from Sight,
> And bids the weary Labourer, Good Night.
> Homewards we move, but spent so much with Toil,
> We slowly walk, and rest at ev'ry Stile.
> Our good expecting Wives, who think we stay,
> Got to the Door, soon eye us in the Way.
> Then from the Pot the Dumplin's catch'd in Haste,
> And homely by its Side the Bacon plac'd.
>
> (*The Thresher's Labour*, 1735)[19]

This sounds not unlike Gay in rhythm and arrangement of sentence elements
along the verse lines, as well as in the introduction of commonplace rural
things of concern to country workers. Certainly what Gay treats as a joke is
not a joke to Stephen Duck, who has risen from being a figure in a pastoral
landscape to the position of speaker who can tell us what that position feels
like. Yet such a change from the pastoral notion of things is presumably
assisted or even in a sense caused by the intervention of Gay, and the "killing
off" of the pastoral high style along with the introduction of common English
things, unromanticized. Crabbe in his introductory lines to *The Village* mentions Duck as the exception ("Save honest DUCK, what son of verse could
share / The poet's rapture, and the peasant's care?").[20] But there was no need
for Crabbe's onslaught on pastoral poetry at the beginning of *The Village*,
except that Crabbe needed, in the Augustan manner, to defy a genre at the
outset of his poem. Gay's work had already denied the validity of pastoral
stylistic and generic conventions.

Yet Gay was fascinated by the eclogue. In 1720 he produced a series of "Eclogues" including "The Birth of the Squire. An Eclogue. In Imitation of the Pollio of Virgil." This is a burlesque of one of Virgil's most famous poems, *Eclogue* IV, connected by traditional Christian readings with the prophecies of Christ's birth. Pope had produced an imitation of that poem in his *Messiah* (1712), called "A Sacred Eclogue, in Imitation of Virgil's Pollio." Pope, who believed that Virgil really had derived his *Eclogue* from a Sybilline prophecy of the birth of Christ, a prophecy containing the same matter as the prophecies of Isaiah, incorporates large passages of Isaiah in his amplification of Virgil. Pope's "Sacred Eclogue" gives one a good idea of how Virgil's poem had been read for centuries. In Gay's version, Virgil's grand and prophetic poem becomes a mock-comic celebration of the birth of an heir to a rural Squire, and the prophecy deals with the child's future feats, from his learning to ride to his becoming Justice of the Peace to his drinking himself to death:

> Methinks I see him in his hall appear,
> Where the long table floats in clammy beer,
> 'Midst mugs and glasses shatter'd o'er the floor. (lines 101–3)

Considering the traditional exegesis of the Pollio Eclogue ("aspice venturo laetentur ut omnia saeclo!") Gay's version is little short of blasphemous. And he makes sure the title informs us of the connection and allusion. This is another example of doing down a genre, a style and a set of ideas. Even Rochester's mock-pastoral songs ("Fair *Chloris* in a pigsty lay") pale beside "The Birth of the Squire."

Gay's affection for Theocritus, who is quoted in the "Proeme" to *The Shepherd's Week*, seems genuine. He uses Theocritus again in *Acis and Galatea* (first published in 1722)[21] and in the "Town Eclogues" (1720) for which Theocritus had supplied a precedent as he had for that earlier urban idyll, "The Toilette" (1716):

> Now twenty springs had cloath'd the Park with green,
> Since *Lydia* knew the blossom of fifteen;
> No lovers now her morning hours molest,
> And catch her at her Toilette half undrest;
> ...
> Around her wait Shocks, monkeys and mockaws,
> To fill the place of Fops, and perjur'd Beaus;
> In these she views the mimickry of man,
> And smiles when grinning *Pug* gallants her fan;
> ...
> With these alone her tedious mornings pass;
> Or at the dumb devotion of her glass,
> She smooths her brow, and frizles forth her hairs,
> And fancys youthful dress gives youthful airs;
> With crimson wooll she fixes ev'ry grace,
> That not a blush can discompose her face. (lines 1–20)

The trials of the elderly beauty (superannuated at thirty-five), often a source of too-easy laughter for the other sex, constitute a common Augustan topic. Yet Lydia arouses some sympathy, particularly when she becomes a speaker, even as we laugh at her (and at her meanness as well as at her boredom and frustration). This eclogue is, like the pastorals of *The Shepherd's Week*, half-in, half-out of a number of feelings and sympathies. Like its heroine, it is sophisticated and self-conscious. We are a world away, it would seem, from Virgil's sincere, single-hearted and attractive passions – and yet we can indeed see real passion. The poem echoes some of the tones and includes some of the elements of Rochester's *Artemisia*, that celebrated discomposer of genre. The echoes here of *The Rape of the Lock* point out to us the elements of eclogue in that poem too. Pope's poem is not only what we loosely call "mock-heroic" – it is mock-a-number-of-things. Partly, it is an eclogue of the town, showing the "simple" works and days and passions of some civilized but not too admirable people who are surrounded by elaborate artificial objects. These people are in love (or some of them are), they soliloquize and pray, they amuse themselves and they take refreshments – but they make tea and mischief instead of wine-bowls or songs. The mock-pastoral elements become clearly visible in the scene of the battle:

> *O cruel Nymph! a living Death I bear*,
> Cry'd *Dapperwit*, and sunk beside his Chair.
> A mournful Glance Sir *Fopling* upwards cast,
> *Those Eyes are made so killing* – was his last:
> Thus on *Meander's* flow'ry Margin lies
> Th'expiring Swan, and as he sings he dies. (v, lines 61–6)

Though the swan image is from Ovid, the tone of languishing love is mock-Virgilian. But the elements of town eclogue, mock-pastoral, are scattered through Pope's bright allusive poem.

Virgil's *Eclogues* remained for the English Augustans one of the most important examples of a genre to be defied and re-used, remodelled. Even the non-comic eclogues have something strange about them – as is the case, for instance, with Collins's *Persian Eclogues* (1742). On second thoughts, however, perhaps a set of poems with the sub-title "Written originally for the Entertainment of the Ladies of *Tauris*" cannot confidently be said to be without comedy. They are exercises in the strange – "Persian Eclogue" is nearly as much of an oxymoron as "Town Eclogue." And we find too that the Preface carries out a deceit, or conceit; the poems, we are told, came from "the Hands of a Merchant, who had made it his Business to enrich himself with the Learning, as well as the Silks and Carpets of the *Persians*. The little Information I could gather concerning their Author, was, That his Name was *Mahamed*, and that he was a Native of *Tauris*." This is a bit too Quixote-like for our gravity; what kind of credence should we give to the works that have come to us by way of a carpet-seller? An ostensibly Roman form is jerked out of shape, becomes something else, when it is written (ostensibly) by a Persian and full of (supposedly) Oriental images, manners and feelings. Camel-drivers and Sultanas are not what we have traditionally meant by pastoral characters; certainly they have little to do with Virgil.

If Virgil's *Aeneid* and his *Eclogues* were peculiarly used by our British Augustans, there is one other great poem (or set of poems) by Virgil that was more seriously employed. The work by Virgil that is most sincerely taken into partnership by our Augustans is the middle work, the *Georgics*. There are historical and social reasons for the work's popularity. It deals with the troubled condition of Rome after an injurious civil war, and not only prays for a return to peace and prosperity but also advocates the means for achieving a better state. The lot of Englishmen after the Civil War and after the later troubles and solution of 1688 was not dissimilar; Virgil's historical perspective was accessible. Moreover, Virgil in the *Georgics* deals not with artificial shepherds, but with the landowning farmer, whom he addresses. As any farmer who actually read Virgil must have been a man of some education and leisure, the English could imagine him as a gentleman. The English dream was the life of the country gentleman; a poem addressed to country gentlemen and dealing with their concerns would certainly be attractive.

But there are more purely literary reasons for the appeal of the *Georgics* to the English in the Augustan Age. John Chalker in his *The English Georgic* says that the *Georgics* was popular in the eighteenth century because "the form itself enabled poets to arrive at the interpretation of very varied experience," and assisted the English poets who drew on it in expressing themselves with "boldness and freedom."[22] Boldness, freedom, variety – these Augustan qualities are the essential qualities of Virgil's poem. The *Georgics* is the Virgilian work that breaks boundaries, defies genre. Virgil here created, as not in his pastorals or his epic, a new and singular kind of poetry. He thought himself that the work was "audacious," asking Augustus Caesar to approve these audacious undertakings: "atque audacibus adnue coeptis" (i, line 40). Dryden translates "audacibus coeptis" as "bold Endeavours"; "coeptis" also has the sense of beginnings, a new enterprise. Virgil's other explicatory passage, at the outset of Book III, gives a larger view of what the poet considers himself to be doing:

> cetera quae vacuas tenuissent carmine mentes,
> omnia iam volgata: quis aut Eurysthea durum
> aut inlaudati nescit Busiridis aras?
> cui non dictus Hylas puer et Latonia Delos
> Hippodameque umeroque Pelops insignis eburno,
> acer equis? temptanda via est, qua *me* quoque possim
> tollere humo victorque virum volitare per ora.
> primus *ego* in patriam *mecum*, modo vita supersit,
> Aonio rediens deducam vertice Musas.
>
> (III, lines 3–11; italics mine)

> All other Themes, that careless Minds invite,
> Are worn with use; unworthy me to write.
> *Busiris* Altars, and the dire Decrees
> Of hard *Euristheus*, ev'ry Reader sees:
> *Hylas* the Boy, *Latona*'s erring Isle,
> And *Pelop's* Iv'ry Shoulder, and his Toyl
> For fair *Hippodamé*, with all the rest
> Of *Grecian* Tales, by Poets are exprest:
> New ways I must attempt, my groveling Name
> To raise aloft, and wing my Flight to Fame.
> I, first of *Romans*, shall in Triumph come
> From conquer'd *Greece*, and bring her Trophies home.
>
> (Dryden, iii, lines 5–16)

It is no little thing to decide to drag the Muses off the Aonian peak and take them home to Rome, or rather to Mantua – an imperial urge indeed. In translating lines 40–1 of this same book, Dryden adds a meaning to "silvas saltusque ... intactos" in rendering the phrase "*Silvan* Lands ... untouch'd by former Hands." Virgil is not only writing about virgin glades; he is also treating a subject virgin to poetry. For the same reason, Horace praised Lucilius and himself for finding a kind of writing unknown to the Greeks, left untouched ("intacti") by them. Certainly Virgil shows himself conscious of being audacious, of trying something new – and Dryden is more than willing to stress these announcements of boldness. Dryden is enthusiastic about Virgil's powers in the *Georgics*. He seems, by implication at least, ready to consider this the poet's greatest work: "Virgil *wrote his* Georgics *in the full strength and vigour of his Age, when his Judgment was at the height, and before his Fancy was declining*" ("Dedication to Chesterfield"). "Vigour" and "Fancy" are again conjoined; Virgil's *Georgics* are the result of strong imagination.

Virgil is aware that in some eyes his choice of subject, the labours of farmers and husbandmen, would seem unsuited to his desire to raise himself from the ground, "me tollere humo." The subject of the poem is the ground, the earth, and the creatures who live and work upon it. But he proclaims that it is precisely in this odd choice of subject that he can rise. The parodic list of common "poetic" topics in the lines from Book iii quoted above includes not only the Ovidian kind of story but also what one might suppose the Virgilian kind of story, the sort of thing that would make a good interlude or illustration in an epic. Virgil, at least for now, dismisses them. He will create something new, something not conventionally "poetic" nor poetically easy. He will create a new sort of poem, with its own deep relation to human experience.

The promise of audacity is everywhere confirmed by the poem itself. The large subject allows the author to pick out various aspects of rural work, in the unprescribed order in which they seem appropriate. Apparently as his flow of mind leads him, he can choose different tones and styles for different topics, and the topics too are his own invention. There is, for instance, no precedent for dealing with the love-life of animals. And Virgil can move us from the comic to the dramatic or pathetic whenever he chooses. As Chalker puts it, "the *Georgics* is a *montage* involving sudden shifts of subject and mood."[23]

The *Georgics* is the great mixed poem of Roman antiquity. The poem includes epic moments and lyric passages, as well as the most minute technical descriptions of common things. Chalker asserts that "the link between the mundane and the heroic ... is the mock-heroic attitude,"[24] and says that Dryden was correct in stressing the mock-heroic elements in his translation. But "mock-heroic" seems a not entirely satisfactory term to cover the variety of tones presented through the voice of the poet. The poet can move from a grand meditative manner to personal biography to the most vivid homely observation. All is under the control of the poet, of the "ego" present in the poem; there is no constraint of genre as such for there is no precedent in genre. But Virgil has created a voice which expresses *humanitas*, and humanity is always present, human beings at work and play; the whole poem celebrates what human beings create. The puzzling qualities of our human life with Nature – which demands so much that is not "natural" – are fully expressed.

What has been called Virgil's "subjective style" works through the *Georgics*, diffusing from the poet's personal voice to the views and feelings of farmer, ploughman, cattleman to the views and feelings of animals, birds and bees – and even of what we call pests.[25] In warning us about the pests, Virgil gives us a close-up view of them. We recognize that they are doing what is in their nature and in their own interest, and momentarily we share their point of view: "The Field Mouse builds her Garner under ground" (Dryden, *Georgics* 1, line 265; see Virgil, 1, lines 181ff). Birds are treated with similar animation. In the description of their rejoicing after rain, Virgil shows his mastery of a variety of styles, from Ovidian reference to Nisus and Scylla, in moderately high style, to the comic picture of the delighted rooks in their homes:

> apparet liquido sublimis in aëre Nisus
> et pro purpureo poenas dat Scylla capillo:
> quacumque illa levem fugians secat aethera pinnis,
> ecce inimicus, atrox, magno stridore per auras
> insequitur Nisus; qua se fert Nisus ad auras,
> illa levem fugiens raptim secat aethera pinnis.
> tum liquidas corvi presso ter gutture voces
> aut quater ingeminant, et saepe cubilibus altis
> nescio qua praeter solitum dulcedine laeti
> inter se in foliis strepitant. (1, lines 404–13)

Where injur'd *Nisus* takes his Airy Course,
Thence trembling *Scylla* flies and shuns his Force.
This punishment pursues th'unhappy Maid,
And thus the purple Hair is dearly paid.
Then, thrice the Ravens rend the liquid Air,

And croaking Notes proclaim the settled fair.
Then, round their Airy Palaces they fly,
To greet the Sun; and, seis'd with secret Joy,
When Storms are over-blown, with Food repair
To their forsaken Nests, and callow Care.   (i, lines 553–62)

Dryden seems to have drawn upon the *Georgics*, if not yet his published
translation of it, in developing his fables in *The Hind and the Panther*. See, for
example, the description of the happy swallows in the Panther's fable, in a
passage which strongly resembles in techniques and tone the Virgilian passage
quoted above:

Who but the *Swallow* now triumphs alone?
The Canopy of heaven is all her own,
Her youthfull offspring to their haunts repair;
And glide along in glades, and skim in air,
And dip for insects in the purling springs,
And stoop on rivers to refresh their wings.
Their mothers think a fair provision made,
That ev'ry son can live upon his trade,
And now the carefull charge is off their hands,
Look out for husbands, and new nuptial bands:
The youthfull widow longs to be supply'd; ⎤
But first the lover is by Lawyers ty'd   ⎬
To settle jointure-chimneys on the bride. ⎦
. . .
Their ancient houses, running to decay,
Are furbish'd up, and cemented with clay;
They teem already; store of eggs are laid,
And brooding mothers call *Lucina*'s åid.
                                        (Part iii, lines 566–84)

Dryden responds very strongly to that particular Virgilian tone and the use
of appreciative and delicate mock-heroic which illuminates the familiar. As
Virgil shows in the description of the birds, he can use the Ovidian sort of
story, like that of Nisus, unseriously; he can also employ myth seriously and
elaborately, as with the working-out of the story of Aristaeus at the end of Book
iv. No style or mode needs to be rejected. The most homely details of everyday
working life in the country can be combined with description of what is exotic
and extraordinary, almost surreal, as in the famous description (in Book iii) of
the Scythians in their frozen world. The poem accommodates historical narrative and contemporary vignettes; it includes town life as well as country life.
The tone can change from the elegiac to the satiric, as in the description of
preposterous new urban wealth:

No Palace, with a lofty Gate, he wants,
T'admit the Tydes of early Visitants.
With eager Eyes devouring, as they pass,

> The breathing Figures of *Corinthian* Brass.
> No Statues threaten, from high Pedestals;
> No *Persian* Arras hides his homely Walls,
> With Antick Vests; which, thro' their shady fold,
> Betray the Streaks of ill dissembl'd Gold.
>
> (Dryden, ii, lines 643–50, cf. Virgil, ii, lines 461–5)

Virgil, Dryden thought, "cou'd have written sharper Satires, than either *Horace* or *Juvenal*, if he wou'd have employ'd his Talent, that way" (*Discourse of Satire*). The *Georgics* might have offered better examples to prove his point than the verse and a half of the third *Eclogue* to which Dryden refers us in his *Discourse*. And in translating the *Georgics*, Dryden gave full credit to the satiric Virgil as well as the others. Pope seems to have attended to Virgil's description of the proud mansion and to Dryden's vivacious translation in writing his own *Epistle to Burlington*, where he presents us with the lively ugliness of the objects and adornments of Timon's villa.

The *Georgics* can be satiric without having to remain so and can be moving at moments without having to dwell on pathos. The self-sustaining poem, making a genre as it proceeds, answers to no rules save those the poet makes. The whole is perfectly constructed, just for this once alone, out of a medley. The Augustans valued it for its variety, its inexhaustible richness. The poem also answered their own desire to live in a humanized and *animated* world. The *Georgics* is a poem of motion and activity, where all creatures and objects have life; cornfields laugh, fieldmice labour to fill their barns, gates are proud.

After Dryden's translation of the *Georgics* we can note an increase in Georgic reference in English poetry. The eighteenth century sees a large output of works in the mode of the *Georgics*. The single-minded straightforward Georgics, those which give serious advice on some aspect of farming, are the least successful, though they did not go without approbation in their own time; among these is John Philips's *Cyder* (1708), praised as an imitation of Virgil "which needed not shun the presence of the original" (Johnson, *Life of Philips*). *Cyder* is a readable poem of some importance. We can see its influence on Pope's *Windsor Forest*, in, for instance, the description of the shot birds who "leave their little Lives / Above the Clouds" (Book ii, lines 175–6) or the evocation of the British Navy sailing "thro' the Ocean vast ... t'extreamest Climes / Terrific," and returning fraught "with odorous Spoils" or "Pearl, and Barbaric Gold" (*ibid.*, lines 653–7). *Cyder* is also an influence on Thomson's *Seasons*, as we can feel when Philips describes a country walk among files of fruit trees loaded with ripe apples, diffusing a scent "than *Myrrh*, or *Nard* / More grateful, or perfuming flow'ry *Beane*!" (*ibid.*, lines 62–3). It is one of the advantages of the Georgic that it licenses the full use of the senses, and heightens the sense experience of ordinary things. As well as the great world of eye and ear, taste and smell come into their own as they do in Thomson, e.g.

Long let us walk,
Where the Breeze blows from yon extended Field
Of blossom'd Beans. *Arabia* cannot boast
A fuller Gale of Joy, than, liberal, thence
Breathes thro' the Sense, and takes the ravish'd Soul.

("Spring," lines 498–502)

John Dyer's *The Fleece* (1757) is another example of serious Georgic, longer than Philips's and less pleasing. It is hard, given the Virgilian example, to say why a poem on sheep-raising and wool would not be possible and successful; when modern students laugh at the bare idea, they perhaps prove only that we have narrowed the boundaries of poetry and have strict prescriptive notions of the poetic. Dyer fails not because of his subject, but because he lacks range and variety. That is, he isn't quite Augustan enough. Even so, there is good stuff in *The Fleece* and some of the best lines are homely, vivid and memorable: "with busy mouths / They scoop white turnips" (i, lines 483–4).[26]

Gay began his career as a writer of a Georgic, or rather of a mock-Georgic poem. His first important work was *Wine* (1708), a comic answer to John Philips's *Cyder*. Had Philips been inspired by wine, Gay contends, he would have equalled his own previous work, but his Muse has suffered from too much cider:

now in *Ariconian* Bogs
She lies Inglorious floundring, like her *Theme*
Languid and Faint, and on damp Wing immerg'd
In *acid juice*, invain attempts to rise.   (lines 123–6)

The mock-Miltonics are derived from Philips's own *The Splendid Shilling* and the *Cerealia* of 1706 in which Philips apparently anticipated his own serious praise of the wine of the apple in the mock-praise (by no less a personage than Ceres herself) of the juice of the barley. Mock versions come first in so many cases.

The mock-Georgic becomes a staple sort of poem – or poetic technique – in the Age of Anne. It releases itself from heavy obligation to be mock-Miltonic and takes a new direction under the guidance of Swift, who published two short mock-Georgic poems, "A Description of the Morning" (1709) and "A Description of a City Shower" (1710). Both are urban Georgics (to use an oxymoron similar to "town eclogue"); we observe times of day and weather signs in the town, and not in the country. "A City Shower" is a very detailed parallel to Virgil's celebrated description of a storm (*Georgics*, i, lines 316–34) and his advice about how to watch for signs of change in the weather (*ibid.*, lines 351–92). Virgil's thunderstorm, vivid and onomatopoeic, causes flooding; water-courses overflow:

The Dykes are fill'd, and with a roaring sound
The rising Rivers float the nether ground;
And Rocks the bellowing Voice of boiling Seas rebound.

(Dryden, i, lines 441–3)

So, most unglamorously, in Swift (who is obviously alluding to Dryden as well as to Virgil):

> Now from all Parts the swelling Kennels flow,
> And bear their Trophies with them as they go:
> ...
> Sweepings from Butchers' Stalls, Dung, Guts, and Blood, ⎫
> Drown'd Puppies, stinking Sprats, all drench'd in Mud,   ⎬
> Dead Cats and Turnip-Tops come tumbling down the Flood. ⎭
>
> (lines 53–63)

It was probably the success of Swift's two short poems that alerted Gay to new possibilities and stimulated him to undertake a more ambitious and different kind of mock-Georgic than his mock-Miltonic parody of Philips. *Trivia, Or, The Art of Walking the Streets of London* (1716), a poem produced in three books and mock-pompously annotated, is a pleasant and pointed exercise in refashioning a genre. The poet tells us how to avoid chimney sweeps, traffic jams, nasty kennels, pick-pockets – how, in short, to survive in the urban, not the rural, world. We observe the signs of the times of the day and of the seasons, as well as weather-signs, but all in terms of the man-made:

> But when the swinging Signs your Ears offend
> With creaking Noise, then rainy Floods impend;
> ...
> The Bookseller, whose Shop's an open Square,
> Foresees the Tempest, and with early Care
> Of Learning strips the Rails; the rowing Crew
> To tempt a Fare, cloath all their Tilts in Blue:
> On Hosiers Poles depending Stockings ty'd,
> Flag with the slacken'd Gale, from side to side. (I, lines 157–66)

The seasons and their changes are evoked through the activities of the town-dweller, who knows country produce only in shops – but that doesn't preclude sensuous enjoyment of fruit and herbs:

> Wallnuts the *Fruit'rer*'s Hand, in Autumn, stain,
> Blue Plumbs, and juicy Pears augment his Gain;
> Next Oranges the longing Boys entice,
> To trust their Copper-Fortunes to the Dice.
>
> When Rosemary, and Bays, the Poet's Crown,
> Are bawl'd, in frequent Cries, through all the Town,
> Then judge the Festival of *Christmas* near. (II, lines 433–9)

The fact that all this advice is pretty useless only adds to the fun. Gay enjoys celebrating, in an unrepentant manner, the artificial way we live now. But there is a real Georgic pleasure in his picture of human urban works and days, a celebration, like Virgil's of contemporary real life. The mock-Georgics never seem so far away from their Virgilian model as the mock-eclogues do – probably because the *Georgics* itself is so encouragingly multifarious.

Gay had already written a light but sincere straight Georgic in *Rural Sports*, "A Georgic" as it announces itself. *Rural Sports* (1713) deals with play instead of work, but it is the real thing, and its influence is felt in Thomson. Pope also had written a sincere Georgic, *Windsor Forest*, which belongs to these early years of Georgic experiment during the Age of Anne; the first part was written in 1704 ("at the same time with the Pastorals," Pope notes) and the poem was completed and the whole published in 1713. *Windsor Forest* is in any part infinitely more animated and interesting than any of the *Pastorals*. Pope has now taken advantage of Virgilian variety, and the poem, capacious and lively, moves through a kind of play of consciousness, touching on major Virgilian *topoi*, such as Nature and the national fate – though the poet feels free not to follow Virgil's poem as if it offered a set pattern. Though Pope never wrote another such poem, the Georgic style and interests can be found frequently in his major works, especially the *Epistles* to Bathurst and Burlington. These latter exhibit an Augustan interest in combining the Horatian with the Virgilian – and the Virgilian means the *Georgics*. *Trivia*, with its bustle, street scenes and comedy, is an Horatian Georgic; it is as if Gay took from both poets the keys that gave him the freedom to create new original and occasional poems, each defining its own genre. Gay and Pope chose the Horace of the *Satires* and the Virgil of the *Georgics* as models because they offered freedom.

Some of the century's greatest poems are large mixed Georgics, which take advantage of the inclusiveness, the elasticity, that Virgil had revealed as possible. Thomson's *The Seasons* is a Georgic poem in four books. It picks up useful elements of eclogue (including the temporal scheme) but it is a Georgic. Some lines even sound, as we are meant to recognize, like loose translations of Virgil (e.g. "Autumn," lines 1235–373; cf. Virgil, ii, lines 458–542). At the same time, *The Seasons* can by no means be classed as an Imitation, still less a translation. It is a bold experiment and is, like Virgil's poem, itself. Cowper's *The Task* (1785) is another Georgic poem – and its very striking differences from *The Seasons* must make us wary of applying "Georgic" as if it were a satisfactory term for a genre. The post-Virgilian Georgic is for our Augustans a poetic idea rather than a genre. *The Seasons* and *The Task* both flourish on their own; the poets succeed, in true Augustan style, in creating genres that work only once and only for themselves.

The Task has in common with *The Seasons* (and with *Trivia*) the capacity to make our modern experience real to us. That is one of the deepest appeals of the Georgic poem in the Augustan Age, that it could take the world, in all its confusing abundance (of objects, plants, people, national crises, history, personal feelings) and bring it into poetry. Cowper's poem is Horatianly chatty while applying itself to humankind, to national contemporary life, and to individual and communal life in the country. *The Task* never loses sight of the value of human activity, mental and physical, or of the vivid beauty and *demandingness* of the external world. Nothing is too high (including God's presence in creation), nothing too low (including taking tea, building a greenhouse) for the poet's mind. Everything has a claim to be a poetic topic, and the poet triumphs in making his medley into a whole. If we think Dyer's subject precluded poetic success in *The Fleece*, we should consider Cowper's triumph in his description of how to grow cucumbers.

Crabbe's *The Borough* (1810) is the last Augustan Georgic poem. In describing the works and days of a small fishing town and its inhabitants, it describes the lot of Mankind, and develops a great variety of topics, views and techniques, all loosely held in place by the poem's inner vision of its own structure. In Augustan manner, Crabbe begins by querying other genres, other styles:

> Cities and Towns, the various haunts of men,
> Require the pencil; they defy the pen:
> Could he, who sang so well the Grecian Fleet,
> So well have sung of Alley, Lane, or Street?
> Can measur'd lines these various Buildings show,
> The Town-Hall Turning, or the Prospect Row?
> Can I the seats of Wealth and Want explore,
> And lengthen out my Lays from door to door?
> (1, "General Description," lines 7–14)[27]

The answer is "yes, I can" – and if Homer could not sing of alleys and streets, if the epic is incapable of this sort of thing, then Horace and Virgil (and Gay and Pope) have shown us how it can be done. Crabbe, like Gay and Pope and Cowper before him, combines Horatian chattiness with Virgilian depth and flexibility. He too, like his predecessors, subsumes elements of the eclogue (and of town eclogue) into the more mobile design with its contemporary themes.

The "models" of the Roman poets' work that the Augustans chose to contemplate most often and found most satisfying were models which encouraged them in their own enterprise of building great genres for themselves, and from the ground upwards. The deconstructions and reconstructions of their Roman predecessors fitted their own desires and ambitions. Horace and Virgil did not offer blueprints; the poems our Augustans admired never threatened the imposition of generic tightness. In an age which had come to question, and profoundly to question, the meaning and value of genre, and which was suspicious of the single-voiced employment of one style, Horace and Virgil looked like companions. But it was the Horace of the *sermones* and the Virgil of the *Georgics* who were closest and most sympathetic.

The *Georgics* in particular, that splendid and passionate and rich mixture, offered not something to be dutifully copied but the deepest encouragement to poetic aspirations. In an era shocked by civil wars, by revolution and the threat of continued revolution, and by social and philosophical change, the contemporary world had come to seem urgent, unignorable and untameable. Old genres were powerless against the excitements, the ferocious diversity of this world; they seemed like a retreat. The way to master this insistent world in poetry apparently lay not in denying aspects of it, or in timidly filtering out a few elements labelled "poetic," but in taking it on – all of it. Living poetry had to be able to deal with the world the poets knew, and to deal with that world meant not to exclude anything; inclusiveness seemed a virtue, a sign of spirit and of life. The *Georgics* offered a high and congenial example of the possibility of mastery and courageous inclusiveness. It was an exemplar of audacity, "audacibus coeptis," and, paradoxically, a model of freedom. Models of freedom were the only sort the Augustans were able to use.

V

Charivari and metamorphosis

English Augustan poets draw on the world, the "real" world. In finding the Horace of the *sermones* and the Virgil of the *Georgics* especially sympathetic, they were picking up the work of two poets who put the material and actual at the centre of poetic experience. For our Augustans, both private emotions (love, hatred, nostalgia, loss) and public feelings (political views, the sense of history) were to be worked out in relation to an external world. Theirs seems at first glance an extremely extroverted kind of poetry; at least, the poet or speaker seems to turn outside the self, to description and narration of things and stories not existing, or not presented as if existing, in the sensibility of the poet or speaker alone. Like Horace's greens and flour, or his pushing street crowds, or Virgil's plough and mice and rooks, the matters referred to seem to have a solid existence in the particular world we all know. However powerful the personality of the poet, or the poet as "I," the existence of what he alludes to does not seem to require to be referred back to him, in the way that, for instance, John Donne's famous "stiff twin compasses" have to be referred to speaker and context to sustain the right reality. Augustan poetry is poetry that presents us with people:

> The would-be wit, whose business was to woo,
> With hat removed and solemn scrape of shoe
> Advanceth bowing . . .
> (Rochester, "Tunbridge Wells," lines 88–90)

> A tatter'd apron hides,
> Worn as a cloak, and hardly hides, a gown
> More tatter'd still; and both but ill conceal
> A bosom heav'd with never-ceasing sighs.
> She begs an idle pin of all she meets,
> And hoards them in her sleeve . . .
> (Cowper, *The Task* I, lines 549–54)

Augustan poetry deals with places:

> To Hounslow-heath I point, and Banstead-down,
> Thence comes your mutton, and these chicks my own:
> From yon old wallnut-tree a show'r shall fall;
> And grapes, long-lingring on my only wall.
> (Pope, *Imitations of Horace, Sat.* II. ii, lines 143–6)

And Augustan poetry deals consummately with things – animals, plants, objects natural and man-made:

> In the Pond,
> The finely-checker'd Duck, before her Train,
> Rows garrulous.
>
> > (Thomson, "Spring," lines 776–8)

> From silver Spouts the grateful Liquors glide,
> While *China*'s Earth receives the smoking Tyde.
>
> > (Pope, *The Rape of the Lock* iii, lines 109–10)

> The hearth, except when winter chill'd the day,
> With aspen boughs, and flowers, and fennel gay,
> While broken tea-cups, wisely kept for shew,
> Rang'd o'er the chimney, glistened in a row.
>
> > (Goldsmith, *The Deserted Village*, 1770)[1]

> When freshen'd Grass now bears it self upright,
> And makes cool Banks to pleasing Rest invite,
> Whence springs the *Woodbind*, and the *Bramble*-Rose,
> And where the sleepy *Cowslip* shelter'd grows;
> Whilst now a paler Hue the *Foxglove* takes,
> Yet chequers still with Red the dusky brakes:
>
> > (Anne Finch, Countess of Winchilsea, "A Nocturnal Reverie")[2]

The poet seems always to be trying to make you see (or taste, hear, feel, smell) something which, he insists, is there in the external world, a *quidditas* not subject to "poetic" distortion, not a momentary product of the mind but part of an observed reality. The poets often present it as their duty to grasp this reality, in defiance of "poetry." "Could he, who sang so well the Grecian Fleet, / So well have sung of Alley, Lane, or Street?" Old genres will have to go because they won't accommodate reality (or enough of it); it remains for the poet in his new self-made genre to give both himself and us a true version of what is. The poet seems to be there to feed us with the world, and he assumes in us as in himself an appetite for it. But if genres must go because they don't assume enough of reality, the converse might be equally true; the production of the real serves as the poet's justification for getting rid of the ties of genre, or stylistic expectations.

Certainly, if we concentrate only on the most visibly extrovert qualities of Augustan poetry, if we stress only the effective observations, we may miss something else of great importance. We do not really go to Augustan poetry – the Augustans did not go to this poetry – for static mimesis of a quiet universe of quiet things. We see in Augustan poetry people, animals, things, mixed up and rioting.

> They might distinguish diff'rent noyse
> Of *Horns*, and *Pans*, and *Dogs*, and *Boyes*;
> And *Kettle-Drums*, whose sullen *Dub*
> Sounds like the hooping of a *Tub*:

But when the sight appear'd in view,
They found it was an *antique* Show,
A *Triumph*, that for *Pomp*, and *State*,
Did proudest *Romans* emulate;
For as the *Aldermen* of *Rome*
For foes at training overcome,
...
Did ride, with many a Good morrow,
Crying, *hey for our town* through the *burrough*.
So when this *Triumph* drew so nigh,
They might particulars descry,
They never saw two things so Pat,
In all respects, as this, and that.
First, He that led the *Cavalcate*,
Wore a Sowgelder's *Flagellate*,
...
Next *Pans,* and *Kettles* of all keys,
From *Trebles* down to *double-Base*,
And after them upon a *Nag*,
That might pass for a forehand Stag,
A *Cornet* rod, and on his Staff,
A Smock display'd, did proudly wave.
...
Then mounted on a Horned *Horse*,
One bore a *Gauntlet* and *Guilt-spurs*,
Ty'd to the *Pummel* of a long *Sword*,
He held reverst the point turn'd downward.
Next after, on a Raw-bon'd Steed,
The Conqueror's *Standard-bearer* rid,
And bore aloft before the *Champion*
A *Petticoat* displaid, and Rampant;
Next whom the *Amazon* triumphant
Bestrid her *Beast*, and on the *Rump* on't
Sat *Face* to *Tayl*, and *Bum* to *Bum*,
The *Warrier* whilome overcome;
Arm'd with a *Spindle* and a *Distaff*,
Which as he rod, she made him twist off;
And when he loyter'd, o'er her shoulder,
Chastiz'd the *Reformado* Souldier.
(Butler, *Hudibras* II, Canto II, lines 587–648)

In the description of the Skimmington-ride in *Hudibras*, Butler gives us the place (streets of a country town) and shows us animals, people and things all appearing unexpectedly in a conglomerate and detailed misrule. This misrule apparently satisfies its actors in its successful creation of total dissonance and fascinating ugliness. Butler is using more than "mock-heroic" adornment in comparing this ugly procession with the *"antique* Show" of a Roman triumph. He indicates that the Roman triumph as historical fact was as absurd as this other civic display, and Roman patriotism (*"hey for our town"*) the most commonplace sentiment of crude country boroughs. Roman triumphs depended on a degradation; so too do Skimmingtons (or as Ralpho would have it, "Ridings"), which depend on the chastisement of a bossy woman and the humiliation of hen-pecked man. The whole affair is misrule celebrating misrule. Butler gives us details enough to choke us (as indeed Sir Hudibras is nearly choked and blinded with the "Orenge-Tawny slime" of the rotten egg thrown by the revellers). For Butler, the Puritan Revolution has the same elegance, beauty and appropriateness as the Skimmington-ride, this "*Antichristian Opera*" as Sir Hudibras calls it in grave reprobation. Sir Hudibras as Puritan knight is a participant at large in the disarray represented doubly in the country people's mock-festival.

Yet there is not, in *Hudibras*, any order appealed to that can counterbalance the energy and fascination of the misrule so celebrated here and throughout the poem. As with the bear-baiting procession and mob (Part I, Canto II) we are involved in the noise and show and festivity. The Skimmington was illustrated by Hogarth (see Fig. 8), and Butler's scene is very Hogarthian; in it, common and sensible objects are presented in detailed spatial relation to one another and are chaotically significant. Things (and people) here display their capacity for riotous transformation. Or rather, we can say, the poet is interested in creating and making us see that sinister festivity, that transforming riot.

Fig. 8

Taking the hint from *Hudibras'* Skimmington, I shall apply the word
"charivari" to a common *topos* of Augustan poetry. "Charivari" implies a
mixture of the celebratory and the violent, enacted by a crowd. The real
charivari is historically rural in origin, springing from medieval village life, but
it is not purely rustic, for it requires a crowd, and somewhere to parade in; as
the idea is related to community and to streets, urban charivari is a natural
development.[3] The origin of historical charivari seems to be satiric; it is our
equivalent of early Roman Fescennine celebration. (In the nineteenth century
Punch called itself "The London Charivari," keeping up the idea of festive
satire.) Historical charivari is a communal corrective or mockery, especially in
regard to marriage and misdeeds in marriage; it has survived into this century,
at least in a light form, for in the New Brunswick village in which I spent part of
my youth, marriages were celebrated by a "shivaree," a mock-epithalamium
of pan-banging and uproariousness under newlyweds' windows. The Augustan literary charivari is most often satiric, though its satire can run in various
ways and through various modes. The advent of the charivari as a *topos* in
Augustan literature, incidentally, seems to coincide with the historical disappearance of such celebrations as Skimmingtons from the urban environment. City dwellers tend not to police each others' sexual conduct in this
manner. But urban literature can, or at least may self-mockingly pretend to do
so.

Like its sociologically observable counterpart in life, the literary charivari
places obstacles in the way of the *hieros gamos*, the happy marriage of order and
graceful fruitfulness, or of its unselfconscious enjoyment. Yet charivari, which
has self-conscious criticism of sexuality as an intellectual motive, has the
sexual energy itself as a motive force.[4] This may be expressed overtly or
covertly, but union is courted as much as denied – or courted and denied at the
same time. The literary charivari often entails the strong presence of a
feminine being, or even of feminine power(s), which may be officially mocked
according to the daily regulations of customary life but which cannot readily
be weakened or overcome. The autogenetic Flecknoe seems to combine
motherhood with fatherhood, and pitches his throne "Where their vast Courts
the Mother-Strumpets keep." *The Rape of the Lock* has Belinda, both bellicose
and belle, at its centre, and the whole action is begun and supervised by Ariel,
a male sprite who can on occasion take on the appearance of "A Youth more
glitt'ring than a *Birth-night Beau*," and is yet an embodiment of solely feminine
nature. "He" was "once inclos'd in Woman's beauteous Mold." Pope's goddess of Dulness, a renewed representative of Butler's "*Amazon* triumphant,"
works in close association with her son, who also combines male (pen) and
female (parturition, embryo, abortion).

Often in literary charivari we can see the strange confluence of male and
female qualities, bearing all down before them, busily engaged by their very
oddly-combined presence in an un-creation or new creation not subject to
ordinary rules and commonplace vision. Things, people, social relations,

places on the map and places on the ladder of rank – all take on a new existence. In Augustan literature, the charivari is often strangely satisfying in itself, both for imagined participants and for readers. Augustan poets keep turning to this *topos* of splendid and perverse and dizzying mess.

MacFlecknoe is entirely charivari. Detailed objects, real people (at least, Shadwell was once in some sense real, though the poet has raised him to the status of a fiction), and very real places (the Thames, Watling Street, the Barbican) are combined in perverse and wild celebration. Things assume their own animation, in spontaneous activity:

> Rows'd by report of Fame, the Nations meet,
> From near *Bun-Hill*, and distant *Watling-street*.
> No *Persian* Carpets spread th'Imperial way,
> But scatter'd Limbs of mangled Poets lay:
> From dusty shops neglected Authors come,
> Martyrs of Pies, and Reliques of the Bum.   (lines 96–101)

Gay's *Trivia* has its moments of unstressed charivari, as the daily activities of groups and individuals in the work-a-day streets of London seem just touched with the fantastic (Gay's poem was presumably one of the influences on Hogarth's *Four Times of Day*). Gay refers momentarily to a real charivari, or strange epithalamium, in a passage which catches a number of other people and activities as well:

> You'll see a draggled Damsel, here and there,
> From *Billingsgate* her fishy Traffick bear;
> On Doors the sallow Milk-maid chalks her Gains;
> Ah! how unlike the Milk-maid of the Plains!
> Before proud Gates attending Asses bray,
> Or arrogate with solemn Pace the Way;
> These grave Physicians with their milky Chear,
> The Love-sick Maid, and dwindling Beau repair;
> Here Rows of Drummers stand in martial File,
> And with their Vellom-Thunder shake the Pile,
> To greet the new-made Bride. Are Sounds like these,
> The proper Prelude to a State of Peace?
> (*Trivia* ii, lines 9–20)

The influence of *Trivia* is evident in parts of the *Dunciad*, a poem which deals, intermittently but pungently, with the daily life of London. The description of the "attending Asses" may have affected Pope's similar vignette in the *Dunciad*: "As when the long-ear'd milky mothers wait / At some sick miser's triple-bolted gate" (ii, lines 247–8). Since asses' milk was considered a restorative for those suffering from venereal afflictions, the asses at the gate indicate that someone wealthy, weak and presumably poxed lies within. Satire on particular types of people does not, however, seem the lines' only or central meaning; rather, they express a diffuse fear that sexual power and sexual weakness are intimately associated. Charivari is an abandoned if nervous washing of dirty (and clean) linen in public. Collective but customarily secret fears about sex and power are evoked from hiding places in psychic depths to find a place in the streets.

It is a leading element of the charivari that it includes – or is even necessitated by – the feminine, as in the instance of the "milky mothers." *MacFlecknoe* is no exception; the coronation of Shadwell takes place "Where their vast Courts the Mother-Strumpets keep" (line 72), and King Flecknoe is both father and mother, giving birth to his own issue. The female power, often emphatically maternal as well as emphatically sexual, appears in the charivari in some strange distorted form, like "the *Amazon* triumphant" in Butler's Skimmington. She appears, that is, in a form officially disapproved, but expressive of something partly desired as well as partly suppressed in daily social life. Male and female powers are combined in unhandsome but powerful union within the charivari. The female may at times actively preside as destroyer and preserver over the charivari's actions and display. She can take a leading part in this parade of malfunctions.

In Garth's *The Dispensary* (a poem to which Pope was much indebted), surgeons and apothecaries battle with the instruments of their arts in Warwick Lane near the Royal College of Physicians. Helmeted with bed-pans and other utensils of their trade, they hurl galleypots and phials at each other, or fire off their enema syringes:

> Then from their levell'd Syringes they pour
> The liquid Volley of a missive Show'r.
> Not Storms of Sleet, which o're the *Baltick* drive,
> Push't on by *Northern* Gusts, such Horrour give.
> Like Spouts in *Southern* Seas the Deluge broke,
> And Numbers sunk beneath th'impetuous Stroak.
> So when *Leviathans* Dispute the Reign,
> And uncontrol'd Dominion of the Main;
> From the rent Rocks whole *Coral* Groves are torn,
> And Isles of *Sea-Weed* on the Waves are born.
> Such watry Stores from their spread Nostrils fly,
> 'Tis doubtful which is Sea, and which is Sky.   (Canto v)

Multiplying strangeness transforms the streets, which seem to contain Leviathans and coral groves as well as enemas and showers of brass weights. Amid this ugly-beautiful battle a new transforming presence abruptly appears:

> While the shrill clangor of the Battel rings;
> Auspicious *Health* appear'd on *Zephir*'s Wings;
> She seem'd a Cherub most divinely bright,
> More soft than Air, more gay than morning Light.
> A Charm she takes from each excelling Fair,
> And borrows C[*eci*]*ll*'s Shape and G[*raf*]*ton*'s Air.
> Her Eyes like R[*anel*]*agh*'s their Beams dispense,
> With C[*hurch*]*ill*'s Bloom, and B[*er*]*kley*'s Innocence.   (Canto vi)

The Goddess of Health is humanized as feminine by her adoption of the qualities of living English women. It is as if these noble ladies in their own beautiful procession had suddenly stepped up to this mess. The illustration by Du Guernier (see p. vi) is a nice representation of the charivari *topos*. Health, undoubtedly feminine, rises triumphant at the centre of the picture. Prostrate at her feet is Discord (who in the poem had taken the shape of the physicians); Discord, definitely unmasked, writhes with her snakes. The combatants, amazed, have ceased fighting; they stop with their phallic weapons poised and pointing suggestively towards the goddess. Yet she visibly commands as their superior, as much maternal dominatrix as Butler's Amazon or Pope's Dulness. The tensions in perceived relations between male and female emerge as tensions between sickness and health, ugliness and beauty, order and mess – but there are no unvarying alignments among these. Everything insists on strange minglings. And everything mingles strangely – now and in England. Cherubs fly gaily over the head of Health as she gestures towards the College, the real London building in a street now associated with fantastic presences.

So, too, under the leadership of their monstrous female mother and head, the Dunces gather in riotous variety and take over London, with its significant places and dubious diurnal activities, on an ordinary day:

> This labour past, by Bridewell all descend,
> (As morning pray'r, and flagellation end)
> To where Fleet-ditch with disemboguing streams
> Rolls the large tribute of dead dogs to Thames,
> The King of dykes! than whom no sluice of mud
> With deeper sable blots the silver flood.
> "Here strip, my children! here at once leap in,
> Here prove who best can dash thro' thick and thin,
> And who the most in love of dirt excel,
> Or dark dexterity of groping well ..."   (II, lines 269–78)

The dishevelled motley group evidently take their appalling "high heroic Games" very seriously (see Fig. 9). After diving in the "sluice of mud," the dirty competitors parade up familiar Fleet Street. They and their works combine in a grotesque new atmosphere, a kind of cloud shedding unpleasant snow:

> Thro' Lud's fam'd gates, along the well-known Fleet
> Rolls the black troop, and overshades the street,
> 'Till show'rs of Sermons, Characters, Essays,
> In circling fleeces whiten all the ways.   (II, lines 359–62)

As in *The Dispensary*, with its spouting enemas vying with whales in coral seas, the energies of Nature are mimicked by the energies of human art, which has its own productions. What we know as the real world, like Warwick Lane or Fleet Street, is unignorably altered in charivari. It is an extraordinary and notable fact that the Augustans chose to parade their own

Fig. 9

malfunctions through the daylight world and the public place. What is urban, stony, monumental and official is challenged by the flow of unofficial disturbance.

Charivari need not be ugly. A fantastic group may reverse customary order, a surreal moment impose itself on the commonplace world, in charivari without ugliness, as in Belinda's journey on the Thames in her "painted Vessel" guarded by the "lucid Squadrons" (*Rape of the Lock*, Canto II). And charivari may emphasize sheer strangeness rather than ugliness, as in Pope's fantasia imagining his sophisticated moneyed society deprived of paper money and thrown back on the use of the real things that money represents:

> A Statesman's slumbers how this speech would spoil!
> "Sir, Spain has sent a thousand jars of oil;
> Huge bales of British cloth blockade the door;
> A hundred oxen at your levee roar."
>   Poor Avarice one torment more would find;
> Nor could Profusion squander all in kind.
> Astride his cheese Sir Morgan might we meet,
> And Worldly crying coals from street to street,
> . . .
> His Grace will game: to White's a Bull be led,
> With spurning heels and with a butting head.
> To White's be carried, as to ancient games,
> Fair Coursers, Vases, and alluring Dames.
> Shall then Uxorio, if the stakes he sweep,
> Bear home six Whores, and make his Lady weep?
> Or soft Adonis, so perfum'd and fine,
> Drive to St. James's a whole herd of swine?
>
>   (*Epistle to Bathurst*, lines 43–62)

The streets of London are weirdly glutted with products, and continually embarrassed by strange processions. Here as in the *Dunciad*, in typical Augustan genre play and parody, Pope twists the epic *topos* of the games to contribute to his charivari. In both poems (as in *MacFlecknoe* and *The Dispensary*) the mock use of classical *topoi* exploits both the epic and the inadequacy of the epic; the epic cannot say enough about complex (and modern) human behaviour. The epic itself questioned neither the competition nor the trophies of its games. In Pope's poem the normal community scene has become visibly abnormal; the fantastic has been imposed on what our dull daily eyes call the real, forcing us to see a reality beneath. The fantasia brings to light a hidden truth about the activities the community customarily agrees to consider "normal" (bribery, capitalistic ownership, gambling).

The capacity to create such shattering charivari was considered one of the marks of the true poet of the Augustan Age. Milton may be credited with being one of the first Augustans to develop the new *topos*, for his scenes in the nether world have many of the symptoms of the neo-Augustan charivari – crowds, celebratory processions, obscenity, monuments, misrule and wild activity. Above all, they present us with a fantastic vision, and surreal effects. So when Satan returns triumphant from Earth, he meets his son Death, and Sin, "his fair Enchanting Daughter" at the foot of the "wondrous Pontifice," the new bridge from Hell. Sin and Death make a procession of only two, but they greet their chief with familial delight and emphatic civic bustle. Sin's speech dedicates the bridge to Satan in a kind of perverse opening ceremony before the King of Hell sends the two off on their imperial mission. Satan, returning to Pandaemonium, makes his way through the midst of an angelic crowd disguised as a "plebeian Angel militant / Of lowest order," and sits invisible on that exalted throne (which Pope will borrow for Cibber) before revealing himself and making his victory speech:

> So having said, a while he stood, expecting
> Thir universal shout and high applause
> To fill his ear, when contrary he hears
> On all sides, from innumerable tongues
> A dismal universal hiss . . .
> . . .
> dreadful was the din
> Of hissing through the Hall, thick swarming now
> With complicated monsters, head and tail
> *Scorpion* and *Asp*, and *Amphisbaena* dire,
> *Cerastes* horn'd, *Hydras* and *Ellops* drear.
>
> (*Paradise Lost*, Book x, lines 504–24)

The inability to speak is the worst penalty, the most dreadful frustration, any Augustan writer can imagine. In the ironic and satisfying metamorphosis of Satan and his legions into serpents, Milton displays an Augustan taste for complicated monsters.

It becomes the Augustan poet's duty to present what is complicated and monstrous as well as the simple and sensuous. Indeed, what is simple and sensuous is often used to set off freakish deformity or unnatural (or undesired) nature. To turn for a moment from poetry to prose fiction, Gulliver, that freakish monster (*Relplum Scalcath* = Lusus Naturae), lives the sensuous life amid complicated monsters in a very Augustan manner. A poet had to prove his quality by presenting in verse some freakish and disturbing festival. Stephen Duck combines sensuous appeal with monstrous activity effectively in "On Mites. To a Lady":

> Dear Madam, did you never gaze,
> Thro' Optic-glass, on rotten *Cheese*?
> There, Madam, did you ne'er perceive
> A Crowd of dwarfish Creatures live?
> The little Things, elate with Pride,
> Strut to and fro, from Side to Side:
> In tiny Pomp, and pertly vain,
> Lords of their pleasing Orb, they reign
> And, fill'd with harden'd Curds and Cream,
> Think the whole Dairy made for *them*.[5]

The charivari often involves human beings seen in close association with animals, whether "Horned *Horse*," "attending Asses" or "*Ellops* drear"; it is natural to reverse the pattern and present animal or insect charivari, the creatures monstrously acting so very humanly.

"A Lady" might be the addressee of a poem "On Mites," and a lady like the Duchess of Grafton might be invoked in the midst of a charivari, but the ladies themselves were not encouraged to write poetry either satiric or grotesque.

Indeed, women poets had a particularly hard time qualifying as "Augustans," not only since the classics were supposedly closed to them, but also because they (legally powerless) were officially supposed ignorant of politics, history, and of the large world that makes a life outside the self. The boldness and appetite which seizes the world and absorbs it into poetry are not "feminine" qualities. Women were supposed to write elegies on the death of pet linnets and so on, weak versions of the sort of lyric verse despised and discarded by the major movements of the period. Significantly, they did not write long poems at a time when the long poem was most valued. They were rarely satirical (satire is critical and aggressive). Nor were women supposed to write poetry derived from the inner self without the strictest self-censorship. Women poets hardly ever attempted the charivari, the daring dispersal of reality in favour of a crazed version of it. They were certainly not encouraged to attempt it; perhaps their contemporaries uneasily felt that if a topic often representing the female powers and sexual unease were seriously invoked by a female, matters would get out of hand. It is a noticeable event when a woman poet tries to break up reality into the fantasy of charivari.

Ann Yearsley, the Bristol milkwoman,[6] did make such an attempt, and successfully, in a poem "Addressed to Ignorance, Occasioned by a Gentleman's desiring the Author never to assume a Knowledge of the Ancients."[7] Ann Yearsley refused to believe that her inferior position (as woman and as uneducated labourer) dictated that classical allusion was not for her. She thought she had a right to draw on the classical deities, stories and characters if she chose. Her retort is expressed in a poem depending on a classical allusion (to Pythagorean metempsychosis) for the basic conceit, a conceit which allows a flow of classical allusions in succession. But she makes it a strange succession. The poet imagines a wild scene which turns out to be the streets of London, full of classical (and some modern) eminent personages who have come down in the world:

> Fair Julia sees Ovid, but passes him near,
>   An old broom o'er her shoulder is thrown;
> Penelope lends to five lovers an ear,
>   Walking on with one sleeve to her gown.

> But Helen, the Spartan, stands near Charing-Cross,
>   Long laces and pins doom'd to cry;
> Democritus, Solon, bear baskets of moss,
>   While Pliny sells woodcocks hard by.

> In Billingsgate Nell, Clytemnestra moves slow,
>   All her fishes die quick in the air;
> Agamemnon peeps stern, thro' the eye of old Joe,
>   At Egysthus, who, grinning, stands there.

Yearsley has displayed her own knowledge while impishly reducing the famous to her own supposed "low" level, allowing herself a mock-slangy familiarity with the ancients. Who knows what anyone is – or was?

Here's Trojan, Athenian, Greek, Frenchman and I,
Heav'n knows what I was long ago;
No matter, thus shielded, this age I defy,
And the next cannot wound me, I know.

Her poem is a declaration of human equality, achieved as the author is seen throwing off repressive circumstances (and repressive precept) by the strength of her good-humoured and aggressive wit. The use of the past and the insight into discrepancy are Augustan – so too is the common detail, unsettled by context, and the use of urban topography. True, mastery of Augustanism by 1787 is a rather melancholy achievement, as the nature of poetry and ideas of what poetry should be were about to alter radically. But Yearsley has proven herself a true Augustan. She has shown that she can, like the great masculine poets of the period, create a fantasia in the streets – a charivari.

The presence of charivari in Augustan poetry is in itself a defiance of genre and of rules of style, and of rules in general. Charivari refuses to heed normative expectations. The Augustan poets showed they could outdo their Roman satiric predecessors in creating not just the satirized crowd but a fantastic riot. And the fantasia of perversity is not offset within the frame of a fable, not treated as mere quick simile; it is what we are made to see and share in. It acts centrally, not ornamentally. The production of concentrated charivari signifies a high point of the poet's power.

We shall fail to understand a good deal of Augustan literature if we don't comprehend its ability to see through to the other side of ordinary things in peculiar and lively reversals, its daring in tackling the extra-ordinary. Augustan literature has its *Alice in Wonderland* quality. That comparison is not perfectly arbitrary; the Augustans are among the authors Carroll knew, and his quixotic White Knight with all his provisions and accessories is visibly a refined descendant of Hudibras. For the Augustans themselves one of the equivalents of our experience of Wonderland and the World through the Looking-Glass was to be found in the experience of Ovid's *Metamorphoses*. Unknown numbers of children must have sat hushed in parlours, kept quiet and amused with the big books, the translations by Sandys (1632) or by Garth and his "Eminent Hands" (1717). Readers could enjoy in these the large detailed engravings which are among the artistic ancestors of Tenniel's drawings. In the frontispiece to Book II of the *Metamorphoses* in Sandys's edition, for instance, we see the weird crowd in a landscape, thronging in a kind of mad procession (Fig. 10). Phaeton falls, his sisters are turning into trees; Cygnus turns into a swan, still with a man's legs. Ocyrhoë, talking to her centaur father (or talking and whinnying in a mixture), gesticulates, still with a human arm, though her head is already the head of a mare extending over the neck of her rather elegant dress. (She looks a little like a chess piece.) The illustrators of Garth's book, Du Guernier, Kirkall and others, imitate something of the pattern and baroque manner of the older illustrator while producing their own versions of the strange happenings and unpredictable shape-changes of the

Fig. 10

Ovidian world (see Figs. 11 and 12). We feel the rush of movement as the
Heliades turn into trees, sprouting uncontrollably. In the frontispiece to Book
VI we see Niobe with her children, the dread celestial archers, and Arachne's
web, and also the comic peasants of Lycia. These were condemned for their
refusal of a drink to the goddess Latona:

Fig. 11

Fig. 12

The Goddess has her wish; for now they chuse
To plunge and dive among the watry Ooze;
Sometimes they shew their Head above the Brim,
And on the glassy Surface spread to Swim.
Often upon the Bank their Station take,
Then spring, and leap, into the cooly Lake.
Still, void of Shame, they lead a clam'rous Life,
And croaking, still scold on in endless Strife.

(Croxall's translation)[8]

The lively figures in the picture are in the course of becoming frogs; we can see that they are croaking.

The tradition of Ovid illustration seems a partial influence upon Hogarth, and at least one aspect of the tradition behind his Skimmington. The animated figures seem to be transforming themselves into some new animal or creature – particularly in the case of the man on the left who waves the horns above his head, or, on the opposite side, the smock waving below another set of horns, a weird figure that seems striving to become something animate on its own account (see Fig. 8). Parts of bodies seem detached in the parts of clothing flourished about, like limbs with a separate existence. Everything, like the triple beast composed of the horse bearing the man and the woman back-to-back, seems to be escaping normal shape.

The tradition of Ovidian strangeness serves other artists of the eighteenth century when interpreting the strangeness in their writers' texts. The charivari is often alluded to, sometimes very directly as in Edward Young's detailed instructions to a painter, a prescription for a picture representing a world in which men had miserably transformed themselves in sensuality, gambling and masquerades.[9] (It should be noted that the new social entertainment of the Augustan Age, the masquerade, is an attempt to create a charivari in real life.) Young wished such a picture done by Hogarth as an illustration to his *The Centaur Not Fabulous*, a moral prose essay by an author who was also a well-known poet, the satirist of *The Universal Passion*. In the event his instructions were followed very effectively by Samuel Wale (see Fig. 13). Wale's illustration to Thomson's *The Castle of Indolence* (see Fig. 14) is not dissimilar to that for Young's treatise, or at least the Knight of Industry somewhat resembles the centaur in facial complacency. This Knight, attired in strange quasi-Elizabethan garb like a masquerade costume, seems to flourish a large checked cloak; when we look closer, we realize it is a net in which he has caught the Wizard of Indolence, now a wretched small dark mass. The cherubic sprite who plays the lyre at the gate of the Castle looks on in petrified Ovidian astonishment. A small crowd seems to have gathered to watch the cruel entertainment. The scene is one of transformation – not yet a charivari, it gives promise of being about to burst into action, with its odd figures, its crowd.

People in crowds do strange things – as they do in Hayman's version of the diving scene presided over by Dulness (see Fig. 9). Dulness perches atop a

Fig. 13

small bridge, in a flighty and insubstantial simulation of a monument, while her sons, in various states of dress and undress, prepare to dive into the ditch into which sewer grates are visibly discharging. A pair of disembodied legs shows that one competitor has already made the plunge into the other dirty

Fig. 14

element, and been transformed. The illustration echoes the Ovid-illustration pattern, with the important exception that here we know all the figures are involved in the same activity. We still have the crowd formed as a large "S"-shaped procession, composed of individuals and groups self-occupied and self-absorbed. In this strange nakedness or semi-nudity of many of the figures (again as in pictures of Ovidian scenes), the touches of contemporary clothing seem odd, as in the man with wig and ruffles on the left, or the parson in black and with a full wig who is standing on the bridge. Georgian clothing itself is made to look like some odd Ovidian regalia, as if it were about to turn into something. Each character is transforming.

The illustrators understood the sense of the strange conveyed by the writers who were their contemporaries. The writers, like the artists who illustrated them, catch the Ovidian meaning in their world where wild festival is an expression of metamorphosis. Augustan poetry intermittently but fully acknowledges the monstrous in life, giving us another way of looking at the real. With such an acknowledgment comes an implicit question (parallel to the philosophical debates of the time) as to what is real. Reality, solid and sure as the stone Johnson kicked to refute Berkeley, may be, if not illusion, at the same time extraordinary Other, the site of the abnormal, the abode of "complicated monsters." According to Boswell's image of Johnson's mind, Johnson lived in a private desperate Colosseum, the haunt of monsters horribly complicated and fierce.[10]

The Augustan poet shows his courage in displaying the monsters of the outer and inner lives. The fantastic power of the poet, like the power of the fantastic in the poem, pushes against the boundaries of what is ordinarily called "real." The poet dares to go beyond, and dares us to go with him, not without risk. The charivari, with its excessive vitality, threatens (perhaps even attractively threatens) to take over "reality" for good, or perhaps it rules another realm from which, like Gulliver, we cannot easily return. Augustan poetry is venturesome, and exploratory; it dares us to cross borders into what is unknown, to break bounds.

This pressing against and breaking through the boundaries of the ordinary can be very explicitly found in other modes and moods than the charivari, above all in the "visionary" verse that comprises a substantial part of Augustan poetry. We might expect to find in religious verse utterances about the desirability of going beyond the world, and we do indeed find it there. Augustan hymnists very frequently defy the world, and urge us to transcend it, e.g.:

> Sweet Fields beyond the swelling Flood
> Stand drest in living Green:
> So to the *Jews* Old *Canaan* stood,
> While *Jordan* roll'd between.
>
> But timorous Mortals start and shrink
> To cross this narrow Sea,
> And linger shivering on the Brink
> And fear to lanch away.
> (Watts, "A Prospect of Heaven Makes Death Easy" [better known as "There is a
> Land of pure Delight"])[11]

Not only should we "la[u]nch away": the visible world, the sensible universe, will itself some day disappear. Devotional writers of the period certainly did not shrink from imagining the end of the world, of Nature itself. They envisage the end of things and time, as Elizabeth Rowe[12] does:

> And when the pillars of the world
> With sudden ruin break,
> And all this vast and goodly frame
> Sinks in the mighty wreck;   ("Hymn III")[13]

Rowe also wrote "The Conflagration. An Ode," a description of the end of the universe after the Last Judgment:

> Each planet from its shatter'd axis reels,
> And orbs immense on orbs immense drop down,
> Like scatt'ring leaves from off their branches blown.

Edward Young treated the same subject in an early work, *The Last Day* (1713). The last book of *The Last Day* ends, of course, with the destruction of creation in God's fire:

> This Globe alone would but defraud the Fire,
> Starve it's devouring Rage: the Flakes aspire,
> And catch the Clouds, and make the Heav'ns their Prey;
> The Sun, the Moon, the Stars all melt away,
> And leave a Mighty Blank: Involv'd in Flame,
> The whole Creation Sinks! the Glorious Frame
> In which ten thousand Worlds in radiant Dance,
> Orb above Orb their wondrous Course advance,
> . . .
> Is crusht, and Lost; no Monument, no Sign,
> Where once so proudly Blaz'd the gay Machine.
> So Bubbles on the foaming Stream expire,
> So Sparks that scatter from the kindling Fire.
>   (*The Last Day*, Book III)[14]

The illustration to this passage by La Vergne and Kirkall (see Fig. 15) is an interesting link between the art of the middle ages and that of Blake. If we look closely at the burning globe, we can make out two burning edifices, and a mountain; the tongues of flame in the cloud represent the planets, which have caught fire from earth. Sun, moon and stars, all melt away. Everything is to go.

The religious experience of the Augustans has never been fully or perfectly treated. I suspect that it is not peripheral but central to Augustan literature. English Christians, whether Anglicans (like Young) or Dissenters (like Watts and Rowe), all believed that this world is destined to end, and that we shall watch its annihilation. Solid joys and lasting treasure are to be found only otherwise, as John Newton says in "Zion, or the City of GOD," that great homesick-for-heaven hymn.[15] The beliefs of generations who are, with at least part of their spiritual selves, not only making ready to launch into heaven but also being prepared to behold the end of all creation must have some profound effect on the poets those generations produce. The effect may be seen

Fig. 15

even among those who officially reject or react against specifically Christian piety. The Deist Thomson expresses, like Watts, the desire to "launch away" (or rather, the need to be ready to do so):

> When even at last the solemn Hour shall come,
> And wing my mystic Flight to future Worlds,
> I chearful will obey, there, with new Powers,
> Will rising Wonders sing . . .
>
> ("A Hymn on the Seasons," lines 108–11)

Thomson ends "Winter" with the end of this world, though, more cheerfully than Young, he emphasizes the "second Birth" of creation, rather than its destruction. But in either case the "real" world we know is transient. The frame of mind which can entertain such thoughts can permit, at one and the same time, the deepest respect for reality – for fact, object, scientific knowledge – along with an odd kind of lack of reverence for it. The religious insight that reality may break in sudden ruin and disappear (or be reformed utterly), or that the diurnal can be outrun, not only allows but encourages a more secular suspicion that reality has a good many cracks in it. There are visions of truth outside of fact.

The "visionary" element can be found in quite secular Augustan poetry, especially in poetry about the poet's calling.

> Ye sacred Nine! that all my Soul possess,
> Whose Raptures fire me, and whose Visions bless,
> Bear me, oh bear me to sequester'd Scenes,
> The Bow'ry Mazes and surrounding Greens;
>
> . . .
>
> I seem thro' consecrated Walks to rove,
> I hear soft Musick dye along the Grove;
> Led by the Sound I roam from Shade to Shade,
> By God-like Poets Venerable made.
>
> (Pope, *Windsor Forest*, lines 259–70)

Pope's vision here is more than mere ornament. It is a statement about his calling which takes him, as we might say, out of himself. He is, in "Raptures" and "Visions," taken out of the bounds of time and space and natural experience of the senses. The passage above is his version of "heard melodies are sweet, but those unheard ..." Hayman's illustrations to those sections of Pope's poetry where he talks about his own calling (Figs. 1, 2 and 3) capture the "Visionary" in an appropriately Augustan manner. Not held within the bounds of historical time and space, the poet Pope is portrayed in a *locus* outside time, in a visionary landscape. In this Other-world, the spirits of the dead, the powers of the mind, and the impulses of the heart can be met and comprehended.

Even Thomson the scientific is not happy unless he can invoke the elements of another reality, gliding in through the fissures of this intelligible world. In "Summer," he wishes to "pierce into the midnight Depth / Of yonder Grove" (lines 516–17); such shadowy places "of wildest largest Growth" are "the Haunts of Meditation," "the Scenes where antient Bards ... Conversed with Angels, and immortal Forms." Thomson as modern Druid is likewise favoured:

> Shook sudden from the Bosom of the Sky,
> A thousand Shapes or glide athwart the Dusk,
> Or stalk majestic on. Deep rous'd, I feel
> A sacred Terror, a severe Delight,
> Creep thro' my mortal Frame: and thus, methinks,
> A Voice, than Human more, th'abstracted Ear
> Of Fancy strikes.
>
> ("Summer," lines 538–44)

Thomson, like Pope, feels himself invisibly companioned in an inspiring haunt suitable to the poet. He too forsakes realism and what *we* might expect to be meant by "good sense" in order to evoke that feeling of piercing through – or into – the bounds of the ordinary, piercing into something else. It is this quality in Thomson, as well as his capacities as a describer of Nature and "the blooming Year," that Collins pays tribute to: "In yonder Grave a DRUID lies." The power and the ambiguities of Collins's poem have been brilliantly discussed by Laurence Lipking,[16] who points out that the poem celebrates Thomson both as an historical figure, given the immortality of fame in that other eternal *locus* of the poet, and as a dead friend, given what all of us must come to in the end, a grave in earth and a monument that may be forgotten. The visionary and the sad reality are played against one another. But Collins as poet himself has a right to call upon the visionary in his "Ode Occasion'd by the Death of Mr. Thomson," as in his other Odes.

What we might expect to be meant by "good sense" (that sedate and quiescent quality) should not mislead us into labelling all such moments as Thomson's encounter with the "thousand Shapes" or superhuman Voice as either frivolous (if we refuse to be impressed) or Romantic (if we are impressed). When we talk about Romanticism historically, we mean something that happened a good while after 1730; if we are using "Romantic" as a loose term to cover almost any emotional ideas, we are using it so generally as to render it meaningless. In England, it is in our "Augustan Age" that we see a developing interest in portraying disturbances of reality, an interest going hand in hand with an interest in portraying all real, i.e. all sensible, things in exact detail and conjuring up their presence. In this period the imposition of another level of reality did not need to have anything to do with either religious belief or accepted myth. That does not mean the poets did not believe in Christianity, or were not religious. As we have seen there is a considerable output of religious writing. But the poets were inclined to play with and transcend the world of Nature in its everyday sense, and to do so on occasions which were not inspired by religion or by accepted or traditional myths. I have found myself, on occasion, adopting the word "surreal" to describe Augustan poetic effects. That is a late word, coming from the realm of modern painting, though it may describe effects in the arts in the entire modern period. The surreal revises reality without religious occasion and without keeping the revision strictly enclosed in fable, like Horace's story of the mice. It may be one central definition of the surreal that it plays with Nature and all aspects of natural and man-made things on occasions not inspired by any traditional story, and with some intention to shock. In that sense, Rabelais gave the West its first modern surreal literary work.

We can see in our Augustans that classical myths such as had been extensively used in the past began to lose ground a bit, or not to come out straight when they were used. Poets of this age are more apt to make us see the strange and novel, and to see it arbitrarily – as in charivari, or in personal meditations on the poet-self. At almost any point, unpredictably, what we know as real may disappear. These poets constantly show us reality cracking; other strange shapes emerge from the fissure and impose themselves upon the mirror of Nature. Surrealism, in short, is the order of the day. Scepticism about genre, as about all orders and boundaries, makes the strict setting off of these strange effects into some containing interlude seem less possible and less desirable. In *The Hind and the Panther*, for instance, Dryden cracked the mould of beast-fable, even while using it, by crossing from vehicle to tenor and back again very rapidly, leaving the doors between them open all the time. (*"Confounding the* Moral *and the* Fable *together"* as Montague and Prior said.) The "story" of the Hind and the Panther refuses to stay in set fable form; an open-ended fable invites history into it, and the two beasts argue about Popes and Councils. The fable sprawls into and superimposes itself on the historical reality of theologians and disputes, and does not merely illustrate something neatly about that historical world. The fantastic refusing to acknowledge proper limits makes this poem by Dryden a large surreal work. It is hardly necessary to add that such elements and techniques are not confined to poetry alone – one need remember only *Gulliver's Travels*, part of whose perennial attraction is the striking and economic surrealism of execution. But such elements, and such techniques for handling the world that comes bursting through the fissures of the normal, are characteristic of much of the best Augustan poetry. Pope worked at altering *The Rape of the Lock*, turning it from a light social satire to another kind of poem. Everyone has remarked the (even baleful) effects of the Cave of Spleen, but the whole work, once Pope had introduced his sylphs, is a surreal poem.

The Augustan poets are struck with their own power to recreate or to create all kinds of reality. The very power that animates, the power that bears the poet to "consecrated Walks," is the power of Fancy, the power that makes one see more than one reality. To many Augustans, Fancy is the faculty that ranges free, whereas Imagination, related to memory, often means only the capacity to recall and recreate images; the usage is logical and it is a pity for us that "fancy" has degenerated into such a light word that we sometimes miss the import of the Augustan poets as they ruminate on what they do. "Fancy" is not limited to the set boundaries of the commonplace, the normal. "Fancy" makes the poet see various realities: the divinely beautiful and mysterious scene, the perverse charivari. The poet's power to create, to see and hear more than is usually meant for mortal eye and ear, is the same power that sees and creates the fantasia. Fancy is thus a disturbing as well as an animating faculty. Poets not only see beyond the real – they see into the real, they see something else, wonderful or frightening. "To see a World in a Grain of Sand";[17] Blake could have come only in this period, with the experience of Augustan imagination at his back.

Augustan poets are always seeing worlds within worlds. They attend to the minute with a sharpness that gives point to even their most playful moments of seeing great wholes within small parts, as in Duck's "On Mites." If the Augustans did not have the microscopic eye, they cultivated very close vision, as Philips does when he makes us see

> Large Shoals of slow House-bearing Snails, that creep
> O'er the ripe Fruitage, paring slimy Tracts
> In the sleek Rinds ...
>
> (*Cyder* I, lines 412–14)

or as Parnell does in "The Flies," when he shows us the dwelling place of his "airy Nation":

> Near a low Ditch, where shallow Waters meet,
> Which never learnt to glide with liquid Feet,
> Whose *Naiads* never prattle as they play,
> But screen'd with Hedges slumber out the Day,
> There stands a slender Fern's aspiring Shade,
> Whose answ'ring Branches regularly lay'd
> Put forth their answ'ring Boughs, and proudly rise,
> Three Stories upward, in the nether Skies.
>
> ("The Flies. An Eclogue")[18]

Philips employs what Virgil of the *Georgics* has taught him about representing the creatures in their own terms. So does Parnell but he carries matters further; in "The Flies" (an ingenious bit of genre-play, a fable diverted into a mock-eclogue), the Virgilian touches are translated into the rendition of another world. The fern and the heavens are given from a fly's-eye point of view. We see, even in this light poem, a strange world we haven't seen before.

Augustan poets are always looking into the real for the strange, and always finding it. What they see most sharply is change, and variety which is an idea inseparable from the concept of change. Change and variety arouse a sense of wonder which may remain amused but which also may rise to more intense feelings. The sense of wonder reaches ecstasy in Cowper. Taking a "Winter Walk at Noon," and observing the "unprolific" winter's impress of "cold stagnation," the poet imagines the forces at work which will alter these withered stems:

a few short months,
And all shall be restor'd. These naked shoots,
Barren as lances, among which the wind
Makes wintry music, sighing as it goes,
Shall put their graceful foliage on again,
And, more aspiring, and with ampler spread,
Shall boast new charms, and more than they have lost.
(*The Task*, vi, lines 140–6)

Cowper's returned spring cannot be the same as the old one; the plants "aspire" and return with "ampler spread," with "new" and "more" charms (apparently these plants share the Augustan urge to expand and conquer). There follows Cowper's lovely descriptive passage about the flowers of spring – flowers recreated and represented by the imagination of the poet who is "actually" looking at a winter landscape. Cowper anticipates the effect of a benevolent metamorphosis. The flowers are rich and animated, from the guelder rose that throws against the sable yew "Her silver globes, light as the foamy surf / That the wind severs from the broken wave" to the jasmine in "The bright profusion of her scatter'd stars." Wonder at and enjoyment of this good riot of variety leads to religious meditation, as Cowper rejects the notion of an automatic law, the planetary machine set going by a remote Deity. He insists that God is present and active in his creation, personally working all the changes, such as that which makes the "uniform, uncolour'd scene" to "flush into variety again." God is there in all the variety:

One spirit – His
Who wore the platted thorns with bleeding brows –
Rules universal nature. Not a flow'r
But shows some touch, in freckle, streak, or stain,
Of his unrivall'd pencil.
...
Happy who walks with him! whom what he finds
Of flavour or of scent in fruit or flow'r,
Or what he views of beautiful or grand
In nature, from the broad majestic oak
To the green blade that twinkles in the sun,
Prompts with remembrance of a present God!   (lines 238–52)

Presumably the present God is to be seen also in the "uniform uncoloured scene" of "stagnation" and the "naked shoots," but Cowper does not wish to deal with that. Cowper's God creates colour, individuation, *quidditas* and incessant variation. Everything moves and shines, reveals its quirks and its essence. That beautiful line "To the green blade that twinkles in the sun" is perfectly Augustan in its simplicity and expressiveness, and its recognition of an entire whole in a small piece of matter. It is also Augustan in its animation; the blade of grass is itself changing, light-giving, twinkling. For Augustan poets, as for Hopkins, things *selve*, are selving, and their selving is revealed in changeableness and the "Pied Beauty" of variation. Hopkins, however, emphasizes that "All things counter, original, spare, strange . . . / He fathers-forth whose beauty is past change."[19] Cowper is much less likely than Hopkins, or than an Elizabethan, to stress the *un*-changing quality of God or Heaven. To an Augustan, unchanging means "stagnation," uniform and uncoloured. Augustans look constantly for the fickle, freckled, swift, slow, sweet, sour, adazzle, dim.

The Augustans know as well as Yeats that man is in love with what vanishes, but they emphasize the traditional fact of transitoriness much less than the idea of an object's (or a person's) interesting capacity for change. Identities may alter; the sweetness or sharpness of things can have an attraction in proportion to their potentiality for metamorphosis. Rochester, as usual, strikes notes that should be attended to if we are to hear properly the literature of the age that follows him. In his poems on love he embraces, or pretends to embrace, the fact of change as a good in itself – or, since it is a fact, why not call it a good?

> Since 'tis nature's law to change,
> Constancy alone is strange.
> ("A Dialogue between Strephon and Daphne")

> If I, by miracle, can be,
> This livelong minute true to thee,
> 'Tis all that heaven allows.
> ("Love and Life")

The law of change is something the Augustans observe constantly. Even in passages which strongly illustrate the Augustan poets' love of the observed real in people, places, things – such as the passages cited at the outset of this chapter – we can see that there is much change. Cowper's Crazy Kate was once not crazy; she exhibits the weird results of change. The elegant scene of Belinda's festive tea-party is about to alter, and the objects in that scene are the product of fascinating transformation: a porcelain teacup was once quite literally *"China's* Earth." In Lady Winchilsea's "Nocturnal Reverie" the progress of evening is shown as a process of beautiful and gradual alteration. The fox-glove turns progressively paler as the shadows gradually darken. This process of good change (paradoxical, as here the good is darkness) signals the advent of reversal and freedom. "Tyrant-*Man*" will sleep and a transformed world will exist for a short space, in which the creatures may keep "Their short-liv'd Jubilee" and the soul (more particularly, perhaps, the soul of a woman freed also from "Tyrant-*Man*") may find itself free for peaceful contemplation. But both "Jubilee" and peace last only "Till Morning breaks, and All's confus'd again."

For Augustan poets, it is a miracle if things can be for a livelong minute true to themselves. People, places, objects are ever undergoing transformations. It is these transformations that the poet delights to show, even in the heart of the commonplace event:

Brisk *Susan* whips her Linen from the Rope,
While the first drizzling Show'r is born aslope,
Such is that Sprinkling which some careless Quean
Flirts on you from her Mop, but not so clean.
. . .
Not yet, the Dust had shun'd th'unequal Strife,
But aided by the Wind, fought still for Life;
And wafted with its Foe by violent Gust,
'Twas doubtful which was Rain, and which was Dust.
Ah! where must needy Poet seek for Aid,
When Dust and Rain at once his Coat invade;
Sole Coat, where Dust cemented by the Rain,
Erects the Nap, and leaves a cloudy Stain.

N o w in contiguous Drops the Flood comes down,
Threat'ning with Deluge this *Devoted* Town.
. . .
The Templer spruce, while ev'ry Sprout's a-broach,
Stays till 'tis fair, yet seems to call a Coach.
The tuck'd-up Sempstress walks with hasty Strides,
While Streams run down her oil'd Umbrella's Sides.
(Swift, "A Description of a City Shower," lines 17–38)

In Swift's urban Georgic, we watch a series of minute transformations within the larger progressive transformation of the storm. Dust fights heroically "for life," then rain and dust intermingle. Clothes are whipped off the line and the poet's coat is altered by the new "cement" of dust and rain. The street scene changes under the threat, as the urban populace take actions which they would not have taken without this assault. Some are forced into pretence, others are transformed by the use of strange implements. The whole city streetscape alters until the violent ending gives us the flooded kennels and their mingled contents. Swift is, like Dickens, an incessant animator; everything, even the dust of the streets, is by the poet metamorphosed into life and activity.

The Augustan poets in their use of the classical authors were constantly engaged in transforming the transformers. Swift plays with and alters Virgil. So does Gay in *Trivia*, where he also picks up and alters by comic replacement the stories and storytelling of Ovid. Ovid, the author of *Metamorphoses*, is the great poet of change and transformation; it is something, even in jest, to dare him at his own game. Gay piles on the changes within the poem; we are always on the move, not only in place, but in time. We move, for instance, from London in frosty weather to a memory of London in the year of the Great Frost, when the Thames froze over. This remembered episode in London's recent history is treated fully, with obvious allusion to Virgil's Scythians. But here, Gay points out, it isn't a foreign place that is miraculously strange – it is the heart of London itself which could not resist weird alteration in a transformation scene:

> The Waterman, forlorn along the Shore,
> Pensive reclines upon his useless Oar,
> Sees harness'd Steeds desert the stony Town;
> And wander Roads unstable, not their own:
> Wheels o'er the harden'd Waters smoothly glide,
> And rase with whiten'd Tracks the slipp'ry Tide.
> Here the fat Cook piles high the blazing Fire,
> And scarce the Spit can turn the Steer entire.
> Booths sudden hide the *Thames*, long Streets appear,
> And num'rous Games proclaim the crouded Fair.
>
> (*Trivia* II, lines 361–70)

Paradoxes emphasize the strangeness. But in Gay's description of the Frost Fair (as is not the case with Virgil on his Scythians) none of the objects or people is strange or alien at all. The wonder is to see the normal transformed into the abnormal and still acting as if this were normal. We have horses on water, wheels making tracks on water, fire burning on the tide and streets on the river. Waterman, horses, wheels, cook, spit, booths are all familiar creatures or things and they are all super-Georgically transformed. From this transformation, Gay moves through a mock-luscious transition ("Let Elegiac Lay the Woe relate, / Soft, as the Breath of distant Flutes") to a mock-Ovidian story, in the tale of Doll the fruitwoman who plied her trade at the ice-fair:

> *Doll* ev'ry Day had walk'd these treach'rous Rodes;
> Her Neck grew warpt beneath autumnal Loads
> Of various Fruit; she now a Basket bore,
> That Head, alas! shall Basket bear no more.
> Each Booth she frequent past, in quest of Gain,
> And Boys with pleasure heard her shrilling Strain.
> Ah *Doll!* all Mortals must resign their Breath,
> And Industry it self submit to Death!
> The cracking Crystal yields, she sinks, she dyes,
> Her Head, chopt off, from her lost Shoulders flies:
> Pippins she cry'd, but Death her Voice confounds,
> And Pip-Pip-Pip along the Ice resounds.   (lines 381–92)

There are a number of changes, in both Doll and her treacherous road, that are still within the ordinary course of realistic nature. But what follows has the sensational unrealism of a newspaper's strange stories, while being a complicated joke. Doll's head is chopped off; so is her customary word after its first syllable and the head, like a ball or an apple skidding along, utters "Pip-Pip-Pip" which is her word still trying to be uttered and / or the noise a round object makes bouncing along the ice. The punning with Doll's last recorded syllable alerts us to the various plays on art and nature, narrative and significance within this sequence. The whole of the little story of Doll, this little mock-mythlet, is an outrageous allusion to the Orpheus story as told by Ovid (*Metamorphoses*, Book XI), and by Virgil in *Georgics* IV.[20] Gay's next lines make the allusion clear ("So when the *Thracian* Furies *Orpheus* tore," etc.). The whole series of Gay's transformations beginning with the great frost culminates in this parodic metamorphosis, which metamorphoses Ovid and Virgil. We are given a startling sequence of transformations, both representational and stylistic, moving to a sick joke. Neither London nor the Latin poets are left untransformed.

Swift had already shown what he could do with use and displacement of the Ovidian tale at length. His "Baucis and Philemon" (1709) is a comic replacement both of Ovid's story and Dryden's version of it in *Fables Ancient and Modern*. Dryden had expanded on Ovid's (quite detailed) description of the interior of the peasants' cottage and the food they offered to the disguised gods, but had paid relatively little attention to the alteration of the cottage into the temple. Dryden had also added to the comedy present in Ovid in the description of the good folks' pursuit of their only goose for dinner. But he remained, as a translator, faithful to both the spirit of the tale and its essential structure. Swift, giving us a version of the story in jaunty tetrameters instead of pentameters, stretches all the comedy to breaking point, and makes a very different story. He deals extensively with the transformation of the cottage (here an English rural cottage) into – not a temple, but an Anglican country church. It is this transformation that is the centre of Swift's poem; he fits every detail of a commonplace house into every detail of a commonplace church. Both sides of the equation are excessively ordinary; the fun is in the process of alteration. Here is metamorphosis observed lovingly in comic slow motion:

> They scarce had Spoke; when, fair and soft,
> The Roof began to mount aloft;
> Aloft rose ev'ry Beam and Rafter,
> The heavy Wall climb'd slowly after.
>
> The Chimney widen'd, and grew higher,
> Became a Steeple with a Spire.
> . . .
> The Groaning Chair was seen to crawl
> Like an huge Snail half up the Wall;
> There stuck aloft, in Publick View,
> And with small Change, a Pulpit grew.
> . . .
> A Bedstead of the Antique Mode,
> Compact of Timber many a Load,
> Such as our Grandsires wont to use,
> Was Metamorphos'd into Pews;
> Which still their antient Nature keep;
> By lodging Folks dispos'd to Sleep.
> ("Baucis and Philemon," lines 51–106)

In Ovid's story, and in Dryden's version of it, the poor peasants are given a splendid temple. Swift's couple are not rewarded by anything so grand, nor do they seem to deserve it. Unlike his classical prototype, Swift's Philemon does not ask to serve the gods, but considers his own comfort: "I'm Old, and fain wou'd live at Ease, / Make me the *Parson*, if you please." He and Baucis lead a shabby, respectable, ignorant and leisurely life until, after uncanonical jealousy and quarrels, they are turned into English churchyard yew-trees. We need not believe that the satire on the Anglican Church and its clerics is the main function of the poem, or the reason for it. The point of this parody-Ovidian tale is to be seen in the comic observation of violent and startling change – change which yet arrives at just another grotesque commonplace.

In Augustan poetry we frequently watch vivid changes from state to state in which neither condition can be seen as preferable. Sometimes (but relatively rarely), alteration is decidedly for the better. More frequently it is in some sense for the worse. But the observation of changes can often mean watching protean change for its own sake, seeing a process which has energies in motion rather than upward (or even downward) progression. Pope's Sir Balaam undergoes a vivid metamorphosis from sober Citizen to "man of spirit" who joins "the well-bred cuckolds in St. James's air." Changeable Balaam (unlike unalterable Job) might seem to be proceeding either through an improvement (social elevation) or through a degeneration (good man corrupted). The joke is that his transformations are from commonplace to commonplace. We watch his changes, the alterations from *a* to *b* to *c*, with great enjoyment, without having to be too impressed by any of his phases. A new phase often seems, if appropriate, inadequate to the energies that wreak transformation. Balaam is ironically blessed by storms at sea, which give him "two rich ship-wrecks." The whirlwinds "sweep / The surge" and Balaam enriched now lives up to his new income with the lavishness his limited imagination allows:

> "Live like yourself," was soon my Lady's word;
> And lo! two puddings smoak'd upon the board.
>
> (*Epistle to Bathurst*, lines 359–60)

The state arrived at is, as with Swift's church, interesting in detail but anticlimactic in relation to the impetus that makes the changes. There is a pointed joke in the original Balaam's being "Constant at Church, and Change" for he is constantly changing.

Pope, a great poet of transformation, is fascinated by the human capacity to undergo metamorphosis in ordinary life. The whole of the *Epistle to Cobham* deals with the instability of personality; the same person in the course of his ordinary life, and without any marked difference in outward fortunes, can be widely various. People can take on almost a different nature with each change of company or activity. The same man can be

> Early at Bus'ness, and at Hazard late;
> Mad at a Fox-chace, wise at a Debate;
> Drunk at a Borough, civil at a Ball,
>
> (*Epistle to Cobham*, lines 132–4)

but neither business or hazard, fox-chase or debate, borough meeting or polite ball is really preferable to any of these other situations. It is impossible to

prefer on moral or aesthetic grounds that kind of madness or wisdom, drunkenness or civility. Pope deals with the capacity for alteration of what we now
call "personality" and its variability in response to social pressure. Social
pressure might so govern our behaviour (and our inner reactions as well as
outer) that we do not have any sense of self. The investigation of this possibility, and the emphasis on the importance of social pressure in relation to the
civilized person's idea of the self, make the *Epistle to Cobham* Pope's most truly
philosophical poem. It marks the discovery of a new idea, the strength of what
we now call "conformity." The self, constantly responding to the need to
conform, becomes a tiny and dubious but very mobile entity. The possibility
that we have no real self, that we are all metamorphosis, troubles Pope even as
it fascinates him. He finds in the poem a kind of answer in the Ruling Passion,
though we are, I think, warned not to take that too seriously, and in any case
the Ruling Passion governs eternal changeability, the varieties of individual
absurdity. "Nature well known, no prodigies remain, / Comets are regular,
and Wharton plain" (lines 208–9). But Wharton the variable will be easy to
understand only when comets are fully understood, and he is subject to the
laws of Nature at her wildest in the way that comets are. The individual is
eternally mutable:

> Know, God and Nature only are the same:
> In Man, the judgment shoots at flying game,
> A bird of passage! gone as soon as found,
> Now in the Moon perhaps, now under ground.　　　(lines 154–7)

God may be always the same, but Pope had his doubts about Nature, at least
about the Nature man lives with and in, which is constantly changing. In the
Essay on Man, Pope attempts to deal with the divine order present in the
universe and reflected in human society. But he does this upon discovering
that the world we know in Nature and ourselves is a world of change, and of
differences. In human nature, the passions, strong and opposing, are necessary, like the warring elements in Nature; we need "The lights and shades,
whose well accorded strife / Gives all the strength and colour of our life" (*Essay
on Man* II, lines 121–2). This "strife", which ensures change, will never be
brought to an end. Nature is itself perpetual change, a pattern, as some of the
ancient Greeks had known, of persistent metamorphosis and opposition:

> See plastic Nature working to this end,
> The single atoms each to other tend,
> Attract, attracted to, the next in place
> Form'd and impell'd its neighbour to embrace.
> See Matter next, with various life endu'd,
> Press to one centre still, the gen'ral Good.
> See dying vegetables life sustain,
> See life dissolving vegetate again:
> All forms that perish other forms supply,
> (By turns we catch the vital breath, and die)

> Like bubbles on the sea of Matter born,
> They rise, they break, and to that sea return.
> Nothing is foreign; Parts relate to whole.
>
> > *(Essay on Man* III, lines 9–21)

The Augustans were attracted to the ancient atomic theory as they knew it, chiefly through Lucretius' *De Rerum Natura*. Unlike the Latin poet, they wished to emphasize the divine inspiring spirit of Genesis which brought the atoms together into a cosmos:

> When Nature underneath a heap
>   Of jarring Atomes lay,
> And cou'd not heave her Head,
> The tuneful Voice was heard from high.
>
> > (Dryden, "A Song for St. Cecilia's Day, 1687")

They believed also that there is a divine care working in and through all these atoms in their ceaseless activity. But just the same, the atoms of perpetual motion and alteration make a rather giddy cosmos. This world of incessant changeful activity is exciting rather than consoling. And a society composed of "jarring int'rests" (*Essay on Man* III, line 293) is more interesting than comfortable. When watching by the sickbed of a friend it is no help to know either that the friend's heir will give the economy a boost by spending, or that "All forms that perish other forms supply."

Yet the essence of Pope's belief as expressed in the *Essay on Man*, that the world of changefulness is good for man, is in some deep sense suited to man and he to it, appears to be held by most Augustans. Most of the poets (and other writers too) emphasize change and activity in our selves and in Nature. The religious Cowper says "By ceaseless action all that is subsists" (*The Task* I, line 367). Inactivity, the refusal to change or to acknowledge change, is always a chief sin in the Augustan view. Crabbe's Dinah undergoes a hideous metamorphosis into mean old-maidishness, a state to which she clings unmovingly.[21] When her lover returns she finds her empty life with the goods her inheritance brought her too pleasant to give up. Her pattern of life is the avoidance of activity:

> Silky and soft upon the floor below,
> Th'elastic carpet rose with crimson glow;
>   . . .
> Above her head, all gorgeous to behold,
> A time-piece stood on feet of burnish'd gold;
> A stag's head crest adorn'd the pictur'd case,
> Through the pure chrystal shone th'enamell'd face;
> And, while on brilliants moved the hands of steel,
> It click'd from pray'r to pray'r, from meal to meal.
>
> > (*Tales*, 1812, "Procrastination," lines 162–79)

Crabbe's portrait of Dinah is a presentation of the same kind of empty life more jokingly and lightly given by Prior nearly a century before. Prior's

"Saunt'ring Jack, and Idle Joan" do as little as possible, either good or bad, and avoid the keenness of either pain or pleasure:

> Without Love, Hatred, Joy or Fear,
> They led – a kind of – as it were:
> Nor Wish'd, nor Car'd, nor Laugh'd, nor Cry'd:
> And so They liv'd; and so They dy'd.

("An Epitaph," 1718)[22]

They lived "a kind of – as it were"; certainly not a life. Crabbe's Dinah does not have a life either; her clock is alive but she is not. Her endeavour to stop time by staying herself unalterable is absurd, for she will not be able to evade the final metamorphosis of death. Those hands of steel, though braced on diamonds, are going to cut her off – but she has already cut herself off from life, and it is ridiculous to be dead before one's time. The irony of the human condition as perceived by the Augustans is that we are all change. If we tire of change and try to attain the safety of changelessness, we ask for the impossible, and fall into stagnation. "Do not suffer life to stagnate."[23] Variety is the law of nature:

> The earth was made so various, that the mind
> Of desultory man, studious of change,
> And pleas'd with novelty, might be indulg'd.
> Prospects, however lovely, may be seen
> Till half their beauties fade; the weary sight,
> Too well acquainted with their smiles, slides off,
> Fastidious, seeking less familiar scenes.

(Cowper, *The Task* I, lines 506–12)

According to Cowper, we are not changeable because our environment changes; God made the world a world of change in order to suit us. Man is by essential nature a change-loving being. Even if we are not at the moment in a process of visible change, we want the world about us to change, and get impatient if it does not. What is unaltering, even if lovely, slides off the wearied sight. Our human impatience for variety has caused all the variety in the universe, and is now forever operating in our own individual search for the unfamiliar.

The Augustan poet's job is to entertain his desultory readers with variety and change; he is also, more important, a recorder of the changefulness of the world, and pleases by his ability to live up to that variableness, matching it indeed with his own transformations. He creatively proves the truth of what Cowper says, that the human mind is the source or cause of all variety, and that Nature reflects us. There is therefore nothing that the mind cannot touch, nothing that poetry cannot include. Wit comprehends all, and wit shows its quickness in expressing transformation.

History offers us a probable, if only partial, explanation for the Augustans' interest in change and instability. A period of revolution and very visible alterations in the nature of things is bound to focus the minds of several generations on change, while a belief in change itself helped bring about

revolution. The wit that we associate with the Augustans was formed by
deeply significant political metamorphoses: "When Kings are cup-boarded
like cheese." Civil War ballads already exhibit an interest in that technique of
poetical transformation which enacts metamorphosis – a degenerative
metamorphosis here when "King" becomes "cheese."

Augustan poetic wit is transformational. One of its simplest and most
effective techniques is the substitution of one noun for another, or a cross-
referencing of nouns so that x is in some sense transformed and metamorphosed into y. "Thus, in a Pageant Show, a Plot is made; / And Peace it self is
War in Masquerade." Dryden's couplet turns Pageant Show into Plot and this
pageant-plot becomes the "Peace" which is "War in Masquerade." The
pageant is transforming itself into war, and the war in equal and reverse action
is disguising itself, re-enters in "Masquerade," like a guest at a foolish but
high-class costume party. To take an example from another poet, consider
"Where London's column, pointing at the skies, / Like a tall bully, lifts the
head and lies." "Column" becomes "bully"; the extension of the simile raises
it from mere decoration to the latter phase of a metamorphosis.

The neat, if often complex, substitution of a later noun for an earlier one can
be noted in Augustan prose as well as poetry, e.g. "the same earnestness which
excites them to see a Chinese, would have made them equally proud of a visit
from the rhinoceros" (Goldsmith, *Citizen of the World*).[24] That same impulse to
transform by metamorphosing substitution affects spoken remarks, as it so
often does in Johnson's memorable sayings; the preaching woman is transformed into the dog on its hind legs. Vivid comparison is of course always a
feature of literature – Aristotle thought the metaphor the soul of the poetic art.
But in the Augustans we can see a habitual interest in comparison as transformation, an interest which affects patterns of verse and patterns of prose
sentences which are designed to make the process of metamorphosis both
pointed and surprising. Goldsmith's Londoners are transformed in the second
part of his sentence into a group "proud of a visit" from a monster – and
London becomes imaginatively transformed, momentarily, into a place where
people are proud of visits from a rhinoceros. But it is the poet who can give us
the most variety, and work the most effective and compact transformations.

The Augustan poet does work such compact transformations, both on the
small scale and on the large; he leaves no turn unturned. The combination of
many minutely observed transformations can make a large fantastic, even
phantasmagoric, scene – as we can see almost anywhere in Pope. Timon's
villa is fantastic, displaying as it does the result of a metamorphosis wrought
on the innocent land by pride, and the poet makes us see how extravagantly
awful the whole is by making us see what has happened to individual objects.
Objects have literally metamorphosed, changed shape; as their shape-
changing is a product of Timon's mind and will, the result is unhandsome:
"Trees cut to Statues, Statues thick as trees." If any good is to be wrought
upon this dissonant fantasia which is Timon's creation, it will have to be done

through yet another metamorphosis, the change brought about by the irresistible energies of Nature herself, who works changes:

> Another age shall see the golden Ear
> Imbrown the Slope, and nod on the Parterre,
> Deep Harvests bury all his pride has plann'd,
> And laughing Ceres re-assume the land.

(Epistle to Burlington, lines 173–6)

What might seem to be a degenerative process, a sad change in the loss of the
buildings and gardens shaped and erected by man, is here celebrated as a
welcome relief. The disappearance of Timon's villa is a victory. The burial of
"pride" in "Deep Harvests" (where it will be deeply buried) is entirely
desirable; it is a rightful triumph over the painstaking stupid processes of
Timon's own transformation-making, when he assumed the right to take over
arable land for his trifling magnificence. Pope here reverses a theme familiar to
us in the poetry of many nations and ages, the lament over transience. "Ubi
sunt qui ante nos / in mundo fuere?" "Where are they before us weren?" If
people of the future should ask such a question about Timon, the answer will
be the eternal answer, "he is gone," but with the addition "and a good thing
too." Pope surprisingly imagines it as one of the consolations of life that many
of our works, like ourselves, will disappear without trace. Some things *ought* to
disappear. "Eripitur persona, manet res": the person is taken, the thing
remains – a plangent thought, but not here. Not only will the person go, but the
thing will go also, in the world's perpetual whirling pattern of change – *and* we
can sometimes take comfort at the thought. If nothing gold can stay, nothing
heavy and pompous can stay either. Life's pattern of transformations, the
world's impermanence, is here defiantly praised – and generously praised, for
the good to be achieved depends on the poet's disappearing too, with all his
generation, in order to allow time to bring in its revenges. But the poet can
forestall time; the poet's wit can create the future metamorphosis in the present
poem.

The Augustan poet most customarily and typically presents himself as the
speaker, the sole unifying point in his self-made genre and as the single point of
vantage where all the metamorphoses and changes fall clearly on the sight. He
stands alone (but with us his readers) in a world of dazzling change. He
records change and also creates it. His poem undergoes stylistic alterations,
and alterations in mood and tone, which capture the kaleidoscopic variety
which he assures us is the full reality. Persons, places and objects, which are all
attracted in enormous numbers into his poem like filings to a magnet or
(Pope's metaphor) like flies into amber, are capable at any moment of subtle or
extreme variation. Not only are there many different objects, but each object
varies from its former self from moment to moment. Augustan objects can be
seen in a different light as they change, or as we move. Newton's theories about
light (like his other theories of motion, attraction and the void) suited the

Augustan mind and interests very well.[25] (It is amazingly fortunate that in each age we get the scientific theories that do suit us.) Newton showed that the white light we think we know is complex and various, the phase of a metamorphosis combining seven other things, a phase which may be metamorphosed back again (as with the rainbow). He had made us see and imagine what Thomson called "The various Twine of Light, by thee [Newton] disclos'd / From the white mingling Maze" ("Spring," lines 211–12). Newton's theory chimes in agreeably with the Augustans' sense of the inner variation of things, of all things trying to become something else, as well as with their love of things which are mixed rather than pure.

For Thomson, light is intensely changeable and a cause of change. The pleasures of looking at landscape are the pleasures of seeing the changes incessantly made by light in relation to the perceiving "I"/eye.

> the downward Sun
> Looks out, effulgent, from amid the Flush
> Of broken Clouds, gay-shifting to his Beam.
> The rapid Radiance instantaneous strikes
> Th'illumin'd Mountain, thro' the Forest streams,
> Shakes on the Floods, and in a yellow Mist,
> Far smoking o'er th'interminable Plain,
> In twinkling Myriads lights the dewy Gems.
>
> ("Spring," lines 189–96)

But the viewing eye is not always comfortable with the changes of light, as in summer's mid-day glare:

> O'er Heaven and Earth, far as the ranging Eye
> Can sweep, a dazling Deluge reigns; and all
> From Pole to Pole is undistinguish'd Blaze.
> In vain the Sight, dejected to the Ground,
> Stoops for Relief; thence hot ascending Steams
> And keen Reflection pain.
>
> ("Summer," lines 434–9)

And sometimes the visual effects received or half-created by the eye are perturbing and phantasmic:

> A faint erroneous Ray,
> Glanc'd from th'imperfect Surfaces of Things,
> Flings half an Image on the straining Eye;
> While wavering Woods, and Villages, and Streams,
> And Rocks, and Mountain-tops, that long retain'd
> Th'ascending Gleam, are all one swimming Scene,
> Uncertain if beheld.
>
> ("Summer," lines 1687–93)

Both the eye and Nature waver; nothing can be counted upon to be constant, including the act of seeing. To observe, mentally or physically, is to experience vicissitude. The poet as central "I"/eye must accept various transformations.

One may even see oneself abruptly metamorphosed, as Cowper does on viewing the world and inadvertently himself on a winter's morning:

'Tis morning; and the sun, with ruddy orb
Ascending, fires th'horizon: while the clouds,
That crowd away before the driving wind,
More ardent as the disk emerges more,
Resemble most some city in a blaze,
Seen through the leafless wood. His slanting ray
Slides ineffectual down the snowy vale,
And, tinging all with his own rosy hue,
From ev'ry herb and ev'ry spiry blade
Stretches a length of shadow o'er the field.
Mine, spindling into longitude immense,
In spite of gravity, and sage remark
That I myself am but a fleeting shade,
Provokes me to a smile. With eye askance
I view the muscular proportion'd limb
Transform'd to a lean shank. The shapeless pair,
As they design'd to mock me, at my side
Take step for step; and, as I near approach
The cottage, walk along the plaster'd wall,
Prepost'rous sight! the legs without the man.

(*The Task* v, lines 1–20)

This passage describes most energetic changes. Clouds crowd together to escape the wind; they turn into a blazing city seen through the bare trees. The spears of grass sticking up above the now-pink snow cast long shadows over the field. The very act of seeing, of being a perceiver and receiving impressions through the senses into the mind, is fantastically metamorphosing. The viewer finds himself a participant in the process of change he sees, he is worked upon. His legs transformed into spindly shapelessness both accompany him and leave him as they walk along the white outside wall of the cottage; the peculiar shadow effect makes it seem as if Cowper had half a *doppelgänger*. "Prepost'rous sight!" Even as nature goes about her quiet daily affairs, we can be made into complicated monsters. Transformation scenes are the order of the theatre of Nature. The poet here shows his understanding of and delight in that process, his willingness to participate in it. And of course the passage exhibits his own ability to create the metamorphosis for us.

In city and in country, in Nature and in Man, change reigns. The Augustan poet's world is fundamentally and not merely occasionally surreal, because objects and people are unstable, always altering, and it is the job of art to capture that instability. That *Alice in Wonderland* quality I referred to earlier applies not just to the grand fantasia, the full charivari, but also to almost every topic – that is, to what fundamental Augustan poetic practices are designed to present. The poets like Swift and Gay who play with Ovidian story do so not only to outdo Ovid but to point out that the ordinary is extraordinary, and that all things are constantly transmogrified. There's no guarantee against metamorphosis at any moment. Mind may turn to Moss, Borough to Ball, column to bully, substance to shadow and shadow to substance.

Metamorphosis in the poetry differs from charivari. Metamorphosis is habitual; charivari is occasional. The one is a process, the other a *topos*. Metamorphosis is an aspect of charivari, or of the description of it, but charivari need not be present in all these metamorphoses. Yet the animation within every metamorphosis, as well as its disjunction from the regular or predictable ("wavering Woods, and Villages," "the legs without the man"), promises or threatens that at some point we will see everything joined together in a wild spree of unrestrained activity. Charivari fulfils the tendency of Augustan poetry by openly celebrating (while parodying) the love of change. The charivari *topos* is on each occasion a large-scale entry into the world of the poem of creatures formally defying the conditions of custom and order, and actively honouring and asserting their relation to metamorphosis. There is not, after all, an enormous distance between individual instances of metamorphosis and disjunction ("the shapeless pair . . . walk along the plaster'd wall") and the communal charivari of strange relations, demonstrated in Butler's and Hogarth's Skimmington, or the legs that disappear into Fleet ditch ("Prepost'rous sight!"), in Dulness's heroic games.

When it is present, the charivari very forcefully and disturbingly (as in the *Dunciad*) reminds us what Augustan poetry is about. It introduces an other world, which has "re-assumed," to use Pope's phrase about Ceres' triumph (and his spelling of the word), the land and the control over ordinary versions of things. There is no assurance that there is any accessible alternative, any good past to go back to or even any good future that can positively be worked for. The poets themselves, however satirically they use the *topos*, are accomplices in the charivari they create. They show it to us at length and with a kind of love, for this violent explosion of energy, of shape-changing, shows us what is to be seen even in the mad procession's absence: The poet accepts disjunction and recombination. Through his power of "Fancy" and through his wit he is able to record the deep truth about the nature of things, the unmaking and remaking of things, including the untuning of the sky, the conflagration of the universe. Reality is always cracking up and admitting new realities, or possibilities. The poet, unflinching – even delighted – in the face of all change, proves himself a loyal citizen of a divine creation and a suitable creator within it.

VI

Metamorphosis, pleasure and pain: the threat of the end

The Augustan poets do not seem to yearn, like Spenser, for the steadfast pillars of Eternity nor do they desire, with Shelley, Eternity's white radiance. The "dome of many-coloured glass" would seem preferable, in Augustan opinion, to a still and steady light. The human mind (or soul) was not made for such perfect stagnation. Edward Young, in whom the characteristic Augustan horror of monotony is clearly visible, stresses the idea that Virtue "gives / To Life's sick, nauseous *Iteration* Change".

> Noble minds
> Which relish Fruits unripen'd by the *Sun*,
> Make their Days Various; various as the Dies
> On the Dove's Neck, which wanton in *his* rays.
> On Minds of Dove-like innocence possest,
> On lightened Minds that bask in Virtue's beams,
> Nothing hangs Tedious, nothing old revolves . . .
> *(Night-Thoughts: Night the Third. Narcissa)*[1]

Change and iridescence are naturally associated with the good; Young can think of no better way of converting readers to virtue than by assuring them it will make existence "Various," and rid them of what is "Tedious" and "old." Life, physical and spiritual, is meant to be variable and many-coloured.

If Life is colourful, so ought literature to be. Poetry, like the perceiving mind, should capture the pleasures of variety. We should attune ourselves to Nature whose variety, as Cowper says, was made to satisfy our own deep love of novelty. Even Johnson can advise us, on occasion, to be chameleons:

There are animals that borrow their colour from the neighbouring body, and, consequently, vary their hue as they happen to change their place. In like manner, it ought to be the endeavour of every man to derive his reflections from the objects about him; for it is to no purpose that he alters his position, if his attention continues fixed to the same point. The mind should be kept open to the access of every new idea, and so far disengaged from the predominance of particular thought, as easily to accommodate itself to occasional entertainment.

(Rambler, No. 5)

Johnson is here talking about a spring walk, but his lesson has wider implications. The human mind should be prepared to vary with the various, to be hospitable to "every new idea" or image; a mind that attempts not to do

159

this, that tries to remain fixed, is unhealthy, going against nature. Mind should change colour. Poetry can make us see the varying and the variegated, treating us to the colour of life. It is very noticeable that Augustan poetry is certainly, and in the most literal sense, very colourful – full of blues and yellows and reds and purples and greens. There is, for instance, the well-known pheasant painted in words by Pope:

> Ah! what avail his glossie, varying Dyes,
> His Purple Crest, and Scarlet-circled Eyes,
> The vivid Green his shining Plumes unfold;
> His painted Wings, and Breast that flames with Gold?
>
> (*Windsor Forest*, lines 115–18)

Colour-words are often modified with other words that capture the exact quality of the hue (such as Butler's "Orenge-Tawny Slime") or the degree and kind of light reflected from the colourful object, in words like "shining." Both such modifications can be observed in Dryden's (pre-*Opticks*) translation of Virgil, e.g. "And set soft Hyacinths with Iron blue, / To shade marsh Marigolds of shining Hue." Thomson, whose interest in colour and light has often been noticed, excels in colour representation, as in his celebration of sunlight's power both to ripen the gems in the earth (an old theory that still held) and to give them (Newtonianly) the colours that we see:

> The lively Diamond drinks thy purest Rays,
> Collected Light, compact;
> . . .
> At thee the Ruby lights its deepening Glow,
> And with a waving Radiance inward flames.
> From thee the Saphire, solid Ether, takes
> Its Hue cerulean; and, of evening Tinct,
> The purple-streaming Amethyst is thine.
> With thy own Smile the yellow Topaz burns.
> Nor deeper Verdure dyes the Robe of Spring,
> When first she gives it to the southern Gale,
> Than the green Emerald shows. But, all combin'd,
> Thick thro' the whitening Opal play thy Beams;
> Or, flying several from its Surface, form
> A trembling Variance of revolving Hues,
> As the Site varies in the Gazer's Hand.
>
> ("Summer," lines 142–59)

As Nicolson notes, "All the colors come together in the 'whitening opal,' which dimly reflects each of them, and which begins to return them to the white light from which they were derived."[2] But the opal is valued, like the "lively Diamond," for its capacity to change colour from moment to moment. It is not its whiteness that makes its value and fascination, but its "trembling Variance of revolving Hues"; the gazer can see in miniature in the palm of his hand all the variety of colour and the motion of light that makes us rejoice in the world.

Thomson was not the only poet to con and catalogue the colours of Newton's spectrum, or elaborate them in the hues of gems and flowers. That the Augustan poets were so near numbering the streaks on their tulips is probably one of the reasons Johnson has Imlac warn against the practice. Colour, variegated colour, is almost an Augustan poetic obsession. Colour represents one of the pleasures of living and perceiving – of being an "I" that is perceiving eye; it is also one of the purest delights we gain from living in a world of change and mingling.

The poet has the responsibility for imitating, representing, the extra-ordinary colourful world. Thomson expresses a sense of ecstasy in seeing, and of frustration in trying to find a language to capture what he sees:

> But who can paint
> Like Nature? Can Imagination boast,
> Amid its gay Creation, Hues like hers?
> Or can it mix them with that matchless Skill,
> And lose them in each other, as appears
> In every Bud that blows? If Fancy then
> Unequal fails beneath the pleasing Task;
> Ah what shall Language do? Ah where find Words
> Ting'd with so many Colours; and whose Power,
> To Life approaching, may perfume my Lays
> With that fine Oil, those aromatic Gales,
> That inexhaustive flow continual round?

("Spring," lines 468–79)

Thomson's frustration is the equivalent of that expressed by other poets (Elizabeth Rowe for a contemporary example[3]) who are trying to describe Heaven. Nature is ineffable. Language is not various enough to keep up with it. Nature, Thomson says, is so full of changes, creating such new mixtures in infinite variety, that Imagination, Fancy, Language quail before her power. The sense experiences she offers are more vivid and multiple than even Fancy can grasp, and if Fancy fails in the effort, what can mere Language do? Words should have "so many Colours" to express Nature; there isn't yet a language colourful enough, varied enough or full enough. The high pleasures which Augustan vision and Augustan poetry offer here seem difficult to achieve and almost impossible to sustain; pleasure itself is a task that wearies and bemuses. Everything is too full and too varying. The best Augustan poetry dwells lovingly on variation, on change and transformation, and approaches multi-coloured reality with language of many colours. But Thomson's passage indicates the trials involved. The entertainment offered by Augustan poetry at its best demands strenuous exertion of energy for both reader and for poet – but particularly of course for the poet. The poet tries to live up to that impossible demand, to reproduce the reality of creation, in its abundance and self-perpetuating variety. Nature is "inexhaustive" but the poet can become exhausted. We feel here too the weight of living that Augustan life, which entails always watching and participating in an endless cycle of changes, of strange transformations and continual motion.

The power that makes change and motion is variously seen in Augustan poetry. It may be divine, like Thomson's Light:

> Efflux divine! Nature's resplendent Robe!
> Without whose vesting Beauty all were wrapt
> In unessential Gloom; and thou, O Sun!
> Soul of surrounding Worlds! in whom best seen
> Shines out thy Maker! may I sing of thee?
> 'Tis by thy secret, strong, attractive Force,
> As with a Chain indissoluble bound,
> Thy System rolls entire . . .
> . . .
> How many Forms of Being wait on thee!
> Inhaling Spirit; from th'unfetter'd Mind,
> By these sublim'd, down to the daily Race,
> The mixing Myriads of thy setting beam.
>
> ("Summer," lines 92–111)[4]

But Pope's Dulness presents another secret, strong, attractive force, also presiding over variety, mixture and changefulness:

> All these, and more, the cloud-compelling Queen
> Beholds thro' fogs, that magnify the scene.
> She, tinsel'd o'er in robes of varying hues,
> With self-applause her wild creation views;
> Sees momentary monsters rise and fall,
> And with her own fools-colours gilds them all.
>
> (*Dunciad* I, lines 79–84)

Dulness too gives colour and variety and life, though hers is a sort of anti-life anti-matter. Yet, there certainly is a perverse majesty in the powers of Dulness; while Thomson's Sun also sees its own "momentary monsters," the mixing Myriads of transient insect life. Both "high" and "low" meet in the re-forming metamorphosing world of the Augustans. At one level we can say the simple and obvious. Thomson is celebrating Light, which gives beauty to the cosmos and is a good thing, whereas Pope is ironically pointing out the confused pseudo-power of Dulness, which produces the useless horrors of bad literature. But there is more to the matter than that; we find at such points an ambiguity in the Augustan perception of that which is the source of creations. The poets are of two minds about the exhausting unstoppable power which works beneath all the visible change and makes life iridescent and mobile. Thomson expresses the obscene side of the source of imagery, mixture and change in his satiric-comic picture of the *"lubber Power"* which urges the country squires to booze it up, and transforms what they sense in their drunkenness:

> earnest, brimming Bowls
> Lave every Soul, the Table floating round,
> And Pavement, faithless to the fuddled Foot.
> Thus as they swim in mutual Swill, the Talk,
> Vociferous at once from twenty Tongues,
> Reels fast from Theme to Theme . . .
> . . .
> So gradual sinks their Mirth. Their feeble Tongues,
> Unable to take up the cumbrous Word,
> Lie quite dissolv'd. Before their maudlin Eyes,
> Seen dim and blue, the double Tapers dance,
> Like the Sun wading thro' the misty Sky.
> Then, sliding soft, they drop. Confus'd above,
> Glasses and Bottles, Pipes and Gazeteers,
> As if the Table even itself was drunk,
> Lie a wet broken Scene; and wide, below,
> Is heap'd the social Slaughter; where astride
> The *lubber Power* in filthy Triumph sits,
> Slumbrous . . .

("Autumn," lines 535–62)

Writers had long noticed the double vision caused by drunkenness; Horace mentions it.[5] But no one had given the perception the detailed attention Thomson gives it here. Drunkenness becomes ominously strong and fascinating; it governs objects, and everything seems caught by it ("As if the Table even itself was drunk"). The poet presents it as a transforming Power. The monstrous transformation process has its own fascination, and cheerfulness as well as variety triumphs until the dead end. As for what the drunkards do under this Power – is it so different from what the poet does? They feel language, "the cumbrous Word," fail them; so at times does he. Their discourse "Reels fast from Theme to Theme"; so does that of James Thomson in *The Seasons*. The *"lubber Power"* does not seem so different from the true powers of vision, imagination and poetry.

As everyone has noticed, Augustan poets frequently employ personifications, and (what now seems to some even more strange) readers of the time evidently enjoyed them. A mid-century critic, presumably Goldsmith, alluding to Thomson's lines

> O Vale of Bliss! O softly-swelling Hills!
> On which the *Power of Cultivation* lies,
> And joys to see the Wonders of his Toil

("Summer," lines 1435–7)

comments

We cannot conceive a more beautiful image than that of the Genius of Agriculture, distinguished by the implements of his art, imbrowned with labour, glowing with health, crowned with a garland of foliage, flowers, and fruit, lying stretched at his ease on the brow of a gently swelling hill, and contemplating with pleasure the happy effects of his own industry.

This is a lot of accessory detail to give the "*Power of Cultivation.*" Donald Davie has said the critic "probably contributes nothing that was not in Thomson's intention. For Thomson could count on finding in his readers a ready allegorical imagination, such as seems lost to us to-day. The loss is certainly ours."[6] It might be added that one of the things that inhibits our reacquiring such an "allegorical imagination" is the insistence of editors of the nineteenth and twentieth centuries on getting rid of eighteenth-century capitals, italics and other expressive signs. If we have to read Thomson in modernized pages, the loss is certainly ours. It is true that such a passage of criticism shows how personifications could be read and responded to. The "*Power of Cultivation*" (a different thing from the power of cultivation) lived in this reader's memory. His allegorical imagination is also in tune with the spirit of Kent's illustrations of *The Seasons.*[7] I think myself that the critic's reading is slightly too pretty for the passage of Thomson. It eliminates the sexuality which is certainly present in Thomson's language, and too many accoutrements embarrass rather than enhance Thomson's *Power*. Thomson rarely softens to the pretty or the charming.

Eighteenth-century readers were accessible to such embodiments of energies. Personifications were real and significant presences. Artists (who were also readers) even drew them so that other readers could either see more clearly or compare their own vision with that of the artist. As we have seen, Hayman drew Dulness (Fig. 9) and Wale the Knight of Industry (Fig. 14). Richard Bentley, Walpole's protégé, who worked closely with Gray over the *Designs by Mr. R. Bentley, for Six Poems by Mr. T. Gray* (1753), was a very intelligent artistic reader of Gray's work.[8] He provides in his illustration for the "Ode on a Distant Prospect of Eton College" (Fig. 16) one of the finest commentaries on the meaning of such allegorical presences in his rendition of a number of the personifications alluded to so feelingly by Gray within a poem that sorrowfully observes the power of the Powers over human life. Gray laments the fatal metamorphoses that wait on us all from the time of our innocent childhood – when all activity is good activity, and pleasure has not yet known the mixture of pleasure and pain which marks adult thought:

> Alas, regardless of their doom,
> The little victims play!
> No sense have they of ills to come,
> Nor care beyond to-day:
> Yet see how all around 'em wait
> The Ministers of human fate,
> And black Misfortune's baleful train!
> Ah, shew them where in ambush stand
> To seize their prey the murth'rous band!
> Ah, tell them, they are men! (lines 51–60)

The picture shows us the innocent children at play, not knowing the truth, the terrible secret, that "they are men" and thus condemned to pain – the poem

Fig. 16

concludes they will know it soon enough. Bentley's children, in a nakedness
not generally characteristic of the playing fields of Eton, are rendered as both
real and universal (as they are in the poem). The nakedness recreates them as
partially personifications themselves. Beside them, in the same frame, at the
same level, and with equal solidity of drawing, is the natural presence of Father

Thames, who has seen "Full many a sprightly race / Disporting on [his] margent green." Benign, pensive and detached, he watches the children who cleave his "glassy wave," play with "the captive linnet" or "chase the rolling circle's speed." Above this group and unseen by them is another group, less solid and undoubtedly menacing. The passions, misfortune and death are holding a charivari of their own, and are moving in over the landscape, apparently choosing their targets in the regardless victims.

Bentley has made an architectural frame for his picture, holding it within (as Walpole's "Explanation" says) "terms representing Jealousy and Madness."[9] The terms on their hard columns compress the children within an enclosure of which they in their freedom are not aware. The figures of Jealousy and Madness seem to metamorphose from stone to flesh as solid as that of the children and the river-god; they unite the upper and lower portions of the picture, that is the real and the symbolic, the natural and allegorical, the present and future – and make us feel that all these are one. They refuse to remain statuesque, but steadily become animate. Madness is particularly threatening, as she turns outward to us and seems to be about to include us in her baleful glance. (It must be acknowledged that in Bentley's picture all the good is innocent male while most of the ills are female.) In the construction and use of the "terms" we are led from monumental figures and the idea of decorative traditions to free and mobile figures, from imagined sculpting of inanimate object to soft flesh to fearful powers. Bentley is an elegant and embellishing artist, but he makes certain we know that the figures Gray refers to in capital letters are no mere figures of speech. What seems at first decorative becomes active, capable of wreaking change – and havoc. The picture reminds us that Personification is not decoration.

The Augustan love of personification was not the effect of a mild liking for a shallow artifice. The use of personification, as of any other literary device, can degenerate. It would seem, however, that the Augustans' particular discovery of personification is an aspect of the Augustan sense of what is powerful and changeable and capable of making change. The Personifications are all agents of metamorphosis, the energies which make metamorphosis inevitable. In them we have momentary glimpses – often somewhat painful glimpses – of the energies of existence. Gray's Misfortune, Jealousy, Age are powers, like Thomson's *"lubber Power"* or *"Power of Cultivation."*

When they are not mere flat instant statements, the Personifications of Augustan poetry often embody not only energy but the two-edged effects of the energies of Nature or the mind. Chatterton jokingly begins "Resignation" (1770), a satire on politicians, with the punning line, "Hail Resignation hail ambiguous Dame." But a number of these personifications could be hailed as ambiguous. Collins, taking his cue from Aristotle and paying tribute to the dramatists, wrote two companion *Odes* (1746), one to Pity and the other to Fear. He is of course trying to investigate the puzzling aesthetic question of how such emotions can be pleasurable when incited and enacted in art. Pity is

the softer of these two passions, gently pleasing (like the Beautiful) in contrast
to her sublime counterpart. So we might think – but a life in Pity's temple
sounds debilitating, if sexually intense.

> There let me oft, retir'd by Day,
> In Dreams of Passion melt away,
>   Allow'd with Thee to dwell.

("Ode to Pity," lines 37–9)

Fear seems really fearful as well as fearsome:

> Thou, to whom the World unknown
> With all its shadowy Shapes is shown;
> Who see'st appall'd th'unreal Scene,
> While Fancy lifts the Veil between:
>   Ah *Fear*! Ah frantic *Fear*!
>   I see, I see Thee near.
> I know thy hurried Step, thy haggard Eye!
> Like Thee I start, like Thee disorder'd fly,
> For lo what *Monsters* in thy Train appear!
> *Danger*, whose Limbs of Giant Mold
> What mortal Eye can fix'd behold?
> Who stalks his Round, an hideous Form,
> Howling amidst the Midnight Storm,
> Or throws him on the ridgy Steep
> Of some loose hanging Rock to sleep:
> And with him thousand Phantoms join'd,
> Who prompt to Deeds accurs'd the Mind:
> And those, the Fiends, who near allied,
> O'er Natures Wounds, and Wrecks preside;
> Whilst *Vengeance*, in the lurid Air,
> Lifts her red Arm, expos'd and bare.

("Ode to Fear," lines 1–21)

Who can doubt that gigantic *Danger* and red-tinged *Vengeance* are *powers*?
Danger moves about and then rests in the manner of Thomson's lubber Power
or Power of Cultivation, having a particular affinity with the latter, as Danger
also rests on and commands a landscape. Piercing through the visionary
"Veil" here means seeing (like a Radcliffe heroine) something almost unbear-
ably awful. Fancy leads to Fear; we come upon *Monsters* – a favourite Augustan
word for something we are commonly required to see in Augustan literary art.
Yet of course the energies of Danger and Vengeance have an awful attraction,
as does Fear herself, an attraction acknowledged in the latter part of the poem.
There the poet addresses Fear, the "mad Nymph" who sitting in her "haunted
Cell" of murder or in her sea-cave "'Gainst which the big Waves beat,"
listening to "drowning Sea-men's Cries in Tempests brought," has a fascination all her own as well as gifts only she can give. The poet sues, amorously, to
the "Nymph" for her favours:

> Dark Pow'r, with sudd'ring meek submitted Thought
> Be mine, to read the Visions old,
> Which thy awak'ning Bards have told.   (lines 53–5)

There is a power of mind, the "Dark Pow'r," which the poet would not be without, which he craves even while he shudders. Hail Fear, hail ambiguous Dame. In Augustan literature, any approach to the central sources of the energies of life or of art, or of the creative powers of the poet's mind, takes us toward something monstrous. It is not only the sleep of Reason that produces monsters. If we look too closely into the causal energies which move this varying world, we must expect to be partly appalled. The universe is haunted by metamorphosis, and the metamorphosing *powers*, including even Fancy herself, are monstrous in themselves or lead to monsters. It is as if, to paraphrase Shelley, the awful shadow of some obscene power hovers over all this change and creativity. The fount of all this transformation, this iridescent instability and free play of energies, may be divine, but one aspect of it is to human sight dismaying and shows us the low and the terrible.

The Augustans are rarely willing to ignore this other side which, like Pope's Cave of Spleen and the "Strange Phantoms" both "Dreadful" and "bright" encountered there, can tell us something about ourselves, our imagination and our world. In this matter the poets are certainly indebted to classical literature. As well as displaying the epic Hades, Latin poets repeatedly entertain us with visions of undersea grots (like Cyrene's home in *Georgics* iv) and underground caverns (like the home of Morpheus in *Metamorphoses* xi, from which the Cave of Spleen is derived). Later poets such as Spenser had amplified the tradition upon which the Augustans draw repeatedly, with their own interest (sometimes it seems almost an obsessive interest) in the underworld of the under-consciousness. In a period when English gardeners introduced open spaces and then contrasted them with enclosed or inverted ones, with hermitages and grottoes, the English Augustan poets seldom lose a chance of showing us what lies *medio in antro* – though the cave may be presented as a garret room, prison cell, or room in Bedlam. What is to be found in these cavernous retreats is not emptiness but unfamiliar potencies. The illustration by Du Guernier of *The Rape of the Lock*, Canto iv, another representation of a personification, recognizes Spleen as a comic Power but as a Power nevertheless (see Fig. 17). The picture reflects the poem faithfully in its surreal effects as it displays the processes of metamorphosis in relation to convolutions of interesting darkness, a darkness which seems to possess a careless fecundity in producing monsters. There is a bright patch in the midst of this darkness, a diagonal rush almost like the stream in Blake's illustration of the Cimmerian vale in *Night-Thoughts* (see Fig. 18). In Du Guernier's picture, Spleen and her attendants brood in a rather bored fashion over monstrous births and re-formings, while in Blake's illustration Darkness with his raven wing broods half-invisibly over disappearances.[10] But the poets are in the same tradition, and their illustrators,

Fig. 17

> *54*
>
> Where darkness, brooding o'er unfinish'd fates
> With raven wing incumbent, waits the day,
> Dread day ! that interdicts all future change!
> That subterranean world, that land of ruin !
> Fit walk, LORENZO, for proud human thought!
> There let my thought expatiate ; and explore
> Balsamic truths, and healing sentiments
> Of all most wanted, and most welcome here.
> For gay LORENZO's sake, and for thy own
> My soul ! " The fruits of dying friends survey ;
> " Expose the vain of life ; weigh life and death ;
> " Give death his eulogy ; thy fear subdue ;
> " And labour that first palm of noble minds—
> " A manly scorn of terror from the tomb :"
> This harvest reap from thy NARCISSA's grave.
>
> As poets feign'd, from Ajax' streaming blood
> Arose, with grief inscribed, a mournful flower ;
> Let wisdom blossom from my mortal wound.
> And first, of dying friends ; what fruit from these ?
> It brings us more than triple aid ; an aid
> To chase our thoughtlessness, fear, pride, and guilt.
>
> Our dying friends come o'er us like a cloud,
> To damp our brainless ardours, and abate
> That glare of life which often blinds the wise:
> Our dying friends are pioneers, to smooth
> Our rugged pass to death ; to break those bars
> Of terror and abhorrence nature throws
> Cross our obstructed way ; and thus to make
> Welcome as safe our port from every storm :
> Each friend by fate snatch'd from us, is a plume

Fig. 18

too. Pope and Young, Du Guernier and Blake are all consciously members of
that Augustan universe of persistent change of all forms: "Like bubbles on the
sea of Matter born, / They rise, they break ..." Du Guernier, whose picture
mingles pain and pleasure for the viewer in a remarkable manner, has
presented two perishable forms of potential being in the two little shapeless
and unnameable creatures (they look bubbly and we think of them as slimy) in
the bright middle patch. In their metamorphosis they have not found any final
form; these two little snarling Nothings are peculiarly horrible. As the illus-

trators knew, comic personifications, like Spleen or Dulness, can be significant expressions of the perverse sublime. Even the most benevolent of Augustan personifications are capable of giving a frisson to the prepared reader, as forces made momentarily visible, and arousing pleasure or awe as they make themselves known. They represent what is underneath or within the objects we see, whether crazed beggars or china teacups, noisy rooks or ship-wrecks, house-bearing snails or whitening opals.

As a passage like Thomson's catalogue of jewels illustrates, the Augustan poets exhibit a love of sensuous pleasure in their poetry, which like that of Elizabethans, gives a high place to pleasure. At moments the poets can even sound rather like Elizabethans, as Smart purposely does in his "A Noon-Piece":

> Their scythes upon the adverse bank
> Glitter 'mongst th'entangled trees,
> Where the hazles form a rank,
> And court'sy to the courting breeze.
> . . .
> On a bank of fragrant thyme,
> Beneath yon stately, shadowy pine,
> We'll with well-disguised hook
> Cheat the tenants of the brook;
> Or where coy Daphne's thickest shade
> Drives amorous Phoebus from the glade,
> There read Sidney's high-wrought stories
> Of ladies charms, and heroes glories.
> ("A Noon-Piece Or, The Mowers at Dinner")

Only the patronizing tone about the *Arcadia* gives the game away here. Moments of Elizabethan play with richness ("For me the Balm shall bleed, and Amber flow, / The Coral redden, and the Ruby glow") or even a mock-Elizabethan sumptuousness come naturally to the Augustans. But with all the glitter and softness and colour and fragrance in the Augustans' poetry, the love of pleasure in their works is closely allied to a sense of pain, or the possibility of pain. The intensity of the one is related to the intensity of the other. In Early Augustan, i.e. Restoration, poetry, the connection of pain and pleasure is most often and most explicitly produced in connection with love and sex:

> Pains of Love be sweeter far
> Than all other Pleasures are
> (Dryden, Song from *Tyrannick Love*, 1670: "Ah how sweet it is to love")

> *Cupid* in Shape of a Swayn did appear,
> He saw the sad wound, and in pity drew near,
> Then show'd her his Arrow, and bid her not fear,
> For the pain was no more than a Maiden may bear;
> When the balm was infus'd she was not at a loss,
> What they meant by their sighing & kissing so close.
> (Dryden, "A New Song," *Sylvae*, 1685)

But poetic images in which ideas of pleasure and pain lie close together are to be found in the discursive and argumentative poetry of the Restoration, as when Dryden in *Astraea Redux* makes the whiteness of "th'approaching cliffes of *Albion*" into the white sheet of public "penitence and sorrow" (lines 250–5), or as when in *Religio Laici* he satirically refers to the Puritan preachers' onslaught on the Bible: "The tender Page with horney Fists was gaul'd" (line 404). Rochester, in what is probably his most famous poem, creates a landscape of torment for that deluded traveller who insists on following Reason, that pleasure-promising shiny *ignis fatuus*. The *ignis fatuus* itself, a popular image with Restoration poets, combines the beautiful and the unpleasant in the shine and glow of marsh gas.

As the age proceeds, the experience of mixed pleasure and pain becomes a more overt topic. In mid-Augustan poetry the close relation of pleasure and pain is observed almost universally, and recreated in lines which themselves give a painful pleasure, or pleasurable pain:

> No armed Sweets, until thy Reign,
> Cou'd shock the Sense, or in the Face
> A flusht, unhansom Colour place.
> Now the *Jonquille* o'ercomes the feeble Brain;
> We faint beneath the Aromatick Pain,

says Anne Finch, in *The Spleen*, A Pindarick Poem (*Miscellany Poems*), addressing a postlapsarian (and modern) malady which heightens and perverts simple sense experiences into complex ones. Sweets shock; jonquils overwhelm. Pope admired the lines, and adopted a phrase in his "Die of a rose in aromatic pain" (*Essay on Man* I, line 200). The sensuous oxymoron is meant to give us a little shock. There are numerous other examples in which sensations of odd pain are allied to sensations of pleasure, e.g. "Stretch'd on the rack of a too easy chair" (*Dunciad* IV, line 342). Many of Pope's lines have a similar effect, combining the pleasurable (in some images, in the music and cadence of the verse) with the disgusting or painful (in other images, often in the final impression), e.g. "And the fresh vomit run for ever green,"[11] or "Where slumber Abbots, purple as their wines." The pleasurable cannot be extracted or separated from the painful, nor the beautiful sundered from what is ugly.

It is not only in Pope that we find this alliance of the high and the disgusting, the beautiful and the painful. Almost any Augustan poet can furnish it, though not in Pope's succinct and brilliant manner. William Falconer, an underrated though uneven poet, gives us in his *Shipwreck* (1762), in a passage influenced by Pope's pheasant, a description of the dying dolphin killed by the sailors and brought on deck:

> Unerring aim'd th'emissive weapon flew,
> And, plunging, strikes the trembling victim thro':
> Th'upturning points his pondrous bulk sustain;
> He strives to disengage himself in vain;

On deck he quivers in extatic Pain:
Now, as the near approach of Death, he feels,
And flitting life escapes in sanguine rills,
What radiant changes strike th'astonish'd sight!
What glowing hues of mingled shade and light!
Not PHOEBUS orient in the rosy dawn,
Decking with countless gems, the dewy lawn,
Or when he paints the west with setting rays,
Such varied beauties, round the sky displays,
As, from his sides, in bright profusion flow,
That, now in gold empyreal seem to glow,
Now beam a flaming crimson on the eye,
And now assume the purple's deeper dye;
Now in pellucid sapphires strike the view,
And emulate the bright celestial hue;
But here, description makes each beauty less,
What terms of Art can Nature's pow'rs express?

(*The Shipwreck* (1762), Canto I, lines 257–77)[12]

Falconer ends this passage by saying, like Thomson, that Nature's colours can hardly be imitated in words. But of course he has, in a Thomsonian manner, run through a catalogue of colours, bright colours, almost the spectrum ("rosy," "gold," "crimson," "purple," "sapphires"). He has also used words to emphasize the quality of colour, the emanation of light, in "radiant," "glowing," "flaming"; these words, especially in this context, suggest a certain violence in the heat of colour. The colours are as lovely and astonishing as those seen in the diamondlike dew of dawn, or in a vivid sunset. It is all very wonderful – but at the same time, very disconcerting. These brilliant colours and glowing effects are seen in an animal in the process of dying, actually suffering its last throes. We are told in such detail about the "trembling victim" at the outset that we might expect the passage to continue in that sympathetic vein, with expressions of pity for the creature "in extatic Pain." But it does not. In pain, in death – behold beauty. The beauty which so strikes the observer's eye is bought at the price of the death of an innocent creature. And if there is any guilt attached to this death, we too share it, for we are engaged in admiring the wonders of Nature's colours in the suffering dolphin. We must not think Falconer merely insensitive, for all else in his poem shows us he is not. Rather, his poem itself has the ambiguous beauty of the dying dolphin, being a poetic work made for our pleasure (and the poet's own) out of his experience of a shipwreck in which most of his companions died.

Falconer's passage on the dolphin is a vivid example of change ("radiant changes"), of metamorphosis which is at once horrifying, sensuously and sympathetically painful, and beautiful. In other passages we have seen the distorting and the painful within the operations of change, affecting observed and observer. Cowper's winter morning turns clouds into burning cities and makes a man look like weirdly truncated legs. The sun in Thomson's observed

summer noon bakes the parched earth and in "dazling Deluge" gives pain to
the eyes – pain vividly noted and recreated. Wherever we turn, there seems to
be no power of Nature or of the Mind that is not threatening as well as
wonderful. The boundless crowded scene of change may "fill the mind," in
Johnson's phrase, but what it fills the mind with is rarely perfectly beautiful or
tranquil, and may be discomforting or disgusting – or uncomfortably lovely,
beautifully disgusting.

Burke, in his *Philosophical Enquiry into the Origin of our Ideas of the Sublime and the
Beautiful* (1757) includes, rather uneasily, things which pain the senses, such as
bad smells, under the sublime – though he does not elaborate or illustrate.
Burke's treatise is much more concerned with the "Sublime" than the "Beautiful," and the author endeavours to find an answer to that complex question,
how it is that we can find enjoyment in the artistic rendition of frightening or
painful things. His work is a most decidedly Augustan aesthetic treatise. Its
date in mid-century defies us to enlist it through historical chauvinism under
the Romantics, but also, and more important, Burke's concerns are Augustan.
He picks up and investigates a theme persistently found in Augustan literature, a motif which Burke illustrates from Milton (his major sublime author)
and which can certainly be found in poetry from Milton onwards: the inter-
relation of pain and pleasure. Burke proposes the use of the word "delight" for
our response to the sublime images, i.e. to pain-giving things, confused, cloudy
and threatening things. He proposes the intensity of our desire for self-
preservation as his explanation for the delight we experience in reading about
murder, hell, darkness, sea-cliffs, thunderstorms, and so on.

As Martin Price has said, the new aesthetic doctrines of the period "mark a
revolt against the tyranny of beauty."[13] Price sees the beginning of the revolt in
Addison's *Spectator* papers on "the Pleasures of the Imagination" (1712).
Addison distinguishes Beauty from what he calls the Great, and also from the
"New or *Uncommon,"* which "bestows charms on a Monster" and gives us
pleasures in fountains and waterfalls "where the Scene is perpetually shifting." Addison himself, rarely an originator, seems merely to have formulated
in his essays the qualities and interests so very apparent in Augustan literature
before his periodical existed. The "tyranny of beauty" and of Renaissance
ideas of the Beautiful had been assaulted in the burlesques, and denied in the
attack on genre, the refusal to put new wine in old bottles. Range, variety,
energy, the mingling of likes with unlikes, had been valued far beyond the
regularly pleasing; *"give the vigorous fancy room."* We may ask if there is any great
Augustan poem of the whole period which is perfectly beautiful, in which some
elements of the ugly, the astonishing, or the overpowering do not mingle.
Pope's *Dunciad* is as notable a phase in what Price calls "the reclamation of the
ugly" as Burke's treatise, and the tyranny of beauty was certainly not a
problem by the time Burke wrote it.

From Milton onwards, the Augustan imagination seems to have little room
for the symmetrical or the pretty. The efforts of the whole movement had

concentrated on including everything, finding *words* for everything – colourful words for the stupendous, the detailed, the shocking, the jagged, the mobile. What is new in Burke is his psychological interest, with its avowed and open focus on the place and value of pain in aesthetic experience. Our feeling for the sublime is related to that great fundamental passion, the fear of death. Persons in conditions of well-fed safety and comfort need, Burke suggests, to have their nervous system reactivated by a simulation of the dangerous or awesome. Burke's physiological explanation may not seem too satisfactory; taken at one level, our need for such artificial stimulus might lead to the roller coaster rather than to Milton. But Burke is touching something close to the heart of all Augustan poetry (that of Rochester, Dryden and Pope as well as that of Gray and Collins) in suggesting that the truly fine experience is the intense experience which has some pain in it. The uncertain, mingled and strenuous seem to an Augustan mind (such as Burke's) obviously preferable in excitement and significance to the clear, limited and sweet. Burke expresses clearly the aesthetic of boundlessness and mixture on which Augustan poetry is so largely based. He also voices some of the fears that affect the psyche encountering the Powers that make change, that wreak metamorphosis. The nature of Augustan Personification, its ambiguous appeal as representative of strong forces and unswerving energies, is conveyed in Burke's discussion of Milton's Death; "all is dark, uncertain, confused, terrible and sublime to the last degree," he exclaims of Milton's personification, the shape that shape had none.[14] As Burke points out, Milton makes us imagine many forms confusedly while settling on none of them specifically; this *power* is not to be bounded by form. In Burke's passage of criticism (which includes the long quotation from Milton), sublimity, shape-changing and death are closely associated. The last power of metamorphosis is a limitless sublime energy; it is also, in Death, the final term, the end of all shape and all life.

In seizing upon Longinus, the critic of the sublime, the Augustans had long declared their interest in and allegiance to effects different from the beautiful, their preference for energy. The sublime for the Augustans represents the highest energy of poetic response the poet could wish to evoke, and which he must evoke by his highest efforts, directing us to the strong energies and forces within life. But the Burkean Sublime (like the sublime of Longinus) has more than a little in common with Pope's anti-Sublime of Dulness. Dulness is also cloudy, uncertain, terrible, unclear and confused to the last degree. Pope was, of course, very conscious of the sublime in Dulness. The relation between the Sublime and the anti-Sublime had occupied him during much of his life.

Nevertheless, too true it is, that while a plain and direct Road is pav'd to their ὕψος [hypsos] or *sublime*; no Track has been yet chalk'd out, to arrive at our βάθος [bathos], or *profound*. The *Latins*, as they came between the *Greeks* and *Us*, make use of the word *Altitudo*, which implies equally *Height* and *Depth*. Wherefore considering with no small Grief, how many promising Genius's of this Age are wandering (as I may say) in the dark without a Guide, I have undertaken this arduous but necessary Task, to lead them as it were by the hand, and step by step, the gentle downhill way to the *Bathos*; the Bottom, the End, the Central Point, the *non plus ultra* of true Modern Poesie!

(*Peri Bathous: Or, Martinus Scriblerus, His Treatise of the Art of Sinking in Poetry*, 1728)[15]

Writing ironically upon the Profound, Pope hit, not too comfortably, on the real resemblance between the Sublime and the Bathetic. The Altitudo may catch us all, going in either direction. In Augustan literature, both the high and the low, the sublime and the disgusting, are often treated in terms of each other. When we wish to be profound, we may touch bottom. Even when the poet most ardently wishes otherwise, the suggestion of the opposing dimension often accompanies the sublimest description, like the shadow of anti-matter. Self-consciousness about style made it difficult indeed for Augustans not to anticipate the reverse effects in both directions. The Augustans felt the connection of "high" and "low," of glorious and disgusting, beautiful and dull. Their sense of these connections is intimately related to their connection of pain and pleasure, and importantly concerned also in their sensitive apprehension of the powers of metamorphosis. The sublime may metamorphose into the bathetic, or the bathetic (dying fish) into the sublime. The bi-formed poet may be caught in the process of becoming a swan, at a moment when the sublime and the bathetic mingle. The ugly can become the beautiful or the beautiful the ugly at any moment in the cycle of Nature's and the mind's changes – as Timon's estate may be rendered beautiful once again. Nothing stays put. And, above all, that power which gives birth to all these changes, wild creations and momentary monsters is a threatening force both sublime and monstrous in itself. To go towards that power, to investigate it, is to invite the danger of metamorphosing oneself to the point of no return. The glorious and the shamefully ugly, the height and the depth, threaten one equally, above or below, first with loss of language and then with loss of consciousness. Loss of consciousness is a menace evoked in the invocation of that threatening power, or powers, whatever they may be called, whether Pope's Dulness or Collins's Fear. The change and changefulness which are seen with the eye of consciousness or in "visionary" glimpses of the unknown alike threaten the self, the central conscious "I," with a fulfilment too climactic to be safe.

Sometimes the poet can be seen flirting with the potential delights of partial loss of consciousness. Thomson in *The Castle of Indolence* (1748) plays daringly with committing the sin most shocking in Augustan eyes, the sin of sloth, *accidie*, inertia. He presents himself as speaker in the castle and grounds of Indolence, busy doing nothing and happy the whole day long, like his lazy companions. Thomson seems to be giving himself a rest after the energy so strongly urged upon us in *The Seasons*; we get away from those active walks, sublime thunderstorms and so on with a vengeance. One can't help liking a poet who can so shamelessly present us with such fullness of lazy luxuriance:

Soft Quilts on Quilts, on Carpets Carpets spread,
And Couches stretch around in seemly Band;
And endless Pillows rise to prop the Head;
So that each spacious Room was one full-swelling Bed.

(Canto I, stanza 33)

Who cannot respond to such surrealistic and voluptuous interior decoration? Thomson here plays with the seductive pleasures of renouncing energy. But so in a way does Collins, in imagining the pleasures of dreaming away the day in Pity's Temple; there too the renunciation of energy also means an oozing away of the self in a sort of gentle continuous orgasm, "In Dreams of Passion melt away." There is a force inertly strong not just in Dulness but in various qualities and states that tempt us with losing part of the responsibility and effort of active consciousness. In Collins's Ode, as in Pope's desire to be borne away by the Muses ("Ye sacred Nine! ... Bear me, oh bear me to sequester'd Scenes"), the loss of some aspects of consciousness entails a sharpening of other functions. But it could be that all faculties are lost, in a last metamorphosis.

Creative powers can fail to support themselves; imagination can be transient like temporary fame. In his reproachful response to the *Dunciad*, Aaron Hill imagines Alexis (Pope) in a dream-vision rapt away by Fancy and shown a visionary topography.[16] Alexis sees the Stream of Life flowing between two shores; it goes shallowly beside "low *Oblivion*'s Shore," and deeply beside the green regions of immortal Fame. Most aspirants are prevented from crossing to the deep side of the stream. One boatman (Pope) is alone able, almost effortlessly, to land among the swans in the green islands, but he is diverted by the gaudy insects on the other side, and steers to the shallow stream that leads to oblivion. Hill's Alexis is the Pope who has been wasting his talents in catching Dunces, trivializing a genius that had nobler possibilities.

Hill's own poem is in its way an extraordinarily inventive, even passionate, use or re-use of images found in both the *Essay on Criticism* and the *Dunciad*. *The Progress of Wit: A Caveat* (1730) is also an extraordinarily self-conscious and self-mocking poem. Supposedly written "By a Fellow of *All-Souls*" (which Hill was not) it is introduced by the ostensible editor, Gamaliel Gunson, "Professor of Physick and Astrology" (i.e. quack doctor) who found the manuscript "*one rainy Day, at the Bottom of a Hackney-Coach.*" Puzzled, fearing treason, he shows it to colleagues, to the Secretary of State, and to a Lawyer. Hill's poem is thus subjected to various parodic readings and interpretations which are encountered by the reader before he reads the poem. That is, the poem is parodied and deconstructed in advance. Disarming or forestalling other satirists (like Pope) seems only a minor object of this strategy. More important, the various readings make us aware of the multitude of possible meanings that hover around the poems, especially those of multiple meanings like the *Dunciad* itself. We see the inescapable perverse busy-ness of interpretation.

He [the Secretary] *was pleas'd, when he came to the following Lines, to read them aloud, to a Young Spark, in Red, and ask'd him, what He thought of the Matter? – I confess, I was almost in a Passion, when this* Feather-Brain *made answer, that it was the liveliest Satire in the World, upon a* Bawdy-House *of his Acquaintance, by the Bank-Side, over the Water! I cite the very Verses . . .*

> Caught by the gulphy *Void*, that gloom'd, below,
> Crowds, from the Currents fair-descending Flow,
> Indrawn, at once, by Darkness swallow'd o'er
> Sunk, from their Sunny Scene, and rose no more . . .
>
> ("To the Reader")

The Lawyer sees in other lines a reference to "*the* Masquerade *in the* Haymarket" and is sure he has found in reference to "*a* dark, bustling, Power, obscurely seen" [Fortune] a libel on a "*great Man, in a certain Assembly*" [Walpole].

The combination of readings dazzles the reader before he has begun the poem proper; even though Gunson's son in college at last supplies the correct frame of reference, the other meanings hide out in the lines when we come to them, refusing to be censored or quite rescinded. Gulfs, darkness, dark bustling Powers, do recall other Augustan embodiments, and other significances. Power, darkness, obscurity, the liquid pull which indraws into darkness – this is the feminine power, the vagina, sexual energy – hence the Bawdy-House by the Bank-Side. Masquerades, carnival activities, are also associated with these energies of sex and death – as is Walpole, the masculine embodiment of the energies of Dulness, the dark, bustling male Power shaping the political ends of England. The *Dunciad* works through all these motifs; Hill's *Progress of Wit* draws our attention to them. As usual in the charivari of Augustan literature, the feminine dominates as the frightening, the sublime, refusing to be limited to the beautiful – indeed refusing limitation. In Hill's poem it is a feminine aspect of the mind who showed Alexis the scene and himself; Van der Gucht's illustration to the poem makes Fancy a goddess very like his Juno in the illustration to *Virgile Travestie*; she stands aloft on her cloud while a laurel-crowned Alexis averts his eyes from the precipice. In Hill's poem, as so often in Augustan poetry, male and female energies (caricatured as Walpole and bawdy-house) combine in the vision of the powers that pulse through life. These uncontrollable powers delight and frighten the creative mind. Consciousness always knows that it is at last subject to that threatening power that presides over all the changes in nature, and will not stay for our debate or exclamation. What Alexis is made to see is frightening:

> Yet, *one* broad Gulph absorb'd the double Tides;
> From *Birth* devolving, *Death*'s blind *Sea*, below,
> Boundless, and formless, snatch'd the mingl'd Flow;
> Both rounding Oceans, backward, seem'd to tend,
> And vast, *beneath*, their sable Surges *blend*:
> But far more dreadful *This*! – whose dark *Profound*,
> A Depth Eternal! Life wants Line to sound:
> Unbottom'd Shade roll'd loose o'er swallow'd Light –
> *Fancy* grew giddy, nor sustain'd the Sight.

The imagery resembles that in Addison's essay *The Visions of Mirzah*, in which the seer beholds the fragile and broken bridge of human life poised over "a prodigious Tide of Water"; passengers keep dropping through the bridge into "the great Tide of Eternity" flowing inescapably beneath them.[17] But in Hill's poem the emphasis is on the two gulfs of Birth and Death; the stream of life leads always to "*Death*'s blind Sea, below," to the caverns measureless to man adumbrated by Johnson in the visionary topography of *Rasselas*, in "a stream which entered a dark cleft of the mountain on the northern side, and fell with dreadful noise from precipice to precipice till it was heard no more."[18] As Hill warns Pope, there is a Profound – there is the *beneath* that threatens – threatens so terribly that Fancy cannot sustain the sight or bear what it knows. This is the real fear that has been played with and yet evoked in Pope's mock-epic. Here, Hill seems to say, is the real meaning of the *Dunciad* – it is not Civilization but Alexander you mourn for, in the intuition of universal darkness. Peri Bathous indeed. For all, "Unbottom'd Shade" waits to "roll loose" – shapeless, unrestrained, the caricature of joyous boundlessness – over "swallow'd Light."

This vale, with its stream and gulf, should become familiar to us in eighteenth-century poetry. It appears again in Young's *Night-Thoughts* (1742–5); in "*Night the Third: Narcissa*" we are enjoined to turn our thoughts "Down their right Channel, through the Vale of Death," and are then asked to imagine the place:

> The Vale of Death! That husht *Cimmerian* Vale,
> Where *Darkness* brooding o'er Unfinisht Fates,
> With Raven wing incumbent, waits the Day
> (Dread Day!) that interdicts all future Change.
> That Subterranean World, that Land of Ruin![19]

In this passage of Young, the stream through that vale seems to be the stream of thought which bears the memory and injunction of the dead. In other passages of Augustan poetry, the emphasis is on the stream of time rolling all towards death and that "dark vale" – an idea that can be put as simply and powerfully as in Watts's hymn: "Time like an ever-rolling Stream / Bears all its sons away."[20] The image or image-cluster contributes to the climax of Johnson's *Vanity of Human Wishes* (1749): "Must helpless Man, in Ignorance sedate, / Roll darkling down the Torrent of his Fate?" (lines 345–6).[21] The idea can be found even in light touches, as in Burns's image in "Tam O'Shanter":

> But pleasures are like poppies spread,
> You seize the flow'r; its bloom is shed;
> Or like the snow falls in the river,
> A moment white – then melts for ever.[22]

The Augustans had a strong intuition of that stream that bears everything fast to oblivion, and felt the paradox of the river which is in its nature lively and changeful leading in its rapidity to unchanging darkness. The image itself combined pleasure and pain. Intuition and images are impressively captured by Blake's illustration (1797) to the lines by Young quoted above (Fig. 18).[23] We see the shape of darkness with raven wing (face and body here occulted by the text) brooding over the Cimmerian vale. At the bottom of the picture the bright stream rushes forth rapidly, almost plunging out at the reader. In it, the faces of the dead and dying can be seen in the process of that last metamorphosis and turbulent hurry to changelessness – a moment white, then melting for ever. They are borne rapidly towards the darkness that shades the edge of the picture, ready to swallow light. Fancy and identity are subject to that final loss of consciousness, the end of self and selving.

In eighteenth-century poetry, metamorphosis is finally associated with the thought of death. The connection can be jestingly made as in Gay's story of dying Doll (another victim of the river, whose consciousness or at least her head remains comically above water). The association can be put seriously, as in Cowper's remark that his shadow reminds him he is "but a shade" – or it can be put with subtle shadings of various tones, as in Pope's contemplation of the death of Belinda at the end of *The Rape of the Lock* ("When those fair Suns shall sett, as sett they must, / And all those Tresses shall be laid in Dust"). Augustan poetry, for all its appetite and energy, is death-haunted. Characters in poems often take on the burden of enacting the loss of consciousness, representing it for us – as, for instance, in the death-bed scenes of the *Epistle to Cobham*, where the characters' styles (linguistic patterns and styles of living) prove inadequate to the occasion, even as they are cut off. The *Epistle to Bathurst* also confronts us repeatedly with death, and with the grim (and grimly absurd) transformations of person into centrepiece of funeral, and then funeral monument. The death of Villers shows us that last transformation in crazily metamorphosed surroundings, no longer "in Cliveden's proud alcove," but "In the worst inn's worst room, with mat half-hung, / The floors of plaister, and the walls of dung" (lines 299–300). It is as if both body and spirit of the dying man had turned inside out, spreading over or creating the surroundings (another ruinous body) in the last involuntary act of metamorphosis. In Crabbe's verse narratives, characters often die in the event, despite or even because of their self-preserving energies and their desire to control life. The deep appeal of "Peter Grimes" arises from its vision of Peter as a consciousness under threat. Peter, quite seriously and even tragically, becomes subject to the sluggish ooze and slime which are the materials of Pope's Dulness. He is indeed a victim of the dull, within and without:

> Thus by himself compell'd to live each day,
> To wait for certain hours the Tide's delay;
> At the same times the same dull views to see,
> The bounding Marsh-bank and the blighted Tree;
> . . .

When Tides were neap, and, in the sultry day,
Through the tall bounding Mud-banks made their way,
. . .
There anchoring, *Peter* chose from Man to hide, ⎤
There hang his Head, and view the lazy Tide   ⎬
In its hot slimy Channel slowly glide;   ⎦
Where the small Eels that left the deeper way
For the warm Shore, within the Shallows play;
Where gaping Muscles, left upon the Mud,
Slope their slow passage to the fallen Flood; –
Here dull and hopeless he'd lie down and trace
How side-long Crabs had scrawled their crooked race;
. . .
He nurst the Feelings these dull Scenes produce.
(*"The Poor of the Borough: Peter Grimes"*)[24]

Grimes seems to have arrived at the point where the stream of life runs into the gulf of death, anticlimactically and sluggishly, and the Fancy is stupefied and anaesthetized. He has come to that downhill stop, that place of rest and inertia which is the Profound, where the only life is the small slimy monsters that reflect the small monsters of his own flickering consciousness.

In another poem in the same sequence, Crabbe gives us another unforgettable and quite different picture of a consciousness under threat. The condemned man in the death-cell in "Prisons" is not, like Peter Grimes, a subject of mental inertia; his vision is of lively sea, not dead stream. His dreams exhibit the feverish efforts of his under-consciousness to relieve him from intolerable anguish, from a state of death-in-life knowingly awaiting only death. His mind in sleep tries to supply pleasure instead of pain, creating change and brightness where all has been so transformed into horror and monotony. Crabbe never wrote anything better than this passage where the prisoner, in dream, is again wandering with his friend and his sweetheart on a holiday afternoon:

The Ocean smiling to the fervid Sun –
The Waves that faintly fall and slowly run –
The Ships at distance and the Boats at hand:
And now they walk upon the Sea-side Sand,
Counting the number and what kind they be,
Ships softly sinking in the sleepy Sea:
Now arm in arm, now parted, they behold
The glitt'ring Waters on the Shingles roll'd:
The timid Girls, half dreading their design,
Dip the small foot in the retarded Brine,
And search for crimson Weeds, which spreading flow,
Or lie like Pictures on the Sand below;
With all those bright red Pebbles, that the Sun
Through the small Waves so softly shines upon;
And those live lucid Jellies which the eye
Delights to trace as they swim glitt'ring by:
Pearl-shells and rubied Star-fish they admire,

And will arrange above the Parlour-fire, –
Tokens of Bliss! – "Oh! horrible! – a Wave
Roars as it rises – save me, *Edward*! save!"
She cries: – Alas! the Watchman on his way
Calls and lets in – Truth, Terror, and the Day.   ("Prisons")[25]

The description is beautiful, sensuous and detailed. There is a touch of the dream-like in "Ships softly sinking in the sleepy Sea," a lovely line with an almost Elizabethan alliteration.

Visionary rest and peace are combined with fervent activity and brightness. We can see in this passage a multitude of the characteristics of Augustan poetry. People and things are active, objects closely observed. The passage is full of bright colours – although here, not the colours of the spectrum but various shades of red, the colour of life. The sun emanates light which is reflected and refracted in a number of ways, from soft shining to "glitt'ring." Everything is beautiful, though the irregularity and oddness of the curious objects examined make against the perfect proportions of beauty; what is lovely in Augustan poetry has always the touch of the strange. Here too things are changeable, delightfully so, like the weeds and jellyfish, and light changes things, like the red pebbles under water. And then – there is that last change within the dream, in which the dreamer's own fear is projected upon his remembered sweetheart, and the soft shining life-giving element becomes menacing. There follows the final terrible change, from dream to bitter awakening. The watchman lets in the day unsought by the dreamer: "Truth, Terror, and the Day" are synonymous. Daylight is often welcomed (in life and in literature) for rescuing us from nightmares, but here the prisoner's real life is a nightmare, from which his subconscious fancy has tried in vain to rescue him. He has in dream been able to roam; now he is brought back to an awful stasis. The prisoner is, and knows he is, imminently and inevitably the subject of that last terrible metamorphosis which cannot be held back, and after which there will be no more. The reader has been made to share the condemned man's consciousness and under-consciousness, his mind and its activities, as he has tried desperately to summon up those wonderful protective images that fail in the end.

Crabbe's prisoner, trying to stave off the end of the dream which means his end by producing vivid descriptions, images, changes is no ill image in itself of what the Augustan poets seem in general to be doing. Their poems, their long poems, seem to be flying forever back to the world, observing its transformations and reproducing them, or transforming the world into new images in a perpetual evasion of The End. That is, according to Burkean ideas, almost all Augustan poems are sublime, or related to the sublime, because in them we find an embodied representation of the fear of death and the efforts to avoid it. Poets appear to stave off the end, turning again and again back to the world and packing it in, collecting more autumn leaves, people, ships, teacups – more things and more plays of transformation appear, and postpone conclusion and closure. The endings of many important Augustan poems are problematic; some readers have felt that Augustan poets start out strong, but don't seem to know how to finish.[26]

The ending of many great Augustan poems is death. That is the ending of *Winter* (1726, first version), the first of Thomson's Seasons, and of *The Seasons* itself. The last season of the year and of life is dreary: "And pale concluding Winter comes at last, / And shuts the Scene" ("Winter," lines 1032–3). After all the pleasure, all the science, the author says that the world is full of injustice and pain, and that there must be more than Nature or we are badly off indeed. Thomson's long poem becomes a consolation:

> Ye good Distrest!
> Ye noble Few! who here unbending stand
> Beneath Life's Pressure, yet bear up a While,
> And what your bounded View, which only saw
> A little Part, deem'd *Evil* is no more:
> The Storms of WINTRY TIME will quickly pass,
> And one unbounded SPRING encircle All.
>
> ("Winter," lines 1063–9)

For the last good season we have to be somewhere else, in another state of existence. Thomson's poem seems to have failed him in a way. The poem and the subject seemed boundless, but the end is death. If that be so, no wonder the poet took so many thousands of lines getting there, postponing that realization over and over by offering us new themes, new topics, new objects, instead of an ending. There seems no reason why any of the parts should have an ending – or indeed why some Season shouldn't stretch out almost forever. As long as the poem sustains itself, we are reprieved from confronting death. This sense of the poem is beautifully borne out in the pictures by Bartolozzi and Tompkins in the great 1797 edition of *The Seasons*. The illustration to "Winter" is called "The Winter of Life" (Fig. 19). A young woman is reading to an elderly couple; through the window the ice and snows of winter are clearly visible, while within all is warm. But the old woman is shrouded in black and seated in shadow, while the old man on whom the light falls looks patient and emaciated. His white hair and sharp nose echo the frosty twigs without the window-pane, and he seems to be about to become one with that cold landscape. Death is imminent – but, we feel, as long as the reading continues, as long as the book lasts, death will wait. The tension within this misleadingly quiet picture comes from the sense that an ending, both to art and life, is inevitable, and yet may be a while suspended.

It might be argued that Thomson, having once begun with his original *Winter*, was stuck with it as the ending to the whole, once he thought of his grand plan. His is not the only sequence of seasons that could be found, however; Thomson chose Winter to be the end, and the ending that had come at length in his first long poem becomes the inevitable end of his giant poem, an end postponed through thousands of lines. Once the whole was written,

Fig. 19

Thomson wrote his "Hymn" (1730) to crown the work and end the whole sequence. The "Hymn" also ends with death, though with the thought of a life after death. But that life ends language. The place of silence where language fails has a secret horror all its own. The hushed recognition that all this activity ends in death and in the failure of human language is finely registered by Hamilton's illustration, the tail-piece to the "Hymn." Called "The Reaper Returning Home" (Fig. 20), it awakens slightly New Testament echoes, but its delicate emphases fall on death and stillness. There is no hint of harvest joviality about the solemn strong-faced reaper illumined only by the moon: we see shadows, finished task, silence and night.

Thomson's next long poem, the less popular *Liberty* (1735–6), also ends with a dying fall. This five-part poem opens among the ruins of Rome. There, the poet has a vision of Liberty who lectures him on the history of the Greeks, the Romans and modern western Europeans, outlining the growth of liberty in each nation and pointing to England's history as the culmination. Although the future of England is shadowed by some doubt about corruption (a jab at Walpole), everything in Liberty's last exclamatory speech seems to be doing superbly well. British cities, canals, trade, ports are fine and flourishing. Yet the ending brings us an unexpected sense of dejection: "The VISION broke; and, on my waking eye, / Rush'd the still RUINS of dejected ROME" (v, lines

Fig. 20

719–20).[27] The poem ends, as it began, with ruins (a pattern that might have
interested Gibbon), and the waking reality of ruin seems to signify something
beyond the vicious influence of Walpole as viewed by Opposition Whigs.
Large statements tend towards ruin.

The age was interested in ruins. A love of ruins as sights of course become
part of the mid and late Augustan aesthetic, but we find ruins as landscapes
earlier, and in unexpected places, like MacFlecknoe's Barbican (*MacFlecknoe*,
lines 66–70). Ruins were interesting not because they signified the past, but
because they expressed what threatened the present. They figure or represent
the constant menace of death, and illustrate the transformation that tends to
decay, the authority of destruction. John Dyer's *The Ruins of Rome* (1740), a
poem probably influenced by Thomson's *Liberty*, was guardedly praised by
Johnson for its descriptive power. The lines that Johnson especially admired
do not merely show us a city that *has* fallen into ruin; it *is* falling into ruin now,
at the present moment:

> Globose and huge,
> Grey-mouldring Temples swell, and wide o'ercast
> The solitary Landskape, Hills and Woods,
> And boundless Wilds; while their vine-mantled brows
> The pendent Goats unveil, regardless they

Of hourly Peril, though the clefted Domes
Tremble to ev'ry Wind. The Pilgrim oft
At dead of Night, mid his Oraison hears
Aghast the Voice of Time, disparting Tow'rs,
Tumbling all precipitate down dash'd,
Rattling around, loud thundring to the Moon:
While Murmurs sooth each awful Interval
Of ever-falling Waters...[28]

The beautiful is also the monstrous ("Globose and huge"); the sublime threatens, but it threatens through change. What gives pleasure also gives pain of mind. The visitor to Rome ("Pilgrim," poet or reader) seems plunged into the midst of a process of degenerative if exciting transformation; each moment brings a new phase, and each phase is peril. The illustration on the title-page of the first edition (Fig. 21) could have been used for Thomson's setting for his vision; ruins rush upon the eye. The spectators in the street are all far below; we look from a height at crumbling columns and precarious blocks. The pediments seem about to fall on the spectators' heads, and every facade is in danger of giving way in this city of ruin. Dyer is most anxious to give the ruinous in the now, the *power* that can be felt to be altering everything, the undersong of the phenomenal – the "Voice of Time."

Fig. 21

The feeling within Dyer's poem and its illustration can be found in Pope's own work as a visual artist. If we look at the drawing by Pope included by Warburton in the posthumous 1745 edition of *An Essay on Man* we see another study of ruin (Fig. 22). It must be admitted that we cannot be at all certain that Pope ever intended this picture to accompany this poem, and Warburton, who includes the illustration, is slightly evasive on that point in his detailed commentary on it:

Fig. 22

The Reader will excuse my adding a word concerning the Frontispiece; which, as it was designed and drawn by Mr. *Pope* himself, would be a kind of curiosity had not the excellence of the thought otherwise recommended it. We see it represents the Vanity of human Glory, in the false pursuits after Happiness: Where the Ridicule, in the Curtain-cobweb, the Death's-head crown'd with laurel, and the several Inscriptions on the fastidious ruins of Rome, have all the force and beauty of one of his best wrote Satires: Nor is there less expression in the bearded-Philosopher sitting by a fountain running to waste, and blowing up bubbles with a straw, from a small portion of water

taken out of it, in a dirty dish; admirably representing the vain business of School-
Philosophy.[29]

Certainly we do see a statement about the vanity of human glory – or of the
vanity of human wishes, to borrow the title of a poem that appeared four years
after this edition of Pope's great poem on Happiness. There is more to the
picture, however, than that general theme. The picture (which strongly
resembles Hogarth's *The Bathos*) expresses the imminence of ruin, and the
immanence of the power that makes for ruinousness. The illustration is an
expressive commentary to counteract what Warburton evidently (and Pope
perhaps) found the too-great optimism of the *Essay on Man*. We are brought up
against stoppage and cessation; we see processes of ruin ending in the dust. An
alternative ending of death and annihilation is supplied to the poem – supplied
before it begins – thus changing its meaning. After all the attacks on the
irreligion of the poem, Pope himself had wished to emphasize the Christian
elements within it. But whatever he and Warburton may have desired for the
poem's interpretation, the picture is not specifically Christian. It is, however,
certainly very Augustan, visually expressing the sense that everything is close
to coming to pieces, the feeling that transformations are fascinating and
potentially lethal. Pope evidently did not keep the vision of the *Dunciad*
cupboarded in one poem. *An Essay on Man* itself holds off the ruinousness which
Pope's picture (inserted by Warburton) permits us to see. The real ending of
any poem is death.

Cowper is undoubtedly a Christian poet. Yet the ending of *The Task* is
similar to that of *The Seasons*, just as both poems have operated at length by
procrastinating an ending. Cowper envisages death as the end, though
the poet is more personal in discussing his own imagined death, and his own
work:

> So glide my life away! and so at last,
> My share of duties decently fulfill'd,
> May some disease, not tardy to perform
> Its destin'd office, yet with gentle stroke,
> Dismiss me, weary, to a safe retreat,
> Beneath the turf that I have often trod.
> It shall not grieve me, then, that once when call'd
> To dress a Sofa with the flow'rs of verse,
> I play'd awhile, obedient to the fair,
> With that light task; but soon, to please her more,
> Whom flow'rs alone I knew would little please,
> Let fall th'unfinish'd wreath, and rov'd for fruit;
> Rov'd far, and gather'd much: some harsh, 'tis true,
> Pick'd from the thorns and briers of reproof,
> But wholesome, well-digested; grateful some
> To palates that can taste immortal truth;
> Insipid else, and sure to be despis'd.
>
>   (Book vi, lines 1000–16)

Cowper imagines himself dead, and then moves back to defence of his poem, which is both unfinished wreath and thorny fruit; his modesty sorts ill, perhaps, with the smugness that seems to make appreciation of the poem a test of spiritual health and taste. Yet the poem itself is nothing without the praise of God, "Whose frown can disappoint the proudest strain, / Whose approbation – prosper even mine" (lines 1023–4). Cowper hopes that God can "prosper" his poem, however humble, as long as the poet's heart is right. But what God thinks of Cowper's heart can be known only after death, and Cowper entertains here no speculations about launching away into immortality. We are left with a strong impression of the poet as dead, "Beneath the turf that I have often trod." Once he "*rov'd*"; poetry is roving, searching, change – but movement comes to an end in sombre stillness just as the poem comes to an end. Cowper did indeed in this poem "rove" far and wide, moving from topic to topic, object to object, in a long and changeable poem that seemed to have no reason to finish. The reader may well be surprised at coming to the end, when the appetitive life (the poet is trying to feed us), the lively wandering and the stylistic variations stop suddenly in the quiet of the grave.

Silence, stasis and death – these ideas are associated by Augustan poets with the idea of the ending of a poem. "Come then, expressive Silence, muse HIS Praise" says Thomson oddly at the end of the "Hymn," imagining an eternity as a kind of blank end sheet. Praising the Muse becomes muse-ing God's praise, something done by Silence, which kills poetry. At the end of *The Castle of Indolence*, that quite different poem, Thomson can find a resolution, a means of flying from the seductions of inertia and loss of consciousness only in reproducing another form of loss of consciousness. The Knight of Arts and Industry razes the castle, destroying the place and disenchanting it to a place of ugliness. The pleasures that were once savoured with a languorous melting intensity are now no more. The salvation of a full and energetic consciousness, capable of making and doing, can be purchased, it seems, only by killing off something else. The former inhabitants of the Castle are transformed; the unrepentant become ugly wretches. Chased by Beggary and Scorn, they are lost swinish things:

> Even so through *Brentford* Town, a Town of Mud,
> An Herd of bristly Swine is prick'd along;
> The filthy Beasts, that never chew the Cud,
> Still grunt, and squeak, and sing their troublous Song,
> And oft they plunge themselves the Mire among.
>
> (Canto II, stanza 81, p. 81)

This last transformation sends pleasure, delightful consciousness, into the ugly mud and mire. Pleasure becomes pain, capacity for sensing beauty is pushed into ugliness, and language becomes brute noise and then earthy silence. The turf of the grave, Silence, the mire – these are the endings, alternate but not so very different, that wait on conclusions.

It is not contended that Augustan poetic endings are weak, unplanned or arbitrary. They are often graceful, even more often powerful; certainly, they belong to their poems. But their appropriateness is related to the various modes in which change and death are acknowledged in all that has gone before. One of the very greatest of Augustan poetic endings is that to Pope's *Dunciad*, an ending that expresses its own finality and the general problem of endings most effectively. After all the games and absurdity, the *Dunciad Variorum* of 1728 ends its third and last book with the prophetic vision of the "Cloud-compelling Pow'r" "Lo! the great Anarch's ancient reign restor'd, / Light dies before her uncreating word" (*Dunciad Variorum*, III, lines 339–40). As we know, Pope revised his poem (repeated and extensive revising is a very Augustan habit). The new poem with its new last book is even more effective than the former, offering us a wider vision of the irrational in the world. The ending, now postponed to the end of a longer poem, is even more effective and elaborately grim. It is in the new book that Pope amplifies the ending through discussing ending, providing a poet-ventriloquist, a sort of Poet Laureate of Dulness, who is faced with the problem of how to celebrate the unspeakable, that which transforms speech to silence and action to stop. The poet-speaker (an ironic dummy who admires what Pope condemns) must at the beginning of Book IV beg the Powers that he praises to suspend their negative final smothering transformation long enough to permit him to get out his last words:

> Yet, yet a moment, one dim Ray of Light
> Indulge, dread Chaos, and eternal Night!
> Of darkness visible so much be lent,
> As half to shew, half veil the deep Intent.
> Ye Pow'rs! whose Mysteries restor'd I sing,
> To whom Time bears me on his rapid wing,
> Suspend a while your Force inertly strong,
> Then take at once the Poet and the Song.
>
> (*Dunciad* [1743], Book IV, lines 1–8)

The ending threatens, the ending that means no more poetry, but the speaker is apparently favoured for a little while; his prayer is briefly answered, and we have the scene of crowds and actions and transformations before the end swallows up everything. The charivari looms large and violently vivid for a little while before it defeats and annihilates itself.

The "Pow'rs" that the Dunciad poet sings are among the most frightening personifications in Augustan literature, the ultimate representatives of the energies that work change until no more change is possible and nothing *is* but sleep, and death, and silence. The poet's voice is, like Dyer's "Voice of Time," a sound ominously telling of great fissure, dislocation and ruin. The Powers continue their transformations until all is completed and nothing remains to be done save make the last metamorphosing leap into darkness and silence. The ventriloquized poet, stupefied with wonders, finds he can no longer keep the darkness at bay:

In vain, in vain, – the all composing Hour
Resistless falls: The Muse obeys the Pow'r,   (lines 627–8)

Chaos is restored, an empire of nothing. "Thy hand, great Anarch! lets the curtain fall; / And Universal Darkness buries all" (lines 655–6). That is the very ending – darkness over all, the smothering of silence and non-entity. The Muse is quelled; ironically, that which created, or seemed to create, the "powers" of personification is itself, or herself, subject to the formless "Pow'r" that kills the word. All the liveliness and variety and dazzling prismatic light of the world go when the powers of the mind that perceive and represent them are transformed into death. The end of the world is the end of the activity of the mind – and of the activity of the poet, any poet.

For years we have singled out the *Dunciad* for special praise among eighteenth-century poems, and every reading must persuade more praise from us. And the last version is better than the first; we need Book IV. If the *Dunciad* remained only a satire on bad writing and bad ideas in writing it would not have the same power to move us. In Book IV we see more of our whole society and thus see ourselves more clearly reflected. Still more important, the revised and final *Dunciad* is not only a great mock-epic but achieves epic grandeur in its confrontation with horror; it is an interior epic, an expressionistic story of the mind's journey to oblivion, of the psyche's deep horror of death as well as a satiric warning of our society's self-destructive follies. We are brought to mourn the idea that the powers of the mind may fail, and all the bright universe turn into a wasteland, left to invisibility and silence. We see in the *Dunciad* a confrontation with endings of all kinds, and the whole idea of An Ending. The poem represents the end of Any Poem, Every Poem, and the end of every poet. Aaron Hill was not being unfair to Pope, was only supplying an obvious reading, when in the *Caveat* he pointed out that the Bathos, the Profound that Pope celebrates and loathes, is really ultimately the gulph of Death "whose dark *Profound*, / A Depth Eternal! Life wants Line to sound."

If we look attentively at Augustan poems, we will see that the rewards of good poetry are, in essence, no better than the reward of bad poetry meted out in the *Dunciad*. All, good poets and bad, tend toward the same end. They all go into the dark, sublimely or inanely; they retreat or are forced into the ground, into the depths and the darkness. Cowper's reward is to rest beneath the turf he once trod, oblivious, and even Thomson in Heaven (or wherever the "future Worlds" are) has to yield to the muse of Silence. The praises of God mused by Silence and the last praise of Dulness sound much alike – they cannot sound at all. The end of the poem seems to bring the poet up against the fearful quiet when his voice must cease, and when all the metamorphoses halt in the last change. Death is the reward of poets – death, and the end of utterance, which are one. Gray's *The Bard* (1757), the story of an heroic poet, the last of his kind, confronted by death, starts very defiantly. The bard goes on magnificently (if a thought too historically) against his conqueror. But the end of the Bard is a bardic suicidal death – which is also the end of *The Bard. A Pindaric Ode.*

> He spoke, and headlong from the mountain's height
> Deep in the roaring tide he plung'd to endless night.

Here is the *altitudo*, both depth and height in one. Gray's sublime archetypal Good Poet meets the end suited to the *Dunciad*'s bad poets, and Pope's ventriloquized bard of Dulness – "endless night."

The poet within Gray's best-known poem, *Elegy Written in a Country Church-Yard*, meets a similar fate. This well-known and much-loved – though not un-parodied – poem is Augustan not only in its concerns, and in its *sui generis* nature (and inimitability) but also in its ending.[30] We are surprised to find what happens to the poet-speaker, who has been speaking to us at length, descriptively, philosophically and movingly about the village inhabitants and the significance of their lives and deaths. Suddenly the implicit "I" becomes "thee"; the poet addressed by himself. We, along with the poet, are invited to imagine his future, which soon becomes a past. If some "kindred Spirit" enquires after the poet's fate, the Swain will give an account of him, as he once was in his life, and then of his disappearance. The end of the poem is the epitaph of the poet himself, the speaker who has become person-in-the past, dead man in coffin, and then only a short poem engraved on a tombstone.

Richard Bentley's illustrations capture the central movement of the poem, its transformation of living observer to dead object distantly observed, and then to object read. In his frontispiece to the *Elegy* Bentley again uses an architectural frame: "A Gothic gateway in ruins with the emblems of nobility on one side; on the other, the implements and employments of the Poor" (Fig. 23).[31] Nobility is hollow and empty; the employments of the poor are associated with life and the fruits of the earth. At first glance the Gothic arch looks solid and even perhaps realistic, or like a real arch with some emblematic objects resting on it. The surreal effect is not fully taken in until the second glance, when we see that the imposing archway is falling into ruin, threatening to drop the remaining cornice and entablature and let go of its shape altogether; like the Ruins of Rome this English gateway is in the process of collapse of form, undergoing metamorphosis now. Within this frame representing the insta-bility of the phenomenal, we see the poet in the churchyard reading a tomb-stone which a rustic is pointing out to him. The poet's shadow, cast along the grave whose monument he observes, indicates and literally foreshadows his own destiny. Like Cowper's, his solid form is really but a shade. He is now living observer; he will soon be in the earth. The dead who are imagined in the poet's meditation and the speaker who so sympathetically imagines them are already being drawn into one.

The tail-piece illustration to the poem comes at the end of a page which contains only "The Epitaph" with this small picture under it (Fig. 24). We see the funeral of the poet, as described in the poem's last verse before the epitaph:

Fig. 23

"Slow thro' the church-way path we saw him born."[32] Under a churchyard tree we see a gap, a cave, like a cross-section opened to us and unrealistically made visible; this is the hole in earth that will be filled in, the grave that yawns for the poet and for us all. Bentley's dark gap in the earth is shored by architectural outlines; he turns the dark gap in earth, in a surreal touch, into an ancient vault, echoing the vaulting in the frontispiece's archway and reminding us that gap and void yawn beneath all the works of man. (The illustration

Fig. 24

of the lonely grave contrasts interestingly with that of Du Guernier to Gay's
"The Dirge" (Fig. 7); Blowzelinda's funeral takes place in a crowded church-
yard, a charivari scene, and everyone seems about to fall into the grave.)
Bentley introduces in his solitary surreal vaulted grave a traditional emblem,
the torch upside down, in the process of expiring. The image of the doused
torch is closely connected with Time's pipe in Hogarth's *The Bathos* or the
philosopher's bubble-pipe in Pope's drawing. The fume of smoke here drifting
up toward the tree is a last indolent manifestation of life just as it flickers out, a
symbol of vanity. Bentley shows us, just as Pope the visual artist shows us in his
picture, that the works of man are always tending toward ruin. Bentley insists
that Gray's whole poem has been tending to this void, this silence, this gap
under the last lines of the poem which are "The Epitaph." If we feel the gap
yawns for us, it is freshly disquieting to turn again to the frontispiece and to
think that the grave being examined under the tutelage of the swain must
really be that of the poet, whose epitaph we are here seeing on stone, not on
the page. The "Explanation" is nicely ambiguous about the identity of
the figures in the frontispiece: "A countryman showing an epitaph to a
passenger" (i.e. passer-by). Once we take in the new meaning, then the
figure whose shadow lies on the grave is not the poet – already departed into

silence and dust – but the passer-by, the reader, who will repeat the poet's experience and his transformations, including inevitably the disappearance into silence.

Bentley is right in seeing that the whole poem acts out (and makes us act out) dying, the move to oblivion. These changes, and the alterations of nouns and pronouns ("me," "they," "us," "thee," "he") are subtle and rapid, so that we do not feel the Poet is merely *speculating* about the way he will be remembered; he seems actually to die in the latter course of the *Elegy*. The ending, problematic and beautifully wrought, is a bathos which is also sublime. The Poet disappears into the dusty ground he has been celebrating. Subject (church-yard) and Speaker (Poet) have become one. The voice vanishes, being replaced by that of the Swain, and that in turn is replaced by the voice of the reader or "kindred Spirit" making out the written verses on the tombstone. We take up the job of making an elegy, through repeating the poet's words in his own epitaph. But *in* the poem, it is the inferior poem only (the epitaph) that remains to be read and re-read. The whole poem, the *Elegy* itself, disappears, along with its speaker-poet. Gray's *Elegy* expresses through its action the sobering thought that few of the poet's words will last – nor does this transience matter overmuch, for he will not remain to care about them. The challenge within the work, whereby the inferior poem (Epitaph) takes over from the superior poem (*Elegy*), is a daring bathos in itself. The exchange also images a resignation under the potential despair a poet feels at contemplating the unlikelihood of being understood, or being read – of surviving, in the secular immortality of fame. God is interested in "merits" and "frailties," but not in poetry. The Poet is indeed equalled in death with the illiterate and the inarticulate, and we are moved because the poet's democratic exhortation within the poem is no mere preaching from a secure position. Of all poems, the *Elegy* most eloquently says that there is no secure position.

Gray's *Elegy*, a work of such strength that even generations of schoolbook editors have not been able to spoil it, is centrally Augustan in its concerns, and gives us some valuable clues to the rest of Augustan poetry.

> For who to dumb Forgetfulness a prey,
> This pleasing anxious being e'er resign'd,
> Left the warm precincts of the chearful day,
> Nor cast one longing ling'ring look behind? (lines 85–8)

On a universal level, that speaks to all; every bosom returns an echo as Johnson said.[33] But that stanza speaks to us about Augustan poetry itself. Just as the rustics erect their frail memorials with ill-spelt inscriptions, so the Poet creates his Epitaph – and so too do poets in general make their verse. Poetry not only staves off "dumb Forgetfulness" in that the poet can hope not to be silent to posterity and forgotten by them; the making of poetry itself also staves off dumb Forgetfulness by being articulate, employing the powers of the mind. It expresses the experience of life which is pleasure and anxiety together – or, rather, the anxiety itself (our primal anxiety for survival) is a source of pleasure, for life itself is the fundamental pleasure. Augustan poetry is about the "pleasing anxious being," and it lives intensely in the warm precincts of day and life. The poetry is a spell against death, oblivion, coldness, night and muteness. Poetry achieves an intensification of life by pulling into itself and comprehending all that is – from the motions of the mind to the structure of rocks; from fans and teacups to hazel trees and thunderstorms; from urban landscapes and individual actions to the progress of history. These things are shown as lively and changing in a world where proof of life, within the mind and outside it, is constant alteration and the capacity to change and move, to rove and gather, to run together and mingle and also to separate. The world's reality is opalescent, changeable and fragile. New changes, fresh realities, continually disrupt and reshape any calm surface.

Augustan poets are perpetually showing us that they understand the "daz-z'ling" or "glitt'ring" qualities of an ever-transforming reality. The great irony, however, is that the force or forces which make for change and variety – the Powers – ultimately dictate oblivion, even the end of the poet and the song. In Augustan poems (both good and bad) the poet seems to be trying with all his might (in the inferior poems the effort results in tedium) to hold at bay that menacing moment of the end. If the poet stops singing the changing world, the poem dies, and he dies. Augustan poets therefore defy endings. They run over them, ignore them, turn them round, or patch up and change and add to them. They will seem to come to a stop, and then, with scarcely a pause for breath, will pick up another topic, another theme, another object, and continue – still triumphantly in the warm precincts of the cheerful day. The unstoppability of a poem is part of its joy and its value. It is almost as if at each moment (until the last one) when an End threatens, the poet flies for succour to some friendly object, some variable and transformation-prone thing and will find relief in that, as Crabbe's condemned prisoner finds relief in the objects within his dream – the jelly-fish and bright red pebbles. And yet each object, each thing, in its own variousness and transformations hints back at that Power behind its own changes which imposes final change.

Weighted with changes, dizzied with transformations and alterations, the Augustan poem finally succumbs to an Ending. Sometimes the ending is as graceful and harmonious as that of *The Rape of the Lock*, which combines an acceptance of death with an assurance of memorial; an acknowledgment of the poet's and his Belinda's fragility under the power of time is blended with a tribute (the more modest for its comic exaggeration) to the poet's power to transform and make metamorphoses. More often, Augustan poems boldly refuse to die without a protest or struggle. Sometimes they die of natural causes, marking their reluctant tailing off. Some poems, after having staved off the End for a long while, at last make the gesture of despairingly and defiantly anticipating it before time. Some poems (*The Bard*) end with a suicide, some (the *Dunciad*) end suicidally. Most poems end less self-destructively, but are emphatic or peculiar in their death-throes, sufficiently to mark the destruction inherent in the end. After the end is Nothing.

> Nothing! thou elder brother even to Shade:
> Thou hadst a being ere the world was made,
> And well fixed, art alone of ending not afraid.
>
> ("Upon Nothing," lines 1–3)

Rochester saw that the only thing at an advantage in relation to change, well placed in that regard as well as utterly stable and secure (well fixed), is Nothing. Only Nothing isn't afraid of Ending or endings. The explicit corollary is that Everything, every thing that has being, is frightened of ending. And that Everything would include poems which celebrate the dance of Matter and Mind above the void.

Rochester was not a Christian (and perhaps not a theist) until his last days, but "Upon Nothing" is less a satire on Christian cosmology and ontology than a witty exercise in paradox. But Samuel Johnson, certainly neither atheist nor Lucretian wit, articulates the fear of ending even better than Rochester did. On an occasion no more (and no less) dramatic than the cessation of his *Idler* as a series of periodical essays, Johnson writes strikingly of "the secret horrour of the last":

This secret horrour of the last is inseparable from a thinking being whose life is limited, and to whom death is dreadful. We always make a secret comparison between a part and a whole; the termination of any period of life reminds us that life itself has likewise its termination; when we have done any thing for the last time, we involuntarily reflect that a part of the days allotted to us is past, and that as more is past there is less remaining.

. . .

An even and unvaried tenour of life always hides from our apprehension the approach of its end. Succession is not perceived but by variation; he that lives to-day as he lived yesterday, and expects that, as the present day is, such will be the morrow, easily conceives time as running in a circle and returning to itself. The uncertainty of our duration is impressed commonly by dissimilitude of condition; it is only by finding life changeable that we are reminded of its shortness.   (*Idler*, No. 103)

"As more is past there is less remaining" – Johnson approaches the mood of Crabbe's condemned prisoner who "Counts up his Meals, now lessen'd by that one." The only mode or escape from the harsh daily knowledge of termination is a mind-controlled changelessness, a lack of variation which will anaesthetize the psyche and permit the illusion of circular time. But time is for mortals linear, not circular; nature will not accommodate us for ever. An escape from the haunting fear of the end through wilful tranquillity is not only, in the Augustan view, wrong but deadening, a rejection of rightful pleasure. "An even and unvaried tenour of life" means unprolific winter, cold stagnation. "Do not suffer life to stagnate." As Johnson's last *Idler* essay so powerfully argues, "succession" and "variation," the changeableness which we value in life and in literature, remind us underneath, and at some deep level at all times and in all places, of life's shortness. The poet rings his changes until the changes bring him round to the end, and his – and our – transience is made manifest. The awesome and dreadful last line must come at length (and in most Augustan poems it *is* at length) to imitate death. The part (poem) reminds us of the whole (life), and termination arrives in both. We all feel "the secret horrour of the last." The Augustan poets felt and reflected this "secret horrour." Through changeableness and variation we move towards the stop. Even small endings presage the great one, and even literary endings evoke muteness and oblivion as they paradoxically utter the call for silence.

VII

Character, style, language: the two voices of Augustan poems

"The secret horrour of the last" is expressed by another Augustan author who also suggests a logical solution to the problem of literary endings:

I am this month one whole year older than I was this time twelve-month, and having got, as you perceive, almost into the middle of my fourth volume – and no farther than to my first day's life – 'tis demonstrable that I have three hundred and sixty-four days more life to write just now, than when I first set out ... at this rate, I should just live 364 times faster than I should write – It must follow, an' please your worships, that the more I write, the more I shall have to write – and consequently, the more your worships read, the more your worships will have to read.

Will this be good for your worships eyes?

It will do well for mine; and, was it not that my OPINIONS will be the death of me, I perceive shall lead a fine life of it out of this self-same life of mine; or, in other words, shall lead a couple of fine lives together.

As for the proposal of twelve volumes a year, or a volume a month, it no way alters my prospect – write as I will, and rush as I may into the middle of things, as *Horace* advises, – I shall never overtake myself – whipp'd and driven to the last pinch, at the worst I shall have one day the start of my pen – and one day is enough for two volumes – and two volumes will be enough for one year. –

(Sterne, *Tristram Shandy*, Vol. IV [1761], ch. 13)[1]

If death comes as the end of a work, then why not allow the work to continue until death?

In no respect are the poems and novels of the Augustan Age more alike than in their approach to the closure of a work, to the End. If poets tend to stave off the End, so too do the novelists, in their lengthy works whose accretions of detail and intercalated narrative serve to retard closure. The ideal Augustan literary work would seem, if we examine Thomson and Cowper and Crabbe – and also Defoe and Richardson and Smollett and Sterne – a work which carries on the business of change and activity as long as possible, allowing the narrator-speaker or author to continue as long as there is breath in his body. Sterne has created in his Tristram a quintessential Augustan writer, who expresses the problems lurking behind Augustan forms and proposes ingenious solutions. And Sterne, like his discursive hero Tristram, is a true Augustan, inventing a *sui generis* literary kind.

Our understanding of both Augustan novels and poetry would be improved by studying both together, and the academic tendency to teach them in separate "courses" does a disservice to the literature of the period and to the

students who are trying to understand it. The novels and poetry of this period
are very closely related – but the poetry came first. Despite the examples
offered by Continental novels, the English novel proper is a product of the
Augustan Age, and does not appear until the Augustan poets have been at
work for two generations or more. Our great novelists are not visible until the
1720s, the period of Defoe's fiction, and, with the exception of Defoe's works,
our first big novels arrive in the 1740s, the exciting decade which saw the
publication of *Pamela, Joseph Andrews, Roderick Random, Clarissa* and *Tom Jones*.
By that time, Augustan poets had long been interpreting contemporary life
and concerns, and had discovered and established literary modes of representing what they knew. To follow nature was to follow the poets. The novelists are
indebted to the poets for what we now call "deep structure" and not merely for
ornament. Novels and poems share the same interests and even the same *topoi*.
Both are expansive and appetitive; we have seen how Fielding's Author at the
beginning of *Tom Jones* picks up the appetite-food *topos* (see above, chapter IV,
pp. 85–6). Augustan novels include many instances of effective charivari: the
Battle of the Church-yard in *Tom Jones*, for instance, or the election in Smollett's *Launcelot Greaves* (1760) – or that finely chilling and outrageous fantasy of
Richardson's Lovelace when he imagines his trial for rape:

we shall see all the doors, the shops, the windows, the sign-irons and balconies (garrets,
gutters, and chimney-tops included) all white-capt, black-hooded, and periwigg'd or
crop-ear'd up by the *Immobile Vulgus*: while the floating *street-warmers*, who have seen us
pass by at one place, run with stretched-out necks, and strained eye balls ... in order to
obtain another sight of us ...   (*Clarissa*, Lovelace to Belford, 25 May)[2]

The novel of the Augustan Age is, like the poems that preceded or accom-
panied it, self-referential, a self-conscious work. Not quite a genre, always *sui
generis*, the novel asserts itself in each case by rejecting other modes of discourse
or narrative. The Romance is particularly useful in this context, a handy
whipping-block, represented as an old-fashioned prose narrative with impossible formulae against which the new unclassifiable piece may reveal its unique
lustre. The novel when at last taken up in the Augustan Age proved the ideal
literary form because it isn't precisely a literary form. It isn't quite a genre. It is
a large loose idea, capable of apparently almost perpetual variation and
innumerable idiosyncrasies. It confines itself to no one typical length, to no one
method of telling or plan or structural division. We can hardly begin an
eighteenth-century novel without being reminded, in a most Augustan
fashion, of questions of style or kind, whether in Defoe's riddling prefaces or
Fielding's mock-authorial commentaries. Fielding, who in his early years
associated himself with the Scriblerians in their most deconstructive moods,
elaborately articulates a number of Augustan insights about the nature of
styles and structures. And in both jest and earnest the "Fielding" of *Tom Jones*
makes a constant case for his own work as *sui generis*: "I am, in reality, the
Founder of a new Province of Writing."[3]

When, however, the new novel emerged, proclaiming itself as a new discovery, Augustan poetry had already been showing what it could do in describing contemporary settings and scenes, managing modern narrative and reproducing colloquial speech. In the production of "character" especially – that is, in the area often thought peculiarly the province of the novelist – the eighteenth-century poets had made sophisticated and memorable advances. Everyone who has read any Augustan poetry recalls it partly in terms of characters whose names and natures stick in our minds, e.g. Hudibras, Achitophel, Flecknoe, Eloisa, Belinda, John Gilpin. The poets had proved themselves capable of rendering, like dramatists, acutely observed characters who speak and move. In the devices of what might be called "objective characterization" Augustan poetry early showed itself particularly rich. We remember, for instance, the fools at Rochester's Tunbridge, or his equally vivid fools, the guests and insistent host at the dinner party Timon could not avoid:

> And now the wine began to work, mine host
> Had been a colonel; we must hear him boast,
> Not of towns won, but an estate he lost
> For the *King*'s service, which indeed he spent
> Whoring and drinking, but with good intent.
> He talked much of a plot, and money lent
> In *Cromwell*'s time. My lady, she
> Complained our love was coarse, our poetry
> Unfit for modest ears; ...
>
> ...
>   "But pox of all these scribblers! What d'ye think:
> Will *Souches* this year any champagne drink?
> Will *Turenne* fight him? Without doubt," says *Huff*
> When the two meet, their meeting will be rough."
> "Damn me!" says *Dingboy*, "The *French* cowards are.
> They pay, but th'*English*, *Scots*, and *Swiss* make war."
>   ("Timon," lines 95–156)

Augustan poetry was in the vanguard in catching the passing of time, the alterations in fashion and the differences between generations; it picked out the antiquated, the passé ("in *Cromwell*'s time") and reinforced examination of the contemporary. Augustan poetry catches verbal manners, the tones and habits of speech appropriate to the character's rank, background, age and individual character. This acuteness is noticeable in the lightest of pieces; indeed, it is often the lightest pieces that take pleasure in exploring such matters:

> So because I had been buying things for my *Lady* last Night,
> I was resolved to tell my Money, to see if it was right:
> Now you must know, because my Trunk has a very bad Lock,
> Therefore all the Money I have, which, *God* knows, is a very small Stock,
> I keep in a Pocket ty'd about my Middle, next my Smock.
> So when I went to put up my Purse, as *God* would have it, my Smock was unript,
> And instead of putting it into my Pocket, down it slipt:
>   ("The Humble Petition of Frances Harris," 1700, lines 3–9)

Swift's "Humble Petition of Frances Harris" is a lighthearted exercise in total colloquialism, by an author uniquely interested in speech patterns and clichés. But we catch the colloquial tone and ordinary voice quite often in Augustan poetry – as we do in Dr. William King's description of the farmer's dinner party, showing the farmer's notion of ostentation and politeness, as well as his idea of what a man who is master of his wife should sound like:

> He said, that the next *Tuesday* noon would show
> Whether he were the Lord at home, or no;
> When their good company he would entreat
> To well-brew'd ale, and clean, if homely, meat.
> . . .
> The guests upon the day appointed came,
> Each bowsy farmer with his simp'ring dame.
> Hoe! *Sue!* cries *Slouch*, why dost not thou appear?
> Are these thy manners when aunt *Snap* is here?
> I pardon ask, says *Sue*, I'd not offend
> Any my dear invites, much less his friend.
> *Slouch* by his kinsman *Gruffy* had been taught
> To entertain his friends with finding fault,
> And make the main ingredient of his treat
> His saying there was nothing fit to eat;
> The boil'd pork stinks, the roast beef's not enough,
> The bacon's rusty, and the hens are tough;
> The veal's all rags, the butter's turn'd to oil;
> And thus I buy good meat for sluts to spoil.
> 'Tis we are the first *Slouches* ever sate
> Down to a pudding without plumbs or fat.
>
> (King, "The Old Cheese")[4]

Poetic narrative may take advantage of multiple narrative possibilities; it can (as it does in this passage from King's poem) move from authorial judgment to a summary of indirect speech (indicating character's discourse) to the renewed use of pure mimetic quotation. Poets take advantage of all their powers of description and their licence to describe through imagery in order to give us character amplified, and character in appropriate setting:

> Stretch'd on the couch of state she pensive lies,
> While oft' the snowy Cambric wipes her eyes.
> Now enter'd *Lucy*, trusty *Lucy* knew
> To roll a sleeve, or bear a *Billet-doux*.
>
> (Gay, "The Funeral. A Town Eclogue," 1720, lines 9–12)

The conversation of characters often maintains the description while allowing us to see that what is described is the product of an individual taste and an individual point of view. This is the case when, for instance, Lady Winchilsea's character Almeria, the silly London lady, describes her uncouth visitor, Ardelia (Lady Winchilsea herself): Almeria bounces about on her coach's cushions, displaying herself to the beaux, one of whom lolls against the carriage and "Thrusts in his head, at once to view the fair, / And keep his curls from discomposing air." Almeria garrulously displays her ill breeding in extended complaint, and criticism of her guest:

> Pitty me then (she crys) and learn the fate
> That makes me Porter to a Temple gate;
> Ardelia came to Town, some weeks agoe,
> Who does on books her rural hours bestow,
> And is so rustick in her cloaths and meen,
> 'Tis with her ungenteel but to be seen,
> . . .
> To her I did engage my coach and day,
> And here must wait, while she within does pray.
> Ere twelve was struck, she calls me from my bed,
> Nor once observes how well my toilett's spread;
> Then, drinks the fragrant tea contented up,
> Without a complement upon the cup,
> Tho' to the ships, for the first choice I stear'd,
> Through such a storm, as the stout bargemen fear'd;
> Least that a praise, which I have long engross'd
> Of the best china Equipage, be lost.
> ("Ardelia's Answer to Ephelia")[5]

Almeria's defects are satirically clear; indolent and spiritually slothful, she will not join her guest in church but prefers to wait in the carriage and talk to beaux. She is totally caught up in conspicuous consumption. Yet Almeria has the courage of her consuming, and we can feel her individual energy in her tones and in her description. She may rise after noon, but she prides herself in her daring all hazards to get at the best china – and she makes us know how heroic such an adventure could feel to a lady who believes in her cause.

Augustan satiric poetry, like all other satiric poetry, very often views mankind as a crowd of grotesques or knaves or fools – or just as a crowd. But Augustan poetry is extremely ready to seize on individuals on whom to focus, and an Augustan crowd commonly individualizes itself very rapidly. Rochester's Tunbridge Wells becomes a collection of individuals. Gay's *Trivia* captures the excitement and estrangement of the walker in the city surrounded by anonymous multitudes – but typically the persons the eye lights on become real persons, like the "waggish Boys" who sweep the street, or "the sallow Milk-maid" who chalks her gains on the doors.

Persons observed are always on the point of springing into personality. This is true in non-satiric and even non-comic poems also. In any crowd in Augustan poetry there is a sense of personal as well as collective life. In Gray's description of the children at play about Eton, the children are shown pursuing a variety of activities, and we are asked to imagine (in the questions directed to Father Thames) how different these children seem to each other, although the observer sees a group and cannot give names. Though the observer looks down from a height, and from a distance of age and time, and cannot know the children individually, the personal is still honoured.

The personal is honoured in instances where we might not expect it at all. Blair's *The Grave* (1743), for instance, is a mournful preachment on *vanitas* and death, combined with Christian consolation – hardly the sort of poem in which we expect lively character sketches. Yet even here the author, when he chances to glance at a human type in order to make a quick illustration of a point (about the vulgar horror of a churchyard) cannot resist individualizing his type:

> Oft in the lone Church-yard at Night I've seen
> By Glimpse of Moon-shine chequering thro' the Trees,
> The School-boy with his Satchel in his Hand,
> Whistling aloud to bear his Courage up,
> And lightly tripping o'er the long flat Stones
> (With Nettles skirted, and with Moss o'ergrown)
> That tell in homely Phrase who lie below;
> Sudden! he starts, and hears, or thinks he hears
> The sound of something purring at his Heels:
> Full fast he flies, and dares not look behind him,
> Till out of Breath he overtakes his Fellows;
> Who gather round, and wonder at the Tale
> Of Horrid *Apparition*, tall and ghastly,
> That walks at Dead of Night, or takes his Stand
> O'er some new-open'd Grave, and, strange to tell!
> Evanishes at Crowing of the Cock.
>
> (*The Grave*, lines 56–71)[6]

Blair's schoolboy is not drawn satirically, in the sense of supplying primarily an example of something needing immediate correction. The child may be wrong, but he is made sympathetic. We see what he does, and know what is going on in his emotions and mind when he panics and then has to seek the safety of his companions and excuse his fear by the ghost story which he himself by now believes. His fear and his bravado in telling his tale are fully developed. What we see in the boy, as well as in the weeping widow of the next lines of Blair's poem, is human nature, human beings in inner life as well as outer gesture.

Sometimes the very essence of a poem is the observation of an individual whose distinct personality becomes more and more noticeable and insistent. The inner life is indicated through the outer life of appearance and gesture. This is the case with Dryden's portrayal of the clown, Cymon, drawn in lines often referred to in the eighteenth century. Cymon exemplifies disturbing dissonance of outer and inner, combining a handsome body with a feeble mind:

> His eldest Born a goodly Youth to view
> Excell'd the rest in Shape, and outward Shew;
> Fair, Tall, his Limbs with due Proportion join'd,
> But of a heavy, dull, degenerate Mind.

His Soul bely'd the Features of his Face;
Beauty was there, but Beauty in disgrace.
A clownish Mien, a Voice with rustick sound,
And stupid Eyes, that ever lov'd the Ground.
He look'd like Nature's Error; as the Mind ⎫
And Body were not of a Piece design'd, ⎬
But made for two, and by mistake in one were join'd. ⎭
. . .
The more inform'd the less he understood,
And deeper sunk by flound'ring in the Mud.
. . .
  His Father, when he found his Labour lost,
And care employ'd, that answer'd not the Cost,
Chose an ungrateful Object to remove,
And loath'd to see what Nature made him love;
So to his Country-Farm the Fool confin'd;
Rude Work well suted with a rustick Mind.
Thus to the Wilds the sturdy *Cymon* went,
A Squire among the Swains, and pleas'd with Banishment.
His Corn, and Cattle, were his only Care,
And his supreme Delight a Country-Fair.
. . .
His Quarter-Staff, which he cou'd ne'er forsake,
Hung half before, and half behind his Back.
He trudg'd along unknowing what he sought,
And whistled as he went, for want of Thought.
          (*Fables*, "Cymon and Iphigenia," lines 50–85)[7]

The passage is so arranged that it is impossible not to feel sympathy for
Cymon. The father's (rather cold-hearted) frustration is entirely secondary to
the misery of the son. The reader catches Cymon's uneasy sense of being at
odds with himself – and his relief at finding an environment which makes no
unanswerable demands. Cymon's dull blankness has some joyousness and
delight of nature about it (unlike, say, that of Peter Grimes). And this is the
story of the transformation of a mind. Love teaches and rescues the "Man-
Child," working an inner alteration of will and understanding:

    What then of alter'd *Cymon* shall we say,
    But that the Fire which choak'd in Ashes lay,
    A Load too heavy for his Soul to move,
    Was upward blown below, and brush'd away by Love? (lines 226–9)

The whole story is taken from Boccaccio, but Cymon is Dryden's distinctive
amplification; the central activity within this section of Dryden's story is the
development of personality in the mind, the invisible growth of character
within. It is such movements of mind that pleased Augustan poets in their
characters. They can show us character within – including the turmoil and the
muddle – both by dramatic means and by the surreal or expressionistic

imagery which is at their command – as in the portrait and development of Pope's Belinda, to choose one of the most famous characters of all.

The poets also developed, particularly in portraying women, modes of subjective narration such as the verse epistle, or the monologue. We have seen Rochester's use of the verse epistle in drawing his sympathetic and complicated character "Artemisia" not as the object of a satire but as subject, who seems to have a life outside the pages she indites and not to have been fully caught or described by this one poem. In a lighter vein, Gay can produce the lovesick jealous monologue of his middle-aged Lydia imagining the (future) married life of her former lover and his new love, Chloe:

> Fly from perfidious man, the sex disdain;
> Let servile *Chloe* wear the nuptial chain.
> *Damon* is practis'd in the modish life,
> Can hate, and yet be civil to a wife.
> He games; he swears; he drinks; he fights, he roves;
> Yet *Chloe* can believe he fondly loves.
> Mistress and wife can well supply his need,
> A miss for pleasure, and a wife for breed.
> But *Chloe*'s air is unconfined and gay,
> And can perhaps an injur'd bed repay;
> Perhaps her patient temper can behold
> The rival of her love adorn'd with gold,
> Powder'd with di'monds; free from thought and care,
> A husband's sullen humours she can bear.
>   Why are these sobs? And why these streaming eyes?
> Is love the cause? no, I the sex despise.
>
>   ("The Toilette. A Town Eclogue," 1716, lines 79–94)

Lydia, forsaken, tries desperately and meanly to put Chloe in her own slighted place, but, however much misery and odium Lydia heaps on her rival, the rival's happiness is too much for this fragile and imaginary revenge. The lack of satisfaction to be found in Lydia's agitated prophecy leads to breakdown and tears. The investigation of inner life and motive by use of such subjective techniques is to be found outstandingly in that great Ovidian heroine-ic poem, *Eloisa to Abelard* (1717), in which, as generations of critics have noted, the heroine's inward and mixed responses affect the outer reality she sees. She feels only "Melancholy" in the landscape around her convent:

> Her gloomy presence saddens all the scene,
> Shades ev'ry flow'r, and darkens ev'ry green,
> Deepens the murmur of the falling floods,
> And breathes a browner horror on the woods.
>
>   (*Eloisa to Abelard*, lines 167–70)

Eloisa's inner activity distorts the church service, even as the tears rising to her eyes distort what she sees:

> One thought of thee puts all the pomp to flight,
> Priests, Tapers, Temples, swim before my sight;
> In seas of flame my plunging soul is drown'd,
> While Altars blaze, and Angels tremble round.   (lines 273–6)

The Augustans are always interested in the mind's power to transform what is exterior into a reflection of the mind:

> About Eight at Night, we enter'd the Court-yard of this handsome, large, old and lonely Mansion, that looks made for Solitude and Mischief, as I thought, by its Appearance, with all its brown nodding Horrors of lofty Elms and Pines about it...
>
> (Richardson, *Pamela*, 1740)[8]

Indeed, the presentation of character in Augustan literature almost always entails showing the mind's power to transform what is exterior into a reflection of the mind. The transforming character is also endowed with savour, *quidditas* – what we now call personality – and the whole modern idea of "personality" seems to come into being in this period.[9] Since antiquity we have become accustomed to the satiric habit of making enemies into characters, but the eighteenth century sees the desire to turn almost everyone into poetic personalities; friends become (as in Goldsmith's *Retaliation*) poetic characters, comic, sympathetic and individual. It is as if reality means getting into a poem, somehow, acquiring dimension as a poetic fiction. A poet has a sort of duty to put himself/ herself and friends into verse, not enshrining them in deep satire or high love poetry but offering quick observation of individual circumstances, activities and traits, all appropriately particularized. What we call *"Person*ification," the person-making trope, is closely related to that interest, that appetite for personality. To the Augustans, evidently, everything – a favourite cat, a sensitive plant, a Muse, or Dulness – is more or less like a person. And the power of person is such that what belongs to person(s) or is apprehended by human beings could in itself be presented effectively as Person. Aspects of the psyche are so many and so various that they can be usefully split off for momentary observation. The Augustan use of personification is not an evasion of human life, but an intensification of what was found to be so real. Personification expressively signals the vitality and centrality of person in an age whose poetry is formed and populated by personalities. Eloisa's "Melancholy" with its gloomy and transforming presence does not divert us from Eloisa's response but adds to it, and makes us feel not only that Eloisa can try to half-objectify a subjective sensation but also that she is herself so rich a person as to give rise to – or split off into – intensely apprehended and active aspects of psychic life.

It is hardly fair to turn to Pope for examples of characterization both objectively and subjectively presented. The case is too easy – we all remember Pope's characters. Pope was not at all singular in being a character-drawing poet. The wealth of the Augustans' poetic characters prefigures the age of the Augustan Novel, and the novelists expand on the poets' discoveries rather than supersede them. The characters in the novels are fitting companions for Artemisia, Cymon, Slouch, Lydia, Eloisa. We recognize their similars not alone in the major characters in the novels, such as the subjectively drawn Pamela, Clarissa, Lovelace, Tristram, or the mock-heroic Parson Adams or Tom Jones, but also in the great population of interesting minor or secondary characters, such as Lady Booby, Lady Bellaston, Lord Fellamar, Win Jenkins, Mr. Grandison, Mr. Orme. Characters from the poems and the novels make good company for each other – but the poets got there first.

The characters within the novels, when they act as narrators (for the whole or for parts of the story), reveal themselves precisely as authorial presences trained in Augustan poetry. Incidentally, a number of such characters are poets themselves: Pamela, Lovelace, Roderick Random. All of these narrating characters are to some degree self-conscious about narration, particularly when the narrative is written. We hear the voice letting us into the secrets of what he or she is making. The voice discusses with us the variety of its styles, questions its own effects. Fielding's Author in *Tom Jones*, as everyone notices, offers us statement in alternative styles ("or in plain English ..."), investigating the capacities of his language, asking what dialect and what register we would choose to hear. But so do the characters as narrators; they are always questioning their effects, re-examining what they have done so far, offering alternatives, continuations or variations. It is an authentication of personality to exhibit such a self-consciousness and sophistication. To enter on the ground of literary fastidiousness and stylistic doubt bespeaks the lively and individual mind. Clarissa Harlowe, that great Augustan writer, constantly notices her own writing, enters into discussion of diction and changes of tone in her own letters and speeches, and those of others. She reconsiders a letter just written as a literary object, and apologizes, Artemisia-like, for tone and closure:

And now, my dear, let me ask you: Have I come up to your expectation? If I have not, when my mind is more at ease, I will endeavour to please you better. For, methinks, my sentences drag; my style creeps; my imagination is sunk; my spirit serves me not...
(*Clarissa*, Clarissa to Anna, 20 March)[10]

Authorial characters are often parodists momentarily, as we see in the letters of Anna Howe and Lovelace and also of Clarissa herself. Roderick Random parodies high styles and low, sardonically mimics the manner of thought and expression of superiors and associates. It is part of the pattern of *Humphry Clinker* that the characters parody one another. The best of such authorial characters engage in self-parody, an activity which displays their wit, a quality aligned in Augustan works with self-consciousness. Clarissa parodies herself, catching up in advance the response she supposes Anna Howe will have to what she has just said and pre-empting criticism with her own commentary on phrases Anna will make fun of: "So that This is but *conditional liking* still, you'll say ..." The capacity for self-parody is a kind of final proof of the intellectual stature of an author. It is an Augustan belief that

no style, no genre, should be taken quite for granted, even one's own. There is
no rest for the witty.

Such consciousness of style is related to a consciousness both of personality
and of "originality" – both concepts of the new age. Any work of any length
depends for its success on a kind of ability to repeat itself, and the concept of
"originality" in literature, the sense of the individual voice and style that
allows us to say "this must be by Pope," "this is surely by Johnson," is
supported by the ability of the author, having found or made his unique style
and manner (or styles and manners), to maintain and reproduce them. Of this
the Augustans were quite aware, and they perceived at once the pitfalls that
lay in wait. They mocked individual bad styles, like Blackmore's bumbling
drone, but they also kept a watch on themselves and showed they noticed their
own habits. Catching somebody and identifying his work by the style became a
favourite literary game (and has remained so). Rochester's Timon comically
conveys his annoyance when a stupid acquaintance praises him for authorship
of a poem he didn't write and in fact despises as "insipid":

> He knew my style, he swore, and 'twas in vain
> Thus to deny the issue of my brain.
> Choked with his flattery, I no answer make,
> But silent, leave him to his dear mistake,
> Which he by this had spread o'er the whole town,
> And me with an officious lie undone.
>
> ("Timon," lines 25–30)

Fools pretend to identify styles, when the game needs more intelligence than
they can muster. Pope also jokes about critic-readers so confident that they
think they can identify him when they are in fact quite capable of attributing to
him "The first Lampoon Sir *Will.* or *Bubo* makes":

> Poor guiltless I! and can I chuse but smile,
> When ev'ry Coxcomb knows me by my *Style*?
>
> (*Epistle to Dr. Arbuthnot*, lines 281–2)

Pope knew he was being Pope, as he occasionally shows in descriptive self-
vindication, in self-quotation, and even in self-mimicry. He was also capable of
departing from the style of Mr. Pope momentarily, in order to throw readers off
the scent:

> Our author told MR. HARTE, that, in order to disguise his being the author of the
> second epistle of the Essay on Man, he made, in the first edition, the following bad
> rhyme:
>> A cheat! a whore! who starts not at the *name*,
>> In all the inns of court, or Drury-*Lane*?
> And HARTE remembered to have often heard it urged, in enquiries about the author,
> whilst he was unknown, that it was impossible it could be POPE's on account of this
> very passage.[11]

Such knowingness about style, like the sensitivity to it, accompanies a strong sense of its individuality. Style is personal – style is a voice. Through a particular style an individual person is created and known – like Pamela with her own idiosyncratic and memorable and energetic style:

All the Matter is, if I could get Needle-work enough, I would not spoil my Fingers by this rough Work. But if I can't, I hope to make my Hands as red as a Blood-pudden, and as hard as a Beechen Trencher, to accommodate them to my Condition.

(Pamela, p. 78)

Through style alone Richardson makes Pamela a physical presence, an achievement which matches that of the great Augustan poets who make themselves, through the expressive, flexible and interesting deployment of personal style, into voices which are also strong physical presences.

Writing means voice. In Augustan novels, as in the poems, the voice – speaking out or musing, reflecting and observing – is capable of going on with infinite and inexhaustive liveliness. The Voice seems to wish never to give over, and endings are staved off as the Voice triumphantly continues. The worst thing that can befall a character in Augustan fiction is not bankruptcy, injury, forced defloration, or imprisonment – but suppression. Being silenced, rendered unable to utter, is the most dreadful torture. To become incapable of discourse is an appalling affliction. Roxana nearly bursts "for want of a Vent" when she cannot express her emotions. Almost every novel has at least one episode in which the central character falls into that most agonizing and dehumanizing predicament, though few suffer as outrageously as Roderick Random, who is stapled to the deck and exposed to the elements and the cannon shot in the midst of a sea-fight, his cries unheeded in the din (*Roderick Random*, chapter 29). Censorship of one's writing is also a torment, estranging self from world, and self from utterance. Mr. B. in trying to dictate Pamela's letter home, and Lovelace in forging letters between Anna and Clarissa are both engaged in a deadly oppression. Such forgery marks the point where parody of style becomes tyranny; there is something murderous in taking over another's voice. But the forging or censoring villains don't get away with it. The real voice is always heard in the end, triumphant over restraint. Characters persist in utterance. Their insatiable appetite is their voice. And that is true too of Young and Pope, of Thomson and Cowper. They, like Pamela or Roderick, absorb life into their discourse and return it again. When forced with the threat of a stop, they seize on the particular and remake it for us, feeling in the particular and in the power of the mind to grasp it that constant source of reassurance that the self is alive.

Augustan works are typically long discursive narratives, each one a discourse that promises never to suppress itself, to be never-ending. If you read Thomson or Cowper for the story, you would hang yourself – and not because they don't have stories. The whole is one large story or a discourse, perpetually triumphing over itself and over the possibilities of suppression. The voice will have its way. Cowper says it is impossible not to write. High and hazardous topics might daunt mere prudence, but "the impulse" will not be denied:

> Sweet is the harp of prophecy; too sweet
> Not to be wrong'd by a mere mortal touch:
> Nor can the wonders it records be sung
> To meaner music, and not suffer loss.
> But, when a poet, or when one like me,
> Happy to rove among poetic flow'rs,
> Though poor in skill to rear them, lights at last
> On some fair theme, some theme divinely fair,
> Such is the impulse and the spur he feels
> To give it praise proportion'd to its worth,
> That not t'attempt it, arduous as he deems
> The labour, were a task more arduous still.
>
> (*The Task* VI, lines 747–58)

Not to try the theme, *not* to utter, would be a much more arduous task indeed. For the Augustans, heard melodies are always sweeter. Those unheard just don't get heard.

The truly Augustan nature of the eighteenth-century novel is itself a topic for a book, but I hope enough has been said here to help remove the distorting notion that lingers in our schools, to the effect that the eighteenth-century novel is "fun" whereas the poetry distinctly is not, but is an entirely different matter concerned with grey and distant things. Novels and poems have deep resemblances. For our immediate purposes here it is important to notice the sense of the personal and the characterful in Augustan poetry, and to consider the meaning and value of voice in that poetry. The voice – the utterance – is personal, urgent and important.

Nevertheless, matters are much more complicated than the last few pages would suggest. The true Augustan poem is rarely, if ever, satisfied with a voice. One extraordinary effect of Augustan poems is that they seem double-tongued. Not only does almost every poem include debate within itself, but also nearly every line speaks in, as it were, two languages. Verses conduct a kind of quick debate internally, a debate rarely capable of quick resolution. A poet's ability to render this effect is related to his highly valued capacity to produce parody, but the poets go beyond the limits of parody in seeking mixed effects. And within the one "style" characteristic of and personal to the poet, a number of styles play and confront each other, with complicated results.

In considering this essential technique or habit of Augustan poetry, its double-tongued utterance, or quality of double-mindedness, I wish to turn for the first time for illustration to a dramatic work, a work by one of the most intelligent and most experimental of Augustan poets. John Gay in the second generation of Augustan poets, like Lord Rochester in the first, is the most outspoken exponent and clearest analyst of the Augustan manner. Gay's *oeuvre* combines a full use of the effects dear to Augustan poets with a creative

scepticism about all effects. *The Beggar's Opera* (1728), a piece outrageously
witty, parodic and utterly stylistically self-conscious, can provide a key to all
the literature of the Augustan period. *The Beggar's Opera* mixes a number of
genres, and combines the sublime and the ridiculous. It imitates nothing,
though it borrows from almost everything; it is definitely, almost defiantly, *sui
generis*. The play crosses boundaries, making itself into an opera by the introduction largely of well-known melodies, supporting various kinds of lyric verse
with varying appropriateness to the speaker/singer.

It is that aspect of *The Beggar's Opera* that I wish to stress here, as illustration
of its doubleness – its combination of lyric with melody, song with situation,
speaker with what is spoken. The piece constantly puzzles and distracts our
emotions and thoughts by arousing conventional (and not unreal) feelings and
expectations in circumstances in which these feelings and expectations cannot
be comfortably indulged. Take, for instance, the "Cotillon" in Act II, scene iv.
Macheath sings this song of two stanzas, each stanza being repeated after his
singing by the chorus of women:

> *Youth's the Season made for Joys;*
> *Love is then our Duty* •
> *She alone who that employs*
> *Well deserves her Beauty.*
> *Let's be gay*
> *While we may,*
> *Beauty's a Flower, despis'd in decay.*
>
> *Let us drink and sport to-day,*
> *Ours is not to-morrow.*
> *Love with Youth flies swift away,*
> *Age is nought but Sorrow.*
> *Dance and sing;*
> *Time's on the Wing,*
> *Life never knows the return of Spring.*[12]

The air is simple, elegant and delicate. It fits unexpectedly but magnificently
with the lyrics, conveying the plangency of the invitation to joy. The verses are
perhaps the nearest thing to the true Horatian note of the *Odes* that we will find
in our Augustan period, and they also possess the grace of seventeenth-century
lyrics, including that resignation to the power of time combined with a refusal
of submission to melancholy which always supplies much of the unexpected
moral strength of such hedonism. The singing/speaking characters here yield
themselves to the universal; they could be on a canvas in a mythological
landscape, illuminated by a serene and haunting light, voyaging to Cytherea
or gathering the roses that will fade.

All this is entirely true – but, of course, we know the verses of the "Cotillon"
are being sung on stage by a highwayman and a large group of whores.
Macheath has sent for them, as if ordering up the wine: "I must have Women.
There is nothing unbends the Mind like them" (II. iii, p. 22). We know the

women by name through Macheath's greeting: they include Dolly Trull, Betty Doxy, Jenny Diver, Mrs. Slammekin, Suky Tawdry. The "ladies" are just about to take wine and gin with their host Macheath, and to gossip about their success in their trade, which includes picking the pockets of their customers. Macheath is about to be betrayed by Jenny and the others. Hedonism, which has its glories in the verses of the song, is disconcertingly presented in its practicalities.

We could say that the song shows Macheath and the doxies romanticizing themselves, assuming an elegance and emotional justification that they cannot really claim – that the song represents only their rationalization of their thievery, gin-sipping and calculated lechery. The prostitutes' beauty is factitious, must be a flower decaying already. When they say "Love" they mean sex and in their case, sex for sale – and their "Love" will not be saleable for long. Indeed they will not know a second spring. All this is also true, and the various ironies are apparent, including the ironic fact that Macheath's youth and beauty seem to be betrayed to the gallows, so his time is shorter than he thinks, and Time's wings are moving much more swiftly than the delicate abstractions of the lyric really mean. Yet what we are most centrally conscious of when we hear the scene complete with its music is that we *are* moved by the song. The beauty of "Youth's the Season made for Joys" still stands, and it retains its plangent significance even while we know while we hear it that it is sung by whores and an easy-going highwayman. We cannot extract the sense of the song, reduce and degrade it through ironic readings, and shove it away. The melody itself touches us before we can stop it. There is no way of repudiating the song. The true reading – or hearing – means that we have to stretch heads and hearts to accommodate both the reality of the song and the reality of the trulls. We are not allowed to hang on to pure satire and dismiss the song, any more than we can hang on to the loveliness of the song and eliminate the vulgarity and crassness of the characters, or the satire on human nature. One effect does not cancel out the other. The whores are made poetic speakers of other aspects of themselves, and of ourselves too. They have different voices in their prose speeches and in their song, and yet the different voices are, as they must be in theatrical performance, the same voice too. Gay himself speaks with double tongue here, making us hear two literary voices together, at once and equally. The two languages of this scene, or this part of it, are disparate and yet related; they work in unison and they work counter to each other at the same time. We must be able to hear both.

We have here come upon an important and common characteristic of Augustan poetry, the combination of disparate languages, disparate voices, working simultaneously both with and against each other. In such a combination of counter-effects *a* cannot be dismissed or cancelled out by *b*. A line or a passage may seem to set up a ventriloquist's dummy to chant against another, or against the ventriloquist-speaker. Sometimes this sense of two voices is brought to the fore of the poem, with some explication of the two sets of views and some overt play of part against part, as if the language belongs to two different parties and divides into halves.

A gentle but sophisticated and very effective example of the use of the two-voice effect as overt subject is Pope's "Epistle to Miss Blount, on her leaving the Town, after the Coronation" (1717). The forced withdrawal of *"Zephalinda"* from town is quickly explained, and there follows a lengthy description of her country surroundings and her life in the country:

> She went, to plain-work, and to purling brooks,
> Old-fashion'd halls, dull aunts, and croaking rooks.
> She went from Op'ra, park, assembly, play,
> To morning walks, and pray'rs three times a day;
> To pass her time 'twixt reading and Bohea,
> To muse, and spill her solitary Tea,
> Or o'er cold coffee trifle with the spoon,
> Count the slow clock, and dine exact at noon;
> Divert her eyes with pictures in the fire,
> Hum half a tune, tell stories to the squire;
> Up to her godly garret after sev'n,
> There starve and pray, for that's the way to heav'n.   (lines 11–22)

After this effective and sympathetic description of *ennui*, the poem continues by imagining Zephalinda's animating imaginings:

> In some fair evening, on your elbow laid,
> You dream of triumphs in the rural shade;
> In pensive thought recall the fancy'd scene,
> See Coronations rise on ev'ry green;
> Before you pass th'imaginary sights
> Of Lords, and Earls, and Dukes, and garter'd Knights;
> While the spread Fan o'ershades your closing eyes;
> Then give one flirt, and all the vision flies.
> Thus vanish sceptres, coronets and balls,
> And leave you in lone woods, or empty walls.   (lines 31–40)

The portrait of Zephalinda is a good example of poetic character-drawing (though Pope is also drawing on the personality of an individual friend). The poem creates for the girl her own setting and atmosphere, and makes us notice her inner state, providing us with a picture of the movements of her mind as well as giving us the imagistic play with her external circumstances amid the plain-work and rooks. The girl looking out the window on the country evening transforms what she sees, and the metamorphosis is vividly described; we see, almost cinematically, the "real" scene (green, woods) becoming the "fancy'd scene" as Court and Town are transferred, through the activity of her mind, into this other (unsuitable) space: "see Coronations rise on ev'ry green." The vision vanishes, the girl is left alone in what is to her emptiness.

But the poem does not end there; the last verse-paragraph concerns the poet himself, who participates in an exactly similar activity:

> So when your slave, at some dear, idle time,
> (Not plagu'd with headachs, or the want of rhime)
> Stands in the streets, abstracted from the crew,
> And while he seems to study, thinks of you:
> Just when his fancy points your sprightly eyes,
> Or sees the blush of soft *Parthenia* rise,
> *Gay* pats my shoulder, and you vanish quite;
> Streets, chairs, and coxcombs rush upon my sight;
> Vex'd to be still in town, I knit my brow,
> Look sow'r, and hum a tune – as you may now.　　　(lines 41–50)

The parallel is closely pointed by phrasing and rhyme words ("eyes/flies"; "eyes/rise"). Rhythm and emphasis work in parallel, though there is some emphasis on reversal. In the section on Zephalinda's fantasy, the set of three nouns belong to her vision and not to the dull reality around her; "sceptres, coronets and balls" are to her not only the most fascinating but the most solid things, even in their absence. The vision conjured up by the poet-speaker is less specific; the solid detail is the triplet of nouns representing the too-solid irritations of a present reality which, in his circumstances, is crowded, not empty: "Streets, chairs, and coxcombs rush upon my sight." Both persons make unconscious efforts of reverie to see what is not there, and each is brought back to the unsatisfactory setting which the eyes cannot choose but see. The reveries are not totally alike, for the girl is dreaming of the Coronation and the poet is imagining her.

The entire poem must, at one level, be taken as the reverie of the controlling Poet, who has conjured up the whole, including the girl's dwelling-place and how she feels about it. But within the poem the girl is given her own voice and language as well as setting. That is, the poem seems to break out into a new language. The first language of description is largely description from Zephalinda's point of view. It is to her that the halls are "Old-fashion'd" and the aunts "dull." In the first long descriptive passage, however, the girl is (objectively) "she." In the verse-paragraph that follows, she becomes "you," and the poem takes on the form of inner debate, concealed debate, as it keeps for a long while to the point of view of the girl – one might call her the heroine. It is "you" that does the dreaming, though what is present in that part of the poem is produced through the enchantments of her mind. The Poet speaks in counterpoint as "I" in the last verse-paragraph; he emerges with another language, less naive, less detailed than the girl's. It is also different in tone: "abstracted from the crew" could not be used about or by Zephalinda. The poet's gestures, and the words used to describe gestures and their context ("Vex'd ... I knit my brow, / Look sow'r"), are different, would not be appropriate to the girl in either her boredom or her pensiveness.

The poem dramatizes, amusingly and affectionately, common but not banal tensions: Female against Male, Town against Country, high things (corona-tions) against low or commonplace things (cold coffee), natural against man-made things. The poem comically presents the female's preference of Town over Country (a commonplace of Restoration drama) by placing the lady in the Country, with the Town in her imagination. There is no moral drawn; Pope, as speaker-character inside the poem, seems indifferent to the country. His imaginings of natural beauty present a lady's eyes and blush. What we have is just *difference* – difference multiplied, for each of these two different people is forced to see something other than what he/she would see. "Zephalinda's" circumstances, and her voice and thoughts, run counter to and yet in unison with those of "Pope," the gallant "your slave" who is struck with memory in the middle of the street. The difference does not mean there is an obviously superior and obviously inferior set of views and language. Indeed we are so made to experience the girl's circumstances and her boredom that, though we may laugh (as Zephalinda does not) at her predicament, we cannot deny the concretely documented reality of what she knows and the way she knows it. Her experience is just as real as that of the poet, her "slave" (who is also funny), and both of them really try, very vividly, to make an unreality real, the absent present, through the transformational powers of the mind. The two visions don't quite match. The fulfilment of the one would not necessarily at all entail the fulfilment of the other. Parallel, they go their separate ways together (a good illustration in itself of the relation between Male and Female). And neither can cancel out the other. They are two; this is a poem about doubleness. But Pope also suggests here that the two, however disparate and separated, can make a whole, though neither character is fully aware of it. The girl's incomplete melody ("Hum half a tune") is perhaps completed when the Pope character in the poem takes up a melody ("and hum a tune"). It may be that we are meant to think of the two humming the same tune, in two halves. The two voices possibly come together, though remaining separate. Half a tune plus half a tune equals the whole song, just as the two voices in the poem make up the whole. Yet the two voices, even in coming together (and in the poem any union is tenuous and visionary), do not make a simple unity or unison. The two voices, even in this gentle and witty poem, are diverse and different; to some extent they are in collision with each other.

If we examine Augustan poetry more minutely, we find that this combination of disparate languages working both in harmony and against one another is a common and even fundamental technique. It is the source of much that is most striking in memorable verses, even in single lines of verse. Take, for example, Pope's "And the fresh vomit run for ever green!" (*Dunciad* II, line 156). It is a voiced line, spoken by a character, being part of Curll's ventriloquized speech of exclamation at seeing his deeds and labours (his shames) recorded on the shaggy tapestry that Dulness gives him as a prize. The occasion parodies Aeneas' viewing of the deeds of himself and the other Trojan heroes recorded in the art of Carthage. The line itself, with its preceding line, is a parody of two lines by Halifax. The whole section is thus a complex pattern of interfolded parodies and references, with older poems, serious poems, lending their language – against their wills – to this peculiar transforming effect. Styles are borrowed for alien substance, matched with matter in conflict with the styles' original nature. But the style borrowed and parodied is not ineffectual: "And the fresh vomit run for ever green" has in rhythm and sound and cadence an effect of haunting grandeur and elegant simplicity. If we change it, for instance, to "And the fresh *Isis* run forever green" we can hear the lilt of language, feel the charm of the diction. There is an appeal to ideas of Nature ("fresh ... green") and a satisfying appeal to undying time ("run for ever"), summoning up Nature's eternal fresh motion as well as the traditional immortality bestowed by art. This sweet and appealing poetic language has of course been subverted by the use of the one noun that changes everything. Fresh green running *vomit* is immensely disgusting; indeed the disgust is so immense as to be oddly satisfying in very intensity, peculiarly almost sublime in its bathos. But the effects of beauty, elegance, simplicity and pathos conjured up by the other "poetic" language do not simply disappear under this impact; they are also fully present, working against and angrily *with* the full meaning of the new poetic line. In miniature we recognize the effect we saw in *The Beggar's Opera*, when the whores sing "Youth's the Season made for Joys" and the audience is simultaneously moved to scorn and joy, to the toughest of cynicism and the most delicate modes of plaintive hedonism. Both are double-voiced statements. We cannot discount the effect of beauty in Pope's line any more than we can in Gay's "Cotillon." Pope's line is an extended oxymoron, maintaining with insistent freshness its power to yield surprise. We are unsettled even while satisfied, as we cannot do away with one element, one language, to concentrate on the other.

Oxymoron is the governing figure of speech of Augustan poetry, the central figure of its poetic thought. In its use the Augustans are related to and indebted to the Elizabethans with whom, and with many Continental Renaissance writers in the Petrarchan mode, we chiefly associate the use of the rhetorical figure, in "cold fire," "sick health" and so on. The Augustans, however, expand the use of oxymoron, exploiting all its possibilities in a much larger use than even the Elizabethans made of it. In its simplest form, oxymoron applies to the use of a word with a companion or modifier that signifies the opposite, or an unlike. When the Greeks called the lemon *glukupikros* (sweet-sour) they were employing oxymoron, and in attributing the lemon tree to Venus and to love (also sweet and sour) they extended their oxymoron metaphorically. The Augustan use of oxymoron does not disdain the primitive forms, such as combination of an adjective with a strikingly unlikely noun, and many unitary effects ("fresh vomit") utilize such contrasts. But the Augustans' extension of oxymoron leads them to a diversified play of parts of speech: noun with unexpected verb, modifying phrase with inappropriate object, object unsuited to verb. Zeugma is a slightly extended and punning form of oxymoron, as in the oft-explained lines of Pope "Or stain her Honour, or her new Brocade... / Or lose her Heart, or Necklace, at a Ball" (*The Rape of the Lock* II, lines 107–9).

Here the metaphorical meaning of both "stain" and "lose" is first emphasized, and then we are asked to attach to it as object, unexpectedly, a noun which works with it in the literal sense only. The shock of inappropriate relation is conveyed. Augustan metaphor and simile and metonymy tend to be worked into some oxymoronic expression, in relationships unique, inappropriate, "unsuitable" according to the conventions of language meanings and customary contexts. Two statements seem to be interfolded and pleated together. Very often the total extended oxymoron depends on our understanding of the two languages involved, and knowing that one of them is in some way traditional in poetry. "Language" includes (in its complete nature) cadences, rhythms and sound. Not just two words but two languages unsuited to each other are forced into unusual association and are visibly – or audibly – present.

"A New Song of New *Similies*" (1728), a light poem attributed to Gay, offers a simple illustration of oxymoron at work in Augustan comparisons, as well as exhibiting that delight in play with cliché which is noticeable in many of the Augustans, especially the Scriblerians.[13] The first quatrain begins "My Passion is as Mustard strong." The simile, like the other similes in the piece, is colloquial cliché; "strong as mustard" is a vulgar commonplace. But the strength of mustard is not the sort of strength we commonly associate with love, and Passion and Mustard are forcefully, nonsensically but intelligibly related, to our surprise. The inversion (adjective after noun) belongs to the poetic language of "Passion" and does violence to the natural order of the cliché. The second verse goes thus:

> Round as a Hoop the Bumpers flow;
> I drink, yet can't forget her;
> For tho' as drunk as *David*'s Sow,
> I love her still the better.

The roundness of (ladies'?) hoops is not the same kind of roundness we associate with bumpers passing round the table; indeed, one "round" is a noun, the other a preposition or adverb. Modern readers will be reminded of the White Knight in Carroll, who was stuck as fast as lightning: "It was all kinds of fastness with me."[14] Nonsense writers of the nineteenth century, such as Hood, Lear and Carroll, are direct inheritors of Augustan forms of language, the interfolding of language in linguistic play. In "A Song of New *Similies*" the linguistic play includes not only oxymoronic unions of one word with another, but also the larger play of theme (passion of love) against the activity of the speaker (drinking), and plays of the thematic subject (love for a lady, who is described) against the incessant and obtrusive vulgar comparisons which have nothing to do with the traditional tones or styles of love poetry. In the last stanza the poet achieves a comic pathos (a triumph of oxymoronic effect, being an oxymoron itself) in his fast-falling similes wrenched away from customary causal functions and references:

Sure as a Gun, she'll drop a Tear
And sigh, perhaps, and wish,
When I am rotten as a Pear,
And mute as any Fish.

The hard-hearted lady's imagined future regret for her lost lover-poet is a common topic in love poetry, and the second line here keeps appropriately to the traditional language for that. And, very Augustanly, the end of the poem means the death of the poet-speaker. Death is customarily and also poetically associated with decay and silence, but the similes here, taken from a language which serves lighter and more casual meanings, are pressed into service to perform a task above their capacity. We do not speak of a corpse as being "mute as a fish"; "silent as a stone" would be the appropriate kind of silence, for fish, if always mute, are still alive. Yet the two languages, here forced together for the joke's sake only, do make a statement and the poem utters in its double-voiced manner.

Such an obviously trifling set of verses ought not to be forced to exemplify too much. Yet this kind of conscious play with the two languages, and with the very elements of poetry and speech, really arises only in the Augustan period. This little poem, first published in 1728, could not have appeared in 1628; we could not expect to find anything quite like it before the Restoration. For more serious illustration of the omnipresence and power of oxymoron in Augustan poetry, I proceed to a list of examples, culled almost at random from the work of major Augustan poets. It will be noticeable that in many cases the oxymoron is extended, and consists of the forced union of different styles, not just of contrasting words. Expectations have to be continually revised.

Fair *Chloris* in a pigsty lay;
    Her tender herd lay by her. (Rochester, "Song," 1680)
And the severe Delights of Truth enjoy'd.
    (Dryden, *Religio Laici*, line 233)

And where *Infallibility* has *fail'd*.   (line 251)
Mean while the South rising with dabbled Wings,
A Sable Cloud a-thwart the Welkin flings,
That swill'd more Liquor than it could contain,
And like a Drunkard gives it up again.
    (Swift, "A Description of a City Shower," lines 13–16)

CORINNA, Pride of *Drury-Lane*,
For whom no Shepherd sighs in vain;
Never did *Covent Garden* boast
So bright a batter'd, strolling Toast;
    (Swift, "A Beautiful Young Nymph going to Bed,"
    1734, lines 1–4)

Her conscious tail her joy declar'd;
The fair round face, the snowy beard,
    The velvet of her paws,
    (Gray, "Ode on the Death of a Favourite Cat," 1748)

Some mute inglorious Milton here may rest,
(Gray, *Elegy Written in a Country Church-yard*, line 59)

In Pastry Kings and Queens th'allotted mite to spend
(Shenstone, "The Schoolmistress")[15]

Sorry Pre-eminence of high Descent
Above the vulgar-born, to rot in State!
(Blair, *The Grave*, lines 154–5, p. 10)

Spend all the pow'rs
Of rant and rhapsody in virtue's praise:
Be most sublimely good, verbosely grand,
(Cowper, *The Task* v, lines 676–8)

A widow'd Aunt was there, compell'd by Need,
The Nymph to flatter and her Tribe to feed;
Who, veiling well her Scorn, endured the Clog,
Mute as the Fish, and fawning as the Dog.
(Crabbe, *The Parish Register*, "Burials," lines 368–71)[16]

In the sad Summer of her slow Decay.   (*ibid.*, line 383)

In lines and phrases such as these we can see the activity of poetic transformation, working metamorphosis after metamorphosis at speed. Oxymoron is wonder-working, giving us a world where kings are pastry, pigs are tender. Some of the passages quoted above offer examples of simple oxymoron, like Dryden's "severe Delights" or Crabbe's "sad Summer" (the latter exhibiting a contrast between customary evocative ideas, a contrast amplified by making summer, rather than autumn or winter, the time of decay). But a number of the passages offer examples of extended stylistic oxymoron, rather than only simple discrete self-contrasting phrase. Both Rochester's "Fair *Chloris*" and Swift's "Beautiful Young Nymph" are presented in two languages, of which one is pastoral and "poetic," the other "vulgar" and colloquially realistic, emerging through strongly accented particularized and unignorable nouns. The oxymoronic style of the whole is substantiated in each case by particular compact phrases of oxymoron, such as "tender herd," "Pride of *Drury-Lane*," and "strolling Toast." Gray's "Ode on the Death of a Favourite Cat" plays with two languages, one suited to pastoral love elegy in the description of a beautiful lady, the other appropriate in reference to a domestic cat. We are pushed quickly from phrase appropriate to the first ("fair round face") to phrase appropriate only to the second ("snowy beard"); the whole effect is substantiated by the unitary oxymoron phrase, in which ideas commonly separate are suddenly welded together – "conscious tail."

The four-line passage quoted from Crabbe's *The Parish Register* depends with more subtlety and less sheer comedy on the forcing together of two styles, classical and colloquial. "Nymph" is derived from classical pastoral tradition and "Tribe" from Georgic tradition. "Tribe" is customarily used like "kind" or "race" to refer to a particular genus or species of animal; here the species is unscientifically all the animals owned by the rich young lady, the pets of this arrogant "Nymph." A Nymph who requires flattery and a tribe that requires to be fed by the needy are presented as paradoxes that seem to demand oxymoron. A "high" language of poetic abstraction and a "low" language of short words and proverbs wrestle oxymoronically together. The two languages here are related to the divergent ways in which the rich young lady evidently thinks of herself and her life, and the opinions or feelings of the indigent Aunt, the employee, about her patroness, herself and her task. The whole passage is a quick piece of character-drawing, a character-drawing which remains objective and yet lets us glimpse the complexities of the inner world. For the Augustans, character implies contrast, and the portrayal of a character usually involves a dynamic contrast between inner and outer, a conflict of values and actions which invites oxymoron in its representation. Here Crabbe runs into effective cliché (rather like the "Song of New *Similies*") in the last line quoted, conveying not what the Aunt directly said or would say but the sort of patterns in which she might habitually think – "Mute as the Fish." The downtrodden Aunt is oddly and oxymoronically both fishy and doggy at the same time. Humanly, actively and privately she veils "her Scorn," but yet, like an animal, she behaves passively, and warily tries to please. She endures "the Clog." The clichés trace deterioration. "Dog" expresses what the Aunt is herself being turned into, and the short harsh word fights strongly against the elegant high-style word "Nymph."

The Augustans' choice of diction has often been commented on. We modern readers tend, on the whole, to admire their use of short, concrete, particularized words, and sometimes feel we must apologize for their use of general or abstract terms or high style. These two strains of language belong together in Augustan literature, and the writers could not do without either. Their love of general or abstract or categorical terms reflects a pleasure in having another linguistic element to play with. The Augustans had and always wished to have literary modes or approaches that counter one another. And general terms, adopted from theology, philosophy, politics, or from the poetical tradition, are words which are just as *real as words* as nouns like "cat" or "*Drury-Lane*," or adjectives like "rotten" or "snowy" or "green." The Augustans liked any language reflective of human thoughts, feelings, suppositions and expectations. Their stylistic acuteness most often led them also to investigate each language or sub-language, to shake well before using, to parody this tongue and set it a-working in relation to some other language. We can see these characteristic Augustan activities in the following passage in which the single line from Dryden's *Religio Laici* quoted above appears in its context:

> Those hours hast thou to Nobler use employ'd;
> And the severe Delights of Truth enjoy'd.
> Witness this weighty Book, in which appears
> The crabbed Toil of many thoughtfull years,
> Spent by thy Authour, in the Sifting Care

Of *Rabbins* old Sophisticated Ware
From Gold Divine; which he who well can sort
May afterwards make *Algebra* a Sport.
                                       (*Religio Laici*, lines 232–9)[17]

Dryden's compliment to his friend Henry Dickinson, who had spent his time
translating Père Simon's *Critical History of the Old Testament*, is mingled with the
critical attitude of Dickinson himself to his author, Simon; indeed in Dryden
the questioning seems to touch the translator's work as well. In this mingled
explanation, tribute and argument, Dryden becomes fascinated by the challenge of producing a language fit to explain the activity of such scholars. The
language of the learned activity itself is exploited and demoted in the lines that
follow:

A Treasure, which if *Country-Curates* buy,
They *Junius*, and *Tremellius* may defy:
Save pains in various readings, and Translations;
And without *Hebrew* make most learn'd quotations.   (lines 240–3)

Dryden sports with the technical language, the jargon of Biblical studies. The
jargon includes the names of two sixteenth-century commentators, names not
entirely familiar to all his readers, though they would be to Protestant
theologians and to their comic and commonplace counterparts, the "*Country-
Curates.*" In the process of employing this technical language, and imitating
the procedures of mind which might employ it, Dryden alludes to another
language altogether. "*Algebra*" (still somewhat esoteric and not the grammar-
school staple it was to become) stands for an abstract and opaque activity
which discounts words. It is an original "gibberish." Algebra is another
language, difficult and dubious, which could become (hyperbolically) a mere
game to a crabbed genius (like Père Simon) who spends strange and almost
perverse energies on languages and interpretations. With a characteristic turn
of Augustan thought, Dryden swerves into questions of language and the use of
language, increasing the jargon effect while lightly mocking the curates. He
turns our attention to a vacuous intellectual activity – or rather, non-activity:
that of making quotations from a language absent to the mind. The idea in
"And without *Hebrew* make most learn'd quotations" (i.e. quotations in or
from the Hebrew) is paradoxical and oxymoronic in itself; we have Hebrewless
Hebrew, unquoted quotations. The intellectual activity described has turned
at last into mirror-play with language, while the poet describing the various
activities has himself maintained mastery and survived without deterioration.

   In this verse-paragraph Dryden has kept up his own use of and play with a
language pertaining to an abstract and specialized field of study, while engaging in his own "sport" with it by introducing another technical language, and
the cautiously absurd ("save pains") language of scholarship ("readings, and
Translations") which proves not to be scholarship at all. And all these
languages of specialized study are bounced off a clear if source-shifting lightly

metaphorical language borrowed from everyday life: "Care," "Sophisticated Ware," "Gold," "a Sport," "*Country-Curates,*" "pains."

This passage, which describes a lively (and grotesque) encounter of tongues is itself an exercise in play with language; in it, the relations of words in likeness and in oxymoronic difference are strongly indicated by the way the poem is set out. We see in this passage how the capitalized and italicized words make a kind of pattern to the eye; we pick up a list of abstract characters (who are yet in some sense characterized) and abstract things: *Rabbins, Algebra, Country-Curates, Junius* and *Tremellius, Hebrew.* Rabbins, curates and commentators are connected, representing different phases of the same or related mental interest and action, while "*Algebra*" comments on "Rabbins" and is paralleled (and replaced) by "*Hebrew.*" Dryden's emphasis, through this deployment of capital letters and italics, is not carelessly produced. The Augustans, most particularly those of the first two generations, marked their stresses emphatically, drawing on all the resources of typography to make their stresses clear upon the page, and this habit is deeply and intimately related to their considerations of diction. We are taught how to read every word, by its appearance on the page, and are educated into looking for its stress and its counterpart. Every word is given its own exact weight as well as flavour; the Augustans (from Milton on) were as self-conscious in spelling as in style and were careful that the word as spelled should reflect its sound; they are exact as to numbers of syllables. "Enjoy'd" for instance is quite obviously only two syllables, while "crabbed" is a full two syllables, the "ed" counting as one. The Augustans write "Heav'n" when they mean the sound "Heav'n" and not "Heav-en"; they write "simp'ring," "thro'," "powder'd with di'monds." No poets ever paid more attention to the sound of their words, or their appearance on the page in relation to each other. It seems absurd to talk about Augustan diction to a class reading either poetry or prose in an edition which has modernized the writers, abolishing (except for occasional whim) most capitals and italics, and often turning all spellings into the modern ones save for the exceptional archaic "o'er" or the like. It seems as great a liberty as taking e. e. cummings in hand, straightening his lines for him and endowing him with a dutiful capital on proper names and at the entrance to a line. We have taken such liberties with our poets that they do not look like themselves. And when we have given them a dull appearance we fancy new readers will find them the more congenial, though they have been deprived of keys to reading. The poets often look strangely subdued in this modern (or pseudo-modern) garb. As Johnson said of modernizing,

An authour's language, Sir ... is a characteristical part of his composition, and is also characteristical of the age in which he writes. Besides, Sir, when the language is changed we are not sure that the sense is the same.[18]

Augustan diction is, as the Augustan habitual use of typographical markers indicates, a strongly conscious diction. The reader, by acknowledging capitals and italics, is made aware of and asked to participate in the writer's exercise of choice. The words must be actively noticed, not allowed to drift over the mind. And the choice of emphasis is never mechanical. Even in the heyday of capitalization, not all nouns are capitalized; we are asked, in the fleeting milli-second of reading response, to record the fact of a capital and its significance. This is not what happens in reading modern German, for instance, in which capitals are the regular dress of all nouns. Sometimes Augustans may capitalize an adjective ("Sophisticated Ware") even, though more rarely, a verb. Participles ("Sifting Care") are capitalized fairly often, emphasizing the verbal activity attached to a noun. The convention of italicizing proper names of persons and places, as if these had some extra nominative significance (particulars registered in the mind of God, as it were), invited meaningful play with other italics attributed at choice to nouns set in action with or against these. Italics (*"Country-Curates," "Algebra"*) seem for the Augustans to concretize general categories or abstract nouns, making them more fully real, while at the same time setting them in an aura of teasing significance.

Augustan diction emphasizes its own work. In the self-conscious diction all devices remind us that these are *chosen* words. It is also a diction in which great attention is paid to the modifiers, such as prepositional phrases, adjectives, participial and adverbial phrases. We are always being alerted to the fact that an innocent-seeming word in its "straight" role may turn double agent, may be about to transform its meaning, to become united with something other. The language may be shifting while we watch. Geoffrey Tillotson has written brilliantly of some of these effects within Pope's poetry, and what he has to say might, *mutatis mutandis*, be applied to the work of other Augustans as well:

Pope's syntax is always as compressed as possible. His meaning is left to grow at leisure out of its confined context. One of his chief methods is the conjunction, the monosyllabic "low" word which lays together in apparently tame concord the strangest of bedfellows.

> Who give th'hysteric, or poetic fit ...

This *or* may represent an *alias* ... another word for the same thing ... On the other hand, the *or* may represent a choice between the two things ... The doubleness of these different meanings is discovered by the reader's analysis of two possible syntactical relationships.[19]

Tillotson provides a painstaking and thoughtful analysis of the origins, meaning and effect upon the reader of one line from Pope, "And Alma mater lie dissolv'd in Port!" (*Dunciad*, III, line 338).

His line requires the co-operation of the reader's memory. After "dissolv'd in" the reader expects "ease" but gets "port" ... "Port" has a reflexive action on "dissolv'd in." The reader has already been at pleasant pains to recognize this verb as figurative. He must now return and allow it its literal meaning since port, unlike rest and ease, is a liquid and therefore a solvent. But the figurative sense persists, since the traditional phrases, dissolv'd-in-rest and -ease, equally apply to the dons of the eighteenth century. This mixture of abstract and concrete in "dissolv'd in" produces a slightly dazed perplexity in the reader, but not until the words have been read a second time. Pope, that is, first requires the reader to work – recognizing (the beginning of) a traditional phrase, linking dons with Morpheus who was the subject of the verb in Ovid and Sandys. He then requires him to start working again, partly undoing his former labour. A line already accepted as complex has to be reaccepted as still more complex and complex in different ways.

Tillotson's analysis here emphasizes the work required of the reader; all good Augustan poetry demands this sort of attention. The second reading of a line or passage, in which the reader is alerted to the duality of the languages, does not cancel out the first reading but amplifies it, creating new relations and new tensions, since no meaning can be ruled out or simply cancelled. The Augustan proclaimed distaste for puns may merely have reflected a feeling that puns of the simple sort were too grossly obvious to be much fun. Complete in themselves, and attention-seeking, puns signify a stop to the work of thought, and the two languages are baulked before they can go anywhere. But Augustan choice of words reflects operations very like those involved in straight punning, as in Pope's use of "Port" in the line just discussed. Tillotson's extensive discussion has still not exhausted all the resources and surprises of language which appear in that one line. "To lie in port" is a phrase used of ships, and indicates the idea of reaching a happy haven, well deserved after the struggle of a journey. Alma mater has made no journey and has no right to a happy haven. The "port" to which a ship comes is transformed into another liquid element, both like and unlike that associated with a sea-port; the university seems to be submerging in a liquid element underneath the resting place, disappearing into what ought to support it and ought not to act as a solvent. There is an oxymoronic relationship between lying in port and being dissolved in it.

Words demand our attention, insistently, in Augustan poetry. What Tillotson refers to as "the doubleness of these different meanings" is almost always present, a *doubleness* that makes us hear two languages at work even as we move from modifier to noun, or verb to modifier. A single noun may itself generate contrast, become an oxymoron on its own. Individual words in Augustan poems, like so many individual characters in Augustan plays and novels, may become visibly double-faced, exerting their energies in acting self-contradictory roles, transforming themselves in taking on a part.

As Tillotson says, Augustan syntax is often compressed – but it is not so always. Indeed, one of the features of Augustan poetry which we find hard to take is the relatively straightforward and sometimes leisurely use of normal English syntax, with articles and prepositions all in place. We are trained on the Metaphysicals and on the late Victorians and the moderns, for whom syntactical arrangements are conventions to be defied for the sake of compression. Augustan poetry may seem at first "unpoetical" because the lines move in accordance with the "rules" of the normal sentence: Modifier + Subject + Verb + Predicate. Copulas and conjunctions are present and accounted for. The occasional inversions are not confusing nor grammatically demanding. This is so, not only because the Augustans wanted to be clear (very few poets haven't wanted to be clear to somebody) but because their best work and fullest effects could not be achieved by muddying syntax. Syntax is the clear transparent frame on which their colourful effects can be displayed and supported. If the elemental language which makes reading possible, i.e. syntactical arrangement, were to become very confusing, then the effects of the *doubleness*, of the dual languages, would be lost in the general murkiness. Syntactical straightness allows us to see the work of transformation, the dynamic criss-cross of language. Oxymoron loses its pungent savour if it comes cooked up in a stew of confusions. With so much going on among the elements themselves (nouns, verbs, adjectives) the elements of syntax, supportive but not too visible, can then be quietly shanghaied into strangeness. They do their normal work but are made to say something unusual in their particular context. Grammatical elements, themselves lucid and glassy, take on the bright colours of what they support: "Die *of* a Rose, *in* aromatic pain"; "Slow rose a form *in* Majesty *of* Mud." Grammar and syntax, elements like copulas, conjunctions and prepositions all make connections. The Augustans want us to see connections and connectedness in a new way. The oxymorons (in *aromatic pain*, in *Majesty* of *Mud*) strike out new connections which are related to ourselves, to our customary ways of seeing and describing, and to our sense-reactions, by the quiet use of normal prepositions, introducing the modifying phrase and connecting it with the strange noun and verb, themselves likewise oddly linked. The verse can pretend in its syntactical normality that the linkage is possible and common – since it fits into the way our mind customarily works along the frame of grammar. Augustan syntax is transformational syntax, masquerading as simple syntax. The use of syntax is itself a kind of oxymoron, double-tongued.

The Augustan "doubleness" is usually associated with irony, but "irony," useful word though it is, is sometimes used too sweepingly to be helpful. Manner and meaning of irony can change from moment to moment, not to say from poet to poet. We associate irony with satire, that is with a moral meaning which the writer already has up his sleeve. Blair's "To rot in State" is an ironic oxymoron conveying a moral point. But there can be "free ironies" not immediately connected with a particular moral meaning. Pope's (or Anne Finch's) phrase "aromatic pain" is connected in Pope's paragraph ultimately with a moral point, but is in itself a "free irony," exhibiting a conflict of ideas and senses and even languages interesting in itself; within the phrase neither "aromatic" nor "pain" is wrong or stupid or calls for demotion in favour of the other. The Augustans made good satirists because their interest in double meanings found room to play within satire, but they did not become interested in the doubleness of language only because they wished to be satirists.

The tendency to doubleness of language is visible in Augustan poems where the effect is not satiric, not what we usually mean by "ironic." In Gray's *The Bard* an imagined speaker utters a bardic language which is (by the poet) translated into rational modern utterance without ceasing to be itself. The reader is in some sort made to imagine that other language behind, within and parallel to the one he knows – and that language too is connected with a strong sense of *person*, for the Bard himself is a character in a story as well as abrupt speaker of the poem. Gray, always a versatile and incessant user of oxymoron (as quotation from his best-known poems shows – "Where ignorance is bliss," "frail memorial erected," "unletter'd muse"), was quite literally interested in other languages, and in the otherness of languages. He studied Welsh, Anglo-Saxon and Icelandic, endeavouring to supply Augustan poetry with more languages and strangeness. In *The Bard* the Welsh language is introduced through rich reference to the "tongue" and "song" of the poets. The whole poem, as it is a confrontation between English King and Welsh Bard, between inane conqueror and powerful (linguistically powerful) victim, is an oxymoronic structure operating in a one-sided debate. The other language, the Bard's real language, plays in its imagined power against the one we know and are reading in the poem – but that is being changed by the fancied infusion of the Bardic. Augustan poets had enjoyed trying out other languages, or creating a simulacrum of other language, from Dryden's day, when Dryden introduced Inca or Indian scenes, characters and names into his plays. Macpherson's Ossianic poetry is all otherness of language, pleasing the public because it offered just the very kind of otherness most readers were best prepared for and most capable of absorbing.

The move into other languages was made literally. The latter part of the eighteenth century saw the production of works which required glossaries to explain foreign or exotic words from another language or sub-language. Chatterton always provided glosses to his "Rowley" poems. Burns's *Poems, Chiefly in the Scottish Dialect* appeared with an extensive "Glossary." It was the era of the dictionary, and the dictionary is a transforming as well as explanatory sort of work; it plays with turning words into each other, and takes them apart in order to put them together again. The notion of words so unfamiliar as to need explanation had its own appeal (an appeal capitalized on by, for instance, Scott in the next and last Augustan generation). Words were allowed their alien presence, and were not to be simplified back into familiar language. When it was complained of Falconer's *The Shipwreck* that the poet included too many technical terms of the parts of a ship and their functions, he found a solution by which to assist his readers without losing what might be called the sailors' dialect. He supplied his own drawing for the next edition's engraved frontispiece, "Elevation of a Merchant-Ship with all her Masts, Yards, Sails & Rigging, more particularly designed for that which is the Subject of the Poem" (see Fig. 25).[20] This dictionary or encyclopaedia solution is intended to amplify the unfamiliar language, making it more real and substantial, rather than

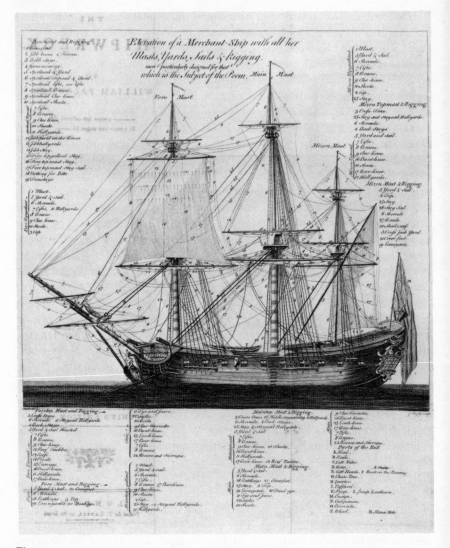

Fig. 25

demoting it through translation into the common language of gentlefolk. We would think Falconer peculiarly representative of his own time did we not recall Dryden's "Account" of *Annus Mirabilis*, drawing attention to his own description of the naval fight "in the proper terms which are us'd at Sea" and decrying reliance on "common notions" and "general terms." We remember the poem with its "dawby Marling" and "strong Tarpawling"; *Annus Mirabilis* was probably one of the poems that encouraged Falconer the sailor to write. And Dryden's literary manifesto of 1667 indicates that keeping to one tongue is too severe a restriction upon poetry.

If we look at Augustan poetry in the light of its two-language tendency, an extraordinary poet like Chatterton can seem much more explicable. A lot of study and some speculation have gone into Chatterton's social position in Bristol, and his psychological state. But, quite simply, Chatterton may also be seen as an extreme case of the two-language tendency. We now have the advantage of being able to see all his work, in Taylor's edition. When we look at the whole of Chatterton's *oeuvre* (and it is amazing that someone who died at seventeen should have an *oeuvre*), we find a very versatile Augustan poet. It is clear that he is an unslavish follower of Rochester and Gay, both of whom he strongly resembles, not least in being an exponent of his own period and an investigator of what might be called his culture's sub-text. He started out with considerable confidence in his heritage and in himself. He participates fully in the techniques and *topoi* of the other Augustans – debate, for instance – and displays a remarkably acute and overt stylistic and generic consciousness, as can be seen in, e.g., "Journal 6th." There is nothing in Chatterton's arrogant short life to indicate that he was ever considerate of other people, but in his poetry he always considers the reader, at least to the extent of engaging him in the discussion of what's going on, and he demands readers sophisticated enough to be entertained by burlesque and parody. He engaged in self-parody; his playlet *The Revenge* (performed at "Marybone Gardens," 1770) is as Taylor notes "a fairly close travesty of the tragic plot of Rowley's *Ælla*."[21] The styles dearest to him awakened in Chatterton the desire to play with them. He parodies Ossian, for instance, taking apart the grand Scottish epic style:

or, to speak in the language of the high-sounding Ossian, "Behold! thou art happy; but soon, ah! soon, wilt thou be miserable. ... Thou art beautiful as the cathedral of Canterbury; but soon wilt thou be deformed like Chinese palace-paling ... But see! riding on the wings of the wind, the black clouds fly. The noisy thunders roar; the rapid lightnings gleam ... and the dropping swain flies over the mountain: swift as Bicker-staff, the son of song, when the monster Bumbailiano, keeper of the dark and black cave, pursued him over the hills of death, and the green meadows of dark men." O Ossian! immortal genius! what an invocation could I make now!"[22]

This passage comes from the surprising *Memoirs of a Sad Dog*, published in *The Town and Country Magazine*, 1770, a piece of prose fiction that puts Chatterton in a direct line with James Joyce and Dylan Thomas.

Chatterton's most extended and elaborate plays with language are to be found in his "medieval" poems, in writing which he impersonates a late-medieval monastic poet. Chatterton was a "forger"; that is, he meant his language impersonation to be undetectable. But beside the joy in deceiving the grown-ups Chatterton exhibits the full licence of pleasure in creating a language which is playable-with. The richness of this (partly made-up) past language had a real appeal, offering the poet a literary language uncontami-nated by predecessors, and the pleasure of articulation in another tongue. The parodic impulse is itself behind the enterprise; one can see in the thorough parodic endeavour illustrated in most of Chatterton's work that parody was a means of the young poet's acquiring control over all his languages.

In one of Chatterton's "medieval" poems, such as "An Excelente Balade of Charitie, as wroten bie the gode Prieste Thomas Rowley, 1464," we can see that normal eighteenth-century usage or poetic custom is commonly maintained.[23] The verse form (rime royal with a final Spenserian or Drydenesque Alexandrine) is unusual, but the syntax is straightforward, laid along the rungs of the verse line in the Augustan manner. Usual and unusual words alternate, though not mechanically; we are asked both to decipher meanings and to appreciate effects, as in the Virgilian–Thomsonian description of a September storm: "The gatherd storme is rype; the bigge drops falle; / The forswat meadowes smethe, and drenche the raine." In reading such lines the reader finds himself mocked for linguistic inefficiency, forced to resort to the Glossary supplied by Chatterton when he first submitted the poem for publication.[24] Some words are not puzzling at all, and some are merely lightly disguised by unusual spelling ("rype," "bigge"). But there are the big puzzlers, the ornate medievalisms ("smethe", "levynne"). We may come upon strange nouns and adjectives, such as "peede chelandri" (pied goldfinch), or the words in "Haste to thie church-glebe-house, ashrewed manne! / Haste to thie kiste, thie onlie dortoure bedde." The reader has to submit to learning a "new" language.

Chatterton's ornate spelling is his version of the typographical play we find elsewhere in Augustan literature. It acts as finger-post to the diction, calls attention to language used. We are set problems in diction as we move from the familiar language to the exotic English, and back. If we become too bewildered by archaic glamour, we will miss what is going on. It is as if Chatterton (not Rowley) were asking us "Can you get the point? Do you understand the poem as efficient narrative? Or are you just going to sit there bemused by strange words?" Once we crack the code of the second language (under Chatterton's tutelage) we can appreciate the playful potential of what at first seemed mystifying, and enjoy the two languages at work within the poem. We can also enjoy the generic mixes, as in the "Excelente Balade" which mingles ballad, satire and Georgic, or "Eclogue the Third" that odd "medieval"-sophisticated comic-serious folkish-literary pastoral. Chatterton is a great exploiter of parodic decorum, and the decorum of play. Each poem, *sui generis*, speaks suitably in its own two languages, setting up a tension and a relation between them. Language, itself always such a subject in Augustan poetry, is in the Rowley poems being made before our eyes, coming at us with fresh unfamiliarity to challenge our powers of association and our knowledge of the way language works. Chatterton's special use of his own "other language" raises the question of diction, always interestingly problematic in Augustan poetry. We can take it that the poet who could write the comic "Elegy I" (published April 1769), which ends "Ye livid comets, fire the peopled skies, / For Lady Betty's tabby cat is dead," was not at all unaware either of the customs of diction, or of the power generated when two kinds of diction collide, are made to play off each other in an oxymoron of styles. And the poet who wrote "Begin, my muse, the imitative lay, / Aonian Doxies sound the thrumming string" ("February. An Elegy"; published February 1770) was no stranger to oxymoron.

Chatterton is not least among Augustan wits. And two-tongued Chatterton illustrates the Augustan poetic ideal, that every utterance should speak twice at the same time. A language should be enriched by another counter-language, a voice by a counter-voice. Whether drawing characters or describing the past, Augustan poets tend to present voices and styles working against each other, in productive conflict. Poems are units defined by contrast of self with self, sense with sense. For the Augustans, there is no poetry without doubleness.

VIII

Augustan voice and Augustan verse

> In POPE, I cannot read a Line,
> But with a Sigh, I wish it mine:
> When he can in one Couplet fix
> More Sense than I can do in Six.

Asked what is the most characteristic sort of verse employed by the Augustans, any reader of moderate experience would reply "the couplet." Despite the example of Milton, and the Miltonic imitations, and even the great experiments in blank verse like Thomson's *Seasons*, the Augustans on the whole disliked parting from rhyme. The couplet, the rhyming pair of basically iambic five-beat or four-beat lines, is indeed a most salient feature of Augustan poetry. The Augustans did not invent the couplet. They had, as they knew, close predecessors among the Elizabethans (Drayton, for instance), and they were delighted to discover that Chaucer had long ago used the couplet, at the beginning of recognizable English poetry. Yet, if the Augustans did not invent couplets, or the iambic pentameter couplet which came to be called the heroic verse, they re-invented or re-discovered it, making it their own so entirely, developing it so thoroughly, that after their period it seemed exhausted. In order to create for themselves, successors in the new age of poetry had to decry the couplet, for there was really nowhere further to take it. It has rarely been used seriously since, for later poets have felt that in that period from Dryden to Johnson it was perfected beyond future possibilities. It is perhaps relatively rare for any school of poetry to exploit a verse form so thoroughly as to render it unusable later. It might be suggested that the Augustans' scorched-earth policy regarding their verse form worked to the disadvantage of their reputation in later periods, when fewer and fewer readers could appreciate a verse pattern not employed by their own contemporaries. The Augustans certainly found the couplet deeply congenial. It answered (and they taught it to answer) all their poetic objects.

A study of the verse form dearest to the Augustan poets is intimately related to the study of all the other characteristic elements of their poetry. The couplet is, as we shall see, the enactment of appetite as well as the perfect expressive form for stylistic self-consciousness. It is the arena of charivari and the instrument of metamorphosis; in its constant and supple use the vividness of insistent life can be felt to keep death at bay. In the couplet the deep figure of

Augustan thought, its oxymoron, finds perfect form, and it can proceed through debate, through paradox, antithesis and parallel. Through the operation of the couplet various languages can play, and the double-voices statement finds a natural pattern.

One might say that the Augustans had binary minds, that they thought in twos. Presumably a series of historical events involving, first, a Civil War (between two chief sides) and then a series of political disputes (involving the same two sides as two national parties historically modified) all leading, however reluctantly, to the evolution of what we now know as the two-party system had something to do with this cast of thought. The emergence of the two-party system in politics is, after all, not a little matter in the history of ideas, or of human behaviour. And by "the two-party system" we mean not the mere existence of two sides (such as Guelfs and Ghibellines in Dante's Italy) but the public acceptance of two groups which will exist simultaneously and in opposition to each other, perhaps for ever. If the Augustan Age is considered in terms of its history, the development of the two-party system and the divided House is its unique contribution to the political ideas of the world, to civilization. We need not be surprised if the literature incorporates and expresses something closely related to that turn of human thought, just as we could not be surprised that the stylistic consciousness bred in the propaganda of national upheaval during the Civil War marked the poetry of the period that followed.

The iambic pentameter couplet, the large couplet, is well suited to the stylistic versatility begotten of acute and appreciative stylistic consciousness. It is extensive enough to rise to the demand for stylistic alteration as it proceeds, while it is a unit still short enough to allow the reader to retain what he knows, and to remember the different languages that have appeared in it. It provides very strong markers in the form of rhyme, and the chime and antagonism inherent in definite rhyme can be useful in pointing up oxymoron and identifying diversity even when the two rhyme words are not themselves involved (as they so often are) in oxymoronic conflict of meaning. Most of the greatest Augustan poems depend on that strong relation of line 1 to line 2:

> Or soft Adonis, so perfum'd and fine,
> Drive to St. James's a whole herd of swine?
>
> (*Epistle to Bathurst*, lines 61–2)

In this example, the conflict between the two lines is clearly marked. The first line of the unit of two is entirely in one language, in an idiom that continues until the middle of the next line where it is overthrown by the last five words. The picture of "soft Adonis" is transformed; he becomes someone driving (like the Prodigal Son) a herd of swine, ridiculously, to St. James's. As so often noted in discussion of the couplet, the alliterative patterns here link diverse elements and stress contrast ("*s*oft . . . *s*wine"), as do the patterns of assonance ("fine," "Drive," "swine"). The rhyme word stretches and extends the diversity between the first subject (Adonis) and the second subject (Adonis with pigs): "fine ... swine." The entire couplet fully expresses an oxymoron also expressed in single pairs of words – "perfum'd swine." In the subtleties of the couplet's tensions rhyme makes unavoidable the relationship between all the various elements syntactically asunder.

In such an example the binary relation of the two lines is impossible to miss. But such a relation still functions in couplets in which the second line is a discourse on and an amplification of the first, rather than a vivid contrast, e.g.

> Or quick effluvia darting thro' the brain,
> Die of a rose in aromatic pain?
>
> (*Essay on Man*, I, lines 199–200)

The first line of this pair is in scientific and abstract language; the second line gains its strength from simple and very strong monosyllables with powerful sensuous or emotional appeal: "Die," "rose," "pain." The darting means death (to die is often considered the effect of a dart), and the effluvia are the source of aromatic pain; thus, if we call the two parts of each line *a* and *b* then we can see a relation between 1*a* and 2*b*, and between 1*b* and 2*a*. There is also the syntactic sequence linking 1*a* and 1*b*, and 2*a* and 2*b*, and the rhyme sound relates 1*b* and 2*b*. Within a couplet single lines themselves tend to be composed of binary sets.

Pope's binary sets are often vividly brought to our attention as central elements in his lines. As we might expect, his contemporaries noticed his techniques, not always with unmixed admiration. The anonymous author of *Pope Alexander's Supremacy and Infallibility Examin'd* (1729) creates a critic who offers (with recollections of Pope's *Guardian* "Receit") "A Curious Receipt, wherein is disclosed, the Art of Writing Poetry with a small Genius, taken from M ARTINUS SCRIBLERUS's writings." The critic claims to have found "the first Secret in *Scriblerus*'s Poesy, namely, That Divine one of Ingemination" – that is, elements linked or twinned by alliteration.[1] The mock-editor modifies this position:

yet must I beg leave to animadvert on one Assertion ... which I take to be erroneous; *viz*. That the *Divine Art of Ingemination of Sounds* in Poesy, was the sole Invention of *Martinus Scriblerus*; whereas, in Justice to the Memory of his Predecessor Mr. *John Grub*, the Great Founder of the Street and Sect, which still bear his Name, I shall venture to affirm, that he was no Stranger to this Mystery. This will most evidently appear by a most curious Fragment of his ... Such is the Beauty of the Allegory, couch'd in the few Lines of our Fragment, and such the Harmony of its Versification, as may justly entitle it to a Place in the next *Edition* of the *Dunciad*. The Verses of Mr. *Grub* are as follow.

> *Thus Trojan Boots ting'd with Tartarean Glue,*
> *Near which the Greasy Great Gambadoes Grew,*
> *While Coaches rumbled round my Roman Nose,*
> *And green Iniquity grew grey in Prose.*

This flight of nonsense verse is clearly intended to show that the tricks and tics of Pope's style are not only recognizable but can function without the operation of meaning. That parody is followed by another,

a Distick written in the Spirit and Stile of our Poet.

> *See Clumsy Cleland lay a Claim to Wit,*
> *From Puzzled Prose, in Poets Praises Writ.*

It is rather pleasing than otherwise that Pope himself did not escape parody (what Augustan writer could hope to do so?). The surprise is that the parody seems so coarse. Alliteration is simplified. The binary elements are aggressively present, acknowledged in the fullness of crudity. But the critics could not capture the secret efficiencies of the Popean style, even though they could identify some of its elements; a couple of the lines (but only a couple) sound *almost* like something Pope could have jotted down on a bad day. The play of part against part is more subtle than the jeering mimics can duplicate – but they do draw attention to it. Pope is especially brilliant in achieving a number of relations of part with and against part, in permutation. His "Ingemination of Sounds" is only one of the devices that suddenly twine and entwine various elements in his couplet. Within any of the units of a line, a single or clearly visible oxymoron may act as a signal for the many complex connections and repulsions between 1 and 2.

Sometimes line 2 of a couplet will be, or seem, merely a logical and grammatical continuation of what has begun in line 1, as when line 2 merely completes a series begun in line 1, e.g.

> She went, to plain-work, and to purling brooks,
> Old-fashion'd halls, dull aunts, and croaking rooks.
>   ("Epistle to Miss Blount," lines 11–12)

These lines exhibit the pull of opposition, however, as well as the pull of likeness. Line 1 contains its own two constituent sets, in contrast; "plain-work" is dull colloquial fact, whereas "purling brooks" is a phrase borrowed from another language, that of traditional (and by now flaccid) pastoral. The pastoral element "interrupts" the series of five noun subjects after the preposition; the brooks represent a different style of thing, represented in a different style. The fourth object (beginning of 2*b*) is also an "interruption" of the sequence, for the "aunts" are, unlike everything else mentioned in the series, human – though they are comically dehumanized by being stuck between the halls (man-made and inanimate) and the rooks (animate but not human). The relation between 1*a* and 2*a* is readily visible; the old-fashioned rooms are where the girl does her plain work, indoors, and she also does it under the eyes of her aunts (whose qualifying adjective colours everything else in the sequence), while the exterior world of pretty brooks (1*b*) bathetically harbours the rooks (2*b*). We have sets of contrasts and antagonisms as well as likenesses: homely and romantic, plain and purling, outdoor world and indoor world. The romantic brooks of the end of line 1 are overtaken by the chiming rhyme word, and the echo of rhyme in the participle, at the end of 2; "purling" becomes "croaking" and we can hardly hear the mock-pastoral brooks for the homely mock-georgic rooks.

We can see in these lines that the couplet has offered the poet rich opportunity (which he has taken advantage of) for variation, display and change. That is what couplets do. This form of verse offers immense opportunity for transformation – indeed, transformation must take place if the result is not to be dull or inane and unpoetic repetition. The couplet is in its nature a transformational form. It is the object of a couplet to metamorphose its first part, its first line. The first line is, even in mere amplification, pushed out of its original place and given new funds of meaning.

It is perhaps too easy to illustrate the couplet's effects in the lines of such a master as Pope. But the couplet continues its work in the poems of any Augustan poet, even in the work of a poet inferior to Pope who works to different thematic purposes. Stephen Duck offers a case in point; nobody would claim that he is either great, or particularly Popean. A couplet like this (from *The Thresher's Labour*),

> We often whet, and often view the Sun;
> As often wish, his tedious Race was run,

is not satiric, nor in any sense urbane. Duck is describing what it feels like to be one of the labourers; he is in earnest, trying to convey the human sensations and emotions involved in the labour. But his couplet works, couplet-like, and he understands its essential dynamics. The first line tells us what the threshers do, through simply describing their physical action; the second tells us what they think of while they act. They pause to whet their scythes because they are tired; they look at the sun for the same reason, as the second line fully explains. "Whet" in 1*a* is the outward visible sign of the inward invisible desire expressed (alliteratively) in the "wish" of 2*a*. Transformational contrast works around the "Sun," so often considered a grand and glorious object. "Race was run" reminds us of Biblical and Miltonic phrasing – but instead of delighting in the sun's race, the threshers wish it were over. The personification allows a relation and contrast of pronouns: "we" for the weary labourers in 1*a* and 2*a* and "his" for the Sun in 2*b* where the sun becomes a kind of opponent. Yet the Sun is also an unreachable familiar; if he would only hurry, their work would lessen. To the Sun is attributed the weariness the labourers feel – his race is "tedious," primarily to them but also, it is suggested (through the positioning of the word) tedious to the Sun himself. The feelings implicit in line 1 have become explicit in line 2, and the great luminary objectively and simply viewed in line 1*b* has been transformed into a tedious source of tedium, who can fulfil his part best by being absent.

The relation of line 1 to line 2 can be seen in couplets even more casual than those cited above, such as Rochester's

The would-be wit, whose business was to woo,
With hat removed and solemn scrape of shoe,
                    ("Tunbridge Wells," lines 88–9)

a couplet taken from an only lightly emphatic descriptive sequence leading to a short drama. These quick lines are not the occasion for large ornament or grand effects. But here too we can see the couplet doing its job of bringing together and pulling apart, with line 2 re-working and transforming line 1. Line 1*a* gives us a seventeenth-century type; line 2 tells us what he does. There is a kind of owl-like sound in line 1 (wou-wit, to-woo) which gives us no great opinion of the "wit." But his "business" (in the theatrical sense) more than meets our expectations of his stupidity. His first business is the removal of his hat. "Hat" relates in sound to "wit" – with comic appropriateness, for both pertain to the head. The nouns in line 1 are all semi-abstract terms ("wit," "business," "woo") relating to large general ideas of human activity. Line 2 offers us the concrete and the utterly particular; the man inadequately expresses his notion of wit and wooing. Line 2*b* completely undoes the pretension of the wit, and reveals him for what he is, and the high notion of "to woo" is reduced to, or rather displaced by, the pseudo-wit's "shoe," which seems the most real thing about him. The oxymoron inherent in the descriptive phrase "would-be wit" (if you would be one, you aren't one) is supported by the oxymoron of "business . . . to woo" and is at length supported and replaced by the new oxymoron in "solemn . . . shoe."

The couplet demands that the poet keep on the move. It gobbles up language at a great rate, and is a most demanding, if satisfying, verse form. It is the more satisfactory in that it is not strictly a verse form, not a closed stanzaic pattern, but a flexible framework allowing perpetual activity. The action of the mind (reader's as well as poet's) in keeping up with the couplet, following the significance and stimulus of its rhymed relationships, is likewise a pleasurable employment and representation of consciousness, active, self-delighting, triumphing over stasis and death. The Augustans were so taken with the couplet, it answered their desires and expectations so fully, that they had a hard time getting away from it. Sometimes they felt guilty about using the couplet. Had not Milton said that rhyme was barbarous, unknown to the ancients? Had the couplet not perhaps a tendency to fetter, to constrain? Shenstone expressed a not uncommon notion when he said "Heroic verse, where every second line is terminated by a rhime . . . is apt to render the expression either scanty or constrained."[2] Any notion of constraint was especially objectionable to the liberty-loving Augustans, and the idea that they were bartering noble freedom for a minor effect, for a "jingle," could arouse special guilt. In his Prologue to *Aureng-Zebe* (1676) Dryden criticizes his own practices most severely. He really knows better; even though he's not bad, according to present taste, as a dramatic poet he should be more like Shakespeare:

But he has now another taste of Wit;
And to confess a truth, (though out of time)
Grows weary of his long-lov'd Mistris, Rhyme.
Passion's too fierce to be in Fetters bound,
And Nature flies him like Enchanted Ground.

("Prologue to *Aureng-Zebe*," lines 6–10)

The reference to the long-loved mistress indicates the seductiveness of the
rhymed couplet – used effectively even here when it is the subject of complaint.
Rhyme was a fatal Cleopatra to which they were content to return even when
they thought they ought to know or do better. It appeals, as it were, libidin-
ously. Two years later, in the Prologue to his unrhymed play *All for Love* (1678)
Dryden says of himself "He fights this day unarm'd; without his Rhyme" – a
line indicating perhaps some uncertainty of his own strength as well as of his
audience's response. Writing without the couplet an Augustan poet might feel
virtuously valorous, but also deprived; who wants to fight unarmed? Dryden
did return to his long-loved mistress. And whatever his theories about
dramatic poetry, Dryden when he wasn't writing for the stage never thought of
leaving off rhyme. All his great nondramatic poems are in couplets. To return
to the couplet is to return home, to come back to where pleasure is. Whatever
their occasional criticisms and doubts, the Augustans' delight and their
full sense of liberty were generally found in the active and transforming
couplet.

Those Augustans such as Thomson and Cowper who did successfully
attempt blank verse did not go free of criticism. There were objections, such as
Johnson's perfectly justified strictures on Thomson's lack of structure and
progression. Augustan blank verse is an odd creature, because, unlike the
blank verse of Milton or Wordsworth, it is so often so conscious of the other
possibility. Much of Augustan blank verse consists visibly of couplets that
have shirked their endings. Take, for example, the work of Blair, not, admit-
tedly, one of the best Augustans but still a poet of some competence. In his *The
Grave* he attempted grand-style blank verse in order to achieve the solemnity
suited to his subject, but despite his gallant attempts he is evidently fighting
the couplet all the way. One passage – though almost any, chosen at random,
would serve for illustration – goes like this:

Rous'd from their Slumbers
In grim Array the grizly Spectres rise,
Grin horrible, and obstinately sullen
Pass and repass, hush'd as the Foot of Night.
Again! the Screech-owl shrieks: ungracious Sound!
I'll hear no more; it makes one's Blood run chill.

(*The Grave*, lines 39–44)

It is so tempting, so easy, to turn this poem-sentence (one might almost say,
turn it *back*) into something like this:

Rous'd from their Sleep
In grim Array the grizly Spectres sweep,
Grin horrible, and obstinate to Sight
Pass and repass, hush'd as the Foot of Night.
Again! the Screech-owl shrieks: ungracious shrill!
I'll hear no more; it makes one's Blood run chill.

The pattern of Blair's (not excellent) lines, their syntax running along the
rungs of the lines themselves, the sound patterns ("grizly ... Grin horrible") –
all seem to demand the couplet, and one feels that it is only through an effort of
will that Blair is keeping from it, restrained by some dutiful sense that the
couplet would not make us grave enough, would not, in this case, be good for
us. But the couplets, like Blair's spectres, are obstinately present, if in ghostly
manner.

Not all Augustan couplets are in iambic pentameter. The second favourite
kind of verse is iambic tetrameter, the medium used indefatigably by Butler
throughout *Hudibras* and employed often by Swift and Gay. The iambic
tetrameter is in itself more or less a burlesque of the iambic pentameter; its
verses are slightly haunted by the "missing" foot. In iambic tetrameter verses
the parts 1 and 2 of a couplet are thrown more closely together, even pushed
abruptly into relation, and the relation becomes more marked through
this hurry. Iambic tetrameter verse is the perfect medium for comic rhyme,
e.g.

> With Basket-hilt, that wou'd hold broth,
> And serve for fight and dinner both.
> In it he melted lead for Bullets,
> To shoot at Foes, and sometimes Pullets.
> ...
> The trenchant blade, *Toledo* trusty,
> For want of fighting was grown rusty,
> And ate into it self, for lack
> Of somebody to hew and hack.
>
> (*Hudibras*, Part 1, Canto 1, lines 351–60)

The rhythm allows occasional variation, and tetrameter permits, as pentameter does not, a liberty with the number of syllables in a line: "Bullets" and
"Pullets," each with an extra weak syllable, extend their respective lines to
nine syllables, as do "trusty" and "rusty" in lines that follow. In both cases the
poet has brought off a rhyme in double syllables, an effect almost always comic
in English largely because of the relative infrequency of such double rhymes in
our language, so that we are bound to notice the effect as almost anomalous, a
conceit of sound. After two nine-syllabled lines we have, as in the last two lines
quoted above, the effect of tumbling downstairs into the shorter eight-syllabled
lines with their very definite hard-sounded rhyme words ("lack," "hack").
Similar liberties are taken by Swift in his iambic tetrameters, e.g.

Aloft rose ev'ry Beam and Rafter,
The heavy Wall climb'd slowly after.

The Chimney widen'd, and grew higher,
Became a Steeple with a Spire.

The Kettle to the Top was hoist,
And there stood fast'ned to a Joist:
But with the Upside down, to shew
Its Inclination for below;
In vain; for some Superior Force
Apply'd at Bottom, stops its Course,
Doom'd ever in Suspence to dwell,
'Tis now no Kettle, but a Bell.

("Baucis and Philemon," lines 53–64)

The first four lines in the passage quoted are nine-syllabled, with double
rhymes thus occurring at the end of the first two couplets; the light tacked-on
syllable acts anticlimactically in each case. These lines are followed by eight-
syllabled lines with strong endings ("hoist," "Joist"). In both passages we can
see that the relation between the lines of a couplet is similar to that in iambic
pentameter couplets, the second line both amplifying and counteracting the
first. Fine language ("The trenchant blade, *Toledo* trusty"; "In vain; for some
Superior Force") is explained, contradicted and parodied by what follows, and
the two-language effect is maintained. What pleases us most in tetrameter,
however, is the effect of ease; the lines seem to be tossed off, without effort,
doing credit to the inventive spontaneity of the poet's mind, and the reflective
spontaneity of his reader.

Ease – or rather the effect of ease – is a quality much valued (some might say
too much) by Augustans. Poetry ought not to smell of the lamp, nor to seem
laboured, or too highly wrought, for such laboriousness detracts from the effect
of contact with a living consciousness enjoying its powers. We lose personality,
and the voice speaking becomes only words read. The verse, if it exhibits its
efforts, ceases to be vital flow, and becomes stagnant. For the Augustans,
complexity that shows its hand was apt to seem pedantic. Iambic tetrameter
verse is ease incarnate. With a couplet squashed into such small compass and
treated so cavalierly, we as readers feel the need for pleasant hurry rather than
for cogitation. The surprises of the short packed lines prepare us to laugh even
before the main joke is sprung.

In iambic tetrameter verse, the most obvious joke is customarily in the
rhyme itself. The tetrameter offers play with rhyme, making us conscious of the
sound of words, and of the ridiculous elements in the nature of words. Some of
the rhymes are truly outrageous in the manner of *Virgile Travestie* (e.g. Swift's
"Your Hero now another Mars is, / Makes mighty Armys turn their Arses"[3])
but they do not have to be so extremely audacious for us to attend to them. The
play with rhyme is another way of making us conscious of diction, as well as
distrustful of all grand styles – it is a natural implement of parody. The

tetrameter verses ostensibly deny themselves room for large serious statements, or for prosodic experiments. Though they really achieve these things, all is brought off with an appearance of casualness, of hurry mixed with ease. We no sooner finish one quick couplet than we are thrust into the next, pelted with quick rhythms and snapping rhymes. The presence of the iambic tetrameter verse in this era acts as an implicit critique of the central iambic pentameter verse pattern. An ill-done or padded-out iambic pentameter couplet may unwittingly display its tendency to slip back into lighter verses. Even large pale blank verse may tempt us to think of this other alternative. Could not Blair, for instance, have written more effectively thus?

> And rous'd from Sleep
> In grim Array the Spectres sweep,
> Grin horrible, and stiff to Sight,
> Pass and repass, as hushed as Night.

"Serious" topics were indeed sometimes treated in iambic tetrameter couplets, as in, for instance, Parnell's "A Night-Piece on Death," an Augustan reference to Milton's tetrameter *Il Pensoroso*. In order to keep comedy from intruding, the serious theme in iambic tetrameter required expression in rhymes less obtrusive than ordinary, but the value of the measure was maintained in its effect of quick expression, as if the thoughts could be thrown away:

> The flat smooth Stones that bear a Name
> The Chissels slender help to Fame,
> (Which e'er our Sett of Friends decay
> Their frequent Steps may wear away.)
> A *middle Race* of Mortals own,
> Men, half ambitious, all unknown.[4]

We can see in Parnell's couplets here, as in all Augustan couplets, the pulls and tensions that make the interest of the relation of part to part. We watch a transformation, quietly done here, from "Stones" through "*Race* of Mortals" to "Men ... unknown." It is the unique quality of tetrameter verses to deny in part their own effects, to insist on a casualness which guarantees the freedom from pomposity. We are moved along too quickly to think of the poet (or of ourselves) getting up a magisterial pose. We are given a new look at the world, and the appropriate feelings are created but not insisted upon or examined. Whether the effect is comic or pathetic, we are induced to think of iambic tetrameter poems as occasional utterances, in the voice of an individual. The high jinks of the comic iambic tetrameter verses (more commonly found than serious tetrameters) signal originality. The very outrageous aggression of such comic verses exhibits an individual (not to say consciously odd) view of the world.

It may be for this reason that the women poets found iambic tetrameter verse so congenial. It is noticeable that their efforts in iambic pentameter rhymed verse are less successful, and, on the whole, they seem to have attempted it less often. The heroic measure was associated with matter thought foreign to women – classical learning, rule over the world. The more memorable poetry of Augustan women poets is usually in iambic tetrameter in which they could be allowed to toss off individual observations and feelings. In this form, too, they could safely exhibit wit without being thought too arrogant. There are exceptions; some of Lady Winchilsea's best work is in iambic pentameter, such as "Ardelia's Answer to Ephelia," or "A Nocturnal Reverie." But even in her case, a number of her poems, and some among the best ("Mercury and the Elephant," "An Invocation to Sleep," "A Tale of the Miser and the Poet") are in iambic tetrameter.

In writing iambic tetrameter verses, Augustan women could dare to be comic – and when they are comic they are most indebted to Swift, who was both directly and indirectly a source of encouragement to women writers and much more important to the female poets than Pope was. Swift's protégée Mary Barber, for instance, wrote some good acute Augustan verse, light verse with a point, such as her poem "Written for my Son, and Spoken by him at his first putting on Breeches":

> What is it our Mammas bewitches,
> To plague us little Boys with Breeches?
> To tyrant *Custom* we must yield,
> Whilst vanquish'd *Reason* flies the Field.
> Our Legs must suffer by Ligation,
> To keep the Blood from Circulation;
> . . .
> Our wiser Ancestors wore Brogues,
> Before the Surgeons brib'd these Rogues,
> With narrow Toes, and Heels like Pegs,
> To help to make us break our Legs.
>
> THEN, ere we know to use our Fists,
> Our Mothers closely bind our Wrists;
> And never think our Cloaths are neat,
> Till they're so tight we cannot eat.
> And, to increase our other Pains,
> The Hat-band help to cramp our Brains.
> The Cravat finishes the Work,
> Like Bow-string sent from the Grand Turk.[5]

The absurdities of feminine dress have been among the topics of satire from time immemorial; Mary Barber carries the war into the enemy's camp in her spirited critique of the absurdity of masculine dress. Giving herself the authority of a male voice (i.e. of her son) she speaks out to the male world. Giving herself the effectiveness of iambic tetrameter lines with emphatic rhymes ("bewitches" / "Breeches") she moves in on the ridiculous, with quick illustrative observation that commands assent. The theme is constriction, which the jaunty and mobile lines defy in their unrestricted expostulation.

A later poet, Ann Yearsley, also turns with effect to iambic tetrameter lines of observant description. In her "Lucy, a Tale for the Ladies," Yearsley shows that she has mastered the art of poetic narrative in couplets. Her story is the story of an unhappy middle-class marriage:

> Now Lucy joyless spends the hour,
> Still Cymon grew more stern and sour:
> She reads, and o'er her prospect mourns;
> He burns her book, her mildness scorns.
>
> . . .
>
> She dies! and Cymon's poignant grief,
> Is finely wrought in bas-relief.
> To prove he does his wife lament,
> How grand, superb, her monument:
> There weeping angels cut in stone,
> The rose snapt off ere fully blown,
> The empty urn – must surely prove,
> Cymon's deep sorrow, and his love.[6]

The lines are unassuming, but nicely formed, with a counterpoint between Lucy's external life and her inner one, and between Lucy and Cymon. The two voices, the two views, are maintained until Lucy's death, which happens abruptly at the beginning of the eight-line verse-paragraph that closes the poem. Lucy, "wife," is transformed to "monument," and we realize Cymon finds the grand inanimate monument a more than satisfactory substitute for the uncomfortable real women. The passage shows a metamorphosis – or perhaps two metamorphoses, the transformation of Lucy into tomb and the transformation of Cymon's feelings into the images. The husband equates his "sorrow and his love" which society expects him to feel (and which perhaps he even persuades himself he must feel) with the expensive decorated memorial which would not be called for had he not, in effect, killed off his wife. His equation (love = expensive tomb) is false, and the false rhyme ("prove"/"love") points the irony. The monument's ornaments constitute a series of light oxymorons (angels weep, the rose doesn't bloom, the urn is empty) pointing to the more significant oxymoron at the centre. Cymon "loves" the monument, not his wife, and the phrasing "grief... in bas-relief" exploits a half pun, showing us that the monument contradicts the assumed grief, and indeed expresses the *relief* that Cymon really feels but cannot acknowledge. The end of the poem employs the dissonance of two languages, the public language of feeling which Cymon keeps for show and the unconscious language reflected in his pleasure in the elaborate monument.

Yearsley's poem is both effective and Augustan, but it comes by its Augustanism by the route of the iambic tetrameter couplet, a verse form which does not demand the public authorial pose and which allows, or even necessitates, the effect of informality. Iambic tetrameter couplets fire quick Parthian shots instead of settling into large discourse. Although the short-line verses allow the full play of most of the major elements that constitute iambic pentameter verses, they are, or pretend to be, unpretentious. The fun of the form is that its unpretentiousness can be drawn to impudence or impertinence, and its casualness, its overt lack of pomposity, can actually assist a large measure of aggression. The iambic tetrameter couplet as a verse form is double-voiced in itself, its tone of unconsidered lightness, of undeveloped refreshing unimportance, speaking against its other and synchronous tone of tough assertions and dismissals. It combines, as it were, a hum with a deconstructive growl.

> What Poet would not grieve to see,
> His Brethren write as well as he?
> But rather than they should excel,
> He'd wish his Rivals all in Hell.
>
> ("Verses on the Death of Dr. Swift," lines 31–4)

Couplets in either iambic tetrameter or iambic pentameter dominate Augustan versification. Between them, they account for many of our major poems in the period, and for the greater part of the work by major poets. Of slightly lesser importance is the quatrain, though the four-line stanza is put through its paces by a number of poets from Rochester to Cowper. The four-line stanza tends to be written in iambic rhythm (with variations) and in meter based either on tetrameter or pentameter. As with couplets, so with quatrains; those based on tetrameter are ostensibly light, more impudent, more ostentatiously anti-pompous and usually more overtly and emphatically comic than those in pentameter. Tetrameter quatrains are likely to have unequal line lengths (lines 2 and 4 shorter than lines 1 and 3), whereas pentameter quatrains tend more often to be metrically regular, with the same number of syllables in all four lines.

Rochester's "Song" of 1676 is a good example of light lyric tetrameter quatrain:

> As *Chloris* full of harmless thought
> Beneath the willows lay,
> Kind love a comely shepherd brought
> To pass the time away.

Here, in fact, lines 2 and 4 are in trimeter, and possess six syllables only in contrast to the eight syllables of lines 1 and 3. This is exactly the basic pattern employed by Cowper in "The Diverting History of John Gilpin" (1782):

> John Gilpin was a citizen
> Of credit and renown,
> A train-band captain eke was he
> Of famous London town.

Both poets are imitating ballad measure, and their stanzas bear a parodic relation to traditional lyric. The quatrain in regular tetrameter is less immediately related to sung verse, and more openly interested in exploiting contrasts, oppositions and relations – like an extended couplet.

Yet as she wasts, she grows discreet,
Till Midnight never shows her Head;
So rotting Celia stroles the Street
When sober Folks are all a-bed.

For sure if this be Luna's Fate,
Poor Celia, but of mortall Race
In vain expects a longer Date
To the Materialls of Her Face.

When Mercury her Tresses mows
To think of Black-head Combs is vain,
No Painting can Restore a Nose,
Nor will her Teeth return again.
(Swift, "The Progress of Beauty," 1719, lines 85–96)

The quatrain offers, as the seventeenth-century poets had shown, a good
mode for exploring conceits. In their poems in tetrameter quatrains the
Augustans were more willing than usual to engage in open puns as well as in
far-fetched transformational images. There is a constant punctuation of what
might be called "punch lines," that is, lines which attack and reinterpret the
language, style, images and cadences used in previous lines. The quatrain
allows an interchange of images and ideas, as well as surprises that can be
worked out through a four-line length. We wait, as in tetrameter couplets, to be
surprised by rhyme sounds, and the rhyme sounds reconnect the two halves of
an oxymoron, as well as exploding in parody the conventional "poetic"
language which can supply half the language and half the rhyme sounds. For
instance, in Swift's stanzas quoted above, "Luna's Fate," "mortall Race,"
"her Tresses mows" – phrases all lifted from the store of poetic convention and
thus carrying a kind of poetical sobriety – are unexpectedly connected with
"the Materialls of Her Face" and "Restore a Nose," strange physical references
which completely reinterpret the other phrases. The basic oxymoron is "rotting Celia," and the conceit is the comparison of a diseased prostitute to the
moon. Swift is maliciously able to manipulate the two halves of a line, as well as
line against line. We do a kind of double-take on reading the first line of the last
quatrain quoted above, because it is Time, Chronos, which is usually thought
of poetically as mowing. Here it is Mercury, an unexpected deity, who mows
Celia's "Tresses" – and then we realize that the god-like power which destroys
through an ageing process is mercury, the mineral taken as a remedy for V.D.
By causing her hair to fall out the remedy, like the disease, is accelerating
rotting Celia's dissolution.

The double languages are working here as hard as ever to produce shock
effects and satisfactory explosions. The diction, wide-ranging if economical,
varies from the high poetic ("Luna," "mortall Race") to the simple nouns for
parts of the body and the most concrete and vulgar reference to a commonplace beauty aid, "Black-head Combs."

While tetrameter quatrains are often comic, and frequently aggressive or at least outrageously conscious of taking liberties with diction and ideas, quatrains in iambic pentameter are used most often for the expression of serious (not necessarily solemn) matters. Shenstone argued in his "Essay on Elegy"

> Heroic metre, with alternate rhime, seems well enough adapted to this species of poetry [i.e. elegy]; and, however exceptionable upon other occasions, its inconveniences appear to lose their weight in *shorter* elegies; and its advantages seem to acquire an *additional* importance.[7]

The "inconveniences" are explained: "The chief exception to which *stanza* of all kinds is liable, is, that it breaks the sense too *regularly*, when it is continued through a long poem." Separate stanzas can seem to the Augustan mind a series of irritating slices; they break the sense, stop the flow of feeling and of thought, and force everything into bounded units. The Augustans were suspicious of intricate or set poetic forms. The heroic quatrain, however, evidently seemed something like a useful compromise between couplet and stanza, and also between couplet and freer verse form. What Shenstone calls "a more dissolute variety of numbers" might, he admits, have "superior advantages," for many admire *Lycidas*, but the disadvantage seems very evident:

> The previous rhime in MILTON's LYCIDAS is very frequently placed at such a distance from the following that it is often dropt by the memory . . . before it be brought to join its partner; and this seems to be the greatest objection to *that* kind of versification.

In reading a quatrain the mind of a reader will be allowed to function fully, with full memory and command of all parts, without, Shenstone feels, being affected by the "air of *constraint*" which can accompany the rhimed couplet. The iambic pentameter quatrain is a satisfactory stanza to this Augustan critic – almost the only tolerable stanza – as it allows complexities and pleasures to function together. It permits a range of mind over space. Both poet and reader can feel unconstrained, but not lost in the dissolute; the mind is still attentive to the rhyme, the sounds not so far apart that we lose one. It is obviously one of the "advantages" of the iambic pentameter quatrain that it keeps the qualities of the heroic couplet. Augustan poets and critics find it hard to imagine a poetry that would not demand the efforts and offer the gratifications of rhyme – rhyme which ensures that patterns of consonance and dissonance are attended to. They disliked the idea of losing anything, of a memory being "cropt," of the mind not enjoying its apprehension and following, fully awake, all the lively transmutations of verse.

A much greater poet than Shenstone had long before discussed the advantages of the iambic pentameter quatrain:

> I have chosen to write my Poem in *Quatrain*'s or *Stanza*'s of four in alternate rhyme, because I have ever judg'd them more noble, and of greater dignity, both for sound and number, then any other Verse in use amongst us . . . I have always found the couplet Verse most easie, (though not so proper for this occasion) for there the work is sooner at an end, every two lines concluding the labour of the Poet: but in Quattrains he is to carry it farther on; and not onely so, but to bear along in his head the troublesome sense

of four lines together. For those who write correctly in this kind must needs acknowledge, that the last line of the Stanza is to be consider'd in the composition of the first.

In his "Account" of *Annus Mirabilis*, Dryden argues for the nobility of this quatrain, and points out its difficulty; the "stanza" seems to be a complication of the couplet. In the poem itself Dryden had shown what the quatrain might do, e.g.

> To see this Fleet upon the Ocean move
> Angels drew wide the Curtains of the skies:
> And Heav'n, as if there wanted Lights above,
> For Tapers made two glareing Comets rise.
>
> (stanza 16, lines 61–4)

In his unusual narrative use of quatrains in *Annus Mirabilis*, Dryden shows how images can be amplified, elaborated and contemplated while the reader is still given the advantages of the patterned relation of section to section, line to line. The long-lined four-line stanza needs, perhaps even more than the iambic pentameter couplet, some variation of rhythm if we are not to be irritated or bored by too tripping a regularity. Dryden not only varies the pauses but alters the stresses, as we can see in this stanza, in which, for instance, the beginning of line 2, "A´ngĕls drĕw wi´de," gives us a trochee and an iamb back-to-back, with something of the falling effect of the dactyl. In iambic pentameter quatrains, as in iambic pentameter couplets, the poet must be conscious of the kind of bustle created by an entirely regular pattern of stresses, and must often want to avoid it, though that chipper busy-ness may at times be desired, and is almost always desired in tetrameter quatrains, especially those playing with obvious comic rhymes.

Gray's *Elegy Written in a Country Church-Yard* is another great Augustan poem written in iambic pentameter quatrains.

> Far from the madding crowd's ignoble strife,
> Their sober wishes never learn'd to stray;
> Along the cool sequester'd vale of life
> They kept the noiseless tenor of their way. (lines 73–6)

This very example, however, brings us up against an interesting problem. It ought to be noted that Gray had an ambivalent attitude to his quatrains. He refers to the poem as in stanzas ("the Stanza's, wch I now enclose to you": letter to Wharton, Dec. 1750).[8] But, when commanding Walpole's supervision of the first anonymous printing by Dodsley (in February 1751), Gray very specifically requested that the poem not be sent out in divisions of verses: "he [Dodsley] must . . . print it without any Interval between the Stanza's, because the Sense is in some Places continued beyond them." Gray's sense of the "inconveniences" of the stanza is evidently like Shenstone's; the separate stanza is objectionable as it "breaks the sense." That Augustan fear – or dislike – of set verse forms emerges. The first printing of the *Elegy* makes it look like the seamless flow of Augustan works in couplets; there are no spaces between the stanzas, whose presence is indicated only by the indented first line of each new group of four. Only later was Gray content to conquer his Augustan aversion to anything that looked like closed form, and to allow his "Stanza's" to be printed with intervals between them.

If we look at the stanza from the *Elegy* quoted above, the one that begins with the famous phrase "Far from the madding crowd's ignoble strife," we can see how Gray had responded to the nobility, the dignity, that Dryden felt this kind of stanza offered. It is certainly serious and elegant; it avoids the burden of too much tick-tock regularity by posing a trochee in place of an iamb in the first foot of the first line, and the regularity of the rest is hushed, smooth and cool, like the sober noiseless lives of the villagers. This particular quatrain deals effectively with what is absent – strife, straying, heat and noise – and makes positive images out of negative conditions. Its greatest triumph is perhaps the word "sequester'd" which in company with "cool ... vale" gives the idea of being secluded, set apart in peace, and yet, perhaps (considering the associations with Hampden, Milton, Cromwell, who have recently been mentioned in the poem) the word carries something of the political import of "sequestration," the idea of something seized, set apart, taken out of one's control for someone else's convenience. It is an ambiguous word, like "cool" and "sober" on which also the stresses fall.

In all such quatrains, rhymed lines work together while being set apart, striving towards each other, their two voices meeting across a slight gap in time. Part of the dynamic effect of the quatrains is caused by our sense, even if an unconscious sense, that these lines would and could be couplets. Indeed, it is not hard to turn them into couplets:

> Angels drew wide the Curtains of the skies:
> For Tapers made two glareing Comets rise
> In Heav'n, as if there wanted Lights above
> To see this Fleet upon the Ocean move.

> Far from the madding crowd's ignoble strife,
> Along the cool sequester'd vale of life
> They kept the noiseless tenor of their way;
> Their sober wishes never learn'd to stray.

To do this is of course to violate the poet's lines and intentions; we realize that although the syntax is exactly the same, and hardly a word needs to be changed, the pattern of relations among images and ideas is made trite by this re-designing. What happens essentially is that the punch lines are spoiled by coming in the wrong places, and the element of suspense on which the quatrain depends has been removed. The point is that we should wait through a quatrain for the completion of a couplet, and this completion involves even larger aggregations of material to be assimilated and played upon than we get in the couplet, or at least in the couplet we can achieve in this fashion. It is, however, worth noting how very much the Augustan quatrain depends on the couplet, to what extent in its more spacious functioning it is patterned like a large couplet. And it *is* made up of two intercutting couplets, which work with and against each other, in two voices. Poems that are intentionally designed in quatrains depend on these two voices, and the couplets themselves, as two rhymed lines thrust together, don't have the same counter-thrusts and complexity that a designed couplet usually does. But in general we may say that the Augustan quatrain is couplet writ large, and that the quatrains are couplets waiting amid complications for their rhyming completion.

The last of the really prominent Augustan verse forms is the so-called "Pindaric Ode." This mode of verse was initiated by Abraham Cowley in 1656, when he produced versions of two Odes by Pindar. Cowley insisted he was not trying to translate: "If a Man should undertake to translate *Pindar* Word for Word, it would be thought that one *Mad-man* had translated *another*."[9] Justice to Pindar, he argues, needs something more than mere copying, or exact Imitation

which being a vile and unworthy kind of *Servitude*, is incapable of producing any thing good or noble ... It does not at all trouble me that the *Grammarians* perhaps will not suffer this libertine way of rendring foreign Authors, to be called *Translation*; for I am not so much enamour'd of the *Name Translator*, as not to wish rather to be *Something Better*, tho' it want yet a *Name* ... I have in these two *Odes* of *Pindar*, taken, left out, and added what I please; nor make it so much my Aim to let the Reader know precisely what he spoke, a[s] what was his *Way* and *Manner* of speaking, which has not been yet ... introduc'd into *English*, though it be the noblest and highest kind of writing in Verse.

Cowley gave Augustan literature not only the lofty manner of Pindar, but also an express assertion of a right to imitate "Way and Manner" rather than to translate, a right emerging in the production of many new and unslavish "imitations" including Pope's of Horace. Cowley himself produced his own modern Pindarics, beginning with his "Ode upon His Majesty's Restoration and Return" (1660); he thus provided full precedent for this big free form, curiously modern as it seemed to Augustans. It was always a noble form, lofty, even high-handed – and associated with poetic verve and freedom (including Cowley's own "libertine way" of rendering his author). Young speaks in terms by now common, even hackneyed, in his "Discourse on Ode" (1728) when he says "Its [an Ode's] conduct should be rapturous, somewhat abrupt, and immethodical to a vulgar Eye," adding, "an humble, tame, and vulgar Ode is the most pityful error a pen can commit."[10] Paradoxically, this nobly arrogant form is also somewhat feminine in being so emotional. Young says (very condescendingly, we may think) that the main "difference from other kinds of Poetry" is "That, *there*, the *Imagination*, like a very beautiful Mistress, is indulged in the appearance of domineering; tho' the *Judgment*, like an Artful Lover, in reality carries its point; and the less it is suspected of it, It shews the more masterly conduct." The Ode that the reader knows and notices would seem then to be the beautiful Mistress, Imagination, in mastery (Young creates a little charivari of his own in describing the Ode). Yet this feminine emotional expressiveness is associated with courage; it is heroic even if (like fair women) it stands at the edge of a precipice:

It holds true in this Province of writing, as in war, "The more danger, the more honour." It must ... (in *Shakespear*'s Style) have hairbreadth 'Scapes; and often tread the very brink of Error ...

The Ode was never immune from parody. One anti-Ode is Oldham's "Satyr. Suppos'd to be spoken by a Town-Hector. Pindarique" (1680). This poem, which came to be called "the Satyr against Vertue," is an absurd hyperbolical praise of vice ranted by a Rochester-like rake who looks down on ordinary sinners:

> In them, sin is but a meer privative of good,
>   The frailty and defect of flesh and blood:
> In us 'tis a perfection, who profess
>   A studied and elaborate wickedness:
> We are the great Royal Society of Vice,
>   Whose Talents are to make discoveries,
>   And advance Sin like other Arts and Sciences.
>   It's I, the bold *Columbus*, only I
>   Who must new Worlds in Vice descry,
> And fix the pillars of unpassable iniquity.[11]

Here are freedom, adventurousness and a libertine way, certainly. Oldham felt compelled to explain that his Muse "only acted here in Masquerade," since "When she an Hector for her Subject had, / She thought she must be Termagant and mad."[12] The satirist certainly knows that "Pindarique" is lofty and noble, and turns it upside down in making it celebrate sin, and plunge bathetically to the base. But the mock-Ode keeps the assertiveness and the running to an extreme position thought typical of an Ode, and even admirable in it. The satirist gives the rapturous utterance to a bullying voice, of one who has tumbled over the brink of error, indeed, and takes advantage (morally) of poetic freedom.

The "Pindaric Ode," so firmly associated with greatness and freedom, answered to the Augustan wish for unconstricted versing, formless form. From the outset, the Pindaric Ode was associated with freedom, lofty manner and intensity of feeling, and with escape from a set or exact verse form. Part of the point of an Augustan Ode is that the reader cannot predict in advance what rhyme pattern may be used; the reading of one stanza or section will not tell us what patterns are to ensue. The stanzas are themselves large and irregular sections or paragraphs of poetry, that may or may not be matched in rhyme scheme or metre by any other such section, and these sections (which often have little to do with the real Greek divisions of Strophe and Antistrophe) are much longer and apparently require us to take much more in than do quatrains or couplets. The poet as speaker makes some kind of intense and solemn utterance which needs to have no fixed limit.

Thou Youngest Virgin-Daughter of the Skies,
Made in the last Promotion of the Blest;
Whose Palmes, new pluckt from Paradise,
In spreading Branches more sublimely rise,
Rich with immortal Green above the rest:
Whether, adopted to some Neighbouring Star,
Thou rol'st above us, in thy wand'ring Race,
   Or, in Procession fixt and regular,
   Mov'd with the Heavens Majestick Pace;
   Or, call'd to more Superior Bliss,
Thou tread'st, with Seraphims, the vast Abyss:
What ever happy Region is thy place,
Cease thy Celestial Song a little space;
(Thou wilt have Time enough for Hymns Divine,
   Since Heav'ns Eternal Year is thine.)
Hear then a Mortal Muse thy Praise rehearse,
   In no ignoble Verse;
But such as thy own voice did practise here,
When thy first Fruits of Poesie were giv'n;
To make thy self a welcome Inmate there:
   While yet a young Probationer,
   And Candidate of Heav'n.

In this, the first stanza or verse-section of Dryden's "To the Pious Memory of
... Mrs. Anne Killigrew ... An Ode" (1686), the poet definitely announces his
poetic intentions as sublime. He is dealing with Heaven, as well as with praise
of the dead; the addressee, who is also subject, is addressed as alive, though in a
higher state of being. The poem exalts itself in bridging the gap between earth
and heaven. This is the kind of lofty and religious subject the Augustans felt
proper to an Ode; unlike their great original, Pindar, they did not spend poetic
time celebrating sports events. The Ode, representing glory and beauty not
contaminated by satire, may at first glance seem very un-Augustan in trying to
free itself and its diction from question. When we read various "Odes,"
however, we find that they don't eschew irony, or satiric criticism; their
problem is finding language for creating a grand past, or future or Otherwhere
in contrast to the mundane present. Odes, like the other Augustan poems, are
written in two voices. In this case, one is the voice of the human, ordinary,
limited and decaying. Odes spend a good deal of time drawing the contrast,
rather than allowing the contrast to emerge in the split-second report of
oxymoron. They point out – as Wordsworth does in the "Immortality Ode" –
the difference between the *there* and the *here*, the sacred and the profane. Their
job is to create space sufficient to deal with these two regions.

Dryden begins the "Ode on Mrs. Anne Killigrew" by creating space,
describing (ostensibly to the deceased lady as his addressee) the place where
she is, which is a place of rising, growth and movement, and then saying that
her space cannot be fixed, cannot be mapped. He locates her variously in
rolling stars, in planets, or with seraphim treading, not golden streets, but "the

vast Abyss." Heaven, or whatever the celestial region entered after death may be called, can be conceived of as in space but cannot be fixed, cannot be described or fully spoken about. Having taken speech to the edge, the Abyss, Dryden asks his newly immortal Anne to cease *her* "Celestial Song" for a while ("a little *space*") in order to give him space and time to praise her. She at least need not worry about having time enough now for her art, whereas he, by implication, must worry about time. His voice is conceived of as the second voice, the contrasting one of "a Mortal Muse," though their voices harmonize when he reminds her that she practised such speech, such poetry, "no ignoble Verse" when she was *here*. Her *voice* once practised poetry, which served to bridge the gap between her life *here* and her life *there*. She is an "Inmate" of heaven now partly because of her good and heavenly-minded poetry when she was a "Probationer" and "Candidate." She has passed her probation, she has been accepted. Dryden, still (like each of his readers) a "Probationer" and "Candidate," still on the ground of the *here*, is attempting to imitate her, though he has not the divine mastery which she must now have achieved *there*, amongst the blest.

Though Dryden's is of course the "real voice" throughout, the controlling voice of the poet, he works by establishing two voices, making Anne's the voice of heavenly music and sublime poetry. The next two strophes or sections amplify the idea: Anne's "Praeexisting Soul" must once have been Sappho's; surely "Brother-Angels at thy Birth / Strung each his Lyre, and tun'd it high." With such advantages, Anne could hardly do less than sublimely, even here on earth. But, as every reader remembers, Dryden's fourth strophe or section turns to the here-and-now, and to discordant notes:

> O Gracious God! How far have we
> Prophan'd thy Heav'nly Gift of Poesy?
> Made prostitute and profligate the Muse,
> Debas'd to each obscene and impious use,
> Whose Harmony was first ordain'd Above
> For Tongues of Angels, and for Hymns of Love?
> O wretched We! why were we hurry'd down
>   This lubrique and adult'rate age,
>   (Nay added fat Pollutions of our own)
> T'increase the steaming Ordures of the Stage?   (lines 56–65)

We move from the sacred to the profane with a vengeance. The "Heav'nly Gift of Poesy" has been profaned, the angelic tongue prostituted. Poetry has undergone a fall, and the poet's historical period, "this age," is signally guilty of ugliness, and distinguished by obscenity. In the first strophe, Anne is in the unmappable space of glorious heaven; here the poet speaks from the revolting space of a dunghill. The "Stage" itself seems the stage of our existence as well as the theatre that flourished under Charles II – or rather, perhaps, that little boxed-in dirty space of polluted theatre is now the stage of the world. The whole poem is an enactment of repentance and redemption. Paying tribute to the heavenly muse, Dryden restores his own tongue, so that at the end he can celebrate the rising of the dead on Judgment Day and claim that "The Sacred Poets first shall hear the Sound." After right hearing, the mortal Muse is rectified, and the poets will "to the New Morning sing." Above and below, *there* and *here*, sacred and profane are brought into new relation as the rising poets (with Dryden surely among their number) follow Anne Killigrew in heavenly humility:

> There *Thou*, Sweet Saint, before the Quire shalt go,
> As Harbinger of Heav'n, the Way to show,
> The Way which thou so well hast learn'd below.

Anne briefly returns from *there* to *here* in order to lead the way back *there* again.

The tribute to Anne Killigrew herself is, incidentally, however hyperbolical, not inappropriate; she did paint and she did write poems – and some of her own poems are Odes. The first Ode in her posthumous book of *Poems* (1686) (the volume in which Dryden's "To the Pious Memory . . ." first appeared) is extremely pessimistic, an unhappy Ode which treats the relation of *there* and *here* in a despairing reversal. The beginning of "The Discontent" defines the irregularity, the ruggedness, of the Ode form as suitable to human experience:

> Here take no Care, take here no Care, my *Muse*,
> Nor ought of Art or Labour use:
> But let thy Lines rude and unpolisht go,
> Nor Equal be their Feet, nor Num'rous let them flow.
> The ruggeder my Measures run when read
> They'l livelier paint th'unequal Paths fond Mortals tread.

After a survey of the various vain wishes of humanity, a survey in terms and imagery suggesting that the writer has attentively read Rochester's "Satyr against Mankind," this Ode ends with the evocation of an entirely negative *there*:

> VI
>
> Is there that Earth by Humane Foot ne're prest?
> That Aire which never yet by Humane Breast
> Respir'd, did Life supply?
> Oh, thither let me fly!
> Where from the World at such a distance set
> All that's past, present, and to come I may forget:
> The Lovers Sighs, and the Afflicteds Tears,
> What e're may wound my Eyes or Ears.
> The grating Noise of Private Jars,
> The horrid sound of Publick Wars,
> Of babling Fame the Idle Stories,
> The short-liv'd Triumphs Noysy-Glories,
> The Curious Nets the subtile weave,
> The Word, the Look that may deceive.
> No Mundan Care shall more affect my Breast,
> My profound Peace shake or molest:

> But *Stupor*, like to Death, my Senses bind,
> That so I may anticipate that Rest,
> Which only in my Grave I hope to find.[13]

In one of the most thorough instances of death and the deathly coming at the end of an Augustan poem, Anne Killigrew's "The Discontent" denies utterly the possibility of any beautiful language, or even of any human one: human language is only babble and miserable noise. Human activity is treachery, or loud and antipathetic charivari. The poet gives up hearing any language, and opts for deafness, insensibility, "*Stupor*" and the Grave. We see that the other place chosen, the solitary wild, is really the same as the grave. The *there* which this poem perversely chooses is a place in contradiction of heaven as it is of the human world. This might be called the Ode opposite to Dryden's. More like his in spirit, and more spiritual, is the poem which follows (or is part of) "An Epitaph on Herself," entitled simply "An Ode":

> Arise my Dove, from mid'st of Pots arise,
> Thy sully'd Habitation leave,
> To Dust no longer cleave,
> Unworthy they of Heaven that will not view the Skies.
> Thy native Beauty re-assume,
> Prune each neglected Plume,
> Till more than Silver white,
> Then burnisht Gold more bright,
> Thus ever ready stand to take thy Eternal Flight.[14]

This more promising seventeenth-century poem, reminiscent in its imagery of Marvell, remains unfinished, the unfinished text on the page giving in itself an impression of the sad abruptness of death – though Anne Killigrew seems to have foreknown and even to have desired her own decease. The latter Ode, in a more characteristically Ode-like manner, develops the idea of ascent to the skies, through the bird image following the movement from here to there, and foretelling a union of earthly song with celestial, of soul with heaven.

It is probable that Dryden read Anne Killigrew's poetry before he composed his Ode celebrating the dead woman as poet. As a number of critics have scornfully pointed out, she did not deserve all that was said of her – but she was not entirely undeserving, either. She, or the idea of her, and even possibly some of her imperfect (but not contemptible) works inspired one of Dryden's best productions, a brilliant and moving poem not surpassed even by Dryden himself in his other Odes, including the more famous *Alexander's Feast: or the Power of Musique* (1697). In that "Ode in Honour of St. Cecilia's Day" we find a similar reciprocal traffic between *there* and *here*: "He rais'd a Mortal to the Skies; / She drew an Angel down" (lines 169–70). It is one of Dryden's favourite motifs, this mutual pull between the two regions which at last succeeds in reuniting them, bringing their two languages into unison. We find this motif also at the end of Dryden's "An Ode, On the Death of Mr. Henry Purcell" (1696):

> The Heav'nly Quire, who heard his Notes from high,
> Let down the Scale of Musick from the Sky:
>   They handed him along,
> And all the way He taught, and all the way they Sung.   (lines 23–6)

Purcell, our delightful emissary from here, teaches not only men but angels, his musical language evidently exceeding theirs. This poem begins with the idea of debate, or rather rivalry between two tongues: "Mark how the Lark and Linnet Sing, / With rival Notes". This earthly competition and dissonance is resolved by the advent of a heavenly language: "When *Philomel* begins her Heav'nly lay, / They cease their mutual spight". The third term which dissolves earthly conflict marks the advent of a new conflict or rivalry, that between the earthly and the heavenly. We are shown the space between the earthly and heavenly (or sublime) languages; the Ode contemplates that space, that "Abyss," the extent of unnamed emptiness separating one from the other. And the Ode then has to find some way of crossing over. In reading an Ode we are faced with the problem of relating the two voices, of earth and heaven, here and there.

  An Augustan Ode characteristically deals with history in some form, mythic history or, more often, real history largely and mythically presented. The Ode was, after all, very much used for current events; it is almost the most journalistic of poetic forms in its turning to the topical, but it seeks to give large archetypal meaning to the history it discusses. The Ode also asks questions about that history – as do, for instance, Collins's "Ode to Liberty" (1746) or Gray's "Progress of Poesy" (1757). In dealing with history, and noting differences between earlier and later, then and now, there and here, an Ode deals with separation and similarity, as well as separation and difference. Characteristically, too, an Ode goes through a number of transient descriptions, unfixed alternatives which replace but do not cancel each other out – as Dryden does with Anne Killigrew's dwelling-place, or Collins with the various abodes of Liberty, or, in the "Ode to Evening," with the various types and phases of evenings. In its rapid superimposed catalogue the Ode deals with all that might be said and provides an effect of fullness, but, except perhaps in the "Ode to Evening," the sense of amplitude is in some way countered by a sense of anxiety as to local and contemporary possibilities. Poet and reader must be willing to enter another state, to speak another language, if the possibilities that apply now and here are to be fully grasped.

  Poets in the Augustan Age most often (and very successfully) used the Ode as a form in which to discuss poetry (music sometimes standing in for poetic art), and to raise serious questions about the alternative languages. Deliberate quotation from other poets serves not only to pay stylistic compliment but also to focus our attention on matters of style; we are made to desire a beautiful and far-reaching language, while at the same time recognizing that we may ourselves fall far short of such language. In the Odes with happy endings, including all of Dryden's, the problems are richly resolved in a union between our language and the beautiful or sublime language, a reconciliation of *there* and *here*. In, for instance, Collins's "Ode to Evening," that lovely unrhymed anomaly among Augustan Odes – and the greatest of the Odes between Dryden and Wordsworth – the poet asks to be taught by Evening herself:

> Now teach me, *Maid* compos'd,
> To breathe some soften'd Strain,
> Whose Numbers stealing thro' thy darkning Vale,
> May not unseemly with its Stillness suit   (lines 15–18)

And evidently the poet is successfully taught by Evening, succeeds in achieving a union between there and here, between beauty and human life, between the life of the Powers and the life of words. Even in poems whose subject is not ostensibly the writing of poetry we find the constant topics, the languages to be reconciled and the new manner to be learned. In any Odes that deal centrally with poetry itself, the union between then and now, or there and here, may not in the end be achieved. Gray's "The Progress of Poesy" ends with a question and a gap: "Oh! Lyre divine, what daring Spirit / Wakes thee now?" In Collins's "Ode on the Poetical Character" at the end of the Epode the poet asks the urgent question,

> Where is the Bard, whose Soul can now
> Its high presuming Hopes avow?
> Where He who thinks, with Rapture blind,
> This hallow'd Work for Him design'd?   (lines 51–4)

We might expect the answer to these queries to be supplied by the poet-speaker himself, but he is not the Bard, nor guilty of presumption and blind rapture. In the Antistrophe he raises this possibility – that he will be the answer to the question and the need – and rejects it as hubristic. The whole poem has an unhappy ending:

> I view that Oak, the fancied Glades among,
> > By which as *Milton* lay, His Ev'ning Ear,
> From many a Cloud that drop'd Ethereal Dew,
> > Nigh spher'd in Heav'n its native Strains could hear:
> On which that ancient Trump he reach'd was hung;
> > Thither oft his Glory greeting,
> > From *Waller*'s Myrtle Shades retreating,
> With many a Vow from Hope's aspiring Tongue,
> My trembling Feet his guiding Steps pursue;
> > In vain – Such Bliss to One alone,
> > Of all the Sons of Soul was known
> And Heav'n, and *Fancy*, kindred Pow'rs,
> Have now o'erturn'd th'inspiring Bow'rs
> Or curtain'd close such Scene from ev'ry future View.   (lines 63–76)

We are left with disruption, not union, and there remains to us only one half of the two-language equation. The earthly language, the language of here and now, seems to fail as it cannot unite with the beautiful language, the heavenly language which Milton could hear, and after hearing utter. *There* and *here* cannot be united or reconciled because Heaven and *Fancy*, those kindred Powers, together have destroyed the space, the ground, on which they could be engaged. Now such union cannot even be seen or imagined; the vision is curtained off and there is no way of passing through that space that separates celestial strains and earthly tongue.

The endings of Odes provided poets with an opportunity to talk symbolically and at large about endings, and about poetic endings which, as we have seen, posed special problems and were of special interest to Augustan poets. In Odes, either the dreaded death which comes at the end of Augustan poems is overcome by a continuation into the supernal or timeless – which is what the reconciliation of the two languages, heavenly and earthly, really means – or the ending is seen as insoluble, unresolvable, because the two voices will not unite. The one voice, the poet's uneven contemporary human voice with its not fully adequate language, is left to trail into silence on its own.

It can be seen that the Augustan "Pindaric Ode," however much it may appear to defy other current forms of poetry and to represent an almost rebellious extreme of the expression of grandeur and imagination, is really working in the same interests, and in much the same way, as other Augustan poems. We find the same concerns in the setting up of opposition, of implied debate, and the relation of two languages – a relation often in Odes made consciously a subject in itself. The Odes were written for readers educated in stylistic consciousness and capable of appreciating the problems of style, or questions about style, raised in these poems.

The Odes were also written for readers trained in rhythm and the effects of rhyme, aware that small changes could make for large pleasures. It is a mistake to think that the Ode threw down or destroyed the couplet, despite the poets' claims for the form's boldness and its irregular numbers. Most "Pindaric Odes" are composed in rhyme (with the remarkable exception of Collins's "Ode to Evening"). And at some point or other in most Odes we come upon couplets, even a profusion of couplets. Sometimes part of a section is a quatrain, e.g.

> Till the sad Nine in Greece's evil hour
> Left their Parnassus for the Latian plains.
> Alike they scorn the pomp of tyrant-Power,
> And coward Vice, that revels in her chains.
> (Gray, "The Progress of Poesy" II. 3, lines 77–80)

It is evident that the poets who wrote Odes intended to offer us a superabundance of the pleasures we get in couplets – including some couplets. Throughout an Ode we have the characteristic Augustan working of idea against idea, sound against sound, tone against tone and voice against voice. The Ode also stood for appetite for language, for expansiveness and liberty. It was the outward and visible sign of an inward daring Muse,

> *Beat not the dirty paths where vulgar feet have trod,*
> *But give the vigorous fancy room.*

It would be a mistake to segregate the "Pindaric Ode" from the rest of Augustan poetry and to consider it a reaction against something more dry, limited and enclosed. The Ode serves the Augustan purpose precisely because the Augustans did not like closed forms; it is of a piece with the rest of their poetic practice.

The Augustans' most celebrated verse mode, the couplet, worked for the poets in place of a closed verse form. Through the attentive use of it, the poets escaped the restrictions of the elaborate and finite stanza. Couplet verse invites and accommodates narrative, and interprets and represents dramatic voices:

> He, puzzled, bites his nail, both to display
> The sparkling ring, and think what next to say,
> And thus breaks forth afresh: "Madam, egad!
> Your luck at cards last night was very bad."

It permits various observation, and can, flexibly, set forth the world and the things in the world, as in Dryden's

> And set soft Hyacinths with Iron blue,
> To shade marsh Marigolds of shining Hue

or

> Round as a Globe, and Liquor'd ev'ry chink,
> Goodly and Great he Sayls behind his Link;

or Gay's

> Or underneath th'*Umbrella*'s oily Shed
> Safe thro' the Wet on clinking Pattens tread.

The couplet is itself only when the effects of sound are properly recognized. Such verse could not be written by poets with dull ears, or for readers who could not hear. We see everywhere on their pages evidence of the Augustans' attention to the sound of words, and of their respect for words. They created a whole set of conventions about typography and spelling to assist the reader. They indicate stresses, and make their words variously emphatic, through the use of capital letters and italics. They spell phonetically, signalling elision ("th'inspiring") and the omission of syllables ("Powder'd with di'monds"). When their works are presented modernized, with the elimination of their "accidentals," the result is that very dull ugliness on the page which the Augustans so disliked. The poems can give an impression of monotony – the last thing the variety-loving Augustans could have wished.

When we get rid of their way of presenting a poem, we are part way to getting rid of their way of reading it. This alteration also imposes the sort of aural murkiness the poets intended to eliminate. The original printed page bearing an Augustan poem is usually the result of a deal of thought, and conveys an intention. The words with their nuances of emphasis (italics, capitals) seem to leap out at us from the page. At the same time, these words make very beautiful patterns on the page – such as many of us, when we first faced Augustan poems in dreary anthologies of tight-packed lines, could not envisage. If the poems look (with their regular iambic pentameter line lengths) symmetrical, they also appear varied, and individual parts seem distinctive down to the very individual line.

A look at a page of an *Horatian Imitation*, for example (Fig. 26), or of Gay's *The Shepherd's Week* (Fig. 27) or his *Fables* (Fig. 28) will help us realize how expansive and vivacious Augustan poems could look, and how immediately attractive they are, attractive to the hand and eye, and also to the ear. These poems, uncramped and unembarrassed, promise interesting pauses between

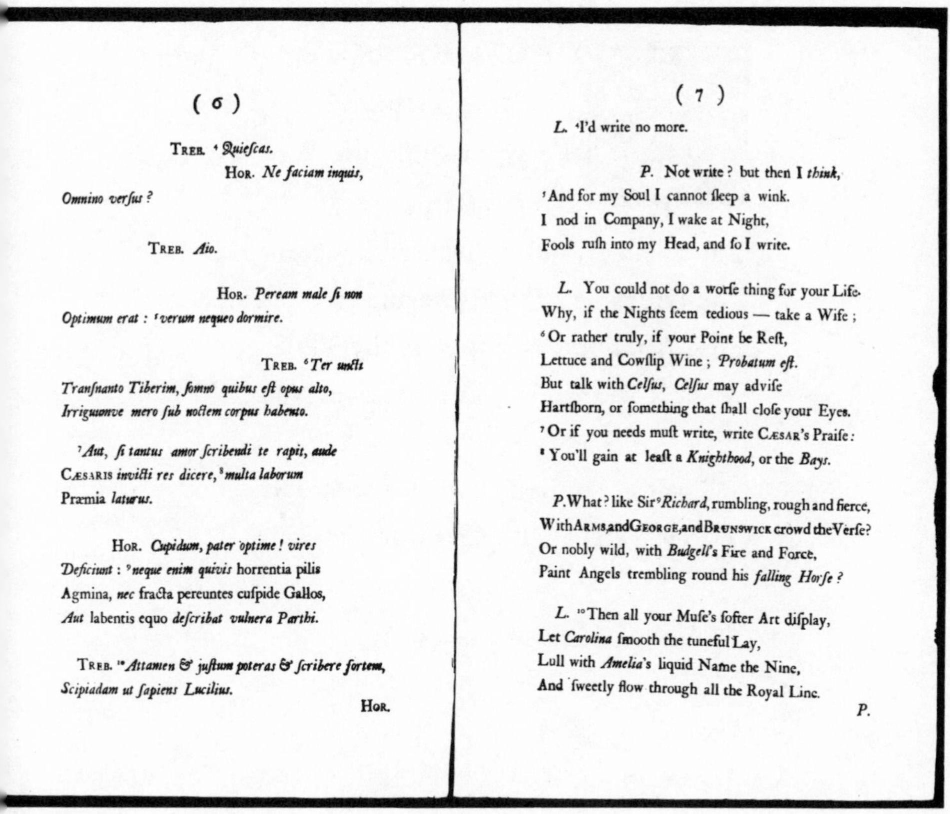

(6)

TREB. ¹ *Quiefcas.*
    HOR. *Ne faciam inquis,*
Omnino verfus ?

TREB. *Aio.*

    HOR. *Peream male fi non*
Optimum erat : ² *verum nequeo dormire.*

    TREB. ⁶ *Ter uncti*
Tranfnanto Tiberim, fomno quibus eft opus alto,
Irriguumve mero fub noctem corpus habento.

    ⁷ *Aut, fi tantus amor fcribendi te rapit, aude*
CÆSARIS *invicti res dicere,* ⁸ *multa laborum*
Præmia *laturus.*

    HOR. *Cupidum, pater optime ! vires*
Deficiunt : ⁹ *neque enim quivis* horrentia pilis
Agmina, *nec* fracta pereuntes cufpide Gallos,
Aut labentis equo *defcribat vulnera Parthi.*

    TREB. ¹⁰ *Attamen & juftum poteras & fcribere fortem,*
Scipiadam ut fapiens Lucilius.
            HOR.

(7)

L. 'I'd write no more.

    P. Not write ? but then I *think,*
¹ And for my Soul I cannot fleep a wink.
I nod in Company, I wake at Night,
Fools rufh into my Head, and fo I write.

    L. You could not do a worfe thing for your Life.
Why, if the Nights feem tedious — take a Wife ;
⁶ Or rather truly, if your Point be Reft,
Lettuce and Cowflip Wine ; *Probatum eft.*
But talk with *Celfus, Celfus* may advife
Hartfhorn, or fomething that fhall clofe your Eyes.
⁷ Or if you needs muft write, write CÆSAR'S Praife :
⁸ You'll gain at leaft a *Knighthood,* or the *Bays.*

    P. What ? like Sir ⁹ *Richard,* rumbling, rough and fierce,
With ARMS and GEORGE, and BRUNSWICK crowd the Verfe ?
Or nobly wild, with *Budgell's* Fire and Force,
Paint Angels trembling round his *falling Horfe ?*

    L. ¹⁰ Then all your Mufe's fofter Art difplay,
Let *Carolina* fmooth the tuneful Lay,
Lull with *Amelia's* liquid Name the Nine,
And fweetly flow through all the Royal Line.
            P.

Fig. 26

SATURDAY;

OR, THE

FLIGHTS.

BOWZYBEUS.

UBLIMER Strains, O ruſtick
Muſe, prepare;
Forget a-while the Barn and Dai-
ry's Care;
Thy homely Voice to loftier Numbers raiſe,
The Drunkard's Flights require ſonorous Lays,
With *Bowzybeus*' Songs exalt thy Verſe,   5
While Rocks and Woods the various Notes rehearſe.

'Twas in the Seaſon when the Reaper's Toil
Of the ripe Harveſt 'gan to rid the Soil;

          Wide

Fig. 27

FABLES.

FABLE XLII.

The JUGGLERS.

A Juggler long through all the town
    Had rais'd his fortune and renown;
You'd think (fo far his art tranfcends)
The devil at his finger's ends.

  Vice heard his fame, fhe read his bill;
Convinc'd of his inferior skill,

U 2

She

Fig. 28

the words, and curves of sound in the words. These poems want to be read –
and to be heard, clearly heard.

The Augustan passion for sound, and for the clear representation of sounded
words ("ev'ry," "thro'"), did not serve some abstract correctness. The major
purpose of phonetic exactness is to make sure nothing gets in the reader's way.
The relations between part and part should be appreciated by the emotions
and the intellect, but that does not entail heavy breaks, or lumbering progress.
On the contrary, the couplet must keep going, and must keep transcending its
own internal pauses and complications. Boundaries are constantly suggested
in order to be o'erleaped.

Rhyme is a boundary mark that does not confine. It pretends to mark
closure but really – or also – marks the beginning of something else, something
contiguous and continuous. The rhyme at the end of a couplet offers its own
satisfactions and posts a boundary mark immediately transcended by the
beginning of a new couplet. We move from bound into new space, new creation
– a move which creates the idea of boundlessness at least as much as does the
large ostentatiously unbounded form of the Pindaric Ode. A couplet provides a
false ending or closure that is at once superseded, an "ending" that we pass
over. There is a deep poetic and psychological satisfaction in encountering this
ending and escaping it. For the Augustans who, as we have seen, felt the secret
horror of the last, and the fear of an ending, the pleasure of constantly
encountering endings and constantly transcending them seems to have been
especially great. We evade the end, we escape death, each time that we pass
through one couplet and enter a new one.

The two-line set is paradoxically complete in itself yet uncompleted –
unitary, yet not discrete. Couplets depend on the relations of binary elements.
They depend, philosophically, on the idea of relating One to Other. We are
formally engaged in relationships of twos. But an Augustan poem is not a
couplet, but *in* couplets; the "two" involved constantly shift. When a rhyme
sound is completed in the second line we do not expect the same rhyme sound
to continue in the next two lines and the next two ... (If a poet occasionally
presents us with a triplet, it is as a surprise, playing upon our expectation of
faster change.) The presence of the two rhymed lines of verse presents the idea
of a perfectly constructed creation that is not yet whole. Augustan couplets
invite other couplets to follow them. They may often be very overtly open-
ended. Rochester's "what next to say" obviously requires something else to
follow at once. But when we see Og "Goodly and Great" we know that the poet
hasn't nearly got through with him yet and there must be punch lines to follow.

The couplet evokes change, play, procedure and movement. Consummately
quotable and memorable, it is not yet in itself finished, but invites capping,
retorting, answering. It suggests part of a process. A really good Augustan
couplet insists expectantly on another rhymed set of two to come after – it
almost requests the reader to begin guessing or inventing what could follow,
what could equal this. Such verse is outward-moving, always reaching toward

addition, always expecting to flush into variety again, and again. The couplet in its context suggests both the inorganic (the artificial, finished, made object) and the organic (the process of growth and change). It gives us both form and flow.

When we look at what the couplet really means, or really meant to the Augustans, we recognize that it is a mobile, not to say restless, mode of writing. Couplet verse shows us at the same time both how to grapple with something and how to let go – it demands letting go. The poet, too, must let go of a perfect couplet and risk writing one less perfect if he is to achieve a poem. Couplet poetry can be, and at its greatest must be, vigorous and demanding. It always seems to need more room. It moves on, as Dryden said Dorset's poetry did, in almost excessive expansion of variety. We are "not kept in expectation of two good lines, which are to come after a long Parenthesis of twenty bad"; the poet is "always bright, even almost to a fault, by reason of the excess. There is continual abundance, a Magazine of Thought, and yet a perpetual Variety of Entertainment; which creates such an Appetite in [the] Reader, that he is not cloy'd with any thing, but satisfy'd with all." Couplet poetry keeps going, amazingly, bringing the riches of the world, covering more space (in the world and on the page). It ingests more and more of the world, and more and more words, into itself. From our vantage point we can say the Augustans found the perfect poetic mode for expressing their appetitiveness and expansiveness. And with such a beautifully developed element as the couplet on which to base their whole procedure they could at once satisfy the desire for formal perfection while doing away with the confines of most poetic forms.

The couplet as a unit and as a part of a whole is also the perfect means for creating transformations. The dynamic alterations within a couplet are strong enough to make a decided impact on the reader; at the same time, the unit is small enough in itself to ensure that important complexities will not be lost to the reader's memory before the working out. The full syntactical presence ensures no unnecessary loss of energy, no halting, as we move towards conflict and changes strongly indicated by transmutations of sound. The couplet is a unit of locution both gracious and under tension. The suspense with which we await the coming of the rhyme ensures that we have some minimal knowledge of tension and are conscious of a resolution involving change. The couplet as constituent unit acts both as a model and as a means of transformation, of metamorphosis.

The couplet is also a unit of locution suggesting or reflecting double-tongued statement. Line 1 and line 2 constitute a kind of dialogue in themselves, the lines suggesting as they do two voices – an effect not diminished by the immediate presence of the next set, lines 3 and 4, as if another voice were cutting in, superimposing itself over what was speaking before. We keep hearing voices in Augustan verse, sometimes the dramatized voices of characters, sometimes the indirect voices of various persons' thoughts, most often the diverse voice of the poet himself as he juggles with two languages.

The Augustans like enriched and sometimes strange harmonies. They start to say something and say something else as well – and as clearly – like melodies in both bass and treble running with and against each other. An idea is not an idea until it is two ideas. A voice becomes two voices, and a statement becomes debate diversified. In Augustan poetry, as in much of Augustan literature altogether, the writers wrestle with the problems and possibilities of language, most constantly and significantly presenting us with two languages that are in opposition to, and yet have a need for, each other.

The experimental vitality of each good Augustan poem, whether in couplets or quatrains or blank verse (or calling itself "Pindaric Ode"), depends on the Augustan love of multiplicity, and the refusal to be set in one direction or couched in one tongue. Having seen, at the beginning of their era, the direst possibilities of stylistic takeover and of pre-emptive strikes against utterance, the Augustans fulfilled themselves by conscious and multiple utterance. Refusing to be depressed by the weight of consciousness acknowledged in their self-consciousness about genre, style and diction, they developed out of that consciousness the idea of originality, and asserted the value of the unique poetic creation. Rather than becoming involved in nervous introspection they turned outward. Their enterprise was an endeavour to grasp this great and strange and metamorphosing universe, without simplifying the external world or losing touch with personality and the inner life. "Rise, kill and eat." They asserted their right to dominion over all creatures, all riches, all spaces and all styles. All that humanity could touch or know or guess at was theirs for poetic subject, and all the transformations and metamorphoses of life.

The Augustan poets wanted, and achieved, rich full utterances in a poetry where the only sign of failure (itself sometimes a topic in that poetry) is the inability to speak, and the only true source of fear is ending and silence. They gave us all the heard melodies they had. Each poet, double-voiced or even multi-voiced, was not just one single harp-bearing bard, but a chorale. What Johnson said of himself and his associates at Pembroke could have been said by the Augustan poets of themselves: "Sir, we are a nest of singing birds."[15] The danger of multi-voiced utterance may be cacophony (as Pope noted in the *Dunciad*) but the poets were willing to take the risk and forgo limpid unison or simple harmony in order to represent the world and our experience of it, and to reconstruct poetry so that it might (in the words of Dryden's detractors) "elevate and surprise." Their programme was ambitious – that each poem should stand on its own feet, be its own kind, its own genre, and tell us some complex truth in such a manner that we experience it as we go. They succeeded, and left us a body of brilliant poetry, which, if we will only let it, can keep surprising and delighting us afresh with its daring beauty and adventurous intelligence.

Notes

Introduction

1. Matthew Arnold makes this remark in an essay, "The Study of Poetry," first published in 1880 as the General Introduction to T. H. Ward's anthology *The English Poets*. See "The Study of Poetry," in *English Literature and Irish Politics*, ed. R. H. Super, Vol. IX of *The Complete Prose Works of Matthew Arnold* (Ann Arbor: University of Michigan Press, 1973), pp. 179–81.

2. See Donald Greene, *The Age of Exuberance: Backgrounds to Eighteenth-Century English Literature* (New York: Random House, 1970). Kenneth MacLean suggests: "That the age of reason might with more justice be called the age of passion"; see his *John Locke and English Literature of the Eighteenth Century* (New Haven: Yale University Press, 1936), p. 38. Steven Shankman has adopted this suggestion in his recent excellent book, *Pope's "Iliad": Homer in the Age of Passion* (Princeton University Press, 1983).

3. See the beginning of "The Fire Sermon" in original typescript, with pen strokes indicating Pound's striking out of the Fresca section, in *The Waste Land: A Facsimile and Transcript of the Original Drafts,* Valerie Eliot, ed. (New York: Harcourt Brace Jovanovich, 1971), pp. 22–7. Eliot later wrote that Pound

> induced me to destroy what I thought an excellent set of couplets, for, said he, "Pope has done this so well that you cannot do it better; and if you mean this as a burlesque, you had better suppress it, for you cannot parody Pope unless you can write better verse than Pope – and you can't."
>
> (Introduction to *Selected Poems of Ezra Pound*, 1928, quoted in *Waste Land* facsimile, editorial note p. 127.)

4. Eliot gives the impression in this essay of having come to praise and remained to blame. Dryden is "the ancestor of nearly all that is best in the poetry of the eighteenth century ... His inspiration is prolonged in Crabbe and Byron." But "Dryden, with all his intellect, had a commonplace mind." "Dryden lacked ... a large and unique view of life; he lacked insight, he lacked profundity" ("John Dryden" [1922], in T. S. Eliot, *Selected Essays* (London: Faber and Faber, 1932), p. 305; p. 314; p. 316). One can hear the echo of Arnold in much of this.

5. See Davie's Clark Lectures 1976, published as *A Gathered Church: The Literature of the English Dissenting Interest, 1700–1930* (New York: Oxford University Press, 1978), especially Lecture 2, "Old Dissent" and Lecture 3, "Dissent and the Wesleyans."

6. See Lady Winchilsea's poem, "A Tale of the Miser, and the Poet. Written about the year 1709" in her *Miscellany Poems on Several Occasions. Written by a Lady* (London: Printed for J. B. and Sold by Benj. Tooke [et al.], 1713), pp. 145–50. A miser digs up his coin, hidden in the days of Charles when wit was in fashion. Now is the time for moneyed men and the poets are no longer valued:

> I hid this Coin, when *Charles* was swaying
> When all was Riot, Masking, Playing;
> When witty Beggars were in fashion,
> And Learning had o'er-run the Nation,

> But, since Mankind is so much wiser,
> That none is valu'd like the *Miser*,
> I draw it hence, and now these Sums
> In proper Soil grow up to *plumbs*. (p. 147)

The Poet, forced to agree that the Miser is right about the present day, must hide his wit where once old Mammon hid his gold,

> Till Time, which hastily advances,
> And gives to all new Turns and Chances,
> Again may bring it into use;
> *Roscommons* may again produce
> New *Augustean* Days revive,
> When *Wit* shall please, and *Poets* thrive. (p. 150)

7. For Donald Greene's dismissal of the term, see his *The Age of Exuberance*, p. 91. Howard D. Weinbrot tackles the use of the term (and the "sloppy scholarship" it encourages) in his *Augustus Caesar in "Augustan" England: The Decline of a Classical Norm* (Princeton University Press, 1978).

I. Appetite, imperialism and the fair variety of things

1. Earl Miner, *The Restoration Mode from Milton to Dryden* (Princeton University Press, 1974), pp. 299–300.
2. In *The Sister Arts: The Tradition of Literary Pictorialism and English Poetry from Dryden to Gray* (Chicago University Press, 1958), pp. 179–80.
3. See, e.g., Raphael's speech to Adam in *Paradise Lost*, Book VIII, lines 66–178.
4. See Edward Niles Hooker, "The Purpose of Dryden's *Annus Mirabilis*," *Huntington Library Quarterly* 10 (1946), pp. 49–67, reprinted in *Essential Articles for the Study of John Dryden*, H. T. Swedenberg, Jr., ed. (Hamden, Conn.: Archon Books, 1966), pp. 281–99.
5. Quoted from *Coopers Hill. Written in the yeare 1640. Now Printed from a perfect Copy; And A Corrected Impression. By John Denham Esq;* (London: Humphrey Moseley, 1655), p. 10. Denham kept revising, correcting and adding to his poem – a very Augustan habit. For an interesting discussion of the political and social meanings of *Coopers Hill*, see James Turner, *The Politics of Landscape: Rural Scenery and Society in English Poetry 1630–1660* (Cambridge, Mass.: Harvard University Press, 1979), pp. 50–61.
6. Passages like this of Pope's *Windsor Forest* have been called "Whig panegyric"; see Cecil A. Moore, "Whig Panegyric Verse: A Phase of Sentimentalism," *Backgrounds of English Literature 1700–1760* (Minneapolis, Minn.: University of Minnesota Press, 1953), pp. 104–44. For a discussion of Pope's relation to his society and its enterprises see Howard Erskine-Hill, *The Social Milieu of Alexander Pope: Lives, Example, and the Poetic Response* (New Haven, Conn., and London: Yale University Press, 1975).
7. See Louis Landa, "Pope's Belinda, the General Emporie of the World, and the Wondrous Worm," in his *Essays in Eighteenth Century English Literature* (Princeton University Press, 1980), p. 197.
8. Quoted from *Dionysius Longinus on the Sublime: Translated from the Greek, with Notes and Observations, and Some Account of the Life, Writings and Character of the Author. By William Smith, A.M.* (London: Printed by J. Watts; And Sold by W. Innys and R. Manby, 1739), pp. 78–80.
   The identity of the Greek author is unknown, and he is nowadays referred to,

depressingly, as Pseudo-Longinus; he may have lived and written as early as the first century A.D. The author of *On the Sublime* quotes Genesis (he had evidently read the Septuagint), and to men of the late Renaissance and Augustan Age his treatise offered a particularly exciting example of the possibilities of blending the Judaeo-Christian and the Hellenic traditions.

9. In *Augustan Satire: Intention and Idiom in English Poetry 1660–1750* (Oxford University Press, 1952), pp. 35–6.
10. See his *Restoration and Eighteenth-Century Poetry 1660–1780*, The Routledge History of English Poetry, Vol. III (Boston and London: Routledge and Kegan Paul, 1981), pp. 68–9.
11. Quoted from *The Dispensary: A Poem In Six Canto's* (London: John Nutt, 1699), Canto II, pp. 20–1. *The Dispensary* was first published in 1699; Garth (later Sir Samuel Garth) kept correcting and adding to it.
12. Quoted from Mark Akenside's *The Pleasures of Imagination. A Poem. In Three Books* (London: R. Dodsley, 1744), Book I, pp. 18–19; p. 13.

II. Some origins of Augustan practice: Civil War verse and its implications

1. I have relied largely on two printed collections. The first is *Rump: Or an Exact Collection of the Choycest Poems and Songs relating to the Late Times. By the most Eminent Wits, from Anno 1639 to Anno 1661* (London: Henry Brome and Henry Marsh, 1662), facsimile edition of 1874, in 2 volumes. The second is *Cavalier and Puritan: Ballads and Broadsides Illustrating the Period of the Great Rebellion 1640–1660*, Hyder E. Rollins, ed. (New York University Press, 1923).
    The ballads quoted in the text of this chapter may be found as follows:
    In *Rump Songs:*
    "The Humble Petition of the House of Commons," Part I, pp. 17–19
    "A Song" ("Know this my Brethren"), I, pp. 14–16
    "Collonel *Vennes* Encouragement to his Souldiers," I, pp. 149–51
    "The Rebellion," I, pp. 291–5
    "The States New Coyne," I, pp. 289–90
    "A Hue and Cry after the Reformation," I, pp. 195–7
    In *Cavalier and Puritan:*
    "Keep thy Head on thy Shoulders" (1641), No. 9, pp. 127–31
    "The World is Turned Upside Down" (1646), No. 15, pp. 161–2
    I am indebted to Rachel Trickett who brought the existence of such verse to the attention of an Oxford graduate seminar which I once attended.
2. See Joseph Frank, *The Beginnings of the English Newspaper* (Cambridge, Mass.: Harvard University Press, 1961), p. 50, and *Cromwell's Press Agent: A Critical Biography of Marchamont Nedham, 1620–1678* (Lanham, Md.: University Press of America, 1980), p. 16.
3. These quatrains are quoted from *A Short History of the English Rebellion. Compiled in* VERSE, by MARCHAMONT NEDHAM; And formerly extant, in his Weekly Mercurius Pragmaticus. (London: 1680), p. 21; p. 4; p. 3; p. 9. The *Short History* was republished at the time of the Popish Plot in 1680 as an anti-Shaftesbury piece. Nedham's last published new works before he died in 1678 were pamphlets against Shaftesbury; "Cromwell's press agent" ended his life as Charles II's journalist.
4. The version of "When the King Enjoys His Own Again" here quoted is taken from Joseph Ritson's *Ancient Songs and Ballads from the Reign of King Henry the Second to the Revolution*, 3rd edition revised by W. Carew Hazlitt, 2 vols. (London: "Printed for Private Circulation," 1877), Vol. II, pp. 368–70.
    C. V. Wedgwood refers to Martin Parker as "London's most popular ballad

monger" in the reign of James I; see *Poetry and Politics under the Stuarts* [first published Cambridge, 1960] (Ann Arbor, Mich.: University of Michigan Press, 1964), p. 26, see also pp. 36–8; pp. 59–61.

5. Wedgwood, *Poetry and Politics*, pp. 130–1.

6. *News from Brussels*. In a Letter From A Neer Attendant on His Majesties Person. To a Person of Honour here. Which casually became thus publique. Printed in the Year, 1660, pp. 6–7. "Hug them ...," p. 4.

7. Quoted from facsimile in *The English Revolution* III Newsbooks, 5 Vol. I (London: Cornmarket Press, 1971), *Mercurius Politicus*, Vol. I, 1650, pp. 33–4.

8. *Mercurius Politicus*, Vol. I, pp. 68–9. The ballad which Nedham supplies for the "Priest" is evidently based on a common Civil War formula (and presumably a very well-known tune).

9. Quoted from *The Poems of John Philips*, M. G. Lloyd Thomas, ed., Percy Reprints No. 10 (Oxford: Basil Blackwell, 1927), pp. 6–7.

10. My translation of comment by Victor Fournel in "Du Burlesque en France et en Particulier du *Virgile Travesti* de Scarron," Preface to Scarron, *Le Virgile Travesti* (Paris: Garnier Frères, 1876), p. xi. The quotation from *Le Virgile Travesti* on p. 50 is also taken from that edition, p. 57; cf. *Aen.* I, lines 92–101.

11. From *Scarronides, or, Virgile Travestie. A Mock-Poem on the First and Fourth Books of Virgil's* A E N A E I S. In English Burlesque. By Charles Cotton, Esq: (London: R. Bonwicke, W. Freeman, Tim Goodwin *et al.*, 1715), bound into *The Genuine Works of Charles Cotton Esq:* Illustrated with many curious Cutts ... (London: R. Bonwicke, Tim Goodwin *et al.*, 1715), pp. 6–8. The illustration faces page 6. Large chunks of Virgil's saucily used poem appear in the lower margin and one's attention is directed to them.

III. Generic self-consciousness: from closed to open forms

1. Pope, *Imitations of Horace*, Epistle II. i, line 108.

2. Rochester's poems were published at different times, many posthumously, and in variant versions; most were passed about in manuscript copies, generally freer in obscenity and scandal than the printed forms. Hayward's prudish edition of the *Collected Works* (1926), and Vivian de Sola Pinto's Muses Library text (1952), more agreeable but still bowdlerized, have both been superseded by David M. Vieth's *The Complete Poems of John Wilmot, Earl of Rochester* (New Haven, Conn.: Yale University Press, 1968). Vieth has done the scholarly bibliographical work which previous editors only pointed to as needing to be done, but he has ruthlessly modernized all "accidentals," claiming "there is virtually no basis for an old-spelling text of Rochester's poems." In presenting the poems so that they look like twentieth-century works Vieth takes a startling liberty. The poems look so unnatural in this guise that I was tempted to follow Barbara Everett's lead in using the Muses Library text, agreeing that "The primary need in presenting a poet is not to obscure his tone; and certain of Rochester's poems ... profit from the retention of that Restoration and Augustan habit of visual literacy, the capitalization of important nouns" ("The Sense of Nothing," in *Spirit of Wit: Reconsiderations of Rochester*, Jeremy Treglown, ed. (Oxford: Basil Blackwell, 1982), p. 15). Nevertheless, as the Vieth edition is truly authoritative and comprehensive, I have reluctantly drawn on it for quotation, only taking the liberty of italicizing proper names, so that the sort of emphasis which Augustan readers were always accustomed to seeing when they read printed poems may not be altogether lacking.

3. The poem in its first appearance has as its full title "Song. Set by Mr. *John Laniere*.

To Lucasta, Going to the Warres" – that is, it emphasizes its literally lyric nature. Lovelace's own poem depends for the effect of its ending on a stressed paradox:

> Yet this Inconstancy is such,
> As you too shall adore;
> I could not love thee (Deare) so much,
> Lov'd I not Honour more.

Lucasta: Epodes, Odes, Sonnets, Songs &c. To Which is Added Aramantha, a Pastorall. By Richard Lovelace Esq. (London: Printed by Tho. Harper, and . . . sold by Tho. Evvster, 1649), p. 3.

4. Jeremy Treglown, in the Introduction to his edition of Rochester's *Letters*, points out Rochester's habit of parody in letter-writing; see *The Letters of John Wilmot Earl of Rochester* (Oxford: Basil Blackwell, 1980), p. 24. There is for instance, the parody of high style in Rochester's nonsense letter to his wife (p. 51), or the satiric parody in a late letter to Savile with a mock-Miltonic treatment of cures for V.D. (pp. 201–2).

5. "His apprehension was quick, and his memory good. He was an everlasting talker. He told his stories with a good grace: But they came in his way too often." Gilbert Burnet, in *Bishop Burnet's History of His Own Time*, 2 vols. (London: Thomas Ward, 1724), Vol. I, p. 94.

6. See Hobbes's appreciative essay, "The Answer of Mr. Hobbes to S^r. Will. Davenant's Preface before G O N D I B E R T," published in *Gondibert: An Heroick Poem; Written by Sir William Davenant* (London: John Holden, 1651), pp. 52–64.

7. Quoted from *The Works of Mr. Abraham Cowley*, 11th edition, 2 vols. (London: J. Tonson *et al.*, 1710), Vol. II, p. 444.

8. See A. L. Korn, *"MacFlecknoe* and Cowley's *Davideis,"* in *Essential Articles*, pp. 170–200. See also Swedenberg's commentary on *MacFlecknoe* in the California *Dryden*, Vol. II, pp. 299–327. In producing *Absalom and Architophel*, too, Dryden could count on at least some of his audience knowing Cowley's serious treatment of the story of King David.

9. Thomas Sprat, "An Account of the Life and Writings of Mr. Abraham Cowley. Written to Mr. M. Clifford," prefixed to first posthumous collected *Works* and here quoted from 1710 edition, Vol. I, p. xxiv. Sprat emphasizes the fact that Cowley's Biblical epic was a very youthful work.

10. Quoted from *The Prose Works of Alexander Pope*, Norman Ault, ed., 2 vols., Vol. I, *The Earlier Works, 1711–1720* (Oxford: Basil Blackwell for Shakespeare Head Press, 1936), pp. 115–20.

11. See prefatory note by Norman Ault and John Butt on "Lines from *Alcander* and the Early Poems," Twickenham edition of *The Poems of Alexander Pope*, John Butt, ed., 11 vols., Vol. VI, *Minor Poems* (London: Methuen, and New Haven, Conn.: Yale University Press, 1964), p. 20.

12. See Joseph Spence, *Anecdotes, Observations and Characters of Books and Men Collected from the Conversation of Mr. Pope and other Eminent Persons of his Time* [first published 1820, Samuel Weller Singer, ed.], reissue with Introduction by Bonamy Dobrée (Carbondale, Ill.: Southern Illinois University Press, 1964), p. 173. For Johnson's remark, see *Life of Pope, Lives*, Vol. III, p. 188. Owen Ruffhead, the biographer, gives us a detailed account of the plan of *Brutus*; unfortunately he doesn't reproduce Pope's own words, though he had "a sketch of this intended piece" lying before him. The plan bears out what Pope told Spence, that the epic "turns wholly on civil and ecclesiastical government," for the Trojan is an Enlightenment hero whose object is

not to conquer and destroy the natives of the new-discovered land, but to polish and refine them, by introducing true religion, void of superstition and all false notions of the Deity . . .

among people who are uncorrupted in their manners, and only want the introduction of useful arts, under the sanction of a good governement, to establish and ensure their felicity.

Ruffhead, *The Life of Alexander Pope, Esq.*, Garland facsimile (New York and London: Garland Publishing, 1974), Vol. II, p. 82. The whole seems like a mixture of *Os Lusiades* and *Robinson Crusoe Part II* filtered through the *Essay on Man*.

13. Everett, "The Sense of Nothing," p. 29; for her discussion of the significance of Artemisia's name, see pp. 29–30.

14. See Warton, *Essay on the Genius and Writings of Pope* [first published 1756], The Fifth edition corrected, 2 vols. (London: W. J. and J. Richardson *et al.*, 1806), Vol. II, p. 153. Warburton is emphatically clear that Bathurst is a speaker:

> The poet represents himself and the noble Lord his friend, as in a conversation ... and it proceeds by way of dialogue, which most writers use to hide want of method; our Author only to soften and enliven the dryness and severity of it.

See *The Works of Alexander Pope Esq. In Nine Volumes Complete. With his Last Corrections, Additions and Improvements; As they were delivered to the* EDITOR *a little before his Death: Together with the Commentaries and Notes of Mr. Warburton* (London: J. and P. Knapton, H. Lintot, J. and R. Tonson, and S. Draper, 1751), Vol. III, pp. 236–7. Warburton makes the dialogue indication quite clear, e.g.:

> B. What Nature wants, commodious Gold bestows,
>   'Tis thus we eat the bread another sows.
> P. But how unequal it bestows, observe,
>   'Tis thus we riot, while, who sow it, starve:
>   ...
> B. Trade it may help, Society extend.
> P. But lures the Pyrate, and corrupts the Friend.   (pp. 239–43)

One can see why Bathurst objected. Subsequent editions in the century perpetuate Warburton's allocation of speeches, though in a late edition "With Notes and Illustrations by Joseph Warton D.D. and Others," Warton registers his own opinion in a note:

> VER. 29 ... What is here put into the mouth of Bathurst might be, with equal propriety, transferred to Pope; and so, indeed, may many other lines.

The Works of Alexander Pope Esq., 9 vols. (London: B. Law, J. Johnson *et al.*, 1797), Vol. III, p. 239. Yet even in his own edition, Warton didn't dare alter the division according to Warburton.

15. Quotation from *Olney Hymns, in Three Books*, by the Rev. John Newton (Burlington: Isaac Neale, 1795), Book III, "On the Rise, Progress, Changes and Comforts of the Spiritual Life," Section III, "Conflict," p. 267. Cowper's contributions are each marked with an anonymous (c) in *Olney Hymns*, first published in 1779.

16. Isaac Watts, "Crucifixion to the World by the Cross of Christ," in *Hymns and Spiritual Songs*, 2nd edition (London: J. H. for John Lawrence, 1709), Book III, No. 7, p. 289.
    The other hymns here quoted are taken from the anthology, *Eighteenth-Century English Literature*, Geoffrey Tillotson, Paul Fussell, Jr., and Marshall Waingrow, eds. (New York: Harcourt Brace Jovanovich, 1969), pp. 1535–7.

17. John Newton, Preface to *Olney Hymns*, p. iv (phrase originally in italics, as is the whole Preface).

18. See Richard F. Jones, "The Originality of *Absalom and Achitophel*," in *Essential Articles*, pp. 201–9; reprinted from *Modern Language Notes* 46 (1931), pp. 211–18.

19. See Earl Miner, *Dryden's Poetry* (Bloomington, Ind., and London: Indiana University Press, 1967), p. 146.
20. Quotations taken from *The Hind and the Panther Transvers'd to the Story of the Country and the City-Mouse* (London: W. Davis, 1687); parody poem on p. 4; Preface, p. A₃r. The authors borrow from the techniques of *The Rehearsall*; critics address Bayes as the ventriloquized poet of the parody poem. Mr. Johnson comments: "Methinks, Mr. Bayes, soft Cheese is a little too coarse Diet for an *Immortal Mouse*: were there any necessity for her eating, you should have consulted *Homer* for some *Celestial Provision*" (p. 5). Dryden was hurt by this attack because he had been "civil" to these two young gentlemen, but young writers of the new age were likely to find parody irresistible, almost a sacred obligation, as Dryden should have known.
21. George Crabbe, *The Village*: A Poem in Two Books (London: J. Dodsley, 1783), Book i, pp. 1–5.
22. Byron, *English Bards, and Scotch Reviewers*. A Satire. (London: James Cawthorn, 1809), line 586, p. 47.
23. Sir Joshua Reynolds persuaded Johnson to read and correct *The Village*; Johnson wrote back his opinion of the piece in these words. Crabbe included Johnson's letter in the Preface to his *Poems* (1807).

IV. The new Augustans and the Roman poets

1. Quoted from *The Works of the Right Honourable Joseph Addison, Esq:* 4 vols. (London: Jacob Tonson, 1721), Vol. iv, p. 187; p. 220. Quotation from the Notes comes from section "On the Stories in the Third Book," p. 237.
2. Quotations from the Preface to *Ovid's Metamorphoses in Fifteen Books*. Translated by the most Eminent Hands. Adorn'd with Sculptures (London: Jacob Tonson, 1717), p. ii; p. viii.
3. Howard D. Weinbrot, *The Formal Strain: Studies in Augustan Imitation and Satire* (Chicago and London: University of Chicago Press, 1969), p. 30.
4. His *Englands Heroicall Epistles* was published in 1619. Fair Rosamond's epistle to King Henry II (first published in 1601) is probably the most famous of these "Heroicall Epistles."
5. The novelist also drew upon Rochester's published letters as models for Lovelace's letters to Belford in *Clarissa*; Lovelace's letters are anti-heroic and mock-heroical epistles.
6. See her article, "'Our unnatural No-voice': The Heroic Epistle, Pope, and Women's Gothic," *The Yearbook of English Studies* 12 (1982), pp. 125–51.
7. Mrs Thrale reports:

I have heard that all the kept Mistresses read Pope's Eloisa with singular delight – 'tis a great Testimony to its Ingenuity; they are commonly very ignorant Women, & can only be pleased with it as it expresses the strong Feelings of Nature & Passion.

Thraliana, the Diary of Mrs. Hester Lynch Thrale (Later Mrs. Piozzi) 1776–1809, Katharine C. Balderston, ed., 2 vols. (Oxford: Clarendon Press, 1942), Vol. i, p. 536.

8. From "Corinna's going a Maying" in *The Poems of Robert Herrick*, L. C. Martin, ed. (Oxford University Press, 1965), pp. 67–9. That Herrick was not read seems a fair inference from the lack of any issues of his works from the early years of the Restoration period to the beginning of the Regency.
9. Pope claimed that this "Ode on Solitude" was written when he was twelve, but the first extant draft dates from 1709, when he would have been twenty-one. The poem seems a reference to, though not a translation of, Horace's Epode ii, "Beatus ille."

10. Quotations from his Preface to *A Poetical Translation of the Works of Horace: With the Original Text, and Critical Notes collected from his best Latin and French Commentators*, 4th edition, 4 vols. (London: A. Millar, 1750), Vol. I, pp. xiv-xvi. Francis's translation of the *Odes* and *Epodes* first appeared in 1743, followed by the translation of the *Satires* and *Epistles* in 1746. Horace had already appeared regularly in English during our period, beginning with the translation by Thomas Creech, *The Odes, Satyrs, and Epistles of Horace. Done into English* (Oxford: J. Tonson and A. Stephens, 1684). There were a number of prose translations of Horace, including Samuel Dunster's *The Satires and Epistles of Horace, Done into English* (London: M. Jenour, for D. Browne and J. Walthoe, 1709); Dunster assures us he has put into English nothing that could be "*offensive to the* modest Reader" (Preface. A$_4$^{r}). This prose version was followed by one by Leonard Welsted in 1726, and there were others before Francis's poetic version, admired by Johnson.

Pope's *Imitations of Horace* came out in a world not only interested in Horace, but familiar with him. Even Latin-less readers (such as ladies) could have read the *Satires* and *Epistles* in various translated versions, and could have caught Pope's allusions (or many of them) at second hand. Interest in translating Horace continued after the era of Pope's *Imitations*. The most notable later translator is Christopher Smart, who produced a prose translation in 1755 and a verse translation in 1767.

11. See *Alexander Pope and the Traditions of Formal Verse Satire* (Princeton University Press, 1982), p. 110.

12. See *The Honest Muse: A Study in Augustan Verse* (Oxford University Press, 1967), p. 96.

13. Horace and Juvenal: The attitude to the two poets involved the political and moral beliefs that fed the definitions of satire. A poet seriously opposed to contemporary earthly powers might be likely to invoke Juvenal as a sort of banner; that does not mean that his work must necessarily be Juvenalian. There were moral anxieties about the propriety or spiritual worth of lashing satires; for a discussion of the age's uneasy relation to satire, see the study by P. K. Elkin, *The Augustan Defence of Satire* (Oxford: Clarendon Press, 1973).

Juvenal was also associated with misogyny, and pornographic misogyny. Juvenal's *Satire VI*, a "bitter invective against the far Sex," was, as Dryden says, "a Commonplace, from whence all the Moderns have notoriously stollen their sharpest Raileries" ("Argument of the Sixth Satyr," *Juvenal*).

14. For a discussion of these illustrations by Cleyn and others see Eleanor Winsor Leach, "Illustration as Interpretation in Brant's and Dryden's Editions of Virgil," in *The Early Illustrated Book: Essays in Honor of Lessing J. Rosenwald*, Sandra Hindman, ed. (Washington, D.C.: Library of Congress, 1982), pp. 175–210.

15. Garth parodies (or rather, burlesques) both this passage and Dryden's translation of it in *The Dispensary*, when Horoscope builds an altar to Disease and brings his offerings:

> Then Flow'rs in Canisters he hastes to bring,
> The wither'd Product of a blighted Spring,
> With cold *Solanum* from the *Pontick* Shore,
> The Roots of *Mandrake* and Black *Ellebore*.
>
> *The Dispensary*, Canto III, p. 32.

16. The episode has been called "the pastoral war": the first full account of it was given by Johnson in his *Life of Ambrose Philips*. The *Guardian* essays praising Philips and slighting Pope (Nos. 22, 23, 28, 30, 32) are believed to be by Thomas Tickell; Pope's *Guardian* No. 40 compares Philips's work with his own and pretends to give the palm to Philips, "with an unexampled and unequalled artifice of irony" (Johnson).

17. Quotations from the Preface of *Pastorals* (London: H. Hills, 1710), pp. 3–4. Philips's emphasis on the soothing is an exaggerated derivation from the theories of Fontenelle in his *Discours sur la Nature de l'Églogue* (1688).

18. "In this poem [*Lycidas*] there is no nature, for there is no truth . . . Its form is that of a pastoral, easy, vulgar, and therefore disgusting; whatever images it can supply are long ago exhausted; and its inherent improbability always forces dissatisfaction on the mind" (Johnson, *Life of Milton*).

19. Quoted from the version in Stephen Duck's *Poems on Several Occasions* (London: John Osborn *et al.*, 1738), pp. 13–14.

20. Crabbe, *The Village*, Book I, p. 3.

21. The date of the opera's composition is uncertain; it was probably written in the winter of 1717–18.

22. See his *The English Georgic: A Study in the Development of a Form* (Baltimore, Md.: The Johns Hopkins Press, 1969), p. 2.

23. *Ibid.*, p. 209.

24. *Ibid.*, p. 27.

25. See Brooks Otis, *Virgil: A Study in Civilized Poetry* (Oxford: Clarendon Press, 1964), ch. 3, pp. 41–96.

26. John Dyer, *The Fleece: A Poem. In Four Books* (London: R. and J. Dodsley, 1757), Book I, p. 29.

27. Quotation from *The Borough: A Poem in Twenty-four Letters* (London: J. Hatchard, 1810), pp. 3–4. The narrative in the twenty-four letters does not seem epistolary in a Richardsonian sense. Crabbe explains the reason for resorting to this device:

> When the reader enters into the Poem, he will find the author retired from view, and an imaginary personage brought forward to describe the Borough for him: to him it seemed convenient to speak in the first person; but the inhabitant of a village in the centre of the kingdom, could not appear in the character of a residing burgess in a large sea-port; and . . . no method appeared to be so convenient, as that of borrowing the assistance of an ideal friend: by this means the reader is in some degree kept from view of any particular place, nor will he perhaps be so likely to determine where those persons reside . . . who are so intimately known to this man of straw.
>
> (Preface, pp. xiv-xv)

The "ideal [i.e. imaginary] friend," the chatty "man of straw," is the Horatian expansive "I" who keeps the poem together. The important point is that the speaker must speak in the first person, but should not be identical with George Crabbe.

V. Charivari and metamorphosis

1. Oliver Goldsmith, *The Deserted Village, A Poem* (London: W. Griffin, 1770), p. 13.

2. Anne Finch, Countess of Winchilsea, "A Nocturnal Reverie," *Miscellany Poems*, p. 291.

3. For a discussion of the development and significance of the charivari in France of the fifteenth and sixteenth centuries, see Natalie Zemon Davis, *Society and Culture in Early Modern France* (Stanford University Press, 1975), ch. 4, pp. 97–123. We may believe that the English use of the charivari followed a similar pattern, and that in both countries it was an urban phenomenon in the Renaissance, and then disappeared from the big cities, remaining in the provinces. By Butler's time, the Skimmington seems to be associated with the rural town, where it remained (surviving in areas of increasing remoteness) to and through the time of Hardy.

4. I have deliberately resisted becoming involved with Mikhail Bakhtin's notions of carnival as developed in *Rabelais and his World* (1965; translation, Hélène Iswolsky)

(Cambridge, Mass.: M.I.T. Press, 1968). Bakhtin is a most brilliant critic, but his notions of carnival, however attractive, are too general, as well as too ideologically loaded, to be helpful specifically in this case. "Charivari," both literal and metaphorical, seems to me to touch upon and define more precisely certain poetic interests of the English Augustan Age.

5. Duck, *Poems on Several Occasions* (1738), p. 113.
6. Ann Yearsley, a poor woman without formal education, married a fellow-labourer and had six children. She worked as a milkwoman and collected leftovers from Hannah More's cook, and it was the cook who brought this milkwoman-writer to Hannah More's notice; More corrected the poems and helped to bring out Years-ley's first volume of poems. Yearsley exhibits a deal of toughness of mind in her works, and is less nervous than the "lady poets" about what is fitting or unfitting. See my article, "Augustan *Women*? Four Poets of the Eighteenth Century," to be published in collection of Clark Library lectures, edited by Alan Roper.
7. In *Poems on Various Subjects*, by Ann Yearsley, A Milkwoman of Clifton near Bristol; Being her Second Work (London: Printed for the Author, Sold by G. G. J. and J. Robinson, 1787), pp. 93–9.
8. Translation of Ovid, *Metamorphoses*, Book VI, lines 370–5, by Samuel Croxall in Garth's *Ovid's Metamorphoses*, p. 192.
9. Young's instructions were:

What, Madam, if, for your modern Academy, *Hogarth* should draw a Centaur, not, as usual, with his bow and arrow, but (what will hit your mark as well) with Harlequin's sabre by his side; in a party-colour'd jacket of pictur'd cards, a band of music before, a Scaramouch-Demon behind him; a Weathercock on his head, a Rattle in his hand, the Decalogue under his feet; and, for the benefit of *your Scholars*, a Label out of his mouth, inscrib'd, as was the Temple of Apollo, with Γνῶθι σεαυτὸν in letters of gold [In ME, Know Thyself]; *They*, your Scholars, will take it in the true philosophic sense, and wonder how it came into the mouth of so ridiculous, and, to them, so foreign a monster.

Young, *The Centaur Not Fabulous*. In Six Letters to a Friend, on the Life in Vogue, 3rd edition (London: A. Millar and R. and J. Dodsley, 1755), p. x. It would seem to be Richardson who found the artist (Wale) to execute the illustration according to Young's design; see T. C. Duncan Eaves and Ben D. Kimpel, *Samuel Richardson, A Biography* (Oxford: Clarendon Press, 1971), pp. 431–2.
10. His mind resembled the vast amphitheatre, the Colisaeum at Rome. In the centre stood his judgment, which like a mighty gladiator, combated those apprehensions that, like the wild beasts of the *Arena*, were all around in cells, ready to be let out upon him.

(A.D. 1769); quoted from *Boswell's Life of Johnson*. Including Boswell's Journal of a Tour to the Hebrides and Johnson's Diary of a Journey into North Wales, George Birkbeck Hill, ed., 6 vols. (New York: Harper & Brothers, 1904), Vol. II, p. 122.
11. Isaac Watts, "A Prospect of Heaven Makes Death Easy," first published in *Hymns and Spiritual Songs* (1707).
12. Daughter of a dissenting minister, she published her first work, *Poems on Several Occasions* (1696), by "Philomela." She married Thomas Rowe, whose uncle had taught Isaac Watts, and was widowed in 1715. Her works were popular on both sides of the Atlantic, and her prose work *Friendship in Death* (1729–33) may have had some influence on the early novel.

After her death Isaac Watts edited her manuscripts and published hitherto unpublished poems; he found some, such as her "Devout Soliloquies," embarras-singly "too near a-kin to the Language of the mystical Writers." Watts is right; there are signs that Elizabeth Rowe was genuinely a mystic, even if he did not wish to think a friend could be guilty of such a thing. See Watts, Preface to *Devout Exercises of the Heart in Meditation, Soliloquy, Prayer and Praise*. By the late Pious and Ingenious

Mrs. Rowe. Review'd and Published at her Request, by I. Watts, D.D. (London: R. Hett, 1738), pp. xxi-xxii.

13. See *The Miscellaneous Works in Prose and Verse of Mrs. Elizabeth Rowe.* The Greater Part now first published, by her Order, from her Original Manuscripts, by Mr. Theophilus Rowe, 2 vols. (London: R. Hett and R. Dodsley, 1739), Vol. i, pp. 33–4; "The Conflagration," p. 89.

14. Edward Young, *A Poem on the Last Day* (Oxford: Edward Whistler, 1713), pp. 71–2.

15. *Olney Hymns*, Book i, "Isaiah," pp. 65–6.

16. See his *The Life of the Poet: Beginning and Ending Poetic Careers* (Chicago and London: University of Chicago Press, 1981), Section iii, "Tombeau," pp. 146–51.

17. *Auguries of Innocence*, quoted from *William Blake's Writings*, G. H. Bentley, Jr., ed., 2 vols. (Oxford: Clarendon Press, 1978), Vol. ii, p. 1312.

18. Thomas Parnell, "The Flies. An Eclogue," quoted from *Poems on Several Occasions* (London: B. Lintot, 1722), pp. 122–3. Thomas Parnell, Bishop of Clogher, was a friend of Pope and Swift; after his death (1718), Pope acted as literary executor, publishing his *Poems*. Parnell had already published his verse translation of the classical pseudo-Homeric mock-epic as *Homer's Battle of the Frogs and Mice* (1717); his interest in miniature creatures and in distortions of proportion or perspective may have influenced Swift. The flies in "The Flies" hold a singing contest between rival swains – a memorable example of generic mockery:

> When thus a Fly (if what a Fly can say
> Deserves attention) rais'd the rural Lay.

19. "Pied Beauty," quoted from *The Poems of Gerard Manley Hopkins*, 3rd edition, W. H. Gardner, ed. (London: Oxford University Press, 1948), p. 74.

20. See Ovid, *Metamorphoses* xi, lines 1–66, and Virgil, *Georgics* iv, lines 520–7. It is in Virgil's version that the severed head calls out "Eurydice" and the hills re-echo the name.

21. In "Procrastination" in *Tales*. By the Rev. George Crabbe, LL.D., 2 vols. (London: J. Hatchard, 1812), see Vol. i, pp. 75–6.

22. "An Epitaph," quoted from *The Literary Works of Matthew Prior*, H. Bunker Wright and Monroe K. Spears, eds., 2 vols. (Oxford: Clarendon Press, 1959), Vol. i, pp. 461–2.

23. Imlac to Nekayah: "Do not suffer life to stagnate; it will grow muddy for want of motion: commit yourself again to the current of the world," in *The History of Rasselas, Prince of Abissinia*, ch. 34, quoted from *The Works of Samuel Johnson, LL.D.*, Arthur Murphy, ed., 12 vols. (London: Thomas Tegg *et al.*, 1824), Vol. iii, p. 397.

24. Oliver Goldsmith, *The Citizen of the World: or Letters from a Chinese Philosopher, Residing in London, to his Friends in the East*, 2 vols. (London: J. Newbery, 1762), Vol. i, No. 44, p. 191.

25. For a discussion of Newton's theories of vision and light and their effect on Augustan literature, see Marjorie Hope Nicolson, *Newton Demands the Muse: Newton's Opticks and the Eighteenth-Century Poets* (Princeton University Press, 1946).

Newton's theories did change the world people felt they lived in. Voltaire, in the fourteenth of his *Letters Concerning the English Nation* (London: C. Davies, 1733), jokes about leaving the Cartesian universe for the Newtonian in travelling from Paris to London:

A Frenchman who arrives in *London*, will find Philosophy, like every Thing else, very much chang'd there. He had left the World a *plenum*, and he now finds it a *vacuum*. At *Paris* the Universe is seen compos'd of Vortices of subtile Matter, but nothing like it is seen in *London* ... According to your Cartesians, every Thing is perform'd by an Impulsion, of which we have very little Notion; and according to Sir *Isaac Newton*, 'tis by an Attraction, the Cause of which is as much unknown to us. (pp. 109–11)

Newton's theory of "attraction" was a philosophical concept, but students interpreted "attraction" as a physical force. A number of passages in Pope's works show his response to this cosmology of pulls and repulsions. The Augustans enjoyed living in a universe of urges across voids.

VI. Metamorphosis, pleasure and pain: the threat of the end

1. Quoted from *The Complaint: or Night-Thoughts on Life, Death & Immortality. Night the Third. Narcissa* (London: R. Dodsley and J. Cooper, 1742), pp. 25–6.
2. Nicolson, *Newton Demands the Muse*, p. 29.
3. See, e.g., her "Soliloquy II":

> I know not what to speak! for human words
> Lose all their pow'r, their emphasis and force;
> And grow insipid when I talk of thee,
> The excellence supreme, the God of gods.
> Whate'r the language of those gods, those pow'rs
> In heav'nly places crown'd; however strong,
> Or musical, or clear their language be,
> Yet all falls short of thee . . .

"Devout Soliloquies in Blank Verse: Soliloquy II," Rowe, *Miscellaneous Works*, Vol. I, p. 193.
4. "the daily Race": in the first published version of "Summer" Thomson's phrase is "the Day-living Race," a coinage that makes transience more emphatic.
5. E.g. "saltat Milonius, ut semel icto / accessit fervor capiti numerusque lucernis," *Satires* II. i, lines 24–5 ("Milonius prances as soon as the heat rushes to his head and the lights multiply").
6. See Donald Davie, *Purity of Diction in English Verse* [first published 1952] (New York: Schocken Books, 1967), p. 40.
7. William Kent, now best known to us as a landscape gardener and architect, was also a painter and illustrator. He supplied four designs illustrating each of the four seasons for the 1730 quarto (a subscription edition) of *The Seasons:* his designs were engraved in Paris by Nicolas Henri Tardieu. The four illustrations are included in Sambrook's critical edition of *The Seasons.* Kent's designs show on the upper half of each picture an allegorical representation of the Season; the area below is reserved for humans, animals and landscapes enjoying or suffering the effects of the season.
8. Son of Richard Bentley the Master of Trinity College, Cambridge, Bentley the younger seems (perhaps in natural reaction against the forceful "Aristarchus") to have been a man of many talents with little capacity for making a career. Walpole apparently planned the publication of Gray's poems with designs by Bentley as a method of assisting both of his friends. Gray, who expected that Walpole would include some of his own poems in an anthology, baulked at the conspicuous isolation of a protégé. He insisted on a change of title, from "Collected Poems of Thomas Gray" (or some such title) to *Designs by Mr. R. Bentley, for Six Poems by Mr. T. Gray:*

I desire it may be understood (wch is the truth) that the Verses are only subordinate, & explanatory to the Drawings, and suffer'd by me to come out thus only for that reason.

Gray to Dodsley, 12 February 1753, *Correspondence of Thomas Gray*, Paget Toynbee and Leonard Whibley, eds., 3 vols. (Oxford: Clarendon Press, 1935), No. 172, Vol. I, p. 371. Despite the alarms of a complicated authorial and personal vanity, and an initial suspicion of Bentley, Gray did co-operate with Bentley and Walpole over the

Designs; Gray sent Bentley (via Walpole) his own pencil drawing of Stoke Manor House to assist the artist in illustrating the *Long Story* (see letter to Walpole, 8 July 1752, No. 168, pp. 362–3).

9. A four-page "Explanation of the Prints" written by Walpole is included (unnumbered) between pages 38 and 39 of *Designs . . . for Six Poems*. Gray was a trifle caustic about this contribution: "if you think it necessary to print those Explanations for the use of People that have no eyes, I could be glad, they were a little alter'd" (to Walpole, 13 February 1753, *Correspondence*, No. 173, Vol. I, p. 372).

10. Robert Halsband comments on Du Guernier's illustrations in the second chapter of his *The Rape of the Lock and its Illustrations 1714–1896* (Clarendon Press, 1980), pp. 9–23.

11. *Dunciad* II, line 156. As the mock note says, Pope's lines here are "A parody of those of a late noble author." Lord Halifax's lines in his "Epistle to Dorset" are: "His bleeding arm had furnish'd all their rooms, / And run for ever purple in the looms" (where also the painful and the pleasurable are deliberately mixed). "Where slumber Abbots": *Dunciad* IV, line 302.

12. Quoted from William Falconer's *The Shipwreck* [2nd edition] (London: A. Millar, 1762), pp. 11–12.

13. See *To the Palace of Wisdom: Studies in Order and Energy from Dryden to Blake* (New York: Doubleday, 1964), pp. 361–2. Addison's three divisions into "what is *Great, Uncommon,* or *Beautiful*" are to be found in the *Spectator*, No. 412 (23 June 1712), one of a series on the "Pleasures of the Imagination." Addison displays an interest in the mingling of pleasure and pain:

> There may, indeed, be something so terrible or offensive, that the Horrour or Loathsomeness of an Object may over-bear the Pleasure which results from its *Greatness, Novelty or Beauty*; but still there will be such a Mixture of Delight in the very Disgust it gives us, as any of these three Qualifications are most conspicuous and prevailing.   (*Spectator*, No. 412)

Finding delight in disgust is an aesthetic activity characteristic of the period. And in the midst of the most traditionally beautiful scenes the eighteenth-century post-*Opticks* viewer can be smitten with the giddy and even painful notion that the beauty he sees is in some sense unreal – there are no colours, the distinctions of light and shade also are provided by ourselves: "In short, our Souls are at present delightfully lost and bewildered in a pleasing Delusion, and we walk about like the Enchanted Hero of a Romance . . ." (*Spectator*, No. 413). *The Spectator*, Donald F. Bond, ed., 5 vols. (Oxford: Clarendon Press, 1965), No. 412, Vol. III, pp. 540–4; No. 413, pp. 544–7.

14. Edmund Burke, *A Philosophical Enquiry into the Origin of our Ideas of the Sublime and the Beautiful* (London: R. and J. Dodsley, 1757), Part II, Section III, "Obscurity," p. 45.

15. Quoted from *The Art of Sinking in Poetry* [facsimile of first edition], Edna Leake Steeves, ed., with notes by R. H. Griffith and E. L. Steeves (New York: King's Crown Press, 1952), p. 6.

16. Aaron Hill's *The Progress of Wit: A Caveat. For the Use of an Eminent Writer*. By a Fellow of *All-Souls*. To which is prefix'd, An Explanatory Discourse to the Reader. By Gamaliel Gunson, Professor of Physick and Astrology (London: J. Welford, 1730); "low *Oblivion*'s Shore," p. 17; "*one rainy Day*," pp. v–vi; "*He was pleas'd*," p. vii; "dark, bustling, Power," pp. viii–ix; "Yet, *one* broad Gulph," pp. 19–20.

17. See *Spectator*, No. 159 (1 Sept. 1711), Bond, ed., Vol. II, pp. 121–6.

18. *Rasselas*, ch. 1, *Works*, Murphy, ed., Vol. III, p. 300.

19. Quoted from *The Complaint: or Night-Thoughts. Narcissa*, p. 19.

20. From the hymn best identified by its first line, "Our God, our Help in Ages past," Watts's "Man Frail and God Eternal" (1719) quoted from *The Psalms of David*

Imitated in the Language of the New Testament, and apply'd to the Christian State and Worship (London: J. Clark, R. Ford, R. Crittenden, 1719), Psalm xc, pp. 229–30.

21. Johnson, *The Vanity of Human Wishes*, quoted from *Samuel Johnson: The Complete English Poems*, J. D. Fleeman, ed. (New York: St. Martin's Press, 1971), pp. 91–2.

22. Robert Burns, *Tam O'Shanter* (1791); quoted from *Poems Chiefly in the Scottish Dialect*, A New Edition Considerably Enlarged, 2 vols. (Edinburgh: Adam Neill and Co. for T. Cadell *jun.* and W. Davies, London, and W. Creech, Edinburgh, 1800), Vol. I, pp. 198–9.

23. Blake illustrated only four of the *Night-Thoughts* in this edition (London: R. Edwards, 1797), and the illustrations surround the text in a manner new in poetry illustration, though it is an extension of eighteenth-century uses of pictorial comment in ornaments, initial letters, tail-pieces, etc.

   Martin Price suggests that "Young seems to have had some influence on his illustrator, Blake" and points to images that Blake picked out for his visual commentary on Young's poem and then used in his own poetry; see Price, *To the Palace of Wisdom*, p. 350.

24. "Peter Grimes," Letter No. 22, *The Borough*, pp. 305–6.

25. "Prisons," Letter No. 23, *The Borough*, p. 326.

26. Particularly Richard Bridgman; see his article "Weak Tocks: Coming to a Bad End in English Poetry of the Later Eighteenth Century," *Modern Philology* 80 (February 1983), pp. 264–79. Bridgman decides that what he sees as weak endings are symptoms of failing religious conviction. Reuben A. Brower has had a general grumble at what he sees as the formlessness of Augustan poetry: see "Form and Defect of Form in Eighteenth-Century Poetry: A Memorandum," in *Eighteenth-Century Studies in Honor of Donald F. Hyde*, W. H. Bond, ed. (New York: The Grolier Club, 1970), pp. 365–82.

27. Thomson, *Liberty*, quoted from Thomson's *Works*, 2 vols. (London, 1763), Vol. I, p. 311.

28. John Dyer, *The Ruins of Rome. A Poem* (London: Lawton Gilliver, 1740), p. 3.

29. Warburton, "Advertisement" in *An Essay on Man. By Alexander Pope Esq. Enlarged and Improved by the Author. With Notes by William Warburton, M.A.* (London: John and Paul Knapton, 1745), pp. v–vi. The lines beneath the engraved picture, "Here in the rich, the honour'd, fam'd and great, / See the false scale of Happiness complete!" refer to Epistle IV of the *Essay on Man*, lines 287–8.

30. An amusing light parody is John Duncombe's *An Evening Contemplation in a College* (1753) which opposes what Duncombe evidently sees as a donnish melancholy in Gray's piece. Duncombe's hero, a Fellow of a college, disappears because he has married ("That day to church he led a blushing bride") and found a patron: "Now by his patron's boundless care remov'd, / He roves enraptur'd thro' the fields of Kent" (p. 11) – boundlessness and roving assertively supplied instead of death and closure.

   Some of Gray's best-known verses are transformed thus, in the comic description of a college:

> The Curfew tolls the hour of closing gates,
> With jarring sound the Porter turns the key,
> Then in his dreary mansion slumb'ring waits,
> And slowly, sternly quits it – tho' for me.
> . . .
> Within these Walls, where thro' the glimm'ring Shade
> Appear the pamphlets in a mold'ring heap,
> Each in his narrow bed till morning laid
> The peaceful fellows of the college sleep.
> . . .

Ev'n now their books from cobwebs to protect,
Inclos'd by doors of glass, in Doric style,
On fluted pillars rais'd, with bronzes deck'd,
They claim the passing tribute of a smile.
Oft are the authors' names, tho' richly bound
Mis'spelt by blund'ring binders' want of care;
And many a catalogue is strow'd around,
To tell th' admiring guest what books are there.

An Evening Contemplation in a College. Being a Parody on the Elegy in A Country Church-Yard. By another Gentleman of Cambridge (London: R. and J. Dodsley, 1753), pp. 5–9. John Duncombe, a Fellow of Corpus, was already involved in the long courtship of Susannah Highmore, parental disapproval and lack of funds being obstacles to their union, so it was natural that he should think of such a happy issue out of the confinement of college bachelorhood.

31. The description is from Walpole's "Explanation of the Prints," in *Designs . . . for Six Poems*.

32. Bentley sent Gray a proof-print of the tail-piece illustration representing the funeral. Gray wrote to Walpole expressing his appreciation of the design and describing a comic mistake on his aunts' part:

> I am surprised at the Print, wch far surpasses my Idea of a London Graving. the Drawing itself was so finished, that I suppose, it did not require all the Art I had imagined to copy it tolerably. my Aunts just now, seeing me open your Letter, take it to be a Burying-Ticket enclosed, & ask, whether any body has left me a Ring? and so they still conceive it to be, even with all their Spectacles on.

Gray to Walpole, 8 July 1752, *Correspondence*, Vol. I, pp. 362–3. The anecdote reminds us that in the eighteenth century invitations to a funeral were sent out almost like wedding invitations now, and that the iconography of death was a feature of common occasions. There is an extra, if grim, humour in the aunts' error – they thought their nephew might have received some small legacy from a dead person, but the design that looked like a funeral ticket really represented in some sense his own death.

33. See Johnson, *Life of Gray*; Johnson had doubts about some of Gray's other poetry, but none at all about the perfections of the *Elegy*, which he praises with great emphasis.

VII. Character, style, language: the two voices of Augustan poems

1. Laurence Sterne, *The Life and Opinions of Tristram Shandy, Gentleman*, Ian Watt, ed., Riverside edition (Boston: Houghton Mifflin, 1965), pp. 214–15.

2. Quoted from Richardson's *Clarissa. Or, The History of a Young Lady: Comprehending the Most Important Concerns of Private Life*, 3rd edition, 8 vols. (London: Printed for S. Richardson, And Sold by John Osborn, Andrew Millar, *et al.*, 1751), Vol. IV, pp. 258–9.

3. See Fielding, *Tom Jones*, Book II, ch. 1, quoted from *The History of Tom Jones, A Foundling*, Sheridan Baker, ed. (New York: W. W. Norton, 1973), p. 59.

4. William King, "The Old Cheese," quoted from *Miscellany Poems. By Several Hands*, 6th edition, 2 vols. (London: Bernard Lintot, 1732), Vol. II, pp. 37–8. King wrote *The Art of Cookery* (1708), in imitation of Horace's *Art of Poetry*, and most of his poems seem to have been about food, e.g. "Apple Pie," "A Panegyric on Beer."

5. Not in *Miscellany Poems*, extant in MS, quoted from *Selected Poems of Anne Finch Countess of Winchilsea*, Katharine M. Rogers, ed. (New York: Frederick Ungar,

1979), pp. 48–9. The poem (*c.* 1690) is a verse letter; it is an interesting example of a poem *by* a woman (not merely a poem *about* a woman) in the Horatian mode.

6. Quoted from Robert Blair's *The Grave* (London: M. Cooper, 1743), pp. 6–7. This edition supplies line-numbering, unusual in the first edition of a new poem.

7. The story is taken from Giovanni Boccaccio's *Decameron*, 5th day, 1st tale.

8. Quoted from Richardson's *Pamela, or Virtue Rewarded*, T. C. Duncan Eaves and Ben D. Kimpel, eds., Riverside edition (Boston: Houghton Mifflin, 1971), p. 102. The copy-text here is the first edition.

9. The word is not used in our modern sense in the eighteenth century, when it alluded to personal reference, as in "descending to personality" in satire, i.e. picking on particular individuals or making abusive personal comments. The inclusion of individuals and their characteristics in poems not necessarily satiric seems linked to the interest in "personality" in our sense. Signs of this rising interest in personality can be seen in the parlour games such as Mrs. Thrale's grade sheet evaluating her friends' qualities, or her and her friends' games of association (first drawn from Goldsmith's *Retaliation*) in which people are likened to dishes of food, colours and fabrics, flowers and animals. See *Thraliana*, Vol. I, pp. 329–31; pp. 347–8; pp. 366–7; p. 414.

10. *Clarissa*, Vol. I, Letter No. 40, p. 279; "So that This is but *conditional liking* still": p. 276.

11. Joseph Warton, *An Essay on the Genius and Writings of Pope*, Vol. II, p. 149.

12. *The Beggar's Opera*. As it is Acted at the Theatre-Royal in Lincolns-Inn-Fields. Written by Mr. Gay. To Which is Added, the Musick Engrav'd on Copper-Plate (London: John Watts, 1728), II. iv, pp. 23–4.

13. This set of verses was first printed in the Pope–Swift Miscellanies. Gay's best and most recent editors, Dearing and Beckwith, do not question the attribution to Gay. They also note that "D'Urfey had published 'A Ballad of Old Proverbs' in Volume IV of *Wit and Mirth*, 1719 ... which includes some proverbial similes ... and which supposes the writer has been jilted" (Gay, *Works*, Vol. II, p. 630).

14. See Lewis Carroll, *Through the Looking-Glass and What Alice Found There*, ch. 8; quoted from edition edited by Roger Lancelyn Green (London: Oxford University Press, 1971), p. 216. The White Knight chapter might be called Carroll's most Augustan piece (as even the parody of Wordsworth's "Resolution and Independence" bears out). The White Knight, with his trappings of mousetraps and his cake dish, is obviously a descendant of Butler's Hudibras, another knight whose appurtenances are strange and strangely used for food-gathering and preparation.

15. Quoted from first edition of William Shenstone's *The School-Mistress, a Poem*. In Imitation of Spenser (London: R. Dodsley, 1742), stanza 25.

16. Crabbe, *The Parish Register*, quoted from *Poems*. By the Rev. George Crabbe, LL.B. (London: J. Hatchard, 1817), pp. 109–10.

17. This passage embodies a compliment to Dryden's friend Henry Dickinson who translated Père Simon's *Critical History of the Old Testament*, though the compliment seems curiously ambivalent. Dryden, still un-reconstructed Anglican, takes Protestant advantage of Simon's attempted defence of the Roman Catholic Church against the Protestants by the application of textual criticism which showed the Bible (on which the Protestants relied) to be a suspect document riddled with varying interpretations. Protestants seized on Simon's statements as exemplifying priestly fallibility, and the French authorities suppressed Simon's book. The Dryden passage thus involves the whole question of the study of language and the interpretation of texts and the Text.

18. See *Boswell's Life of Johnson* (A.D. 1784), Vol. IV, p. 364. Johnson was referring to Lord Hailes's modernizing of the language of "the ever-memorable John Hales of

Eton." Fleeman also quotes this passage in his Introduction to Johnson's *Complete English Poems*. Fleeman's Introduction constitutes an able defence of the retention of capitals, old spelling and italics in editions of eighteenth-century works.

19. Geoffrey Tillotson, *On the Poetry of Pope*, 2nd edition (Oxford: Clarendon Press, 1950), pp. 150–1; "His line requires," p. 154.

20. Falconer's drawing: The frontispiece for the 1762 edition, drawn by "Auctor," engraved by Bayly, is a large fold-out picture. That in the third edition is more modest. The copy of the 1769 edition in the Stanford Rare Books collection (from which Figure 25 is photographed) belonged to Mrs. Boscawen; the fly leaf is inscribed by her as "The Gift of Mrs Jane Falconer Widow of the ingenious Author who was Shipwreck'd in The Aurora Man of War in their Voyage to India 1770."

21. See Donald S. Taylor, note on *The Revenge*, in *The Complete Works of Thomas Chatterton*, Vol. II, p. 1106.

22. Quoted from *Memoirs of a Sad Dog*, in *The Complete Works*, Vol. I, pp. 654–5. Taylor's note explains references: the dark cave is a sponging-house; the hills of death refer to the area around Tyburn, called Deadly Never Green, and to the parks around (the haunt of highwaymen and footpads). Chatterton has thus equated heroic with criminal activity (in an Augustan manner) and has also made the language which originally referred to the rural and savage move back to describing the urban, while the style itself doesn't appear to notice the alteration of venue.

23. Chatterton sent this poem in the summer of 1770 to *The Town and Country Magazine*, which rejected it; Chatterton could not, however, have known about the rejection, which occurred after his death. Actually Chatterton had done extremely well for a teen-aged poet in getting his works published. Before his death a number of works had appeared in the magazines (including *Town and Country* which published *Memoirs of a Sad Dog*), and he had several Burlettas acted in "Marybone Gardens."

24. See Chatterton's covering letter "To the Printer of the Town and Country Magazine": "Sir, / If the Glossary annexed to the following piece will make the language intelligible; the Sentiment, Description, and Versification, are highly deserving of the attention of the literati." *Town and Country* in the rejecting acknowledgment printed in its August issue said "The pastoral from Bristol . . . has some share of merit; but the author will, doubtless, discover upon another perusal of it, many exceptionable passages" (Taylor, *Complete Works*, Vol. II, pp. 1113–14). Evidently the editor didn't quite enjoy the game he was asked to play.

VIII. Augustan voice and Augustan verse

1. See [? George Duckett], *Pope Alexander's Supremacy and Infallibility Examin'd: and the Errors of Scriblerus and his Man William Detected. With the Effigies of His Holiness and his Prime Minister, Curiously engrav'd on Copper* (London: J. Roberts, 1729), "Appendix. A Curious Receipt," p. 5; "yet must I beg leave," pp. 6–7.

   The Cleland referred to is not John, the author of *Fanny Hill*, but William Cleland, supposed author of the "Letter to the Publisher," in praise of Pope and the poem, which prefaces the *Dunciad Variorum*. The "Effigies . . . Curiously engrav'd" show Pope as a monkey and Cleland as an ass. "Gambadoes" (in mock-poem) are gaiters or large boots attached to a horse's saddle for the benefit of a rider, hence suitably if nonsensically twinned with "Trojan Boots."

2. Shenstone, "A Prefatory Essay on Elegy" prefixed to his "Elegies"; quoted from *The Works in Verse and Prose of William Shenstone, Esq.*; Most of which were never before printed, 2 vols. (London: R. and J. Dodsley, 1764), Vol. I, pp. 8–9.

3. From Swift's "Directions for a Birthday Song, Oct. 30, 1729," lines 29–30.

4. Parnell, "A Night-Piece on Death," *Poems on Several Occasions*, p. 154.

5. Mary Barber, *Poems on Several Occasions* (London: C. Rivington, 1734), pp. 13–14.
6. Yearsley, *Poems on Various Subjects*, pp. 128–30.
7. Shenstone, "A Prefatory Essay on Elegy," *Works*, Vol. 1, pp. 7–8. "The chief exception", "The previous rhime": p. 9.
8. Gray, letter to Wharton, December 1750, in *Correspondence*, Vol. 1, p. 335; "he must ... print it without any Interval": letter to Walpole, 11 February 1751, p. 341.
9. Abraham Cowley, Preface to "Pindarique Odes, Written in Imitation of the Stile and Manner of the Odes of Pindar," *Works* (1710), Vol. 1, pp. 183–4. (This Preface is printed in italic type; I have taken it out of italics for ease of reading.)
   In his general Preface to his works, Cowley comments further:

   > For as for the *Pindarick Odes* ... I am in great doubt whether they will be understood by most *Readers* ... The *Figures* are unusual and *bold*, even to *Temerity*, and such as I durst not have to do withal in any other kind of *Poetry:* The Numbers are various and irregular, and sometimes (especially some of the long ones) seem harsh and uncouth ... And tho' the *Liberty* of them may incline a Man to believe them easie to be composed, yet the Undertaker will find it otherwise.   The Preface of the Author, Vol. 1, p. lxi.

10. Edward Young, "Discourse on Ode," *Ocean. An Ode*. Occasion'd by His Majesty's late Royal Encouragement of the Sea-Service. To which is prefix'd, An Ode to the King: And a Discourse on Ode (London: Tho. Worrall, 1728), p. 19; pp. 21–2.
11. "A Satyr against Vertue," quoted from John Oldham's *Satyrs upon the Jesuits*. Written in the Year 1679. Upon Occasion of the Plot, Together with the Satyr against Vertue, And Some other Pieces by the same Hand (London: Joseph Hindmarsh, 1681), p. 113. ["A Satyr against Vertue" is numbered consecutively with the rest of the book but has a separate title-page bearing the date 1680.] Oldham's poem had already appeared anonymously in *Poems on Several Occasions*. By the Right Honourable the Earl of R—. Printed at Antwerp, 1680.
12. See "An Apology for the preceding Poem, by way of Epilogue, to be annexed," p. 115; also in Rochester, *Poems* (Antwerp). Some readers evidently had not understood the poet's ventriloquism or his satire, perhaps because the poem had been attributed to the wicked Earl; Oldham goes to great lengths to explain, not only in his Epilogue but also in the "Advertisement" to his own volume. The "Satyr. Suppos'd to be spoken by a Court Hector. Pindarique" had been, he says, published without his knowledge or consent, and no intelligent reader could take it at face value as expressing his own views:

    > As for the next Poem (which is the most liable to censure) though the World has given it the Name of the *Satyr against Vertue*, he declares 'twas never design'd to that intent, how apt soever some may be to wrest it ... 'Twas meant to abuse those, who valued themselves upon their Wit and Parts in praising Vice, and to shew, that others of sober Principles, if they would take the same liberty in Poetry, could strain as high rants in Profaness as they.
    >   *Satyrs*, p. A₃ᵛ (taken out of italics)

13. "The Discontent," *Poems. By Mrs. Anne Killigrew* (London: Samuel Lowndes, 1686), p. 51; p. 56.
14. "An Ode," *Poems*, pp. 82–3. Anne Killigrew's "An Epitaph on Herself" reads "When I am Dead, few Friends attend my Hearse, / And for a Monument, I leave my VERSE" (p. 82). Her monument, however, has been not her own verse but Dryden's great poem about her. There are indications within the Ode that he had read her poems and seen her paintings. David M. Vieth thinks that Dryden in his Ode was making fun of both Anne and her poetry – a view I do not share (see his "Irony in Dryden's Ode to Anne Killigrew," *Studies in Philology* 62 (January 1965), pp. 91–100). Dryden's Ode seems, rather, a positive response to the Odes by his subject. The Ode was certainly a kind of poem she liked. As her tombstone's epitaph (also published in the volume) asks, *Aut quis canat, nisi Poëta sui similis?:*

"What Verse can celebrate her Fame, / But such as she herself did frame?" (b3^v; b4^v).

One of the most interesting poems in Anne Killigrew's book is another Ode, "Cloris Charmes Dissolved by Eudora," a wild poem describing a journey through "Sorrows Land" with its poisoned flood and "The Terrors of the Cursed Wood." More nightmarish and more personal than the Renaissance allegory from which it is drawn, this imperfect but original poem can serve us as a useful reminder of the "Gothic" strain in the literature of the whole Augustan Age. It is a mistake to be arbitrary about the advent of Romanticism or the "pre-Romantics." On a lighter note, Killigrew's image of the Alps at the beginning of her poem "To the Queen" may have influenced Pope in the creation of a famous passage of the *Essay on Criticism* (lines 225–32).

15. Boswell, *Life of Johnson*, Vol. 1, p. 88.

Index